ORACLE/SQL

A Professional Programmer's Guide

Tim Hartley
University of Hartford

Tim Martyn
Hartford Graduate Center

McGraw-Hill, Inc.

New York   St. Louis   San Francisco   Auckland   Bogotá
Caracas   Lisbon   London   Madrid
Mexico   Milan   Montreal   New Delhi   Paris
San Juan   São Paulo   Singapore
Sydney   Tokyo   Toronto

Library of Congress Cataloging-in-Publication Data

Hartley, Tim.
　　ORACLE/SQL : a professional programmer's guide/ Tim Hartley, Tim Martyn.
　　　　p.　　cm.—(J. Ranade IBM series)
　　Includes index.
　　ISBN 0-07-040775-4 (cloth)—ISBN 0-07-040767-3 (soft)
　　1. Relational data bases.　2. Oracle (Computer file).
　　3. SQL (Computer program language).
　　I. Martyn, Tim.　II.Title.　III. Series
QA76.9.D3H3652　1992
005.75'65—dc20
　　　　　　　　　　　　　　　　　　　　　　　　　　　　　91-42887
　　　　　　　　　　　　　　　　　　　　　　　　　　　　　CIP

1 2 3 4 5 6 7 8 9 0　DOC/DOC　9 8 7 6 5 4 3 2

ISBN　0-07-040775-4　{HC}
ISBN　0-07-040767-3　{PBK}

The sponsoring editor for this book was Jerry Papke.

Printed and bound by R. R. Donnelley and Sons.

Subscription information to BYTE Magazine:
Call 1-800-257-9402 or write Circulation Dept.,
One Phoenix Mill Lane, Peterborough, NH 03458.

For our parents

Contents

Acknowledgments

We gratefully acknowledge the following individuals who played various roles in helping us bring this book to press. They are Mohammad Bat-haee, Michael Danchak, Rod Dehner, Al Gaspar, Joel Kagan, Roger Mehrmanesh, Bob Mumford, Lamont Rogers, and Gary Trail.

Tim Hartley acknowledges the University of Hartford for providing support for this endeavor by granting his petition for a reduced teaching load.

Tim Martyn expresses his gratitude to the Hartford Graduate Center for supporting his sabbatical leave. He acknowledges Judy Rohan and his colleagues and the CIS faculty for their encouragement.

Martyn's previous acknowledgment to the Arch Street Institute of Cognitive Science, which he reacknowledges, generated a substantial number of inquiries regarding its members and their scholarly activities. In response, he notes that the founders and charter members primarily consist of survivors of Catholic grammar schools whose research activities support such projects as the Hartford Hooker Day Parade and the Crusade to Elect an Irish Pope. (Unfortunately, the Vatican has yet to subsidize any of their projects.) Requests for additional information (and donations) can be forwarded to George B. Bartlett at 85 Arch Street in Hartford. Finally, George should be acknowledged for his valuable commentary on our previous DB2 text, his contributions to the Hooker Day Parade Committee, and his generosity in providing free golf lessons to all members of the Arch Street Institute.

Preface

A number of books have been published on the ORACLE Database Management System (DBMS). Most of these books present a comprehensive overview of the ORACLE DBMS, SQL, and other software products marketed by the ORACLE Corporation. The authors of this text have elected to restrict their attention to the ORACLE version of SQL as executed from within a SQL*Plus environment.

SQL is a relational database language which is utilized by a number of ORACLE products. These include SQL*Plus, SQL*Form, SQL*Calc, SQL*Menu, SQL*Graph, SQL*Report, and preprocessors for conventional programming languages (Pro*COBOL, Pro*C, Pro*PASCAL, Pro*FORTRAN, Pro*PL/I, and Pro*ADA). SQL is also utilized by over 40 other relational database management systems. These include DB2, SQL/DS, INGRES, dBASE IV, SYBASE, and RdB.

This text is based on our previous text, *DB2/SQL: A Professional Programmer's Guide* (McGraw-Hill, 1989), which described IBM's DB2 version of SQL. The current text will indicate which ORACLE statements are compatible with the DB2 version of SQL.

This text has specific objectives and is written for a specific audience. We describe these objectives and audience below.

SQL Objective

SQL is a complete database language. It has statements to

1.   Initially create a database

2.   Create the underlying physical objects

3.   Create the logical objects (tables and views)

4.   Define authorization and other management controls

5.   Retrieve and manipulate data in the database

This text will focus on the last task, the retrieval and manipulation of data in the database. It will present a comprehensive discussion of SELECT, INSERT, UPDATE, and DELETE statements. Other statements in the language (e.g., the CREATE TABLE and CREATE VIEW statements) are described to provide insight into the rules and behavior of the SELECT statement and other data manipulation statements.

Any SQL statement can be issued interactively using SQL*Plus. The same SQL statement (with minor modification) can be embedded within an application program written in some traditional programming language (e.g., COBOL, FORTRAN, C). In fact, a desirable feature of SQL is that it allows a programmer to test a statement in an interactive environment before embedding the statement within an application program. This text will restrict its attention to "interactive" SQL. Professional programmers who need to learn the additional SQL statements relevant to "embedded" SQL can consult the ORACLE reference manuals.

To summarize, the primary objective of this text is to present a comprehensive examination of the data retrieval and data manipulation statements in the ORACLE version of SQL.

SQL*Plus Objective

SQL*Plus is a front-end software tool which allows users to submit SQL statements and examine the results. It has some report formatting capabilities and other useful facilities which allow users to save and reexecute SQL statements. This text will cover most of the concepts and facilities pertaining to SQL*Plus. However, the presentation will not be exhaustive.

Audience

A wide variety of people may interact with the ORACLE DBMS. These may be database administrators, systems analysts and designers, systems programmers, application programmers, and "users" (the "customers" who hope to benefit from the system). This book is specifically written for professional programmers and users. Both groups require an in-depth knowledge of SQL's data retrieval and manipulation statements.

In general, this text can be read by any person who has attained a basic level of computer literacy. As such, it can serve as an introduction to SQL for anyone interested in the subject. The authors have used a preliminary version of this book as the primary text in many professional training seminars. It has also been used as a supplemental independent-study tutorial in a graduate-level database course where the content and primary text focused on the theory of relational database. It has been well received in both educational environments. The positive criticism provided by students has helped the authors in preparing the current version of this text.

SQL Versions

This text is written for Version 6 (V6) of ORACLE. However, if you are using Version 5 (V5) of ORACLE, most of this text will apply. We make comments where differences exist.

Organization of Text

This book adopts a tutorial format. A topic is presented by introducing a sample query and the SQL statement that satisfies the query. Usually this is enough to give the reader a basic idea about the syntax and behavior of the SQL feature under consideration. Thereafter, a list of pertinent comments is presented. These comments present details on syntax. However, *the primary intention of the comments is to highlight the more important, and sometimes subtle, logical issues relating to the behavior of a SQL statement*. This will be a constant theme throughout the text. SQL's syntax is easy. But, SQL also provides the opportunity for logical errors. Where appropriate, the comments will emphasize the possible difference between (1) the query you may have intended to execute and (2) the query actually executed by the system in response to your SQL statement.

This text is organized into an Introduction and six major parts, some of which can be skipped, depending on your background knowledge, your status (user or programmer) or particular objectives. We briefly outline each part below.

Introduction: The Database Environment

This Introduction is written for the reader who has no previous exposure to relational database concepts. It describes the fundamental concepts of relational database systems and the evolution of SQL and introduces ORACLE. This section is strictly conceptual. There are no behavioral objectives to be mastered by doing exercises. These concepts are important but are not critical. We encourage anyone who has no previous exposure to relational databases to read this section. However, you should not be discouraged if you have a problem understanding any of the points made in this section. Just carry on. This book really begins in Chapter 1.

Part I: Selecting Data from a Single Table

This section introduces the SELECT statement. In particular, we restrict our attention to retrieving data from a single table. You will learn how to retrieve any rows and/or columns from a table, specify the sequence of the result, utilize the Boolean operators (AND, OR, and NOT), and perform basic calculations.

Many users are allowed only to examine, but not modify the database. Also, many users will be restricted to querying a single table. Such users should find practically everything they need to know in these chapters. For this reason, the chapters in this part of the text have more of a tutorial flavor than subsequent chapters. We expect that most professional programmers will skim the sample queries and bypass the narrative comments.

Part II: ORACLE Built-in Functions

ORACLE provides a collection of built-in functions which serves a variety of purposes. Each function performs a specific task such as a computation or a string manipulation. The special topic of date/time processing using built-in functions is also described.

Part III: SQL*Plus

This part of the book describes the SQL*Plus front-end to the ORACLE DBMS. No new SQL statements are introduced. Instead, we introduce SQL*Plus commands which facilitate report formatting and other housekeeping tasks.

Part IV: Data Definition and Manipulation

This section introduces the CREATE TABLE statement to provide background information on the ORACLE data types and the basic concepts of database integrity. This information is necessary for a proper understanding of the INSERT, UPDATE, and DELETE statements described in detail.

Part V: Accessing Multiple Tables

This section covers all aspects of the SELECT statement that were omitted in Parts I and II. In particular, it introduces queries that require access to multiple tables. This part of the text presents a comprehensive discussion of the join operation; subqueries; recursive processing; and the union, intersection, and difference operations.

Part VI: More about ORACLE

This section introduces the SQL statements that allow you to share your data with other users of the system. It covers the CREATE VIEW statement and the GRANT and REVOKE statements. It includes a brief examination of the transaction concept and ORACLE's Data Dictionary.

Philosophy

Our objective has been to write a text that teaches a few important topics (hopefully) very well. We solicit your feedback in the form of positive criticism regarding errors, changes, or enhancements that might be made to future printings or editions of this text. Your comments can be addressed to the authors at The Hartford Graduate Center, 275 Windsor Street, Hartford, CT 06120.

Introduction

This section introduces the following topics:

* Basic concepts of a Data Base Management System (DBMS).

* The characteristics of a "relational" DBMS.

* The evolution of SQL.

* The ORACLE relational DBMS.

* ORACLE's compatibility with DB2.

* ORACLE's front-end product, SQL*Plus.

This introduction provides a conceptual background by presenting the history and evolution of database technology. There are no behavioral objectives for this chapter. The intention is to set a context for our discussion of the ORACLE version of SQL. Users with some ORACLE experience, or experience with any other SQL-based relational DBMS, may choose to skip this section and begin reading Chapter 1.

Relational Database Concepts

What is a database?

Many people use the terms "file" and "database" as though they were synonymous. However, there is an important difference. A file is a collection of records where each record is composed of multiple data items called "fields." A database usually encompasses many files and, furthermore, provides facilities to capture relationships that exist between records. Hence, a database system transcends a file system by providing the designer with facilities to represent relationships between records. We present a simple example to illustrate this point.

Consider two files, an EMPLOYEE file and a DEPARTMENT file. An EMPLOYEE record contains fields for employee number, name, address, and department name. A DEPARTMENT record contains fields for department name, location, and phone number. (See Figure I.1.) Now consider a request to retrieve the name and address of every employee, stored in the EMPLOYEE file, and their respective departmental locations and phone numbers, stored in the DEPARTMENT file. In a traditional file system this query would involve considerable effort. Both files would first have to be sorted in department name sequence. Then an application program would follow a match-merge process to extract the desired data. The key point is that considerable work is required by application programs. This is because a file system cannot capture the "employee-works-in-department" relationship which exists between the two record types. A database system can.

```
+-----------------------------------------------------------+
|                                                           |
|     DEPARTMENT file                                       |
|     +--------+--------+--------+                           |
|     | DEPT   | DLOC   | DPH    |                           |
|     +--------+--------+--------+                           |
|                                                           |
|                                                           |
|     EMPLOYEE file                                         |
|     +--------+--------+--------+--------+                  |
|     | ENO    | ENAME  | EADDR  | EDEPT  |                  |
|     +--------+--------+--------+--------+                  |
|                                                           |
+-----------------------------------------------------------+
```

Figure I.1: Traditional file system.

Traditional database products, which evolved during the 1970s, captured relationships by allowing the database designer to represent the data and relationships as a tree or network structure. (A tree is just a special type of network.) Figure I.2 reflects such a network structure for our simple example. The figure denotes a database consisting of two record types which are related on a one-to-many basis. A department may have many employees, and an employee works for one department. The database system would usually implement this relationship by using internal pointers to link together a given department record with all its associated employee records. Then an application program would issue commands to the database system which effectively instruct the system to follow the pointers and return the desired data. This process, whereby the application program "navigates" its way through the network, is better than the sort-match-merge process of traditional file processing. However, there are a number of negative issues associated with network databases.

A network structure is often too rigid from the database designer's point of view. And the navigation process is complex from a programmer's point of view. Finally, because the application programs which navigate the database are written in traditional high-level languages (COBOL, FORTRAN, etc.) it is obvious that these early database systems are not at all user-friendly. The current generation of relational database systems address these problems.

What is a relational database?

The relational approach to database was proposed by E. F. Codd in 1970. However, commercial products did not appear in the marketplace until the early 1980s. The remainder of this section presents the basic concepts of relational database. We describe these ideas from a user viewpoint. Codd and others have developed a solid theoretical foundation of relational theory.

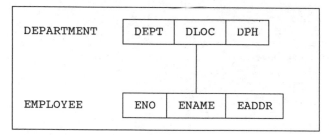

Figure I.2: Network database.

A relational database must fulfill at least two objectives. The first is that the system must present the data in tabular format to the user. In the simple example described above, the user would see the database as a collection of two tables. Figure I.3 illustrates an EMPLOYEE table and a DEPARTMENT table. We have two tables instead of two records types. An individual row in a table corresponds to a record occurrence; and a column in a table corresponds to a single field in a record. In fact we will often use the terms "row" and "record" interchangeably. Likewise we will use the terms "column" and "field" interchangeably.

Note that unlike the previous network design there is no explicit mapping between the tables. Instead the EMPLOYEE table contains a column (EDEPT) to indicate which department the employee works in. This observation might lead to the mistaken conclusion that a relational database is just a friendlier presentation of the old classical file concept. However, this is definitely not the case. The second major feature of relational databases clearly distinguishes relational database systems from file systems and earlier network type database systems.

DEPARTMENT table

DEPT	DLOC	DPH

EMPLOYEE table

ENO	ENAME	EADDR	EDEPT

Figure I.3: Relational database.

The second major feature of any relational database is its support of a "set-at-a-time" query language. This requires some explanation. With traditional systems the query language was "record-at-a-time" oriented. This meant that the query language was capable of expressing a query to retrieve only a single record. Therefore, in order to retrieve a set of records, the programmer would have to write code to repeatedly execute a query statement. For example, if you wanted to retrieve all the employees in the Data Processing Department, and there were 200 such employees, a query statement (to get the "next" record for an employee in the DP Department) would be executed 200 times. Each execution would retrieve one record and return it to the application program.

With a relational system the process is considerably easier because the query language is much more powerful. The language is powerful enough to request any subset of rows and columns. When the user issues a query, the system collects all the data and returns it to the user. The user issues only one query (without multiple iterations), and the system returns all the desired data.

Another important point is that relational languages for commercial database products are user-friendly. One does not need to be a professional programmer to access the database. A computer literate user can sit at a workstation and enter a statement in the query language. The system will extract the desired rows and place them on the display screen.

A number of query languages for relational databases have been developed. This book presents a tutorial on SQL, the most popular relational language. The user will find that SQL is indeed a simple but powerful set-at-a-time database language. Before we describe the evolution of the SQL language, we present a simple SQL statement to illustrate the aforementioned points.

Figure I.4 shows a SELECT statement which will retrieve specified rows from the EMPLOYEE table. In this case it retrieves only those rows where the EDEPT value is "DP". You would enter this statement if you wanted to display all information about employees who work in the DP Department. We will discuss the details of the SELECT statement in Part I of this text. For the moment we merely note that this command is indeed quite simple and would retrieve and display all the desired rows.

```
SELECT *
FROM EMPLOYEE
WHERE EDEPT = 'DP'
```

Figure I.4: Sample SQL statement.

SQL: A Database Language

Evolution and Standards:

SQL (Structured Query Language) was initially defined by D. D. Chamberlin and others during the late 1970s. It was originally called SEQUEL (Structured English QUEry Language) and was developed in conjunction with IBM's relational database prototype, System R. System R is the ancestor of IBM's commercial relational database products DB2 and SQL/DS. The ORACLE Corporation also modeled their commercial DBMS on this prototype. SEQUEL is the ancestor of all the different commercial versions of SQL.

Over the past decade many vendors have introduced SQL-oriented relational database products. Earlier versions of these products had a strong SQL flavor but were quite idiosyncratic. In response to this situation, the American National Standards Institute (ANSI) has established an "official" standard. This official ANSI SQL standard, which is currently being revised, is similar to SQL as understood by ORACLE. However, there are some differences. One reason for these differences is that the data processing community has unofficially adopted another de facto standard which is based on IBM's relational database product, DB2. We refer to this unofficial standard as the "DB2" standard. It happens that there is considerable overlap between the DB2 and ANSI standards. All this means is that there is a lot of confusion on the standards issue. Today many vendors of relational database products, including the ORACLE Corporation, offer a DBMS product which they claim or imply to be DB2-compatible and to also conform to the ANSI standard. In reality, all such claims are only partly true.

This book will present a discussion of SQL which is specific to the ORACLE product. It will not examine the ANSI SQL standard. (In fact, some database authorities believe that any attempt to entice or force vendor conformity to the ANSI standard is a lost cause. We believe there is merit in their argument.) However, we will have occasion to reference the DB2 standard. This is because the ORACLE Corporation has devoted considerable effort to make their version of SQL compatible with the version of SQL used with the DB2 product. In particular, those SQL statements which retrieve and update application database tables are almost identical. We say "almost" identical for a number of reasons.

1. The ORACLE version of SQL offers a number of features which are not present in the DB2 product. Many of these features enhance the power of the language and will be described in this book. However, many users may choose not to use these enhancements in order to write SQL statements which can be executed, without modification, on either product. In many circumstances, this is a reasonable policy. To assist readers who wish to adopt this policy, we will identify those ORACLE-specific SQL statements which are not compatible with the current version of DB2 (V2.2). A double-line box will enclose those sample query SQL statements which are unique to ORACLE. (See Sample Query 1.13.) Those SQL statements which will run on both ORACLE and DB2 will be enclosed by a single line box. (See Sample Query 1.1.) Because ORACLE is indeed quite (but not 100%) compatible with DB2, most of the sample queries are enclosed by a single line box.

2. The DB2 version of SQL has some features which the current version of ORACLE does not implement. These DB2-specific features will not be addressed in this text. If you are interested in examining the DB2 version of SQL, we refer you to our companion text, DB2/SQL: A Professional Programmer's Guide, also published by McGraw-Hill (1989).

3. Both ORACLE and DB2 will continue to evolve as the ORACLE Corporation and IBM make new releases of these products available to their customers. Enhancements to SQL will occur as part of this process. Because new releases of ORACLE and DB2 will occur at different times, many SQL enhancements for the DB2 product will not be implemented in the most recent version of the ORACLE product. However, it is reasonable to expect that many DB2 enhancements will subsequently appear in the ORACLE product. For this reason we will occasionally comment on DB2 features which we believe may eventually be implemented in ORACLE. Because our oracle is imperfect, we note that such comments are clearly speculative.

Embedded SQL:

ORACLE supports "embedded" SQL. This permits application programs written in COBOL, FORTRAN, C, PASCAL, etc. to contain SQL statements. This means that a production information system with batch and/or on-line programs can also interface with ORACLE. ORACLE supports embedded SQL with its precompiler software products: Pro*COBOL, Pro*FORTRAN, Pro*C, Pro*PASCAL, etc.

Embedded SQL statements are similar to the interactive SQL statements presented in this text. However, there are some significant differences. For example, an embedded SQL statement must identify a memory location where the data are to be placed after being extracted from the database. Furthermore, because these traditional programming languages are record-at-a-time oriented, special SQL statements are required to process a query that returns multiple rows. (This detracts from the previously mentioned set-at-a-time advantage of SQL. Note that the source of this problem is the host language, not SQL.) As mentioned in the Preface, this book restricts its attention to interactive SQL. However, we note that a knowledge of SQL statements as presented in this book is a necessary prerequisite for writing embedded SQL.

Efficiency Considerations:

Ideally, in a relational database environment, application programmers and users do not have to concern themselves with the machine efficiency. This task falls to the database administrator who establishes the database and specifies possible data access paths by creating indexes. (Chapter 14 will discuss this issue.) Each SQL statement is processed by a system component, called the "optimizer," to determine the most efficient way to satisfy the objective of the statement. This is an ideal scenario. To date, no vendor of any relational DBMS product produces a perfect optimizer. In particular, this applies to ORACLE and has implications for those who write SQL statements.

We will see that a single query can have many different SQL solutions. Hence a programmer/user occasionally has some options in writing SQL statements. This might be desirable if the optimizer would always choose the most efficient data access path. However, this is not the case. Therefore, the ORACLE reference manuals contain documentation describing SQL efficiency techniques. This documentation will reflect changes (presumably improvements) in future product releases.

Some of the comments in this text will address these SQL efficiency considerations. However, we do not elaborate on this issue because the optimizer improves with each new release of the system. Our objective is to teach SQL per se. This text will present the various ways of expressing a query objective. After reading this text you are advised to consult the ORACLE documentation to become aware of the idiosyncratic behavior of the current optimizer.

USING SQL*Plus to ACCESS ORACLE

The ORACLE DBMS can be accessed from many different software products (e.g., SQL*Plus, SQL*Forms, SQL*Report, and application programs using embedded SQL). The most popular way to interactively execute ad hoc SQL statements is to use SQL*Plus. SQL*Plus is sometimes called a "front-end" to ORACLE. The user indirectly submits SQL statements to ORACLE by directly interacting with the SQL*Plus product. This is illustrated in Figure I.5.

We emphasize that SQL*Plus is a separate software product that is used to enter SQL statements and display the selected data. SQL*Plus also provides a variety of additional facilities (e.g., commands for report formatting) which are not part of the SQL, but which the user will find very useful. The primary goal of this text is to teach the ORACLE version of SQL. We will describe some, but not all, of the additional facilities provided by the SQL*PLUS front-end in Chapters 2 and 8. Appendix A presents an overview on accessing SQL*Plus from your host operating system, entering SQL statements, and exiting from SQL*Plus.

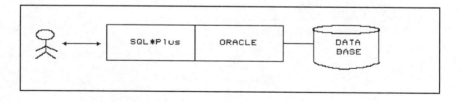

Figure I.5: Accessing ORACLE via SQL*Plus

I

SELECTing Data from a Single Table

Practically every user and programmer will be required to retrieve data that were previously stored in the database. For this reason, Part I of this text is devoted to introducing the SELECT statement, which is used for database retrieval. More specifically, we restrict our attention to selecting data from a single table. This is because many users will be limited to the relatively simple task of querying data located in a single table. Therefore, we have endeavored to encapsulate everything this audience needs to know in this part of the text. Discussion of queries that reference multiple tables is postponed until Part V of the text.

The Sample Database

This text introduces the reader to SQL by presenting a series of sample queries against a small but realistic application database. This is an academic database designed to support the information processing requirements of a mythical college. This design consists of seven tables that will be introduced as we progress through the text. (See Appendix B for a summary of this design.) All sample queries in the first six chapters will reference the same table. This is the COURSE table, which contains one row for each course in the curriculum. It is necessary that you understand the structure and content of this table in order to avoid any confusion pertaining to the illustrated sample queries.

The COURSE Table

The entire COURSE table is shown in Figure PI.1 along with a description of each column indicating its name, data type, length, and content. You should simply assume that this table exists in the database and that you have been granted permission to examine its content. You are advised to scan Figure PI.1 and then note the following points.

- Any reference to a column requires that you know and correctly enter the precise column name.

- References to some columns require a knowledge of actual stored values. For example, the CDEPT column will contain "THEO" to represent the Theology Department, "PHIL" to represent the Philosophy Department, and "CIS" to represent the Computer and Information Science Department.

- The description of data type and length is informal. A more formal presentation of SQL data types is given in Chapter 14. A proper understanding of the topics covered in Part I requires only that you comprehend the following points pertaining to SQL data types.

Introduction to SQL Data Types

In general, the database can contain three kinds of data: (1) numeric, (2) character string, and (3) date/time. The COURSE table contains two numeric columns, CRED and CLABFEE. The other four columns, CNO, CNAME, CDESCP, and CDEPT, contain character string data. Date/time data types will not be introduced until Chapter 10.

We will see that certain types of database operations can be applied only to certain data types. In particular, arithmetic should be performed only on numeric data and pattern matching should be applied only to character string data.

Different numeric columns can vary in length. This determines the range of values which may be stored in particular numeric columns. Chapter 7 will address specific issues involving operations on numeric columns.

Columns defined as a character string data type may also be of different lengths. Chapter 6 will address specific issues which involve the processing of character string data.

COURSE Table Description

Column Name	Data Type	Length	Content
CNO	Character	3	Course Number: A unique "number" used to identify each course
CNAME	Character	22	Course Name: The name of each course will also be unique
CDESCP	Character	25	Course Description: Each course should have a unique description
CRED	Number	not speci- fied	Credits: An integer value which represents the number of credits a student earns by passing a course
CLABFEE	Number	5 (max.)	Course Labfee: A decimal value that represents the labfee paid by each student who takes the course (Maximum value = 999.99)
CDEPT	Character	4	Department Identifier: This identifies the academic department that offers the course

COURSE Table Sample Data

CNO	CNAME	CDESCP	CRED	CLABFEE	CDEPT
T11	SCHOLASTICISM	FOR THE PIOUS	3	150.00	THEO
T12	FUNDAMENTALISM	FOR THE CAREFREE	3	90.00	THEO
T33	HEDONISM	FOR THE SANE	3	.00	THEO
T44	COMMUNISM	FOR THE GREEDY	6	200.00	THEO
P11	EMPIRICISM	SEE IT-BELIEVE IT	3	100.00	PHIL
P22	RATIONALISM	FOR CIS MAJORS	3	50.00	PHIL
P33	EXISTENTIALISM	FOR CIS MAJORS	3	200.00	PHIL
P44	SOLIPSISM	ME MYSELF AND I	6	.00	PHIL
C11	INTRO TO CS	FOR ROOKIES	3	100.00	CIS
C22	DATA STRUCTURES	VERY USEFUL	3	50.00	CIS
C33	DISCRETE MATHEMATICS	ABSOLUTELY NECESSARY	3	.00	CIS
C44	DIGITAL CIRCUITS	AH HA!	3	.00	CIS
C55	COMPUTER ARCH.	VON NEUMANN'S MACH.	3	100.00	CIS
C66	RELATIONAL DATABASE	THE ONLY WAY TO GO	3	500.00	CIS

Figure PI.1: COURSE table information.

Organization of Chapters

The first four chapters provide an introduction to the structure of the SELECT statement and the fundamentals of using SQL*Plus. You will learn the basic structure of the SELECT statement (Chapter 1), how to enter SQL statements and format the output display using SQL*Plus commands (Chapter 2), how to display the output in some desired sequence (Chapter 3), and how to specify complex retrieval conditions using the Boolean operators (Chapter 4). Professional programmers will be able to skim these chapters. The narrative comments are primarily directed to the "rookie" user who needs to learn the logical aspects of query specification in addition to the syntax of the SELECT statement.

Chapter 5 presents the notion of a synonym, a technique for saving keystrokes when entering SQL statements. This chapter also serves to introduce the notion of defining an object in the database, as synonyms must be defined to the system.

The next two chapters concern pattern matching (Chapter 6) and arithmetic expressions (Chapter 7). Professional programmers may also skim these chapters. However, the narrative addresses subtle points that should be read in order to obtain a comprehensive understanding of these topics.

1

The SELECT Statement

This chapter introduces the fundamental concepts and structure of the SELECT statement. This is by far the most frequently used SQL statement. Its purpose is to retrieve data from the database. In this chapter you will learn how to display an entire table or display just some specific rows and/or columns of a table. You will find that the sample queries are almost self-explanatory. In fact, some are so "obvious" that you may be tempted to skip reading the comments pertaining to each sample query. This might be appropriate for experienced professionals. However, users should not yield to this temptation. The commentary on each sample will highlight subtle issues which are important. Understanding these points will prove beneficial to those users who choose to master the more advanced topics covered later in this book.

This chapter covers only the SELECT statement. Chapter 2 will present the details of using SQL*Plus to execute SELECT statements. We recommend that rookie users adhere to the following sequence.

- Read Chapter 1 for conceptual purposes only.

- Read and execute the examples in Chapter 2 to get acquainted with using SQL*Plus.

- Return to Chapter 1 and, using your knowledge of SQL*Plus, execute the sample queries and exercises.

- Proceed to Chapter 3.

Display an Entire Table

The goal of the first sample query is to display the entire COURSE table (i.e., display every column in every row). This can be achieved by coding the simplest of all possible SELECT statements.

Sample Query 1.1: Display the entire COURSE table.

```
SELECT *

FROM    COURSE
```

CNO	CNAME	CDESCP	CRED	CLABFEE	CDEPT
T11	SCHOLASTICISM	FOR THE PIOUS	3	150.00	THEO
T12	FUNDAMENTALISM	FOR THE CAREFREE	3	90.00	THEO
T33	HEDONISM	FOR THE SANE	3	.00	THEO
T44	COMMUNISM	FOR THE GREEDY	6	200.00	THEO
P11	EMPIRICISM	SEE IT-BELIEVE IT	3	100.00	PHIL
P22	RATIONALISM	FOR CIS MAJORS	3	50.00	PHIL
P33	EXISTENTIALISM	FOR CIS MAJORS	3	200.00	PHIL
P44	SOLIPSISM	ME MYSELF AND I	6	.00	PHIL
C11	INTRO TO CS	FOR ROOKIES	3	100.00	CIS
C22	DATA STRUCTURES	VERY USEFUL	3	50.00	CIS
C33	DISCRETE MATHEMATICS	ABSOLUTELY NECESSARY	3	.00	CIS
C44	DIGITAL CIRCUITS	AH HA!	3	.00	CIS
C55	COMPUTER ARCH.	VON NEUMANN'S MACH.	3	100.00	CIS
C66	RELATIONAL DATABASE	THE ONLY WAY TO GO	3	500.00	CIS

Comments:

1.   The asterisk (*) following "SELECT" is an abbreviation for "all columns." The left-to-right column sequence of the output is determined by the order in which the columns were initially specified in the CREATE TABLE statement. (The CREATE TABLE statement will be described in Part IV of this text.)

2.   The "FROM COURSE" clause identifies the table. Your system will undoubtedly have many tables. Each table has a unique name. This name follows "FROM" in the query.

3. "SELECT" and "FROM" are keywords in SQL. A keyword always has a specific unalterable meaning in the language. In this case it means that these words will always imply the selection of data from a database table. Table names and column names are not keywords. They are established, according to certain rules, by the person who issued the CREATE TABLE statement. One of the rules is that a table or a column cannot be given the same name as any keyword. For this reason keywords are also called "reserved words." Your ORACLE reference manual will contain a list of SQL keywords.

4. You could have entered this statement as a "one-line" statement. Entering the following line would produce the same result.

    SELECT * FROM COURSE

   Throughout this text we will usually begin the FROM clause on a new line. This will enhance readability of the SQL code. In practice you may find it easier to type just one line. The key point is that, regardless of how you type the statement, it is interpreted as a single statement.

5. Observe that the rows of the displayed output are not sorted. This is because

   a. Tables do not have any predefined sort sequence.
   b. The SELECT statement does not contain an ORDER BY
      clause.

   In general, you can never assume the displayed result will be in any particular sequence unless you explicitly designate some sort sequence by using the ORDER BY clause. We will examine this clause in Chapter 3.

6. This statement does not contain a WHERE clause. In the next example we will see that a WHERE clause is used to select just some of the rows from a table. The point we wish to emphasize here is that the absence of a WHERE clause means that ORACLE will retrieve all rows from the table.

WHERE Clause

Most real-world databases have tables which contain too many rows to be examined visually by the user. With the exception of small tables, you will rarely want to display an entire table. Instead, you will use the WHERE clause in the SELECT statement to display just those rows that you want to see. (WHERE is another SQL keyword.) The next sample query illustrates this clause.

Sample Query 1.2: Display all information about any course with a zero labfee. (More precisely, select just those rows from the COURSE table where the CLABFEE value is zero. Display every column of these rows.)

```
SELECT  *

FROM    COURSE

WHERE   CLABFEE = 0.00
```

CNO	CNAME	CDESCP	CRED	CLABFEE	CDEPT
C33	DISCRETE MATHEMATICS	ABSOLUTELY NECESSARY	3	.00	CIS
C44	DIGITAL CIRCUITS	AH HA!	3	.00	CIS
P44	SOLIPSISM	ME MYSELF AND I	6	.00	PHIL
T33	HEDONISM	FOR THE SANE	3	.00	THEO

Comments:

1. The WHERE clause follows the FROM clause. Again, we could have entered the SELECT statement in one line. The following statement is equivalent to the one shown above.

    SELECT * FROM COURSE WHERE CLABFEE = 0.00

2.   The syntax of the WHERE clause is

WHERE condition

The condition in our example is "CLABFEE = 0.00". It is the condition which specifies which rows are to be retrieved. Examine the entire COURSE table and then observe the result. Four of the rows in the COURSE table have CLABFEE values equal to zero. These rows form the displayed result. Only rows which match the WHERE condition are displayed.

3.   CLABFEE was defined as a numeric field. Hence, this is an example of a "numeric" compare. This means the system compares on mathematical value rather than on a character-by-character basis. The following WHERE conditions are all equivalent and would select the same four rows as the original example.

WHERE CLABFEE = 0

WHERE CLABFEE = 0.0

WHERE CLABFEE = 00.00

4.   Numeric values can contain a leading minus sign (-). However, no other punctuation is permitted.

5.   Our example compares on an "equals" (=) condition. Other comparison operators are

"less than" (<)
"greater than" (>)
"less than or equal to" (<=)
"greater than or equal to" (>=)
"not equal" (<>) or (!=)

6.   Our example illustrates a "simple" WHERE condition. It references only one column (CLABFEE) and does not contain any Boolean operators such as AND, OR, and NOT. We will study the Boolean operators in Chapter 4.

The next sample query contains a WHERE clause to select rows based on CDEPT value. This query is similar to the previous one, with one important exception. The CDEPT column contains character data. This means that the comparison value must be enclosed within apostrophes.

Sample Query 1.3:   Display all information about any course which is offered by the Philosophy Department. (More precisely, select just those rows from the COURSE table where the CDEPT value is "PHIL". Display all columns.)

```
SELECT *

FROM    COURSE

WHERE   CDEPT = 'PHIL'
```

CNO	CNAME	CDESCP	CRED	CLABFEE	CDEPT
P11	EMPIRICISM	SEE IT-BELIEVE IT	3	100.00	PHIL
P22	RATIONALISM	FOR CIS MAJORS	3	50.00	PHIL
P33	EXISTENTIALISM	FOR CIS MAJORS	3	200.00	PHIL
P44	SOLIPSISM	ME MYSELF AND I	6	.00	PHIL

Comments:

1.   Syntax: The character string must be contained within apostrophes. Our example illustrates WHERE CDEPT = 'PHIL'. (Note that this is not the case with numeric data. The previous example referenced CLABFEE. That WHERE clause did not contain apostrophes.)

2.   Comparison of character string data is performed on a character-by-character basis. Two strings are equal only if

    (i)   both strings are the same length, and

    (ii) corresponding characters match exactly.

3.   DB2 Compatibility: We will describe the ORACLE data types in Chapter 14. However, a preliminary comment is appropriate at this point. ORACLE stores character string data in variable-length format. This means no trailing blanks are stored with the data (unless such blanks are explicitly entered, something which usually occurs by accident, not design). For example, some rows have a CDEPT value of "CIS", not "CIS ". This means that the following WHERE clause will not select any rows from the COURSE table.

```
        WHERE CDEPT = 'CIS '
```

We emphasize this point to note a special DB2 compatibility problem. DB2 allows character string data to be stored in variable or fixed-length format. The compatibility problem lies with the fixed-length format which will store trailing blanks. If the CDEPT column were fixed length with a maximum length of four, the "CIS" would be stored as "CIS ". In DB2 the fixed-length character comparison operation works such that a match would occur on both the following WHERE clauses. They are *not equivalent in ORACLE*.

```
        WHERE CDEPT = 'CIS'
        WHERE CDEPT = 'CIS '
```

4.   The previous examples illustrate "full" character string comparisons. This means that a row is selected only if every corresponding character matches each other. In Chapter 6 we will discuss "partial" character string comparisons. This will help you search for any character string pattern regardless of its position within the column.

5.   Reminder: Very often something called "number" is defined as a character string. Such is the case with the "course number" (CNO) column. Real-world systems contain part numbers, policy numbers, Social Security numbers, etc., stored as character data simply because no calculations are to be performed with these values. Also, they sometimes contain alphabetic characters. When these "numbers" are stored as character strings, you must use apostrophes in the WHERE clause.

Exercises:

1A. Display all rows where the labfee is less than $150.

1B. Display all rows where the number of credits exceeds 3.

1C. Display all information about courses offered by the Theology Department.

1D. Display all information about the Relational Database course.

1E. Display the row for course number P44.

Usually we compare character data using the equals (=) condition. Occasionally we would like to compare character data using the other comparison operators (<, >, <=, >=, <>). Consider the following sample query which requires such a comparison.

Sample Query 1.4:   Display all information about courses having CNAME values which follow "HEDONISM" in alphabetic sequence.

```
SELECT *

FROM    COURSE

WHERE   CNAME > 'HEDONISM'
```

CNO	CNAME	CDESCP	CRED	CLABFEE	CDEPT
T11	SCHOLASTICISM	FOR THE PIOUS	3	150.00	THEO
P22	RATIONALISM	FOR CIS MAJORS	3	50.00	PHIL
P44	SOLIPSISM	ME MYSELF AND I	6	.00	PHIL
C11	INTRO TO CS	FOR ROOKIES	3	100.00	CIS
C66	RELATIONAL DATABASE	THE ONLY WAY TO GO	3	500.00	CIS

Comments:

1.   The system will compare each CNAME value with the character string "HEDONISM". All CNAME values contain just the standard characters (A to Z). This means that the evaluation will be based on the conventional alphabetic sequence.

2.   A special case exists when the character strings being compared contain digits, special symbols, and both upper- and lowercase letters. ORACLE will evaluate a character sequence according to the sequence specified by the EBCDIC or ASCII codes. These codes specify the collating sequence for all characters found within the system. Figure 1.1 illustrates the EBCDIC sequence and the ASCII sequence.

      The EBCDIC code is used by IBM mainframe systems. Almost all other systems (DEC, SUN, IBM PC, etc.) use the ASCII code. The sample data found in the COURSE table has all uppercase character strings. The sequencing of this data will be the same for both the ASCII and EBCDIC codes.

Within the EBCDIC code you will note that special characters (&,?,+, etc.) will sort before lowercase letters, which in turn sort before uppercase letters, which in turn sort before the digits. With the ASCII code the separation of character types is not as distinct. However, most of the special characters precede the digits. Following the digits are the uppercase letters and then the lowercase letters.

When comparing character data using an operator other than equals, the system examines the two strings on a character-by-character basis beginning with the leftmost character of each string. Comparison continues until an inequality is encountered or, if the strings are of unequal length, one of the strings has been exhausted. In this case the shorter of the two strings is considered to be "less than" the longer string.

Listed below are the some character strings sorted according to both the EBCDIC and ASCII sequences.

!!!FIDO!!!	!!!FIDO!!!
jessie	3M
julie	77aaaaaaaAAAAAAAAA
Jessie	JEssie
JEssie	JULIE
JULIe	JULIe
JULIE	Jessie
Zeek	Zeek
3M	jessie
77aaaaaaaAAAAAAAAA	julie
EBCDIC Sort Sequence	**ASCII Sort Sequence**

Exercises:

1F. Display every row where the course number is less than "P01".

1G. Display every row where the course name is greater than "RATIONALISM".

	EBCDIC		ASCII	
(Low)	Symbols:	. < (+ ...	Symbols:	! $ % & (...
	Lowercase:	a b c d e ...	Digits:	0 1 2 3 4 ...
	Uppercase:	A B C D E ...	Uppercase:	A B C D E ...
(High)	Digits:	0 1 2 3 4 ...	Lowercase:	a b c d e ...

Figure 1.1: Hierarchy of EBCDIC and ASCII characters.

Displaying Specified Columns

All of the previous examples selected every column. This was because the statement began with "SELECT *". In practice we usually want to examine just some specified columns. The current example illustrates how to achieve this objective. We simply specify the column names after "SELECT". Only those specified columns are displayed.

Sample Query 1.5:   Display the CNO, CNAME, and CDEPT values (in that order) for every row in the COURSE table.

```
SELECT CNO, CNAME, CDEPT

FROM    COURSE
```

CNO	CNAME	CDEPT
C11	INTRO TO CS	CIS
C22	DATA STRUCTURES	CIS
C33	DISCRETE MATHEMATICS	CIS
C44	DIGITAL CIRCUITS	CIS
C55	COMPUTER ARCH.	CIS
C66	RELATIONAL DATABASE	CIS
P11	EMPIRICISM	PHIL
P22	RATIONALISM	PHIL
P33	EXISTENTIALISM	PHIL
P44	SOLIPSISM	PHIL
T11	SCHOLASTICISM	THEO
T12	FUNDAMENTALISM	THEO
T33	HEDONISM	THEO
T44	COMMUNISM	THEO

Comments:

1.   Syntax: Each column name must be separated by a comma. You may optionally include one or more spaces before or after the comma.

2.   You must know the names of the columns. Usually you are
     working with a familiar database, and therefore this
     will not be a problem. Otherwise you must do one of the
     following.

     a.   Ask somebody who knows. ("Poor show.")

     b.   Issue a statement beginning with "SELECT *". The
          output will display all the names of the columns.
          (Again, "Poor show." You are wasting computer
          resources, especially if the table has many rows.)

     c.   Examine the documentation that the database
          administrator should have produced and made
          available to you. This should contain the names of
          the columns that you can access.

     d.   Let's assume that documentation is not available,
          and you correctly reject the first two approaches.
          Then you must examine the ORACLE's Data Dictionary.
          Information about tables and columns is stored in
          the Data Dictionary. Certain dictionary features
          will be presented at appropriate points in our
          examination of SQL. In Chapter 13 we will present
          DESCRIBE, a SQL*Plus command, which can be used to
          display the column names for a specified table.
          Chapter 26 concludes this text by presenting an
          overview of the Data Dictionary.

3.   This example happens to select the three columns in the
     same left-to-right order as was established by the
     database administrator; this is the same order which is
     displayed when you issue a query beginning with
     "SELECT *". This is not required. Columns can be
     displayed in any left-to-right order. See the next
     sample query.

4.   Note that the current query did not have a WHERE clause.
     Hence all rows of the COURSE table are retrieved. But
     only the three specified columns are displayed.

This next example produces essentially the same result as the previous example. The content is the same. The only difference is the specification of the left-to-right column sequence.

Sample Query 1.6:   Display the CDEPT, CNAME, and CNO values (in that order) for every row in the COURSE table.

```
SELECT  CDEPT, CNAME, CNO

FROM    COURSE
```

CDEPT	CNAME	CNO
CIS	INTRO TO CS	C11
CIS	DATA STRUCTURES	C22
CIS	DISCRETE MATHEMATICS	C33
CIS	DIGITAL CIRCUITS	C44
CIS	COMPUTER ARCH.	C55
CIS	RELATIONAL DATABASE	C66
PHIL	EMPIRICISM	P11
PHIL	RATIONALISM	P22
PHIL	EXISTENTIALISM	P33
PHIL	SOLIPSISM	P44
THEO	SCHOLASTICISM	T11
THEO	FUNDAMENTALISM	T12
THEO	HEDONISM	T33
THEO	COMMUNISM	T44

Comments:

1. The SELECT clause specifies the left-to-right ordering
    of the displayed columns. The example shows that CDEPT
    is the leftmost column, followed by CNAME and then CNO.

2. Again we have no WHERE clause. Hence all rows are
    retrieved.

3. You can specify any valid COURSE column name after
    "SELECT" as long as the COURSE table is referenced in
    the FROM clause. You can even enter the same column name
    more than once. This means that the following query is
    valid.

```
        SELECT CDEPT, CNAME, CLABFEE, CLABFEE, CLABFEE
        FROM COURSE
```

    This is obviously redundant. But it is valid and will
    produce three identical CLABFEE columns. (There is a
    situation where this does make sense. In some systems
    the result of the query may be passed onto an external
    program for further processing. This external program
    may then perform different calculations on the same
    data.)

Exercises:

1H. Select course name and description, in that order, for
    every course.

1I. Select department, course number, labfee, and credits,
    in that order, for every course.

Display Some Subset of Rows and Columns

This next example combines the previously described techniques to select some subset of rows (using the WHERE clause) and some subset of columns (by explicitly specifying column names after "SELECT"). The example does not introduce any new SQL reserved words.

Sample Query 1.7:   Select the CNO, CDEPT, and CLABFEE values for every course with a CLABFEE value less than $100.

```
SELECT  CNO, CDEPT, CLABFEE

FROM    COURSE

WHERE   CLABFEE  <   100.00
```

CNO	CDEPT	CLABFEE
C22	CIS	50.00
C33	CIS	.00
C44	CIS	.00
P22	PHIL	50.00
P44	PHIL	.00
T12	THEO	90.00
T33	THEO	.00

Comments:

1. This example illustrates the general format of a typical SELECT statement. This is

        SELECT col1, col2, ..., colN
        FROM   table-name
        WHERE   condition

2. In the current example the WHERE condition referenced CLABFEE, and we happened to select CLABFEE to be displayed in the output. It is not necessary to display a column used in a retrieval condition. The following example which retrieves all three credit courses displays only the course name and description. It may not be reasonable to display the CRED column because it will be the same for all displayed rows.

        SELECT CNAME, CDESCP
        FROM   COURSE
        WHERE   CRED = 3

3. Remember that no punctuation is allowed in numeric constants. Therefore, even though we are comparing on 100 dollars, the example does not show a "$" before the "100."

Exercises:

1J. Select course number and labfee for all courses where the labfee exceeds $100.00.

1K. Select the course names of all CIS courses.

Observe that the displayed output for all previous sample queries did not contain any duplicate rows. This can occur. Consider the next sample query.

Sample Query 1.8:   Display every academic department which offers courses. (Select every row of the COURSE table. Display just the CDEPT column.)

```
SELECT  CDEPT

FROM    COURSE
```

CDEPT
CIS
CIS
CIS
CIS
CIS
CIS
PHIL
PHIL
PHIL
PHIL
THEO
THEO
THEO
THEO

Comments:

1.   This sample query does realize the objective of displaying every department which offers courses. However, because a department offers many courses, there are many duplicate rows in the displayed output. The system does not automatically remove duplicate rows from the output display. You must use the reserved word "DISTINCT" to prevent duplicate rows from being displayed. This will be described in the next sample query.

2.   You should recognize when duplicate rows can possibly occur. This implies that you know some facts about the content of the COURSE table. Let us assume that our mythical college has established a reasonable policy that course numbers, course names, and course descriptions must be unique. (Chapters 14 and 15 will describe how the system can enforce this policy.) Assuming that our sample COURSE table reflects this policy, you can be certain that duplicate rows will not be displayed under the following circumstances.

   a.   The SELECT clause contains CNO, CNAME, or CDESCP. (Or, a "SELECT *" implicitly references these columns.)

   b.   The WHERE clause compares the CNO, CNAME, or CDESCP columns using an equals (=) comparison operator. This implies that only one row can be selected.

   All of our previous sample queries and exercises met one of these conditions. Hence, duplicate rows never appeared in any of the previous output displays. The current example references only CDEPT. No reference is made to CNO, CNAME, or CDESCP. Hence duplicates can and do occur in the result.

3.   General Advice: Examine each SELECT statement (prior to execution) to see if it references a "unique" column which will inhibit duplicate rows from being displayed. If this is not the case, you should anticipate duplicate rows in the output display.

Exercise:

1L.   Select every row. Display just the course labfees. (Do not attempt to remove possible duplicate rows.)

DISTINCT Keyword

The next sample query is identical to the previous one with the additional stipulation that the displayed output does not contain any duplicate rows. We use the keyword "DISTINCT" to achieve this objective.

Sample Query 1.9:   Display every academic department which offers courses. Do not display duplicate values.

```
SELECT DISTINCT CDEPT

FROM    COURSE
```

CDEPT
CIS
PHIL
THEO

Comments:

1.   Syntax: The keyword "DISTINCT" must directly follow "SELECT" separated by one or more spaces.

2.   Only duplicate rows will be removed. In this example the row consists of a single column. The next sample query will display multiple columns. We will see that a row is considered to be a duplicate of another row only if every column value in the first row matches every corresponding column value in the second row.

3.   You are not required to remove duplicate rows. The previous sample query, by displaying the duplicate rows, indicated how many courses were offered by various academic departments. (Chapter 8 will introduce the COUNT function which would better serve this purpose.) The use of DISTINCT is entirely contingent on the user's objective.

The next sample query selects just some rows and displays multiple columns. Such queries are less likely to produce duplicate rows. However, as the example illustrates, duplicate rows can occur.

Sample Query 1.10: For each course with a labfee less than $100, display the academic department which offers the course and the number of awarded credits.

```
SELECT  CDEPT, CRED

FROM    COURSE

WHERE   CLABFEE < 100.00
```

CDEPT	CRED
CIS	3
CIS	3
CIS	3
PHIL	3
PHIL	6
THEO	3
THEO	3

Comments:

1. The SELECT statement did not reference any of the "unique" columns (CNO, CNAME, CDESCP). Hence duplicate rows can be present in the displayed result.

2. You could simply decide whether you want to see duplicate rows and then include or exclude DISTINCT according to your decision. This is an acceptable approach. However, the use of DISTINCT asks the system to do some extra work to remove the duplicate rows. Therefore, if the result is large, and you can determine that it will not contain duplicate rows, it is better to avoid asking the system to do the unnecessary work of removing nonexistent duplicate rows.

Sample Query 1.11: Same as previous sample query. However, do not display duplicate rows.

```
SELECT DISTINCT CDEPT, CRED

FROM    COURSE

WHERE   CLABFEE < 100.00
```

CDEPT	CRED
CIS	3
PHIL	3
PHIL	6
THEO	3

Comment:

Only rows which were complete duplicates of other rows were not displayed. (The reader should closely examine the results of this query as compared to the previous one.) The key concept is that DISTINCT does not refer to any individual column. It refers to the entire row.

Exercises:

1M. Display the set of all course labfees. Do not display any duplicate values.

1N. Display the credits and labfees for all CIS courses. Allow duplicate rows to be displayed.

1O. Display the credits and labfees for all CIS courses. Do not display any duplicate rows.

Displaying Constant Data

It is possible to incorporate constant data into a column of the result table. The next sample query shows the inclusion of a character string which serves to describe the result table.

Sample Query 1.12: Display the course number and name of every course which has a labfee over $100. Include a third column in the result table which shows "EXPENSIVE" in each row.

```
SELECT CNO, CNAME, 'EXPENSIVE'

FROM    COURSE

WHERE   CLABFEE > 100
```

CNO	CNAME	'EXPENSIV
T11	SCHOLASTICISM	EXPENSIVE
T44	COMMUNISM	EXPENSIVE
P33	EXISTENTIALISM	EXPENSIVE
C66	RELATIONAL DATABASE	EXPENSIVE

Comments:

1. The constant to be displayed in the result table is specified in the SELECT clause. Any constant, numeric or character, can be specified.

2. The constant is shown redundantly in each row. This is the only option SQL provides. It would probably be desirable to include "EXPENSIVE" just once as a report title for the result table. However, you would have to use the SQL*Plus report generator facilities to achieve this objective. (See the TTITLE command described in the next chapter.)

3. The system will generate a column header for the constant data. This column header is not very elegant. The next sample query will show how to produce a more meaningful column header.

Column Aliases

The column names were used as the default column headings for each of the previous sample queries. The ORACLE version of SQL permits a variation of the SELECT clause to contain a "column alias" which can serve a number of purposes. One such purpose, the specification of a column heading, is shown in the next sample query.

   A column alias is simply another name for a column. A column alias for a specified column is entered in the SELECT clause immediately after the column name. The system will then use the column alias in the column heading.

Sample Query 1.13:   Display the course number, name, and labfee for all philosophy courses. The corresponding column headings should be displayed as "CN", "COURSE_NAME", and "CLABFEE".

```
SELECT CNO CN, CNAME COURSE_NAME, CLABFEE
FROM    COURSE
WHERE   CDEPT = 'PHIL'
```

CN	COURSE_NAME	CLABFEE
P11	EMPIRICISM	100.00
P22	RATIONALISM	50.00
P33	EXISTENTIALISM	200.00
P44	SOLIPSISM	.00

Comments:

1.   Syntax: The column alias follows the column name separated by one or more spaces. (Do not use a comma to separate the column name from its alias.) The sample query specifies CN as an alias for the CNO column and COURSE_NAME as an alias for the CNAME column. No alias was defined for the CLABFEE column.

2. Do not make the column alias longer than the size of the data in the column. For example, do not use CNUMBER as an alias for the CNO column. The alias will be truncated showing just "CNU". This is because the length of the CNO column is three.

3. DB2 Compatibility: The column alias feature is an ORACLE extension. It will cause a syntax error in DB2. Therefore, for reasons specified in the introduction to this text, you should try to avoid its use.

Chapter 2 will present the COLUMN command which can be used with a standard SELECT statement to realize the report formatting objective of this sample query. The COLUMN command is unique to the SQL*Plus system and hence it is also specific to the ORACLE product. However, the COLUMN command is a separate report formatting command. Its use allows the SELECT statement to retain a standard form.

As mentioned above, a column alias can serve other objectives which will be described later in this text. In some of these cases the benefits gained by using an alias may be worth the cost associated with nonstandard statements. Also, the documentation provided with the ORACLE product provides a number of examples which utilize column aliases. Hence, we reiterate our philosophical position that you should understand the ORACLE extensions, but avoid their use unless significant benefits can be realized.

4. Qualification of Column Names: You can use the name of a table as a prefix qualifier for any of its columns. The table name precedes the column name separated by a period. We rewrite Sample Query 1.11 to illustrate this point.

```
SELECT DISTINCT COURSE.CDEPT, COURSE.CRED
FROM    COURSE
WHERE   COURSE.CLABFEE < 100.00
```

In this example, the qualification serves no real purpose. However, Chapter 17 will illustrate a case where qualification is necessary.

Summary

This chapter has introduced the basic structure of the SQL SELECT statement. We showed three clauses of this statement.

```
SELECT  column names
FROM    table name
WHERE   condition
```

The query is formulated by

1. Identifying the table which contains the desired data. The table name is placed in the FROM clause.

2. Identifying the columns to be displayed. The column names are placed in the SELECT clause. ("SELECT *" will display all columns.)

3. Coding a condition in the WHERE clause which specifies the row selection criteria. The absence of a WHERE clause means that every row will be selected.

   We also introduced the keyword DISTINCT, which, when placed in the SELECT clause, will inhibit the display of duplicate rows. We emphasized the semantic implications of using DISTINCT.

Summary Exercises

The following exercises all pertain to the STAFF table, which has four columns. These are ENAME, ETITLE, ESALARY, and DEPT.

1P. Display the entire STAFF table.

1Q. Display all information about any employee whose yearly salary is less than $1000.

1R. Display all information about any employee who is employed by the Theology Department.

1S. Display the names and titles of all staff members.

1T. Display the name and salary of any employee whose salary exceeds $1000.

1U. Display the name and title for any staff member whose name is less than MARK in alphabetic sequence.

1V. Display the titles of all staff members. Do not show duplicate values.

Chapter

2

An Introduction to SQL*Plus

The sample queries introduced in Chapter 1 presented SELECT statements in a "standard form." This standard form does not illustrate the actual screen images observed by a user who is using the SQL*Plus facility to enter SQL statements. The primary goal of this chapter is to introduce the reader to some of the editing and report formatting facilities of SQL*Plus. After reading this chapter you will be able to use SQL*Plus to execute SQL statements and display the retrieved data in a simple report format.

No new SQL statements are presented in this chapter. Hence, you will not find any new sample queries. Instead, this chapter introduces a new class of statements which are properly referred to as SQL*Plus "commands." Most SQL*Plus commands are very simple to learn and execute. However, there is a conceptual distinction between SQL "statements" and SQL*Plus "commands" which should be understood. After introducing some basic SQL*Plus commands we conclude this chapter by describing these important conceptual distinctions.

The information presented in this chapter is just enough to get you started. You will be able to use SQL*Plus to execute the SQL statements and exercises presented in the next five chapters. In Chapter 11 we will return to SQL*Plus and present more report formatting commands and other commands which will be helpful for "housekeeping" purposes.

(If you have installed the sample database available for this text, you are encouraged to execute each of the sample SQL statements and SQL*Plus commands presented in this chapter.)

Entering SQL Statements

Assume you have just signed onto SQL*Plus as illustrated in
Appendix A and the system has displayed the SQL prompt as
shown below.

        SQL>

The system is now waiting for you to enter your first SQL
statement. Assume you would like to execute the following
SELECT statement (shown in "standard form").

        SELECT CNO, CRED
        FROM   COURSE
        WHERE   CDEPT = 'CIS'

One way to execute this statement using SQL*Plus is to follow
a four-step procedure.

        1. Position the cursor after the SQL prompt.
        2. Type the entire SELECT statement.
        3. Type a semicolon (;) at the end of the statement.
        4. Press the Enter key to execute the statement.

Prior to step 4 the last line of the screen image should
contain

        SQL> SELECT CNO, CRED FROM COURSE WHERE CDEPT= 'CIS';

After pressing the Enter key, the system executes the
statement and displays:

        CNO   CRED
        ---   -----
        C11   3
        C22   3
        C33   3
        C44   3
        C55   3
        C66   3

        6 records selected

Comments:

1. Placing a semicolon at the end of the SELECT statement
    is necessary. However, the semicolon is not part of the
    SELECT statement. (This is why the semicolon was not
    shown in the sample queries of Chapter 1.) The purpose
    of the semicolon is to indicate the termination of the
    SELECT statement. In SQL*Plus all SQL statements must be
    terminated by a semicolon.

2. SQL statements can be entered on multiple lines. This is
    necessary if the statement is too long to fit on one
    line. Using multiple lines also enhances readability (as
    illustrated in the sample queries presented in Chapter
    1). Simply type each line of the SQL statement and press
    the Enter key. Each time you press the Enter key, the
    system will prompt you for the next line. Place the
    semicolon at the end of the last line. This terminates
    the statement. Instead of prompting you for the next
    line, the system executes the statement. We demonstrate
    this with the previous example.

    Position the cursor after the SQL prompt and type just
    the SELECT clause and press the Enter key.

    SQL> SELECT CNO, CRED

    Because there is no semicolon at the end of the line,
    the system prompts for the second line of the statement
    by displaying a "2". Type the FROM clause on this line
    and press the Enter key.

    2   FROM COURSE

    Again, because there is no semicolon at the end of the
    line, the system prompts for the third line by
    displaying a "3". Type the WHERE clause, followed by a
    semicolon, and press the Enter key.

    3   WHERE CDEPT = 'CIS';

    The system, having detected the semicolon, will execute
    the statement and produce the same result shown on the
    previous page.

    It is not necessary to decompose a SQL statement by the
    separate clauses as shown in this example. It is
    required only that each line end with a complete word
    before pressing the Enter key.

Editing an SQL Statement

Preliminary Comment:

SQL*Plus provides some simple editing commands which are easy to learn. However, these commands are not very powerful. This is because SQL*Plus provides a line editor, not a full-screen editor. This is only a minor problem because SQL*Plus provides a way (via the EDIT command) for you to utilize other editors which may be found in your host operating system. Fortunately many SQL statements are quite short. This means that it is often easier to retype the entire statement or to use the following line editor commands.

The LIST Command:

Assume you have just executed the previous SELECT statement, the result has been displayed, and the cursor is positioned after the SQL prompt. You can request the system to display the previous SELECT statement after the SQL prompt by using the LIST command. Simply type "LIST", or "L" as an abbreviation, without a semicolon and press the Enter key. The system will respond by displaying the previous SQL statement.

```
---------------------------------------
SQL> LIST
  1  SELECT CNO, CRED
  2  FROM   COURSE
  3* WHERE  CDEPT = 'CIS'
---------------------------------------
```

Comments:

1. Syntax: LIST is a SQL*Plus "command," not an SQL "statement." A SQL*Plus command does not require a semicolon to terminate the command. However, a semicolon may be placed after the command without any effect. Occasionally a long SQL*Plus command extends beyond one line. When this happens, use a hyphen (-) to continue the command onto the next line.

2. Note that a semicolon is not shown at the end of line 3. This is because the semicolon is not part of the SELECT statement.

3. The system can display the previous SQL statement because it always saves this statement in an internal location called the "SQL Buffer." This buffer contains only the previous SQL statement. It does not contain any SQL*Plus commands which may have been entered after the most recent SQL statement.

4.   Observe the asterisk (*) after the "3" in the third
      line. It indicates that line 3 is the "current line" of
      a multiple-line SQL statement. You can make any line the
      current line by typing the line number after the LIST
      command. For example, to make Line 2 the current line
      and display it, you would enter "LIST 2" or "L2". The
      result is shown below.

```
SQL> LIST 2
  2* FROM COURSE
```

Our discussion of the CHANGE command will illustrate the
usefulness of this feature.

The RUN Command:

Assume, somewhat unrealistically, you wanted to reexecute the
previous SQL statement without making any change. Simply
enter "RUN", or "R" as an abbreviation, and press the Enter
key.

```
------------------------------------
SQL> RUN
  1   SELECT CNO, CRED
  2   FROM    COURSE
  3*  WHERE   CDEPT = 'CIS'
------------------------------------

CNO    CRED
---    -----
C11     3
C22     3
C33     3
C44     3
C55     3
C66     3

6 records selected
```

Comments:

1.   Observe that RUN will list the SQL statement before
      displaying the result table.

2.   When you use RUN to reexecute the previous statement you
      normally expect the same result. However, you might
      observe a change in a multiuser environment. This is
      because another user (who has update privileges on the
      COURSE table) might change the data sometime between the
      first execution and subsequent reexecution of the same
      statement. This cannot occur if you are on a single-user
      system (e.g., Professional ORACLE) or you are the only
      user who has update privileges on the table. (Update
      privileges will be discussed in Part VI of this text.)

The CHANGE Command:

Occasionally you will want to make a small change to the
previous statement and then execute the modified statement.
Or, more frequently, you will make a typing error when
entering an SQL statement and wish to correct it without
retyping the entire statement. This can be done with the
CHANGE command.

Assume you have just entered LIST and the result is the same
as the previous example. The last few lines of the screen
appear as

```
SQL> LIST
  1   SELECT CNO, CRED
  2   FROM    COURSE
  3* WHERE   CDEPT = 'CIS'
```

You would like to change this statement to display the CNO
and CRED values for philosophy courses. Substituting "PHIL"
for "CIS" in the third line (which happens to be the current
line) will do the job. The CHANGE command, which always
applies to the current line, will replace "CIS" with "PHIL".

```
-------------------------------
SQL> CHANGE /CIS/PHIL/
  3* WHERE   CDEPT = 'PHIL'
-------------------------------
```

After entering this command, you immediately see the altered
line. You may also see the effect of the CHANGE command by
listing the current statement.

```
SQL> LIST
  1   SELECT CNO, CRED
  2   FROM    COURSE
  3* WHERE   CDEPT = 'PHIL'
```

You can now use the RUN command to produce the following
result.

```
SQL> RUN
  1   SELECT CNO, CRED
  2   FROM    COURSE
  3* WHERE   CDEPT = 'PHIL'

CNO    CRED
---    -----
P11       3
P22       3
P33       3
P44       6
```

Comments:

1.   Syntax: The general syntax for the CHANGE command is

> CHANGE /old string/new string/

CHANGE can be abbreviated as "C". The slash (/) is called a "delimiter" and is used to separate the "old string" from the "new string." Any character not present in the old or new string can serve as a delimiter. The "C" can optionally be followed by one or more spaces. The following examples are all equivalent to the previous example.

```
C /CIS/PHIL/
C *CIS*PHIL*
C/CIS/PHIL/
```

2.   If you want to change a line which is not the current line, you must first use the LIST command to set the desired line to the current line. For example, assume the screen shows

```
SQL> LIST
  1  SELECT CNO, CRED
  2  FROM    COURSE
  3* WHERE   CDEPT = 'PHIL'
```

If you wanted to display CLABFEE values instead of CRED values, you would first enter "L1" to make line 1 the current line, make the change, and then enter "LIST" to display the entire statement.

```
SQL> L1
  1* SELECT CNO, CRED
SQL> C /CRED/CLABFEE/
  1* SELECT CNO, CLABFEE
SQL> LIST
  1  SELECT CNO, CLABFEE
  2  FROM    COURSE
  3* WHERE   CDEPT = 'PHIL'
```

3.   The CHANGE command can be used to delete characters from the current line. To remove "CNO," from line 1 you could enter either "C /CNO,//" or "C /CNO,/".

4.   The CHANGE command can change only the current line and only one occurrence of a string in that line. For example, if the current line were "SELECT CNO, CLABFEE", and you wanted to change it to "SELECT XNO, XLABFEE", you would enter "C /CNO, C/XNO, X/" or enter the "C /C/X/" command twice.

The DEL Command:

Assume you wanted to delete the WHERE clause (the third line) of the previous example. You would use "L3" to make the third line the current line. Then you would use the DEL (the "delete") command to delete that line. It would then be wise to list the entire statement to verify the change. This is illustrated below.

```
--------------------------------
SQL> L3
   3* WHERE CDEPT = 'PHIL'
SQL> DEL
SQL> L
   1   SELECT CNO, CLABFEE
   2*  FROM    COURSE
--------------------------------
```

The INPUT Command:

Assume you wanted to insert a new line in an SQL statement. You would use the INPUT command to insert the new line after the current line. The general form of the INPUT command is

    INPUT text

The keyword INPUT can be abbreviated as "I". The following example shows the insertion of a new line to specify additional columns to be displayed. The insertion occurs after the first line. LIST is entered for verification purposes.

```
--------------------------------------
SQL> L1
   1*  SELECT CNO, CLABFEE
SQL> I ,CNAME, CDESCP, CDEPT
SQL> L
   1   SELECT CNO, CLABFEE
   2   ,CNAME, CDESCP, CDEPT
   3*  FROM    COURSE
--------------------------------------
```

Note that the system will automatically renumber the lines. Another variation of this command will allow you to insert multiple lines after the current line. You need only to type "I" and press the Enter key. The system will prompt you for the next line. Enter each line and press the Enter key. Entering an empty line (just the Enter key) terminates the insertion process.

The APPEND Command:

Assume a listing of the current SQL statement shows

```
SQL> LIST
  1   SELECT CNO, CLABFEE
  2*  FROM    COURSE
```

The previous example inserted a new line to select additional columns. We could have realized the same objective by appending the column names to line 1. This would be done by using the APPEND command. The APPEND command appends a character string to the end of the current line. Its general form is

    APPEND text

The keyword APPEND can be abbreviated as "A." There must be a space between "A" and "text." The following example shows the use of APPEND to realize the same objective as the previous example used to illustrate the INPUT command.

```
-----------------------------------------------------
SQL> L1
  1*  SELECT CNO, CLABFEE
SQL> A , CNAME, CDESCP, CDEPT
  1   SELECT CNO, CLABFEE, CNAME, CDESCP, CDEPT
SQL> LIST
  1   SELECT CNO, CLABFEE, CNAME, CDESCP, CDEPT
  2*  FROM    COURSE
-----------------------------------------------------
```

The EDIT Command:

Many users will be familiar with some editor which is provided with their host operating system. To use such an editor you simply enter "EDIT" and press the Enter key. The contents of the SQL buffer are accessed by the host editor. You could use the editing facilities of this editor to modify the current SQL statement. Then, after following the normal "save and exit" procedure for the editor, the SQL prompt is redisplayed.

A variation on the EDIT command allows you to edit any file without exiting SQL*Plus. The format of this variation is

    EDIT filename

The syntax of "filename" must conform to a valid file name according to the rules of the host operating system.

Simple Report Formatting

SQL*Plus provides commands which can be used to display data retrieved by a SELECT statement in the form of a traditional report. However, SQL*Plus is not a comprehensive report generator. (The ORACLE Corporation offers another software product, SQL*Report, which serves this purpose.) In this section we introduce some simple commands to produce report titles, modify column titles, and edit column data. In Chapter 11 we return to report formatting and describe how to establish control breaks and perform summary arithmetic at control breaks. Before presenting specific commands we make some general statements.

1.   Each of the following report formatting commands must be entered *before* executing the SELECT statement which retrieves the data for the report.

2.   The effect of each command lasts until you explicitly "undo" the command or you exit from SQL*Plus. We note that the effect does not carry over to the next terminal session. If you want this to happen, you must reenter the same commands. In practice you will find that you want to have some of the same SQL*Plus commands in effect for every terminal session. This can be done by placing these commands in the login.sql file. (See Appendix A.)

3.   We usually think of a report as being printed on one or more pages of paper. A paper report is called a "hard copy." In the following discussion we use the term "report" to refer to the output display as shown on the terminal screen. In Chapter 8 we will present the SPOOL command, which can be used to generate a hard copy which is a mirror image of the report displayed on the screen.

We begin by discussing the TTITLE (top title) and the BTITLE (bottom title) commands which can be used to generate a title on the top and bottom of each page of the report.

The TTITLE and BTITLE Commands:

The next example shows a report displaying all information about philosophy courses. The TTITLE command is used to produce a report title with "PHILOSOPHY COURSES" positioned in the center of each page. The BTITLE command is used to show "END OF PAGE" at the bottom left side of each page.

```
----------------------------------------------------------
SQL> TTITLE CENTER 'PHILOSOPHY COURSES'
SQL> BTITLE LEFT   'END OF PAGE'
SQL> SELECT * FROM COURSE WHERE CDEPT = 'PHIL';
----------------------------------------------------------
```

```
                      PHILOSOPHY COURSES

CNO CNAME                 CDESCP                CRED CLABFEE CDEPT
--- --------------------  --------------------  ---- ------- -----
P11 EMPIRICISM            SEE IT-BELIEVE IT        3  100.00 PHIL
P22 RATIONALISM           FOR CIS MAJORS           3   50.00 PHIL
P33 EXISTENTIALISM        FOR CIS MAJORS           3  200.00 PHIL
P44 SOLIPSISM             ME MYSELF AND I          6     .00 PHIL

END OF PAGE
```

Comments:

1. Syntax: The keywords TTITLE and BTITLE are followed by the keyword LEFT, CENTER, or RIGHT, which is followed by a character string within apostrophes. LEFT, CENTER, and RIGHT have the obvious effect of positioning the character string text on the left, center, or right side of the title lines. If the character string does not contain any embedded spaces or special symbols, then the enclosing apostrophes become optional.

2. It is possible to generate multiple title lines by using the keyword "SKIP". For example, to produce the following two-line centered top title

        PHILOSOPHY
        COURSES

    you would enter

    SQL> TTITLE CENTER 'PHILOSOPHY' SKIP CENTER 'COURSES'

    The keyword SKIP forces subsequent title data to be displayed on the next print line.

3. The keyword "OFF" can be used to disable a previously defined title (e.g., BTITLE OFF). Thereafter, the title can be enabled with the keyword "ON" (e.g., BTITLE ON). To permanently remove TTITLE, enter "TTITLE CLEAR".

The COLUMN Command:

The COLUMN command has a number of different variations which serve many different purposes. Below we present two variations. The first uses the FORMAT option to edit column data. The second uses the HEADING option to explicitly designate column headings.

Before discussing these options it is useful to reexamine the output display for Sample Query 1.1. Notice that data from each row fits onto one line of the report. And, the column headings are wide enough to hold the full column names. This is no accident. In order to produce this "pretty" report, certain COLUMN commands (shown on the following page) had to be entered before executing the SELECT statement. What if these commands had not been entered? Then the first few rows of the output display would look like

```
CNO CNAME                         CDESCP                      CRED
--- ------------------------      ------------------------  ----------
    CLABFEE CDEP
    ---------- ----
T11 SCHOLASTICISM                 FOR THE PIOUS                  3
        150 THEO
T12 FUNDAMENTALISM                FOR THE CAREFREE               3
         90 THEO
T33 HEDONISM                      FOR THE SANE                   3
          0 THEO
T44 COMMUNISM                     FOR THE GREEDY                 6
        200 THEO
 .       .                            .                          .
 .       .                            .                          .
```

Comments:

1. The length of each displayed row exceeds the width of the screen and is "wrapped" onto a second line of the screen.

2. The column header for department id is "CDEP" instead of the full column name, CDEPT.

3. The width of many columns exceeds that of displayed data. In particular, the CRED and CLABFEE columns have a width of 10, the default for unformatted numeric columns.

4. The values in the CLABFEE column do not show decimal accuracy.

(If you are using the sample database, then you won't see this "ugly" report because COLUMN commands are in effect. They were entered via the "login.sql" file. You can undo their effect by entering "CLEAR COLUMNS". Later, you would reenter the COLUMN commands shown on the next page.)

The FORMAT Specification:

This section describes the COLUMN command with the FORMAT specification. The general format is

COLUMN column-name FORMAT format-specification

We note three circumstances where you might want to use this option: (1) to reduce the width of a column, (2) to increase the width of a column, and (3) to edit column data. We begin by showing the FORMAT specifications which were used to produce the output shown in the sample queries presented in Chapter 1. (These commands are in the login.sql file for the sample database.)

```
------------------------------------
SQL> COLUMN CNAME    FORMAT A20
SQL> COLUMN CDESCP   FORMAT A20
SQL> COLUMN CRED     FORMAT 9999
SQL> COLUMN CLABFEE  FORMAT 999.99
SQL> COLUMN CDEPT    FORMAT A5
------------------------------------
```

Comments:

1. There is no COLUMN command for the CNO column. This is because the default is acceptable. The data (e.g., "C11") are three characters long. The column name "CNO" is also three characters long. Hence the column heading fits nicely above the data.

2. The CNAME column has a specification of "A20". The "A" stands for "alphanumeric" -- any character string. The "20" represents the width of the column. The data have a maximum length of 22. But none of the actual values reach this length. If we reduce the column width of this column and other columns, we can help prevent the wrapping effect. The A20 specification saves two spaces.

3. The CDESCP column has a maximum length of 25. We specify "A20" for the same reason as we did for CNAME.

4. The CRED column, which contains integer numeric values, has a specification of "9999". Each "9" represents a position containing one digit. Most realistic credit values are just one or two digits. We use four positions to show the entire column name, "CRED". Hence, the specification shows four 9s.

5.   The CLABFEE column can contain five-digit numeric values
      with two-digit decimal accuracy. Recall that the system
      uses a default width of 10 for unformatted numeric
      values. Also, note that the unformatted report did not
      show the decimal accuracy because all stored values have
      decimal values of zero (.00); the rounding process,
      which SQL*Plus applies to all numeric values, caused
      this result. The specification "999.99" will only use
      seven columns. The system will set aside space for five
      digits, a decimal point, and a possible negative sign.
      Decimal alignment occurs on the period (.) showing the
      result with a two-digit decimal accuracy.

6.   The CDEPT column contains data having a maximum length
      of four characters. In the unformatted report, this
      caused a truncation of the last character of the column
      name, displaying just "CDEP". The "A5" specification
      allows enough room for the full column name.

   Figure 2.1 presents an overview of some of the more popular
FORMAT symbols. (Other specifications for the DATE data type
will be shown in Chapter 10.) Figure 2.2 shows a number of
examples which illustrate these FORMAT specifications. To
summarize the use of the FORMAT specification, we make the
following observations.

1.   The default specifications usually allow enough room for
      data to be displayed, but column names may be truncated.
      This occurred with the CDEPT column. You can use a
      FORMAT specification to increase the width of a column.
      But this action might force the wrapping of a row onto
      a second line of the report.

2.   You can use a FORMAT specification to reduce the width
      of a column. Then you need to be concerned about
      truncating the column name.

3.   Sometimes a data value can exceed the width designated
      by a FORMAT specification. For example, this would occur
      if the CNAME specification were A20 and we selected a
      CNAME value with a length of 22. This will cause either
      a truncation or wrapping for character string data. If
      this occurs with numeric data, the system will display
      pound signs (#).

4.   Chapters 7 and 8 will show how to produce columns which
      contain the results of calculations. The COLUMN command
      can be used to format the data in such columns.

```
A    Character string
9    Numeric digit
0    Display leading zeros indicator
.    Decimal point indicator
,    Comma indicator
$    Leading dollar sign indicator
```

Figure 2.1: Symbols used in FORMAT specifications.

FORMAT Specification	Stored Value	Displayed Result
A5	ABC	ABC
	ACBDEXYZ	ABCDE (wrap)
		XYZ
999	25	25
	1.27	1
	1.67	2
	1299	*###*
	-225	-225
999.99	25	25.00
	1.27	1.27
	-1.27	-1.27
	10.276	10.28
	1299	*#######*
	-123.45	-123.45
	0	.00
99,999.99	25	25.00
	7810.276	7,810.28
	567810.276	*#########*
$99,999.99	25	$25.00
	7810.276	$7,810.28
09999	-25	-00025
	10.876	00011
$09,999.99	25	$00,025.00
	-7810.276	-$07,810.28

Figure 2.2: Sample COLUMN FORMAT specifications.

The HEADING Specification:

In Sample Queries 1.1 through 1.12 column names were
displayed as the default column headings. Sample Query 1.13
showed the use of a column alias to display a different
column heading. A more direct way to display an alternative
column heading for a designated column is to use the HEADING
specification in the COLUMN command. The general syntax is

        COLUMN column-name HEADING 'heading-specification'

We show an example of customizing two column headers.

```
-----------------------------------------------------------
SQL> COLUMN CDEPT    HEADING 'DEPT.'
SQL> COLUMN CLABFEE FORMAT 99,999.99
SQL> COLUMN CLABFEE HEADING 'SIX-CREDIT¦   LABFEE   '
SQL> SELECT CNO, CLABFEE, CDEPT FROM COURSE WHERE CRED = 6;
-----------------------------------------------------------

CNO SIX-CREDIT DEPT.
        LABFEE
--- ---------- -----
P44        .00 PHIL
T44     200.00 THEO
```

Comments:

1. The first COLUMN command simply established "DEPT." as
    the column heading for the CDEPT values. Note that this
    heading is within the "A5" specification of this column.
    If the width of the heading-text exceeded the FORMAT
    specification, truncation would occur.

2. The second COLUMN command uses the FORMAT specification
    to widen the column containing the CLABFEE values. We do
    this because we intend to use the next COLUMN command to
    establish a column heading which is 10 characters wide.

3. The third COLUMN command establishes a two-line column
    header. The vertical bar (¦) is used to force the
    wrapping of the column header. The top line has the 10-
    character string "SIX-CREDIT"; the bottom line is
    "   LABFEE   ". Note the embedded spaces in the bottom
    line to center it with the top line.

Disabling/Enabling and Clearing COLUMN Specifications:

To disable the existing specifications for the CLABFEE column, use the "OFF" option.

    SQL> COLUMN CLABFEE OFF

The system still remembers the COLUMN specifications. To enable the specifications for CLABFEE, use the "ON" option.

    SQL> COLUMN CLABFEE ON

To permanently remove all specifications for CLABFEE, use the "CLEAR" option.

    SQL> COLUMN CLABFEE CLEAR

Finally, it is possible to clear the specifications for all columns. This requires the use of a new SQL*Plus command. This is the CLEAR command, which has a number of options. We show the option used to clear specifications for all columns.

    SQL> CLEAR COLUMNS

Obviously, you want to think twice before you execute the CLEAR command.

Displaying Current Column Specifications:

We have presented the FORMAT, HEADING, and CLEAR options for the COLUMN command. Other options will be presented later in the text. In practice, many columns will have many specifications, which are easy to forget. Any time you would like to inquire about the current specifications for a column, you only have to enter "COLUMN" or "COL" followed by the column name. To inquire about the COLUMN specifications for the CDEPT column, you would enter

    SQL> COLUMN CDEPT

The system will display

    column   CDEPT ON
    heading   'DEPT.'
    format   A5

It is easy to inquire about all COLUMN specifications. Simply enter "COLUMN" and press the Enter key. The system will display the status of all columns.

Summary

This chapter introduced a very small subset of a large number of SQL*Plus commands. We saw the "tip of the iceberg" of the facilities provided by SQL*Plus. These included

1.   Commands to edit the SQL Buffer: LIST, CHANGE, DEL, INPUT, APPEND, RUN, and EDIT.

2.   Commands to produce report titles: TTITLE and BTITLE.

3.   Selected specifications of the COLUMN command for report formatting: FORMAT, HEADING, ON, OFF, and CLEAR.

We reiterate the objectives of this chapter. The first was to provide enough information so that you can use SQL*Plus to execute SQL statements and generate a readable report. A second objective was to emphasize the conceptual difference between entering SQL statements and SQL*Plus commands. This is important. Figure 2.3 shows the relationship between the SQL*Plus product and the ORACLE DBMS engine. We note that SQL*Plus will pass SQL statements to the ORACLE DBMS for execution. The DBMS returns "raw data" to SQL*Plus. SQL*Plus will use the information specified by the report formatting commands to display the data in a desired report format.

We note another important fact for the professional programmer who will embed SQL in some high-level language (e.g., COBOL, C). Only SQL statements, not SQL*Plus commands, can be embedded in application programs. Programmers who are using SQL*Plus to prototype embedded SQL statements must recognize this fact. Finally, SQL*Plus commands do not apply to other relational database systems. (However, they are similar to some of the ISQL commands in SQL/DS.) For these reasons, we believe it is better to use the standard form when illustrating most SQL statements and to present SQL*Plus commands as a separate topic. More SQL*Plus commands will be presented in Part III.

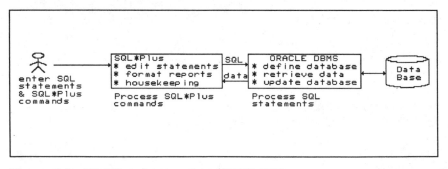

Figure 2.3: SQL*Plus front-end to ORACLE DBMS.

Chapter

3

Sorting the "Result" Table

Whenever you display more than a few rows, it is usually desirable to have the result displayed in some specific row sequence. This objective can be realized by including an ORDER BY clause in the SELECT statement. This chapter will present five sample queries which demonstrate the simplicity and flexibility of the ORDER BY clause.

Before presenting the sample queries, a simple but very important point needs to be emphasized. The process of executing a SELECT statement effectively identifies a table which constitutes the displayed output. We call this table the "result table." Very often this result table consists of just a single column and/or a single row. Nevertheless, it is still a table. The content of the result table happens to be derived from the table specified in the FROM clause. But it is a different table. We emphasize this rather obvious point because sorting applies to the result table only. The result table is a temporary table, and it disappears when the next SQL statement is executed. The key point is that you can make no assumptions about the sequence of the underlying table referenced in the FROM clause. As stated in Chapter 1, this "permanent" table has no inherent row sequence. This is not changed by the query which contains an ORDER BY clause.

ORDER BY Clause

The first sample query illustrates the ORDER BY clause to sort the result table by a single column. Note that this clause is merely appended to a standard SELECT statement.

Sample Query 3.1:   Display the entire COURSE table. Sort the output display by the CLABFEE values.

```
SELECT  *

FROM    COURSE

ORDER  BY  CLABFEE
```

CNO	CNAME	CDESCP	CRED	CLABFEE	CDEPT
T33	HEDONISM	FOR THE SANE	3	.00	THEO
P44	SOLIPSISM	ME MYSELF AND I	6	.00	PHIL
C33	DISCRETE MATHEMATICS	ABSOLUTELY NECESSARY	3	.00	CIS
C44	DIGITAL CIRCUITS	AH HA!	3	.00	CIS
P22	RATIONALISM	FOR CIS MAJORS	3	50.00	PHIL
C22	DATA STRUCTURES	VERY USEFUL	3	50.00	CIS
T12	FUNDAMENTALISM	FOR THE CAREFREE	3	90.00	THEO
P11	EMPIRICISM	SEE IT-BELIEVE IT	3	100.00	PHIL
C11	INTRO TO CS	FOR ROOKIES	3	100.00	CIS
C55	COMPUTER ARCH.	VON NEUMANN'S MACH.	3	100.00	CIS
T11	SCHOLASTICISM	FOR THE PIOUS	3	150.00	THEO
T44	COMMUNISM	FOR THE GREEDY	6	200.00	THEO
P33	EXISTENTIALISM	FOR CIS MAJORS	3	200.00	PHIL
C66	RELATIONAL DATABASE	THE ONLY WAY TO GO	3	500.00	CIS

Comments:

1.   Syntax: When used, the ORDER BY clause is always the last clause in any SELECT statement.

2.   The sort occurs in ascending sequence. This is the
       default sequence used by ORACLE. We could have
       explicitly requested an ascending sort sequence by
       including the ASC parameter in the ORDER BY clause. The
       following ORDER BY clause is equivalent to the one shown
       in the example.

           ORDER BY CLABFEE ASC

       The ASC parameter is rarely used in practice. Its only
       purpose is to enhance readability of a query by
       explicitly indicating an ascending sort sequence.

       It is possible to display output in a descending row
       sequence. The next sample query will illustrate the DESC
       parameter to achieve this objective.

3.   The sort field, CLABFEE, is numeric. Hence the sort
       reflects a sequence based on mathematical value. If
       there were negative values in the CLABFEE column, they
       would have appeared before the zero and positive values.
       We can also sort on character string columns. The next
       sample query will illustrate sorting on a character
       column.

4.   There are duplicate values in the CLABFEE column. We can
       make no assumptions about the sort sequence within
       matching values. Sample Query 3.3 will illustrate
       sorting on multiple columns to establish a second-level
       sort field within matching values.

5.   Note that the sort column of this query is not the left-
       most column. Most users typically establish the sort
       column as the leftmost column. This example illustrates
       that you can sort on any column.

6.   Finally, we emphasize that sorting applies to the
       displayed result only. The data within the stored table
       remain unchanged.

Exercise:

3A.   Display the entire COURSE table. Sort the result by the
       CDEPT column in ascending sequence.

Descending Sort

The next sample query demonstrates the use of the DESC parameter to produce a result which is sorted in descending sequence.

Sample Query 3.2:   Select the course number, name, and credit of any course which is offered by the Computer and Information Science Department. Sort the result by course number in descending sequence.

```
SELECT CNO, CNAME, CRED

FROM    COURSE

WHERE   CDEPT = 'CIS'

ORDER BY CNO DESC
```

CNO	CNAME	CRED
C66	RELATIONAL DATABASE	3
C55	COMPUTER ARCH.	3
C44	DIGITAL CIRCUITS	3
C33	DISCRETE MATHEMATICS	3
C22	DATA STRUCTURES	3
C11	INTRO TO CS	3

Comments:

1.   Syntax: DESC follows the column name in the ORDER BY
     clause. One or more spaces must separate the column name
     and the DESC parameter. (A comma cannot be used as a
     separator.)

2.   The sort column (CNO) contains character data. Recall
     that the ASCII and EBCDIC codes specify the sequence for
     character data. Review the comments for Sample Query
     1.4.

3.   Within the COURSE table every CNO value is unique. Hence
     the row sequence was completely determined.

4.   DB2 Compatibility: Unlike the preceding sample query,
     this query displays just some columns. This situation is
     no problem for ORACLE. However, there is a restriction
     which applies to DB2. In the DB2 version of SQL, the
     ORDER BY clause can reference only a column which is
     specified in the SELECT clause. For example, the
     following statement, which is valid in ORACLE, is
     invalid in DB2 because CLABFEE is not specified in the
     SELECT clause.

```
SELECT  CNO, CNAME, CRED
FROM    COURSE
WHERE   CDEPT = 'CIS'
ORDER BY CLABFEE
```

Exercise:

3B. Display the course name and labfee for all courses
     offered by the Philosophy Department. Sort the result by
     course name in descending sequence.

Sorting on Multiple Columns

Recall in Sample Query 3.1 that the sort column (CLABFEE) contained nonunique values. For this reason the row sequence was not completely determined. The next sample query illustrates that the ORDER BY clause may reference multiple columns. We will see that proper specification of multiple columns in the ORDER BY clause permits complete determination of the row sequence in any desired order.

Sample Query 3.3:   Display the department id and name of every course. Sort the result by department id. Within each department, sort by course name.

```
SELECT CDEPT, CNAME

FROM    COURSE

ORDER BY CDEPT, CNAME
```

CDEPT	CNAME
CIS	COMPUTER ARCH.
CIS	DATA STRUCTURES
CIS	DIGITAL CIRCUITS
CIS	DISCRETE MATHEMATICS
CIS	INTRO TO CS
CIS	RELATIONAL DATABASE
PHIL	EMPIRICISM
PHIL	RATIONALISM
PHIL	SOLIPSISM
THEO	COMMUNISM
THEO	FUNDAMENTALISM
THEO	HEDONISM
THEO	SCHOLASTICISM

Comments:

1. Terminology: This example has two sort columns (fields). There are different ways of expressing the sort relationship between the two columns. The following statements are equivalent.

    a. CDEPT is the major sort field, and CNAME is the minor sort field.

    b. CDEPT is the primary sort field, and CNAME is the secondary sort field.

    c. CDEPT is the first-level sort field, and CNAME is the second-level sort field.

    d. The sort sequence is CNAME within CDEPT.

2. Syntax: The "ORDER BY" is followed by the major sort field which is followed by the minor sort field. The sort field column names must be separated by a comma.

3. Both the major and minor sorts default to ascending sequence. We can mix ascending and descending sequences within the different sort fields. (See Sample Query 3.5.)

4. Both the major and minor sort fields contain alphanumeric data. This is not necessary. (See Sample Query 3.5.)

5. There is no practical limit on the number of sort fields. The following ORDER BY clause is valid and would establish a four-level sort sequence.

    ORDER BY CRED, CLABFEE, CDEPT, CNAME

Exercise:

3C. Display the CNAME, CNO, and CRED columns (in that order) for every row in the table. Sort the displayed rows by CNO within CLABFEE. (CLABFEE is the major sort field, and CNO is the minor sort field.)

ORDER BY Column-number

The ORDER BY clause can also reference a column by its relative position in the output display. This is a convenience which can save you keystroke effort. The next sample query produces an output display which is sorted by the second column.

Sample Query 3.4: Display the CNO, CLABFEE, and CRED values, in that order, for all courses. Sort the result by the second column (i.e., CLABFEE).

```
SELECT CNO, CLABFEE, CRED

FROM    COURSE

ORDER BY 2
```

CNO	CLABFEE	CRED
T33	.00	3
P44	.00	6
C33	.00	3
C44	.00	3
P22	50.00	3
C22	50.00	3
T12	90.00	3
P11	100.00	3
C11	100.00	3
C55	100.00	3
T11	150.00	3
T44	200.00	6
P33	200.00	3
C66	500.00	3

Comments:

1. The use of a relative column number is not necessary in this example. The following equivalent clause will achieve the same objective.

    ORDER BY CLABFEE

    The use of relative column numbers is an acceptable convenience for use with one-time ad hoc queries. For statements which will be saved for future execution, it is better to explicitly name the column in the ORDER BY clause. This enhances readability and is not affected by a reordering of column names in the SELECT clause. This is especially true for SELECT statements to be embedded in application programs.

2. In future chapters we will present built-in functions and calculated columns. Display columns generated by these techniques could be referenced by their relative column position.

3. The DESC parameter can be used with relative column numbers. The following clause is valid.

    ORDER BY 2 DESC

Exercise:

3D. Display the entire COURSE table sorted in descending sequence by the third column.

The final sample query in this chapter illustrates that all of the previously described variations of the ORDER BY clause can be incorporated within a single clause. This clause references both column numbers and names. This example is not very realistic. However, it does demonstrate the flexibility of the ORDER BY clause.

Sample Query 3.5:   Display the CDEPT, CLABFEE, and CRED values, in that order, for all courses. CDEPT is the first-level sort field (ascending); CRED is the second-level sort field (descending); and CLABFEE is the third-level sort field (descending).

```
SELECT CDEPT, CLABFEE, CRED

FROM    COURSE

ORDER BY CDEPT, 3 DESC, CLABFEE DESC
```

CDEPT	CLABFEE	CRED
CIS	500.00	3
CIS	100.00	3
CIS	100.00	3
CIS	50.00	3
CIS	.00	3
CIS	.00	3
PHIL	.00	6
PHIL	200.00	3
PHIL	100.00	3
PHIL	50.00	3
THEO	200.00	6
THEO	150.00	3
THEO	90.00	3
THEO	.00	3

Comments:

1. This sample query sorts on three columns. The ORDER BY clause

    *   References some columns by name (CDEPT and CLABFEE) and another by relative column number (CRED is identified as the third column).

    *   Sorts one column (CDEPT) in ascending sequence and two columns (CRED and CLABFEE) in descending sequence.

2. Note that none of the displayed columns contain unique values. Hence duplicate rows can (and do) appear in the output display. Because this result is sequenced, it is easier to detect duplicate rows. Recall that duplicate rows can be removed from the displayed output by specifying DISTINCT in the SELECT clause.

Exercise:

3E. Display the CDEPT, CLABFEE, and CNAME values of all three credit courses. Sort the output result. CDEPT is the first-level sort field (ascending); CLABFEE is the second-level sort field (descending); CNAME is the third-level sort field (ascending).

Summary

This chapter has expanded on the fundamental structure of the SELECT statement by including the ORDER BY clause.

```
SELECT column-name(s)
FROM    table-name
WHERE   condition
ORDER BY sort-column(s)
```

The result table can be sorted on any column(s). The ORDER BY clause can reference the column name or relative column number. The default sort sequence is ascending (ASC). A descending sequence can be established by using the DESC parameter.

We conclude with some final comments regarding the terms "sort" and "sequence." We have casually used these terms as though they were synonymous. However, to be precise, the objective of all previous sample queries was to display the result table in some specified row sequence. The system may have to execute a sort utility to achieve this objective. Part IV of this text will examine indexes. There we will note that the system can sometimes utilize an index to avoid execution of a sort utility. At this point you should not focus on the internal processes which the system follows to produce the output in row sequence. However, you should be aware that the ORDER BY clause usually requires the system to do more work. This could be significant if the number of selected rows is large. Therefore, you are advised to exercise judgment in use of the ORDER BY clause.

Summary Exercises

The following exercises all refer to the STAFF table. The column names are ENAME, ETITLE, ESALARY, and DEPT.

3F.   Display the entire STAFF table. Sort it by employee name.

3G.   Display the name and salary of any employee earning less than $1000. Sort the result by salary in descending sequence.

3H.   Display all information about employees who work in the Theology Department. Sort the result by employee title.

3I.   Display the department id, employee name, and salary for all employees. Sort the result by salary within department.

3J.   Display the department id, employee title, and salary for all staff members. Let department id be the major sort field (in ascending sequence) and salary be the minor sort field (in descending sequence).

4

Boolean Connectors: AND - OR - NOT

Row selection in the previous chapters was based on a single condition. In this chapter we present the use of Boolean connectors to facilitate row selection based on multiple conditions. The first 12 sample queries illustrate the classical Boolean connectors of AND, OR, and NOT. The remaining sample queries introduce the keywords IN and BETWEEN. You will learn that you can do without IN and BETWEEN because the classical operators provide the expressive power to formulate any row selection criteria. However, you will also find that IN and BETWEEN are very useful because they provide a more compact way of expressing certain row selection conditions.

AND Connector

The first sample query illustrates the AND connector. The AND is placed between two row selection conditions within the WHERE clause. The intent is to request the system to select an individual row only if both of the conditions are satisfied.

Sample Query 4.1:   Display all information about any CIS course which has a zero labfee.

```
SELECT *

FROM    COURSE

WHERE   CLABFEE = 0

AND     CDEPT = 'CIS'
```

CNO	CNAME	CDESCP	CRED	CLABFEE	CDEPT
C33	DISCRETE MATHEMATICS	ABSOLUTELY NECESSARY	3	.00	CIS
C44	DIGITAL CIRCUITS	AH HA!	3	.00	CIS

Comments:

1. Logic: The example shows two conditions which are connected by the AND Boolean connector. These two conditions are

    a. CLABFEE = 0

    b. CDEPT = 'CIS'

    Note that each of the output rows matches both conditions. Observe that the COURSE table contains additional rows which match just one or the other, but not both, of these conditions. There are philosophy and theology courses which have zero labfees. Likewise, there are computer and information science courses with nonzero labfees. These rows were not selected because they met only one of the two specified conditions.

2.   Syntax: The primary requirement is that individual
      conditions be syntactically correct. The sample query
      shows the conditions written on separate lines. This is
      not required, but it enhances readability. Recall that
      a SELECT statement is free form and can be written on
      any number of lines. Therefore, each of the following
      statements is equivalent to the current example.

```
          SELECT *
          FROM    COURSE
          WHERE   CLABFEE = 0 AND CDEPT = 'CIS'

          SELECT *
          FROM    COURSE
          WHERE   CLABFEE = 0 AND
                  CDEPT = 'CIS'

          SELECT *  FROM COURSE
          WHERE   CLABFEE = 0 AND CDEPT = 'CIS'

          SELECT *  FROM COURSE
          WHERE   CLABFEE = 0
                  AND
                  CDEPT = 'CIS
```

3.   The order in which the conditions are specified should
      have no effect on the performance. The following
      compound WHERE conditions should execute with the same
      efficiency and will produce the same result.

```
          WHERE CLABFEE = 0 AND CDEPT = 'CIS'

          WHERE CDEPT = 'CIS' AND CLABFEE = 0
```

Exercise:

4A.   Select all information about three-credit courses
      offered by the Philosophy Department.

Like the previous sample query, the following example connects multiple conditions using AND. This time both of the conditions reference the same column (CLABFEE). The intention is to select rows where the CLABFEE value falls within a certain range.

Sample Query 4.2:   Display all information about any course having a labfee which is strictly between zero and one hundred dollars.

```
SELECT  *

FROM    COURSE

WHERE   CLABFEE > 0

AND     CLABFEE < 100
```

CNO	CNAME	CDESCP	CRED	CLABFEE	CDEPT
T12	FUNDAMENTALISM	FOR THE CAREFREE	3	90.00	THEO
P22	RATIONALISM	FOR CIS MAJORS	3	50.00	PHIL
C22	DATA STRUCTURES	VERY USEFUL	3	50.00	CIS

Comments:

1.   Logic: The example selected rows where the CLABFEE value was strictly greater than zero and strictly less than one hundred. Note that rows with CLABFEE values of 0 and 100 were not selected.

2.   Syntax: The column name must be specified in both conditions. The following WHERE clause is invalid and will cause an *error*.

         WHERE CLABFEE > 0 AND < 100

Exercise:

4B.   Display all information about any course which has a labfee between and including $100 and $500.

Multiple ANDs

It is possible to connect multiple conditions using many AND connectors. The next example illustrates four conditions which are AND-connected. In this case a given row will be selected only if it matches all four of the specified conditions.

Sample Query 4.3:   Display all information about any three-credit philosophy course which has a labfee strictly between zero and one hundred dollars.

```
SELECT  *

FROM    COURSE

WHERE   CLABFEE > 0

AND     CLABFEE < 100

AND     CDEPT = 'PHIL'

AND     CRED = 3
```

CNO	CNAME	CDESCP	CRED	CLABFEE	CDEPT
P22	RATIONALISM	FOR CIS MAJORS	3	50.00	PHIL

Comment:

For all practical purposes there is no limit on the number of conditions which can be used in a WHERE clause.

Exercise:

4C.   Select all information about any three-credit theology course with a labfee between and including $100 and $400.

OR Connector

Like the AND connector, the OR connector will connect
multiple conditions within a WHERE clause. However, OR
connectors have a different impact on the logic of the row
selection process. Assuming that just two conditions are OR-
connected, a given row will be selected if it matches either
or both of the specified conditions. The next sample query
illustrates this point.

Sample Query 4.4:   Display all information about any course
offered by the CIS or PHIL Department.

```
SELECT *

FROM    COURSE

WHERE   CDEPT = 'CIS'

OR      CDEPT = 'PHIL'
```

CNO	CNAME	CDESCP	CRED	CLABFEE	CDEPT
P11	EMPIRICISM	SEE IT - BELIEVE IT	3	100.00	PHIL
P22	RATIONALISM	FOR CIS MAJORS	3	50.00	PHIL
P33	EXISTENTIALISM	FOR CIS MAJORS	3	200.00	PHIL
P44	SOLIPSISM	ME MYSELF AND I	6	.00	PHIL
C11	INTRO TO CS	FOR ROOKIES	3	100.00	CIS
C22	DATA STRUCTURES	VERY USEFUL	3	50.00	CIS
C33	DISCRETE MATHEMATICS	ABSOLUTELY NECESSARY	3	.00	CIS
C44	DIGITAL CIRCUITS	AH HA!	3	.00	CIS
C55	COMPUTER ARCH.	VON NEUMANN'S MACH.	3	100.00	CIS
C66	RELATIONAL DATABASE	THE ONLY WAY TO GO	3	500.00	CIS

Comments:

1.   Logic: The OR is an "inclusive" OR. This means that a
row is selected under the special case where it matches
on both of the specified conditions. This cannot happen
in the current example because both conditions specify
a different "equals" compare on the same CDEPT field.
The next sample query will illustrate a situation where
some rows will match on both conditions.

2.   Syntax: As with the AND Boolean operator, the free
     format of SQL allows flexibility. The following
     statements are equivalent to the current sample query.

```
SELECT *
FROM    COURSE
WHERE   CDEPT = 'CIS' OR CDEPT = 'PHIL'


SELECT *
FROM    COURSE
WHERE   CDEPT = 'CIS' OR
        CDEPT = 'PHIL'


SELECT * FROM COURSE
WHERE   CDEPT = 'CIS' OR CDEPT = 'PHIL'


SELECT *
FROM    COURSE
WHERE   CDEPT = 'CIS'
        OR
        CDEPT = 'PHIL'
```

3.   Both conditions refer to the same CDEPT column. However,
     as with the AND connector, this column must be
     explicitly specified in each condition. This means that
     the following WHERE clause is *invalid*.

         WHERE CDEPT = 'CIS' OR 'PHIL'

4.   The order in which the column names are specified should
     not affect performance. The following compound WHERE
     clauses should execute with the same efficiency and
     produce the same result.

         WHERE CDEPT = 'PHIL' OR CDEPT = 'CIS'

         WHERE CDEPT = 'CIS'   OR CDEPT = 'PHIL'

Exercise:

4D. Display all information about every course offered by
     the Philosophy or Theology Department.

The next sample query illustrates a situation where it is possible for a given row to match on both conditions. This demonstrates the "inclusive" behavior of the OR connector.

Sample Query 4.5:   Display all information about any CIS course or any course with a zero labfee.

```
SELECT *

FROM    COURSE

WHERE   CLABFEE = 0.00

OR      CDEPT = 'CIS'
```

CNO	CNAME	CDESCP	CRED	CLABFEE	CDEPT
T33	HEDONISM	FOR THE SANE	3	.00	THEO
P44	SOLIPSISM	ME MYSELF AND I	6	.00	PHIL
C11	INTRO TO CS	FOR ROOKIES	3	100.00	CIS
C22	DATA STRUCTURES	VERY USEFUL	3	50.00	CIS
C33	DISCRETE MATHEMATICS	ABSOLUTELY NECESSARY	3	.00	CIS
C44	DIGITAL CIRCUITS	AH HA!	3	.00	CIS
C55	COMPUTER ARCH.	VON NEUMANN'S MACH.	3	100.00	CIS
C66	RELATIONAL DATABASE	THE ONLY WAY TO GO	3	500.00	CIS

Comment:

This SELECT statement will display any row which has a CLABFEE value of zero or a CDEPT value of "CIS". Observe that all courses having a labfee of zero are selected, regardless of their department id. And all CIS courses are selected, regardless of their labfee. Also, rows which match both conditions will be selected. Note that a row which matches both conditions, like the rows with CNO values of "C33" and "C44", will occur only once in the output display.

Exercise:

4E.   Select all information about any course which is offered by the Theology Department or is worth six credits.

Multiple ORs

As with the AND connector, it is possible to connect any number of conditions using multiple OR connectors. The next example illustrates four conditions which are OR-connected. In this case a row will be selected if it matches any of the four specified conditions.

Sample Query 4.6:   Display all information about any course which has a labfee equal to 50, 100, 150, or 200 dollars.

```
SELECT  *

FROM    COURSE

WHERE   CLABFEE = 50

OR      CLABFEE = 100

OR      CLABFEE = 150

OR      CLABFEE = 200
```

CNO	CNAME	CDESCP	CRED	CLABFEE	CDEPT
T11	SCHOLASTICISM	FOR THE PIOUS	3	150.00	THEO
T44	COMMUNISM	FOR THE GREEDY	6	200.00	THEO
P11	EMPIRICISM	SEE IT - BELIEVE IT	3	100.00	PHIL
P22	RATIONALISM	FOR CIS MAJORS	3	50.00	PHIL
P33	EXISTENTIALISM	FOR CIS MAJORS	3	200.00	PHIL
C11	INTRO TO CS	FOR ROOKIES	3	100.00	CIS
C22	DATA STRUCTURES	VERY USEFUL	3	50.00	CIS
C55	COMPUTER ARCH.	VON NEUMANN'S MACH.	3	100.00	CIS

Comments:

1.   For all practical purposes, there is no limit on the number of conditions which can be OR-connected.

2.   Note that the CLABFEE column must be explicitly referenced in each of the four conditions. Sample Query 4.13 will introduce the IN operator which offers a more compact way of expressing this query.

Exercise:

4F.   Display all information about any course which has a labfee in the set {0.00, 90.00, 150.00}.

NOT Keyword

All previous examples specified conditions which explicitly identified, in a positive sense, the rows to be selected for display. The next sample query introduces the use of the NOT keyword which allows you to indicate those rows which you do not want selected for display. When a WHERE condition identifies rows which are not to be selected, the system assumes that you want to select all the other rows.

Sample Query 4.7:   Display the course name and department id of any course which is not offered by the CIS Department.

```
SELECT  CNAME, CDEPT

FROM    COURSE

WHERE   NOT CDEPT = 'CIS'
```

CNAME	CDEPT
SCHOLASTICISM	THEO
FUNDAMENTALISM	THEO
HEDONISM	THEO
COMMUNISM	THEO
EMPIRICISM	PHIL
RATIONALISM	PHIL
EXISTENTIALISM	PHIL
SOLIPSISM	PHIL

Comments:

1. Syntax: The NOT operator can be placed before any
    legitimate conditional expression. The current example
    has a single condition which is negated by use of NOT.
    The format of the WHERE condition is

        WHERE NOT (conditional expression)

    Later in this chapter we will see more complex examples
    where NOT is used in conjunction with WHERE clauses
    which contain multiple conditions.

2. The following statement is equivalent to the current
    example. It uses the special "not equals" comparison
    operator (<>).

        SELECT *
        FROM   COURSE
        WHERE   CDEPT <> 'CIS'

3. Avoid making the common mistake of placing the NOT
    before a comparison operator. The following WHERE clause
    is *invalid* because the NOT immediately precedes the
    equal sign.

        WHERE CDEPT NOT = 'CIS'

4. If you are familiar with the basics of set theory, it
    may be helpful to think of NOT as a keyword which
    identifies the complement of a subset of rows from a
    table. The condition (CDEPT = 'CIS') effectively
    identifies a subset of rows from the COURSE table. By
    placing a NOT before this condition, you are requesting
    the system to select the complement of this subset.

Exercise:

4G. Select the course number, name, and labfee of any course
    with a labfee other than 100.

The next sample query shows a WHERE clause with two conditions, each of which is negated by use of NOT, and subsequently AND-connected. We will classify this WHERE clause as "complex," because, unlike all the previous WHERE clauses, it contains two different Boolean operators (NOT and AND). Our comments on the logic of this sample query serve as a prelude to the following detailed discussion on the hierarchy of Boolean operators.

Sample Query 4.8: Display the name and department id of all courses with the exception of those courses offered by the CIS and PHIL Departments.

```
SELECT CNAME, CDEPT

FROM    COURSE

WHERE   NOT CDEPT = 'CIS'

AND     NOT CDEPT = 'PHIL'
```

CNAME	CDEPT
SCHOLASTICISM	THEO
FUNDAMENTALISM	THEO
HEDONISM	THEO
COMMUNISM	THEO

Comments:

1.   This is the first sample query where we have utilized two different Boolean operators (NOT and AND). This raises the question of hierarchy of execution, which will be addressed on the following page. With respect to the current example, we merely note that the system evaluates the NOT before the AND. This means that the WHERE clause is the AND of two negated conditions. Therefore, the system will select any row which meets both of the negated conditions. If a row has a CDEPT value not equal to "CIS" and it is also not equal to "PHIL", it will be selected.

2.   We must always be careful when we are composing queries which use multiple different Boolean operators. For example, many people would articulate the current sample query as

>   "Select course names and departments for courses which are not offered by the CIS or PHIL Department."

This statement may be grammatically correct. However, note that using "or" in the above English-language statement may entice the careless user to code an OR into the WHERE clause. The resulting SELECT statement (shown below) appears innocuous on initial inspection. But when we consider the precise meaning we observe that it is a rather silly way of selecting every row from the COURSE table.

```
SELECT  CNAME, CDEPT
FROM    COURSE
WHERE   NOT CDEPT = 'CIS'
OR      NOT CDEPT = 'PHIL'
```

Any CIS course would be selected by the second expression (NOT CDEPT = 'PHIL'), and any PHIL course would be selected by the first expression (NOT CDEPT = 'CIS').

3.   Observe that the problem identified above and subsequent logical problems described on the following pages are only indirectly related to SQL. The primary source of such problems is the ambiguous use of natural language and a careless approach toward the semantics of the Boolean operators. This transcends not only SQL but any other structured computer programming language.

Exercise:

4H.   Select the course number and labfee for any course which has a labfee other than $100 and $200.

Hierarchy of Boolean Operators

Whenever a WHERE clause contains more than two conditions which are connected by different Boolean operators, the system must decide on the order of execution. If the WHERE clause does not contain any parentheses, the system will follow a specific sequence. This sequence is defined by a hierarchy which dictates that

NOTs are evaluated first

ANDs are evaluated next

ORs are evaluated last

If you have programmed in any other language, you will recognize that this is the same hierarchy that you most likely encountered in that language. If SQL is your first computer language, then you should pay close attention to the next four sample queries, which illustrate the hierarchy of Boolean operators.

Sample Query 4.9:   Display all information about any theology course which has a zero labfee, or any course (regardless of its department and labfee) which is worth six credits.

```
SELECT    *

FROM      COURSE

WHERE     CDEPT = 'THEO'

AND       CLABFEE = 0

OR        CRED = 6
```

CNO	CNAME	CDESCP	CRED	CLABFEE	CDEPT
T33	HEDONISM	FOR THE SANE	3	.00	THEO
T44	COMMUNISM	FOR THE GREEDY	6	200.00	THEO
P44	SOLIPSISM	ME MYSELF AND I	6	.00	PHIL

Comments:

1. Logic: Observe the effect of the AND being evaluated before the OR. A given row will be selected if it meets either or both of the following conditions. (This is because these conditions are OR-connected.)

    a.   CDEPT = 'THEO' AND CLABFEE = 0

    b.   CRED = 6

    The system will examine each row of the COURSE table. If a given row has both a CDEPT value of "THEO" and a CLABFEE value of zero, it will be selected. The first row (course number of "T33") was the only row which met this condition. Furthermore, if a given row has a CRED value of 6, it will also be selected. The last two rows (course numbers "T44" and "P44") met this condition. The COURSE table does not contain any rows which match both of the above conditions. If it did, such rows would have been selected.

2. Syntax: We cannot arbitrarily change the order of the conditions. Consider the following statement, which is not equivalent to the sample query.

    ```
    SELECT * FROM COURSE
    WHERE  CDEPT = 'THEO'
    AND    CRED = 6
    OR     CLABFEE = 0
    ```

    This query would select any six-credit theology course or any course with a zero labfee (regardless of its department and credits).

3. The following two statements are equivalent to the current example. The first reorders the conditions without affecting the logic. The second makes use of parentheses which will be explained on the next page. The parentheses are superfluous, but they help readability.

    ```
    SELECT * FROM COURSE
    WHERE  CRED = 6
    OR     CDEPT = 'THEO' AND CLABFEE = 0
    ```

    ```
    SELECT * FROM COURSE
    WHERE  (CDEPT = 'THEO' AND CLABFEE = 0)
    OR     CRED = 6
    ```

Use of Parentheses

SQL permits the use of parentheses to override the Boolean operator hierarchy. Parentheses make explicit the order of evaluation and enhance readability. The next sample query incorporates the same three conditions as the preceding sample query. This time we illustrate the use of parentheses to change the order of system evaluation. The two conditions adjacent to the OR are enclosed within parentheses. This means that they will be evaluated first. Note that the semantic meaning of this sample query is very different from the preceding one. The only syntax change, the parentheses, effectively changes the semantic meaning of the WHERE clause.

Sample Query 4.10: Display all information about theology courses which have a zero labfee or are worth six credits.

```
SELECT  *

FROM    COURSE

WHERE   CDEPT = 'THEO'

AND     (CLABFEE = 0 OR CRED = 6)
```

CNO	CNAME	CDESCP	CRED	CLABFEE	CDEPT
T33	HEDONISM	FOR THE SANE	3	.00	THEO
T44	COMMUNISM	FOR THE GREEDY	6	200.00	THEO

Comments:

1.   Logic: Observe that the parentheses cause the OR to be evaluated before the AND. The effect is that a given row will be selected if it meets both of the following conditions.

```
CDEPT = 'THEO'
CLABFEE = 0 OR CRED = 6
```

Therefore, this example, unlike the previous, will select only theology courses. Furthermore, these theology courses must meet at least one of the conditions, CLABFEE = 0 or CRED = 6. Observe the displayed result. Note that the row for course number P44, which was present in the previous example, is absent. This is because it is not a theology course.

2. Syntax: The two conditions which are OR-connected within the parentheses are written on one line. This enhances readability, but it is not necessary. The following query is equivalent to the current example.

```
SELECT * FROM COURSE
WHERE   CDEPT = 'THEO'
AND     (CLABFEE = 0
OR      CRED = 6)
```

3. If we observe that we want six-credit theology courses or zero labfee theology courses, we might have written the following equivalent statement.

```
SELECT * FROM COURSE
WHERE   (CDEPT = 'THEO' AND CRED = 6)
OR      (CDEPT = 'THEO' AND CLABFEE = 0)
```

Some individuals would find this statement to be a more explicit representation of the query objective. Note that the parentheses are not required in this statement. The default hierarchy will produce the same result.

4. General Recommendation: Always utilize parentheses to make explicit the logic of your WHERE clause.

Exercises:

4I. Select all information about any six-credit philosophy course, or any course with a labfee which exceeds $200 (regardless of its department id or credits).

4J. Select all information about any three-credit course with a labfee which is less than $100 or greater than $300.

The next sample query involves all three of the Boolean operators. Recall the hierarchy is NOT, followed by AND, followed by OR. Note that this example does not adhere to the recommendation specified on the previous page; parentheses are absent. This will force you to think about the hierarchy. Again, this is a tutorial example. In practice, you should use parentheses.

Sample Query 4.11:   Display all information about all non-CIS courses or any course (regardless of department) which has a zero labfee and is worth three credits.

```
SELECT  *

FROM    COURSE

WHERE   NOT CDEPT = 'CIS'

OR      CLABFEE = 0

AND     CRED = 3
```

CNO	CNAME	CDESCP	CRED	CLABFEE	CDEPT
T11	SCHOLASTICISM	FOR THE PIOUS	3	150.00	THEO
T12	FUNDAMENTALISM	FOR THE CAREFREE	3	90.00	THEO
T33	HEDONISM	FOR THE SANE	3	.00	THEO
T44	COMMUNISM	FOR THE GREEDY	6	200.00	THEO
P11	EMPIRICISM	SEE IT - BELIEVE IT	3	100.00	PHIL
P22	RATIONALISM	FOR CIS MAJORS	3	50.00	PHIL
P33	EXISTENTIALISM	FOR CIS MAJORS	3	200.00	PHIL
P44	SOLIPSISM	ME MYSELF AND I	6	.00	PHIL
C33	DISCRETE MATHEMATICS	ABSOLUTELY NECESSARY	3	.00	CIS
C44	DIGITAL CIRCUITS	AH HA!	3	.00	CIS

Comment:

In this example, the hierarchy of operations happens to fit the objective of the sample query. However, it is better to make the logic explicit by using parentheses. The following equivalent statement does so.

```
SELECT *
FROM    COURSE
WHERE   NOT CDEPT = 'CIS'
OR      (CLABFEE = 0 AND CRED = 3)
```

The above parentheses are superfluous. However, they emphasize that any given row (even a CIS row) will be selected if it has a zero labfee and is worth three credits. To perhaps overdo the use of parentheses, we rewrite the statement with parentheses enclosing the first condition to emphasize that we want the system to evaluate the NOT condition first.

```
SELECT *
FROM    COURSE
WHERE   (NOT CDEPT = 'CIS')
OR      (CLABFEE = 0 AND CRED = 3)
```

Exercise:

4K. Select all information about any course with a labfee which is not greater than $100 or any other course, regardless of its labfee, which is offered by the Theology Department and is worth six credits.

The next example illustrates the use of parentheses to override the default hierarchy. In this example, the NOT is evaluated last.

Sample Query 4.12:   Display all information about every row in the COURSE table except any CIS course which has a zero labfee.

```
SELECT  *

FROM    COURSE

WHERE   NOT (CDEPT = 'CIS' AND CLABFEE = 0)
```

CNO	CNAME	CDESCP	CRED	CLABFEE	CDEPT
T11	SCHOLASTICISM	FOR THE PIUS	3	150.00	THEO
T12	FUNDAMENTALISM	FOR THE CAREFREE	3	90.00	THEO
T33	HEDONISM	FOR THE SANE	3	.00	THEO
T44	COMMUNISM	FOR THE GREEDY	6	200.00	THEO
P11	EMPIRICISM	SEE IT - BELIEVE IT	3	100.00	PHIL
P22	RATIONALISM	FOR CIS MAJORS	3	50.00	PHIL
P33	EXISTENTIALISM	FOR CIS MAJORS	3	200.00	PHIL
P44	SOLIPSISM	ME MYSELF AND I	6	.00	PHIL
C11	INTRO TO CS	FOR ROOKIES	3	100.00	CIS
C22	DATA STRUCTURES	VERY USEFUL	3	50.00	CIS
C55	COMPUTER ARCH.	VON NEUMANN'S MACH.	3	100.00	CIS
C66	RELATIONAL DATABASE	THE ONLY WAY TO GO	3	500.00	CIS

Comments:

1.   The logic expressed in this example is straightforward. We simply write a condition to identify the rows we do not want. This is

```
CDEPT = 'CIS' AND CLABFEE = 0
```

Then we negate this condition by placing a NOT in front of the entire condition which must be enclosed by parentheses.

```
NOT (CDEPT = 'CIS' AND CLABFEE = 0)
```

2.   Consider the reason the following condition without
      parentheses will not achieve the desired objective.

           NOT CDEPT = 'CIS' AND CLABFEE = 0

      The absence of parentheses means the NOT will be
      evaluated first, but it applies only to the first
      condition. This is equivalent to the following
      condition.

           (NOT CDEPT = 'CIS') AND CLABFEE = 0

      Only non-CIS rows with zero labfees would be selected by
      this condition. Observe that the current sample query
      selected some rows for CIS courses and some rows with
      nonzero labfees.

3.   The sample query could have been expressed a number of
      other ways. The following conditions are logically
      equivalent to the current example.

           (NOT CDEPT = 'CIS') OR (NOT CLABFEE = 0)

           CDEPT <> 'CIS' OR CLABFEE <> 0

      These clauses are no better than the original. We are
      merely illustrating logical equivalencies. To restate a
      point we made earlier, the issue of logic per se
      transcends SQL. You must be careful whenever you are
      writing complex queries.

Exercise:

4L.   Select all information about any course except three
      credit philosophy courses.

IN Keyword

The next sample query introduces the use of IN. This provides a convenient way of asking the system to select a row if a given column contains any value in a specified set of values.

Sample Query 4.13:   Display the course number, description, and credits for any course which is worth two, six, or nine credits.

```
SELECT CNO, CDESCP, CRED

FROM    COURSE

WHERE   CRED IN (2, 6, 9)
```

CNO	CDESCP	CRED
T44	FOR THE GREEDY	6
P44	ME MYSELF AND I	6

Comments:

1. Syntax: The set of values must be enclosed within parentheses with commas separating each value. These values can be numeric (the current example) or character. Character values must be enclosed in quotes. (See next sample query.) The values in the current example happen to be written in sequence. This helps readability, but it is not required. For all practical purposes there is no upper limit on the number of values that constitute the comparison set.

2. While the IN keyword is useful, it is also superfluous. This is because any condition using IN can be replaced with an equivalent sequence of OR conditions. The following statement is equivalent to the current example.

```
SELECT CNO, CDESCP, CRED
FROM    COURSE
WHERE   CRED = 2
OR      CRED = 6
OR      CRED = 9
```

NOT IN

The next example illustrates use of the NOT IN phrase which, as you would expect, is the converse of IN. It will instruct the system to select a row if a given column value contains any value other than a value in a specified set of values.

Sample Query 4.14: Display the course name, description, and department id of any course which is not offered by the Theology or Computer and Information Science Department.

```
SELECT  CNAME, CDESCP, CDEPT

FROM    COURSE

WHERE   CDEPT NOT IN ('THEO', 'CIS')
```

CNAME	CDESCP	CDEPT
EMPIRICISM	SEE IT - BELIEVE IT	PHIL
RATIONALISM	FOR CIS MAJORS	PHIL
EXISTENTIALISM	FOR CIS MAJORS	PHIL
SOLIPSISM	ME MYSELF AND I	PHIL

Comments:

1. Logic: The NOT IN phrase, like IN, is useful but superfluous. The current example could have contained any of the following equivalent WHERE clauses.

    ```
    WHERE NOT CDEPT = 'THEO'
    AND   NOT CDEPT = 'CIS'

    WHERE CDEPT <> 'THEO'
    AND   CDEPT <> 'CIS'

    WHERE NOT (CDEPT = 'THEO' OR CDEPT = 'CIS')
    ```

    It is permissible to place a NOT before a condition containing IN. The following WHERE clause is also equivalent to the current example. Notice that NOT appears before "CDEPT" instead of "IN".

    ```
    WHERE NOT CDEPT IN ('THEO', 'CIS')
    ```

    Using NOT IN appears to be more compact and comprehensible. This is especially true if there are a large number of values to be examined.

2. Syntax: Because CDEPT contains character data, the specified values ('THEO', 'CIS') must be enclosed within parentheses and the system will perform a character-by-character compare.

BETWEEN Keyword

The next sample query illustrates the use of BETWEEN to
identify a range of values. A row will be selected if a given
column has a value within the specified range.

Sample Query 4.15:   Display the course name and labfee of
any course with a labfee between, and
including, 100 and 200 dollars.

```
SELECT  CNAME, CLABFEE

FROM    COURSE

WHERE   CLABFEE BETWEEN 100.00 AND 200.00
```

CNAME	CLABFEE
SCHOLASTICISM	150.00
COMMUNISM	200.00
EMPIRICISM	100.00
EXISTENTIALISM	200.00
INTRO TO CS	100.00
COMPUTER ARCH.	100.00

Comments:

1.   Note that BETWEEN really means "between and including."
The system will select rows which match the extreme
values.

2.   The BETWEEN keyword is also superfluous. An equivalent
WHERE clause can always be written using an AND
connector. The current WHERE clause could have been
rewritten as

```
WHERE CLABFEE >= 100.00
AND   CLABFEE <= 200.00
```

Observe that the above approach required that the column
name (CLABFEE) be specified in both conditional
expressions. The use of the "BETWEEN____AND____"
phrase provides another approach which some users might
find more attractive.

3. Although it may be grammatically correct to say "where labfee is between 200 and 100," it would be silly to code the following WHERE clause.

        WHERE CLABFEE BETWEEN 200.00 AND 100.00

    The system would interpret this clause as the following AND-connected clause, which would always produce a "no hit" situation.

        WHERE CLABFEE >= 200.00
        AND   CLABFEE <= 100.00

    There is no number which is greater than 200 and less than 100. Hence, when using BETWEEN, always reference the smaller value first as the example illustrates.

Exercise:

4M. Display all information about any course which has a labfee equal to any value in the following set of values. {12.12, 50.00, 75.00, 90.00, 100.00, 500.00}

4N. Display all information about every course where the labfee is not one of the following. {12.12, 50.00, 75.00, 90.00, 100.00, 500.00}

4O. Display the course number and labfee for any course with a labfee between and including 50.00 and 400.00 dollars.

NOT BETWEEN

NOT BETWEEN is used to select rows where a given column value falls outside of a specified range. The next sample query is the converse of the previous. It will display every COURSE table row which was omitted from the previous result.

Sample Query 4.16:   Display the course name and labfee of any course with a labfee less than $100 or greater than $200.

```
SELECT CNAME, CLABFEE

FROM    COURSE

WHERE   CLABFEE NOT BETWEEN 100 AND 200
```

CNAME	CLABFEE
FUNDAMENTALISM	90.00
HEDONISM	.00
RATIONALISM	50.00
SOLIPSISM	.00
DATA STRUCTURES	50.00
DISCRETE MATHEMATICS	.00
DIGITAL CIRCUITS	.00
RELATIONAL DATABASE	500.00

Comments:

1.   Note that the NOT BETWEEN will exclude extreme values from the result. This is because it is the negation of the result which would have been produced by the BETWEEN. (More formally, it yields the complement of the set identified by the BETWEEN condition.)

2.   The following WHERE clause is equivalent to that of the current example.

        WHERE CLABFEE < 100
        OR   CLABFEE > 200

Note that the comparison operators are "strictly greater than" and "strictly less than." The is because the NOT BETWEEN clause excludes extreme values from being selected.

Also, as with any conditional expression, a NOT can precede the condition. Therefore, we could place the NOT before the column name instead of coding the NOT BETWEEN phrase. Hence the following WHERE clause is equivalent to that of the current example.

        WHERE NOT CLABFEE BETWEEN 100 and 200

3.   Again, the BETWEEN phrase must always reference the smaller value first. If we were to enter the following WHERE clause

        WHERE CLABFEE NOT BETWEEN 200 AND 100

the system would interpret this as

        WHERE CLABFEE < 200
        OR   CLABFEE > 100

Every value must match this condition, which means that all rows would be retrieved. This is obviously not the query objective.

Exercise:

4P. Display the course number and labfee of any course with a labfee which is less than $50 or greater than $400.

The next sample query shows that BETWEEN can also be used to identify a range for character string data.

Sample Query 4.17:   Display the name and labfee of any course with a course name beginning with the letter "D".

```
SELECT CNAME, CLABFEE

FROM    COURSE

WHERE   CNAME BETWEEN 'D' AND 'DZZZ'
```

CNAME	CLABFEE
DATA STRUCTURES	50.00
DISCRETE MATHEMATICS	.00
DIGITAL CIRCUITS	.00

Comments:

1.   Recall the ASCII and EBCDIC coding schemes described earlier in the comments for Sample Query 1.5. Under the realistic assumption that no course name which begins with "D" will be greater than "DZZZ", this example effectively retrieves every course with a course name beginning with the letter "D". Again, we assume that all character values stored in the database are in uppercase.

      It is important that you understand the idea of a character sequence. Note that if "DZZZ XXX" were a legitimate course name, it would not be selected by the SELECT statement because it is greater than "DZZZ".

2.   The intent of this query is to have the system search for a character string pattern in the CNAME field. This pattern is a "D" followed by any string. We will see in the next chapter that the LIKE keyword provides a far more convenient way of searching for character string patterns.

Exercise:

4Q.   Display the course name and description for any course with a description which begins "FOR".

ROWNUM and ROWID Pseudo-Columns

ORACLE provides pseudo-columns which can be selected from any table. (A pseudo-column is a column which is not really stored in the table but can be referenced in a SELECT statement which references any table.) We present two pseudo-columns below. These are ROWNUM, which indicates the order in which a row was selected from a table, and ROWID, which indicates the physical location of the row on the disk. Subsequent chapters will present other pseudo-columns.

Sample Query 4.18:   For courses having a labfee less than $100, display the course number preceded by ROWNUM and ROWID pseudo-columns. Do not display more than five rows.

```
SELECT  ROWNUM, ROWID, CNO

FROM    COURSE

WHERE   CLABFEE < 100

AND     ROWNUM <= 5
```

ROWNUM	ROWID	CNO
1	000022E8.0001.0001	T12
2	000022E8.0003.0001	T33
3	000022E8.0005.0001	C22
4	000022E8.0006.0001	C33
5	000022E8.0007.0001	C44

Comments:

1. The COURSE table has seven rows with a labfee value less than 100. The "ROWNUM <= 5" condition restricted the display to five rows. This technique will be very useful if you need to select a limited number of rows from a very large table.

2. We do not explain the ROWID value. It will vary from system to system contingent on your hardware platform. ORACLE allows you to reference rows using the ROWID. This is a clear violation of logical data independence. For this reason we will not reference ROWID in any future sample queries.

3. DB2 Compatibility: DB2 does not support any features comparable to ROWNUM and ROWID. A theoretical argument can be made that these keywords inhibit data independence. We are silent on this debatable issue.

The last example in this chapter does not introduce any new concepts or techniques. The sole purpose is to illustrate that any of the aforementioned techniques can be used within a single SELECT statement. The only reason that this statement is longer than previous statements is because of the relative complexity of the query objective. Examine each line of code within the statement, and observe that each implements one of the SQL constructs presented earlier in this text.

Sample Query 4.19: Display the department id, course name, and labfee of any three-credit CIS, THEO, or MGT course with a labfee between, and including, $50 and $300. Sort the result by course name within department id sequence (ascending).

```
SELECT CDEPT, CNAME, CLABFEE

FROM    COURSE

WHERE   CDEPT IN ('CIS', 'THEO', 'MGT')

AND     CLABFEE BETWEEN 50 AND 300

AND     CRED = 3

ORDER BY CDEPT, CNAME
```

CDEPT	CNAME	CLABFEE
CIS	COMPUTER ARCH.	100.00
CIS	DATA STRUCTURES	50.00
CIS	INTRO TO CS	100.00
THEO	FUNDAMENTALISM	90.00
THEO	SCHOLASTICISM	150.00

Exercise:

4R. Display the department, course number, and description for any computer science or theology course with a labfee which is less than $100 or greater than $400. Sort the results by course number within the department.

Summary

This chapter presented the formulation of more complex WHERE clauses by use of the traditional Boolean operators. We described the syntax and behavior of AND, OR, and NOT.

WHERE cond1 AND cond2: A given row is selected only if both cond1 and cond2 are true.

WHERE cond1 OR cond2: A given row is selected if either cond1 or cond2 or both are true.

WHERE NOT cond: A given row is selected if cond is not true (is false).

When a complex WHERE clause contains more than two individual conditions, you are encouraged to use parentheses to make explicit the order of evaluation. Otherwise the traditional hierarchy of evaluation applies. This means that NOTs are evaluated first, followed by ANDs, followed by ORs.

Two other useful keywords were presented which can help in the formulation of more compact and readable code. These are BETWEEN and IN, both of which can be prefaced by NOT. These are summarized below.

WHERE col BETWEEN val1 AND val2: A given row is selected if its col value is within the range specified by val1 and val2.

WHERE col NOT BETWEEN val1 AND val2: A given row is selected if its col value falls outside the range specified by val1 and val2.

WHERE col IN (val1, val2, ..., valn): A given row is selected if its col value equals any of the specified values.

WHERE col NOT IN (val1, val2, ..., valn): A given row is selected if its col value does not equal any of the specified values.

Finally, we bring your attention to the fact that no double boxes appeared anywhere in this chapter. DB2 and ORACLE are compatible with respect to the behavior of AND, OR, NOT, IN, and BETWEEN.

Summary Exercises

The following exercises all refer to the STAFF table. The column names are ENAME, ETITLE, ESALARY, and DEPT.

4S.   Display all information about any member of the Philosophy or Theology Department.

4T.   Display all information about any member of the Theology Department whose salary exceeds $52.

4U.   Display the name of any staff member whose salary is greater than or equal to $52, but less than or equal to $1000.

4V.   Display the name and title of any staff member assigned to the Theology Department who earns $51 or $54.

4W.   Display the name and salary of any staff member whose salary equals one of the following values: 51, 53, 100, 200, 25,000.

4X.   Display the names and salaries of staff members who earn less than $100 or more than $1000. Sort the result in ascending sequence by name.

4Y.   Display the department id of every department which employs a staff member whose salary exceeds $5000. Do not show duplicate department ids.

5

Synonyms

This chapter is dedicated to those with poor typing skills who will appreciate the opportunity to reduce the number of keystrokes required to express an SQL statement. One such opportunity is the creation of synonyms for table names. Synonyms usually serve as abbreviations for long table names. Synonyms also serve purposes which are beyond the scope of this text.

This chapter also provides the opportunity to give a sneak preview of some important ideas related to ORACLE concepts and facilities which will be covered later in this text. The first pertains to creating database objects (tables, views, indexes, synonyms, etc.) by using some version of the CREATE statement. We introduce the CREATE SYNONYM statement, which is one of the simplest statements in SQL.

The second idea pertains to ORACLE's Data Dictionary. This is a special collection of tables which ORACLE maintains for its own purposes. However, you will often find it helpful to display the contents of these tables. We describe one such table, USER_SYNONYMS, which will contain information about the synonyms you create using CREATE SYNONYM.

The CREATE SYNONYM Statement

We will create a synonym, "C", to be used as an abbreviation
for the COURSE table. This will be done by executing a CREATE
SYNONYM statement. Thereafter, C can be substituted for
COURSE in formulating SQL statements.

Sample Statement 5.1:   Create a synonym called "C" for the
COURSE table.

```
CREATE SYNONYM C FOR COURSE
```

System Response:

The system should display "Synonym created" as a message
indicating successful creation of the synonym.

Comment:

Now that the synonym has been created, it can be used
like any valid table name in an SQL statement. Consider
the following sample query, where "C" is used in place
of "COURSE".

Sample Query 5.2:   Display the course number and credit
value of courses offered by the
Philosophy Department.

```
SELECT CNO, CRED

FROM    C

WHERE   CDEPT = 'PHIL'
```

CNO	CRED
P11	3
P22	3
P33	3
P44	6

Comments:

1. This example created a "private synonym." Private
    synonyms are local to each username. This means that if
    another user (a person using a different username) has
    access to the COURSE table, that user cannot validly
    reference the synonym C unless that user explicitly
    issues the same CREATE SYNONYM statement.

    This other user could also create a different synonym
    for the same table. For example, assume this other user
    executed the following statement.

        CREATE SYNONYM CX FOR COURSE

    Under this circumstance, the system would recognize the
    other user's CX synonym and reject references to C by
    that user. Likewise, it would recognize your C synonym,
    but reject your reference to CX. Note that, because
    synonyms are local, there is no problem when multiple
    users create synonyms which happen to have the same
    name. This means that another user could also create a
    C synonym which may be associated with the COURSE table
    or an entirely different table.

    Aside: We have yet to discuss the GRANT statement, which
    enables user A to permit user B access to user A's
    table. This topic will be covered in Chapter 24.

2. The system remembers your synonyms for the entire
    terminal session and even after you sign off. The same
    synonyms are available the next time you sign on. You do
    not have to reissue the CREATE SYNONYM statement.

3. The system will let you create multiple synonyms for the
    same table. However, it will reject any attempt to
    create the same synonym for two different tables.

4. What if you no longer need a particular synonym?
    Synonyms can be dropped. The following statement would
    remove the C synonym.

        DROP SYNONYM C

5. ORACLE supports "public synonyms," which are synonyms
    which can be referenced by any user. Only the database
    administrator can create a public synonym.

USER_SYNONYM Table

What if you forget your private synonyms? There is an easy way to ask the system to display them. Simply select all the data found in a special table called USER_SYNONYM.

Sample Query 5.3: Determine your private synonyms and related information by displaying some columns in the USER_SYNONYM table.

```
SELECT SYNONYM_NAME, TABLE_OWNER, TABLE_NAME

FROM    USER_SYNONYM
```

SYNONYM_NAME	TABLE_OWNER	TABLE_NAME
C	U48989	COURSE

Comments:

1. Most of the tables presented in this book are "application" tables containing data related to a business application. Our business application contains data necessary to manage a mythical college. These data are of direct interest to the user. These application tables are explicitly created with the CREATE TABLE statement (to be described in Chapter 14).

    In addition to application tables, ORACLE maintains a set of "system" tables. This set of tables is collectively known as the "Data Dictionary." These Data Dictionary tables are part of the system. Our present intent is to introduce just one such table, the USER_SYNONYM table.

2.   The USER_SYNONYM table will contain one row for each
      private synonym that you create. In order to determine
      which synonyms are currently in effect, you merely
      examine the contents of the USER_SYNONYM table. The nice
      thing about this approach is that you use the standard
      SELECT statement to examine the table. In effect, there
      is nothing new to learn. Like any table, you must know
      (1) the precise table name, (2) the precise column
      names, and (3) the meaning of the data in the columns.
      The USER_SYNONYM table is described below.

      SYNONYM_NAME: The name of the synonym.

      TABLE_OWNER: The username of the creator of the
                      table. (You can be granted access to
                      another user's table and then create a
                      synonym for that table. In this case the
                      username would be different from the
                      username of the person who created the
                      synonym.)

      TABLE_NAME: The name of the table.

3.   ORACLE automatically keeps USER_SYNONYM (and other
      dictionary tables) updated. Whenever you issue a CREATE
      SYNONYM statement, the system automatically inserts a
      new row into this table. Whenever you issue a DROP
      SYNONYM statement, the system automatically deletes a
      row from this table.

4.   DB2 Compatibility: DB2 supports a "catalog" which is
      similar in spirit to ORACLE's Data Dictionary but is
      considerably different in detail. This is why we noted
      that you must know the "precise" table and column names.
      DB2 has a table (SYSIBM.SYSSYNONYMS) which contains
      information about synonyms.

5.   You can use SYN as an abbreviation for USER_SYNONYMS.

6.   In Version 5 of ORACLE, the private synonyms are stored
      in a table called PRIVATESYN.

Synonyms as Column Qualifiers

Synonyms, like table names, can be used to qualify a column name in the SELECT and WHERE clauses.

Sample Query 5.4:   Display the course number, name, and credit value for any course with a $500 labfee.

```
SELECT C.CNO, C.CNAME, CRED

FROM    C

WHERE   C.CLABFEE = 500
```

CNO	CNAME	CRED
C66	RELATIONAL DATABASE	3

Comments:

1.   In addition to referencing the synonym C in the FROM clause, this sample query uses C as a column qualifier in the SELECT and WHERE clauses. A synonym can be placed anywhere in the SELECT statement that the corresponding table name can be placed. This means that it can be used to qualify column names.

2.   The current sample query uses a synonym to qualify some, but not all, of the column names. This works the same for synonyms as it does for queries in which the table name is used to qualify columns.

3.   Note that when using a synonym, a reference to the table name which the synonym represents will be invalid and cause an error. Only the name, table name or synonym, which appears in the FROM clause may be used to qualify columns.

4.   The qualification of a column name in this example is unnecessary and serves no real purpose. However, in our discussion of the join operation we will note that qualification of column names is sometimes necessary. (See Sample Query 17.1.) Synonyms will be very useful in this context.

Summary

This chapter introduced the CREATE SYNONYM statement. Its primary purpose is to construct an abbreviation for a table name. The general syntax for this statement is

CREATE SYNONYM synonym FOR table-name

Once created, a synonym can be substituted for the table name in any SQL statement. We noted that private synonyms are local to your username and that they remain in effect until they are explicitly dropped. The general syntax of the DROP SYNONYM statement is

DROP SYNONYM synonym

There are two kinds of synonyms, private and public. Private synonyms are created by users for their own purposes. Information about your private synonyms is kept in a special Data Dictionary table called USER_SYNONYM. You can query this table to determine which synonyms are currently in effect.

Public synonyms can be created only by the DBA. Any user can reference a public synonym to access the table corresponding to the synonym. How do you discover which public synonyms the DBA has made available for your exploration of the database? The answer can be found by exploring another data dictionary table called ALL_SYNONYMS. (See Exercise 5F.)

You don't need to worry about the accuracy of these dictionary tables. The CREATE SYNONYM causes the ORACLE to insert a row in the appropriate dictionary tables; the DROP SYNONYM causes the system to delete a row from the appropriate tables.

In Chapter 23 we will discuss a special type of table known as a "view." (In fact, the dictionary tables described above really are views.) We mention this here for the purpose of stating that a synonym can also be created for a view. Whenever we have mentioned "table" in this chapter, the term "view" could have been used.

Finally, note that synonyms can be created only for table or view names. Although it might be desirable, synonyms cannot be created for column names.

Summary Exercises

5A. Display all the synonyms currently in effect for your username.

5B. Create an arbitrary synonym.

5C. Display all your synonyms. Note the new row.

5D. Drop the previously created synonym.

5E. Display all your synonyms. Note that the row for the previous synonym is removed.

5F. Make a preliminary exploration of your database by displaying the ALL_SYNONYMS table. (The SYNONYM_NAME column will contain the names of synonyms which you can reference in SELECT statements.) Don't expect to understand the purpose or content of these tables. We are simply suggesting that you apply your current knowledge of the SELECT statement for random exploration.

One more suggestion: The number of rows in ALL_SYNONYMS may exceed the number of lines on your terminal screen. Therefore, the second time you examine ALL_SYNONYMS you might want to use a WHERE clause to restrict the number of rows displayed. For example, to display just the public synonyms for tables created by user "U1111," you would enter

```
SELECT *
FROM    ALL_SYNONYMS
WHERE   TABLE_OWNER = 'U1111'
```

Pattern Matching

There are times when we would like to retrieve information from rows having similar, but not necessarily equal, values in a given column. As an example, suppose we wished to display information about all introductory courses. One approach is to examine the CNAME column in the COURSE table for course names with the words "INTRODUCTION" or "INTRODUCTORY" or perhaps even "INTRO". In this case we want to select rows based on some pattern. SQL provides a method for identifying patterns. It is not necessary to specify or even know a complete column value in order to identify a row for selection.

LIKE Keyword

SQL allows us to provide partial information by using the keyword LIKE. The LIKE keyword is used in the WHERE clause in place of the comparison operator. The general format is

    WHERE column-name LIKE 'pattern'

Column-name identifies the column to be searched for the pattern. The pattern is a character string (enclosed within apostrophes). Pattern matching applies only to character string columns. Pattern matching is not valid for columns which contain numeric or date data types.

SQL must be given some idea of where the partial string of characters is located. It could be found in the leftmost or rightmost positions, or possibly somewhere in the middle of the column. We specify the location of the character string by including special wildcard characters in the pattern. These wildcard characters are the percent sign (%) and the underscore character (_). Each wildcard character will be explained in the following sample queries.

Use of Percent (%) Symbol

The first sample query in this chapter illustrates the   use
of the percent sign (%) in the pattern string. This symbol is
interpreted as a wildcard which can represent any character
string of any length. In particular, it also represents the
empty string of length zero.

   The following example will search the CNAME column for
character strings which have 'INTRO' as the five leftmost
characters. The percent sign is used to represent the
remaining characters.

Sample Query 6.1:   Display the course number and name of all
introductory courses. (More precisely,
display the CNO and CNAME values of any
row which has a CNAME value beginning
with "INTRO".)

```
SELECT  CNO, CNAME

FROM    COURSE

WHERE   CNAME LIKE 'INTRO%'
```

CNO	CNAME
C11	INTRO TO CS

Comments:

1.   The pattern string "INTRO%" contains one percent sign at
     the end. This means that any number of characters
     following "INTRO" will be considered to be a match.
     However, the characters "INTRO" must be found in the
     column as the leftmost characters. After these five
     characters, SQL will consider anything found in the
     column to meet the selection criteria.

     If the following character strings were present in the
     CNAME column, they would all match the pattern used in
     the current example.

     "INTRODUCTION TO COMPUTERS"
     "INTRO TO COMPUTERS"
     "INTRO. TO COMPUTERS"
     "INTRODUCTORY COMPUTER SCIENCE"
     "INTRODUCTION TO COMPUTERS"
     "INTRO TO INTRODUCING"
     "INTRO"

2.   Note that a CNAME value of "INTRO" matches the pattern.
     This is because the percent symbol also represents the
     empty string.

3.   The following CNAME values would not match the "INTRO%"
     pattern.

     "AN INTRODUCTION TO CIS"
     " INTRO TO COMPUTERS"

     Both of these character strings contain "INTRO", but not
     as the leftmost five characters. The pattern for the
     current example requires such.

Exercise:

6A. Display all information about any course which has a
     description beginning with the string "FOR THE".

The next sample query is similar to the preceding. This time we are examining the rightmost part of a character string.

Sample Query 6.2:   Display all CNAME values which end with the letters "CISM".

```
SELECT CNAME

FROM    COURSE

WHERE   CNAME LIKE '%CISM'
```

CNAME
SCHOLASTICISM
EMPIRICISM

Comments:

1.   The placement of the percent sign at the beginning of the pattern informed the system that the desired characters would be found in the rightmost positions of the column. Zero or more characters preceding "CISM" is considered to be a match. Again, note that because the percent symbol matches the empty string, a CNAME value of "CISM" would match the current pattern.

2.   It is unlikely that a character column will have trailing blank characters in the rightmost positions. However, it is not impossible. This can occur if a terminal operator explicitly enters trailing blanks when updating a table. Therefore, it is possible for the CNAME column to contain "SCHOLASTICISM ". The pattern '%CISM' would not match on this value because the last four characters "ISM " do not match "CISM".

Exercise:

6B.   Display the course name and description of any course having a description which ends with the letter "E".

The next sample query illustrates the use of multiple percent symbols.

Sample Query 6.3:   What are the names of courses which have the letters "SC" appearing anywhere in the name?

```
SELECT  CNAME

FROM    COURSE

WHERE   CNAME LIKE '%SC%'
```

CNAME
_____
SCHOLASTICISM
DISCRETE MATHEMATICS

Comments:

1.   The pattern will match on the string "SC" anywhere within the CNAME column. In particular, it will match these characters if they occur in the middle of the string. "DISCRETE MATHEMATICS" was such a match. Because the percent symbol matches on the empty string, the pattern also matches on strings which begin or end with "SC". Hence "SCHOLASTICISM" was a match.

2.   Any number of percent symbols can occur within a pattern string. The following will match on any CNAME value which begins with "F"; has an embedded blank, followed by "OO"; and ends with a period.

WHERE CNAME LIKE 'F% %OO%.'

Exercise:

6C.   Display the course number and description of any course with a period, hyphen, or exclamation mark anywhere in its description. (<u>Hint:</u> You will need to use multiple conditions to satisfy this query.)

Use of Underscore (_) Symbol

Previous examples illustrated the percent sign as a wildcard symbol which could represent a substring of any length. The next sample query introduces another wildcard symbol, the underscore (_), which will always represent exactly one character position.

Sample Query 6.4:   Display course name and department id of any course which has the letter "H" present in the second position of its department id and is exactly four characters long.

```
SELECT  CNAME, CDEPT

FROM    COURSE

WHERE   CDEPT LIKE '_H_ _'
```

CNAME	CDEPT
SCHOLASTICISM	THEO
FUNDAMENTALISM	THEO
HEDONISM	THEO
COMMUNISM	THEO
EMPIRICISM	PHIL
RATIONALISM	PHIL
EXISTENTIALISM	PHIL
SOLIPSISM	PHIL

Comments:

1. The difference between the percent sign and the underscore is twofold. First, the percent sign allows any number of characters to match while the underscore allows only one. Second, the percent sign is considered a match if zero characters are found. The underscore always requires exactly one character to be present.

2. The CDEPT column has a maximum length of four characters. The positions of the underscore characters in the pattern permit the first, third, and fourth characters to be of any value, including blanks. The one character present in the pattern, the letter "H", must be found precisely in the second position of the column for a match to occur.

Exercise:

6D. Display the course name and department id of any course with a three-character department id.

Mixing Wildcard Symbols

The next sample query illustrates the use of both of the
wildcard symbols in the same pattern.

Sample Query 6.5:   Display the names of courses which have a
vowel as the second letter of their name.

```
SELECT  CNAME

FROM    COURSE

WHERE   CNAME LIKE '_A%'

OR      CNAME LIKE '_E%'

OR      CNAME LIKE '_I%'

OR      CNAME LIKE '_O%'

OR      CNAME LIKE '_U%'
```

CNAME
_____
FUNDAMENTALISM
HEDONISM
COMMUNISM
RATIONALISM
SOLIPSISM
DATA STRUCTURES
DISCRETE MATHEMATICS
DIGITAL CIRCUITS
COMPUTER ARCH.
RELATIONAL DATABASE

Comments:

1.   This example demonstrates a combination of the wildcard
        characters. The underscore implies that any character
        can appear in the first position. Each pattern is
        defined with a vowel in the second position, thereby
        identifying specific values acceptable for a match. The
        remaining positions of the column may be any value of
        any length as shown by the use of the percent sign.

2.   The example showed a series of patterns, all to be
        tested against the same column. It might seem that there
        should be some shorthand method of specifying this
        request. Unfortunately, there is no abbreviated method
        available.

3.   A pattern string may contain any number of wildcard
        symbols. For example, the following WHERE clause will
        match on any course name with an "E" in the second
        position and an "I" in the sixth position and is at
        least 10 characters long.

            WHERE CNAME LIKE '_ E _ _ _ I _ _ _ _ %'

4.   Be careful when combining wildcard characters. You might
        be tempted to use the following WHERE clause to satisfy
        Sample Query 6.4.

            WHERE CDEPT LIKE '_H%'

        However, this pattern is not equivalent to '_ H _ _'
        because it will match on any string with an "H" in the
        second position which is at least two characters long.
        The sample query objective required a length of exactly
        four characters.

Exercise:

6E.   Display the name and description of any course where the
        description has "THE" in the fifth, sixth, and seventh
        positions, and an "A" in the tenth position.

NOT LIKE

The last sample query of this chapter illustrates the NOT
LIKE phrase. As you would expect, this is used to select rows
which do not conform to a specified pattern.

Sample Query 6.6:   Display the names of all courses which
do not have a vowel as the second letter.

```
SELECT  CNAME

FROM    COURSE

WHERE   CNAME NOT LIKE '_A%'

AND     CNAME NOT LIKE '_E%'

AND     CNAME NOT LIKE '_I%'

AND     CNAME NOT LIKE '_O%'

AND     CNAME NOT LIKE '_U%'
```

CNAME
SCHOLASTICISM
EMPIRICISM
EXISTENTIALISM
INTRO TO CS

Comments:

1. The NOT LIKE phrase is similar in spirit to the NOT IN and NOT BETWEEN described in the previous chapter. NOT has the effect of selecting every row which does not match the pattern string.

2. This query could have been expressed in other ways. The example shows the NOT keyword placed immediately before the LIKE keyword. However, that is not a requirement. The WHERE clause could have been formed with the NOT before the column name.

```
WHERE NOT  CNAME LIKE ' _A%'
AND    NOT  CNAME LIKE '_E%'
AND    NOT  CNAME LIKE '_I%'
AND    NOT  CNAME LIKE '_O%'
AND    NOT  CNAME LIKE '_U%'
```

Another equivalent WHERE clause is

```
WHERE NOT
    (CNAME LIKE ' _A%'
OR CNAME LIKE '_E%'
OR CNAME LIKE '_I%'
OR CNAME LIKE '_O%'
OR CNAME LIKE '_U%')
```

This approach simply negates the entire WHERE clause shown in Sample Query 6.5 by enclosing the conditions in parentheses and placing a NOT in front of the entire compound condition.

Exercise:

6F. Display the course name and description of any course which does not end with an "E" or an "S".

Summary

The WHERE clause can contain the keyword LIKE to test for a pattern in a character string. The general format is

        WHERE column-name LIKE 'pattern'

The pattern must be enclosed in apostrophes and may contain two special wildcard characters. The percent sign (%) represents any string of any length. The underscore (_) represents exactly one character.

   The ORACLE reference manuals specify that LIKE may be used only to inspect columns containing character data. However, the ORACLE automatic data type conversion facility will allow columns containing numeric and date data types to be examined as well. In Chapter 9 we identify other instances where this facility may affect queries. (We advise against relying on this facility and recommend caution if you choose to capitalize on this feature.)

   DB2 Compatibility: Note that DB2 supports fixed-length data types that offer true trailing blanks. This means that '%S' will not find a match if the data are stored as 'CIS '.

Summary Exercises

The following exercises all refer to the STAFF table. The column names are ENAME, ETITLE, ESALARY, and DEPT. The ENAME, ETITLE, and DEPT columns contain character string data.

6G.   Display all information about any staff member whose name begins with the letters "MA".

6H.   Display all information about any staff member whose title ends with the digit 1, 2, or 3.

6I.   Display the name and title of any staff member who has the letter "S" occurring anywhere in both name and title.

6J.   Display the department id of any department which has the letter "E" in the third character position. Do not display duplicate values.

6K.   Display the name of any staff member whose name has the letter "I" in the 5th position. Display the result in ascending alphabetic sequence.

7

Arithmetic Expressions

This chapter presents some of the computational facilities supported by SQL. We introduce the formulation of arithmetic expressions which can be used to display columns containing calculated results. (Chapters 8 and 9 will present ORACLE's built-in functions which provide additional computational facilities.)

You will discover that it is easy to perform basic calculations with data retrieved via a SELECT statement. However, we note that SQL was not designed as a language to support complex mathematical processing. SQL is really a database language which also supports some basic computational facilities. For this reason you will find that the following sample queries illustrate relatively simple calculations.

The ability to perform calculations on the data and derive values from existing information is useful in formulating and answering "what-if"-type questions. This would prove beneficial to a college administrator involved with budgetary forecasting. We present a variety of "what-if" sample queries which require calculations involving the CLABFEE column.

Sample Query 7.1:   Suppose that we are interested in the impact of increasing the labfee charges for all CIS courses. What would be the labfee for each CIS course if its current labfee is increased by $25? Display each CIS course name followed by the current labfee and the adjusted labfee.

```
SELECT CNAME, CLABFEE, CLABFEE + 25

FROM    COURSE

WHERE   CDEPT = 'CIS'
```

CNAME	CLABFEE	CLABFEE+25
INTRO TO CS	100.00	125
DATA STRUCTURES	50.00	75
DISCRETE MATHEMATICS	.00	25
DIGITAL CIRCUITS	.00	25
COMPUTER ARCH.	100.00	125
RELATIONAL DATABASE	500.00	525

Comments:

1.   Syntax:

The SELECT clause begins "SELECT CNAME, CLABFEE" (which produces the first two columns of the output display) followed by "CLABFEE + 25", which is an arithmetic expression. This arithmetic expression caused the system to calculate and display the third column with the desired adjusted labfee values. There are many details to be addressed regarding writing correct arithmetic expressions. However, for the moment, we will simply describe an arithmetic expression as a meaningful combination of column names, constants, and arithmetic operators. Usually, but not always, the formation of a "meaningful" arithmetic expression is quite simple.

Below is a list of valid SELECT clauses which, in addition to containing column names, contain one or more arithmetic expressions. They illustrate the standard arithmetic operators of addition (+), subtraction (-), multiplication (*), and division (/).

a.   SELECT CNAME, 25.00 + CLABFEE

b.   SELECT CNAME, CRED * 2

c.   SELECT CLABFEE + 25, CLABFEE * 2.3

d.   SELECT CLABFEE + 100.00, CRED - 1, CNAME

e.   SELECT CLABFEE * CRED / 10

The above clauses show spaces between the arithmetic operator and the operands. This may improve readability, but it is not necessary.

2.   Logic:

The calculation involved adding a constant value of 25
to the CLABFEE value for each row in the COURSE table.
It is important to realize that the system performs the
calculation in a temporary storage area and has no
effect on the data stored in the COURSE table. The
SELECT statement only displays data or data derived by
some calculations. It never changes the data stored in
a table.

3.   Column Headings for Calculated Columns:

A column which contains values produced by an expression
has no predefined column name. Hence, the system uses
the arithmetic expression as the column heading. The
current   example   shows   that   the   system   produced
"CLABFEE+25" as the column heading for the third column
containing the results of the calculation.

4.   Display Format for Calculated Columns:

Observe that the calculated results are integer values.
Whenever the result of a calculation is an integer, the
system, by default, will display the result as an
integer. Subsequent sample queries will illustrate
arithmetic expressions which produce decimal values.
Also, we will demonstrate the application of SQL*Plus
commands to format calculated columns.

Sample Query 7.2:   What would be the labfee for CIS courses
if labfee charges were reduced by $25.75?

```
SELECT  CNAME,  CLABFEE,  CLABFEE - 25.75

FROM    COURSE

WHERE   CDEPT = 'CIS'
```

CNAME	CLABFEE	CLABFEE-25.75
INTRO TO CS	100.00	74.25
DATA STRUCTURES	50.00	24.25
DISCRETE MATHEMATICS	.00	-25.75
DIGITAL CIRCUITS	.00	-25.75
COMPUTER ARCH.	100.00	74.25
RELATIONAL DATABASE	500.00	474.25

Comments:

1.   This example demonstrates the subtraction operation.
     There are two CIS courses which have zero labfees.
     Subtracting $25.75 from these labfees produced negative
     values which were accurately presented in the result.
     The system automatically displays any negative value
     with a minus sign. Note that the calculated values show
     the correct values with the appropriate decimal
     accuracy.

2.   The column involved in the expression may be used in the
     WHERE clause. It might have been a good idea to avoid
     any negative labfees derived by this example by
     eliminating any course with a labfee of less than $25.75
     from consideration. The following statement would do so.

```
SELECT  CNAME, CLABFEE, CLABFEE - 25.75
FROM    COURSE
WHERE   CDEPT = 'CIS'
AND     CLABFEE >= 25.75
```

Sample Query 7.3:   What would be the labfee for each CIS course if its current labfee were multiplied by 2.375?

```
SELECT CNAME, CLABFEE, CLABFEE * 2.375

FROM    COURSE

WHERE   CDEPT = 'CIS'
```

CNAME	CLABFEE	CLABFEE*2.375
INTRO TO CS	100.00	237.5
DATA STRUCTURES	50.00	118.75
DISCRETE MATHEMATICS	.00	0
DIGITAL CIRCUITS	.00	0
COMPUTER ARCH.	100.00	237.5
RELATIONAL DATABASE	500.00	1187.5

Comment:

This example illustrates multiplication which happens to generate some decimal results. Observe that the system will still display integer results as integers; only decimal results will be displayed with decimal accuracy. The system does not automatically align a column of decimal values on the decimal point.

By default, the system will display decimal values with an accuracy of 10 column positions, and it will automatically round the decimal value at the last decimal position. (See Sample Query 7.5.) Obviously, these default actions often produce a less-than-desirable display. Subsequent sample queries will illustrate SQL*Plus formatting commands to produce a more attractive report.

Sample Query 7.4:   For each philosophy course, divide the credits in half. Display the course name, credits, and the result of dividing the credits in half.

```
SELECT  CNAME, CRED, CRED/2

FROM    COURSE

WHERE   CDEPT = 'PHIL'
```

CNAME	CRED	CRED/2
EMPIRICISM	3	1.5
RATIONALISM	3	1.5
EXISTENTIALISM	3	1.5
SOLIPSISM	6	3

Comment:

Again, observe that the calculation produced some decimal values and the default formatting rules applied.

Exercises:

7A.   What would be the credit value for each philosophy course if its current credit value were doubled? Display each course number, current credit, and adjusted credit values.

7B.   What would be the labfee of a theology course if each such course were charged $10.50 per credit? Display the course number and the adjusted labfee.

7C.   Assume that any course with a nonzero labfee will have its labfee decreased by 50 percent. Display the course number, and current and adjusted labfees for such courses.

All previous arithmetic expressions contained a constant. This is not always the case. Consider the next example.

Sample Query 7.5: What is the average labfee per credit hour for courses offered by the CIS department?

```
SELECT  CNAME, CLABFEE / CRED

FROM    COURSE

WHERE   CDEPT = 'CIS'
```

CNAME	CLABFEE/CRED
INTRO TO CS	33.3333333
DATA STRUCTURES	16.6666667
DISCRETE MATHEMATICS	0
DIGITAL CIRCUITS	0
COMPUTER ARCH.	33.3333333
RELATIONAL DATABASE	166.666667

Comments:

1. In this example we derived information using two different values stored in the database. (There are no constants in the expression.) The labfee for each course was divided by the number of credits for that course to produce the calculated value we requested -- the average labfee per credit. The system operates on a row-by-row basis. For each row selected, the CLABFEE value is divided by the CRED value.

2. Note that the calculation is accurate within 10 column positions, and the decimal values are automatically rounded at the last decimal position. We now describe how to modify this default format.

Formatting Calculated Columns

In Chapter 2 we introduced the COLUMN command to format displayed columns. This same command can be used to format columns produced by arithmetic expressions. Simply place the expression, exactly as written in the SELECT clause, after the keyword COLUMN followed by desired specification(s). We demonstrate this facility with the following example, which formats the same calculations performed in the first four sample queries.

Sample Query 7.6: For each CIS and philosophy course, display the following calculations with the specified report formatting.
    (a)   CLABFEE + 25: Display six digits with two-digit decimal accuracy.
    (b)   CLABFEE - 25.75: Display as a four-digit integer.
    (c)   CLABFEE * 2.375: Display seven digits with three-digit decimal accuracy.
    (d)   CRED/2: Display two digits with one-digit decimal accuracy. Also, present the column heading as "HALF-CRED".

```
COLUMN   CLABFEE+25      FORMAT 9999.99
COLUMN   CLABFEE-25.75   FORMAT 9999
COLUMN   CLABFEE*2.375   FORMAT 9999.999
COLUMN   CRED/2          FORMAT 9.9    HEADING   'HALF-CRED'

SELECT CLABFEE + 25, CLABFEE - 25.75, CLABFEE * 2.375,
       CRED/2
FROM   COURSE
WHERE  CDEPT = 'PHIL'
```

CLABFEE+25	CLABFEE-25.75	CLABFEE*2.375	HALF-CRED
75.00	24	118.750	1.5
225.00	174	475.000	1.5
25.00	-26	.000	3.0
125.00	74	237.500	1.5

Comments:

1. Observe that the COLUMN command operates as described in Chapter 2.

2. There are other techniques to specify format editing for calculated columns. These other techniques are appropriate when the expression is very long. This will be discussed in Part III of this text.

Hierarchy of Arithmetic Operators

All previous arithmetic expressions contained just one arithmetic operator. It is common practice to formulate an expression which has multiple arithmetic operators. Consider the following examples where COLA, COLB, and COLC represent numeric columns in some table.

   a.   COLA + COLB + COLC + 100

   b.   COLA * COLB * 2

   c.   COLA + COLB - COLC

When an expression contains multiple arithmetic operators, the system must determine the sequence of operations. For the above examples it does not make any difference. For example, in (c) the system could add COLA and COLB to produce an intermediate result which it then subtracts COLC from. Or, it could subtract COLC from COLB and then add this result to COLA. Either way, the result is the same. Using parentheses notation, we note that

   (COLA + COLB) - COLC = COLA + (COLB - COLC)

This equivalence does not always occur. Consider the following examples.

   d.   COLA + COLB * COLC

   e.   COLA / COLB * COLC

The order of execution for these expressions is significant. Assume COLA = 10, COLB = 5, and COLC = 2. Then (d) evaluates to 30 if you do the addition first and then multiply; it evaluates to 20 if you multiply first and then add. Expression (e) evaluates to 4 if you divide first and then multiply; it evaluates to 1 if you multiply first and then divide. You can specify the desired sequence by use of parentheses. However, if the expression does not contain parentheses, the system will follow a standard hierarchy of arithmetic operations.

The hierarchy of arithmetic operators is defined as

* Multiplication and division operations are evaluated first in a left-to-right scan of the expression.

* Then addition and subtraction operations are evaluated in a left-to-right scan of the expression.

* The order of evaluation can be changed by enclosing an expression, or part of an expression, in parentheses. Expressions within parentheses are evaluated first according to the order of the operators just mentioned. After evaluating within the parentheses, the operators outside are then evaluated.

This is the same hierarchy that applies to high-school algebra and many other computer programming languages. This means that expressions (d) and (e) above would be interpreted as

    COLA + (COLB * COLC)

    (COLA / COLB) * COLC

It is strongly recommended that you use parentheses to make explicit the desired order of execution. We rewrite expressions (a) through (e) after substituting the aforementioned values.

    a. 10 + 5 + 2 + 100   evaluates to 117

    b. 10 * 5 * 2   evaluates to 100

    c. 10 + 5 - 2   evaluates to 13

    d. 10 + 5 * 2   evaluates to 20

    e. 10 / 5 * 2   evaluates to 4

You are advised to examine to following expressions to verify your understanding of the order of execution as specified by the hierarchy.

    (10 + 5) * 2   evaluates to 30
    10 / (5 * 2)   evaluates to 1
    10 + 5 * 10 + 2   evaluates to 62
    (10 + 5) * (10 + 2)   evaluates to 180
    (10 + 5 * 10) + 2   evaluates to 62
    (10 + 5) * 10 + 2   evaluates to 152

The next sample query requires writing an arithmetic expression with multiple arithmetic operators. Their order of execution is significant. Parentheses are used to make this explicit.

Sample Query 7.7.1:   What would be the average labfee per credit hour for CIS courses if the labfee were increased by $25.00?

```
SELECT  CNAME,  CLABFEE,  CRED,  (CLABFEE+25)/CRED

FROM    COURSE

WHERE   CDEPT = 'CIS'
```

CNAME	CLABFEE	CRED	(CLABFEE+25)/CRED
INTRO TO CS	100.00	3	41.6666667
DATA STRUCTURES	50.00	3	25
DISCRETE MATHEMATICS	.00	3	8.33333333
DIGITAL CIRCUITS	.00	3	8.33333333
COMPUTER ARCH.	100.00	3	41.6666667
RELATIONAL DATABASE	500.00	3	175

Comment:

This query required that the addition of 25 to each labfee be performed before the division by the number of credits. We enclosed this addition operation in parentheses to ensure that it was performed first. Had we not done this, the result would have been radically different. (See the next query.)

Sample Query 7.7.2: Erroneous attempt at previous sample query. Observe what happens if you forget necessary parentheses.

```
SELECT  CNAME, CLABFEE, CRED, CLABFEE+25/CRED

FROM    COURSE

WHERE   CDEPT = 'CIS'
```

CNAME	CLABFEE	CRED	CLABFEE+25/CRED
INTRO TO CS	100.00	3	108.333333
DATA STRUCTURES	50.00	3	58.3333333
DISCRETE MATHEMATICS	.00	3	8.33333333
DIGITAL CIRCUITS	.00	3	8.33333333
COMPUTER ARCH.	100.00	3	108.333333
RELATIONAL DATABASE	500.00	3	508.333333

Comment:

The absence of parentheses in the expression means that the division is performed first. This is not consistent with the objective of the query.

Exercise:

7D. For any course with a labfee less than $200, display its course number and its adjusted labfee which is $35 more than 150% of the current labfee.

Floating-Point Numbers

ORACLE supports floating-point notation, also called "scientific notation" or "exponential notation." Usually this notation is used to represent very large or small numbers. These are the type of numeric values used by astronomers and nuclear physicists. A business application may occasionally require such values, but usually the conventional decimal notation satisfies its requirements. Below we present a brief description of floating-point notation.

Floating-point notation represents numeric values using exponential notation with 10 as the base value. The following examples illustrate floating-point constants which can be used in SQL arithmetic expressions.

	Floating-Point Number	Decimal Equivalent
a.	123E+06	123,000,000
b.	1.234E+10	12,340,000,000
c.	1.2E+20	120,000,000,000,000,000,000
d.	123E-06	.000123
e.	1E+00	1

You can use floating-point notation when writing arithmetic expressions. SQL*Plus will normally display the calculated results in conventional notation unless the size of the result exceeds the default or specified width for numeric columns.

SQL*Plus has a FORMAT model which can be used with the COLUMN command to display any numeric result in floating-point notation. (See ORACLE Reference Manual.)

The next two sample queries illustrate the use of floating-point notation in arithmetic expressions and the displaying of large calculated values in floating-point notation.

Sample Query 7.8: Assume you would like to double the labfee for the relational database course. Use a floating-point constant in an arithmetic expression to perform this calculation.

```
SELECT CNAME, CLABFEE, CLABFEE * 2E0

FROM    COURSE

WHERE   CNAME = 'RELATIONAL DATABASE'
```

CNAME	CLABFEE	CLABFEE*2E0
RELATIONAL DATABASE	500.00	1000

Comment:

Even though a floating-point number was used in the expression, the result was displayed in conventional notation because it could be represented in less than 10 column positions.

Sample Query 7.9: For each philosophy course, multiply the credit value by one trillion.

```
SELECT CRED, CRED * 1000000000000

FROM    COURSE

WHERE   CDEPT = 'PHIL'
```

CRED	CRED*1000000000
3	3.00E+12
3	3.00E+12
3	3.00E+12
6	6.00E+12

Comment:

Even though conventional numeric notation was used in the expression, the result was displayed in floating-point notation because result values exceeded 10 column positions.

Calculated Conditions

All previous examples have shown arithmetic expressions placed within a SELECT clause. Arithmetic expressions can also occur in WHERE conditions. (The intent is to have the system display a given row only if it meets criteria which are to be determined by some calculation.) Such a condition is called a "calculated condition."

Sample Query 7.10: Which CIS courses have an average labfee per credit hour value greater than $30?

```
SELECT  CNAME, CLABFEE / CRED

FROM    COURSE

WHERE   CDEPT = 'CIS'

AND     CLABFEE / CRED > 30
```

CNAME	CLABFEE/CRED
INTRO TO CS	33.3333333
COMPUTER ARCH.	33.3333333
RELATIONAL DATABASE	166.666667

Comments:

1. The condition "CLABFEE / CRED > 30" contains an arithmetic expression "CLABFEE / CRED" which is evaluated for each row. If the result is greater than 30, the row is selected.

2. The example also displays the evaluation of "CLABFEE / CRED". This is not necessary, but it helps you verify the result.

3. An expression may appear on either side of the operator in a WHERE clause. In the present query the condition could have been expressed as

```
WHERE CDEPT = 'CIS'
AND   30 < CLABFEE / CRED
```

Sorting by a Calculated Column

It is possible to display a result which is sorted by a column, the values of which are produced by an arithmetic expression. We described the general sorting technique in Chapter 3. We now further describe how the ORDER BY clause may be used. When sorting a calculated column we have two options: (1) specify the relative position of the column as it appears in the SELECT clause (review Sample Query 3.4), and (2) use the entire expression in the ORDER BY clause.

Sample Query 7.11:   What would be the labfee for each computer science course if we increased it by $25? Order the result by the adjusted labfee value.

```
SELECT  CNAME, CLABFEE, CLABFEE+25

FROM    COURSE

WHERE   CDEPT = 'CIS'

ORDER   BY CLABFEE+25
```

CNAME	CLABFEE	CLABFEE+25
DISCRETE MATHEMATICS	.00	25
DIGITAL CIRCUITS	.00	25
DATA STRUCTURES	50.00	75
INTRO TO CS	100.00	125
COMPUTER ARCH.	100.00	125
RELATIONAL DATABASE	500.00	525

Comments:

1. In this sample query we specified the expression in the ORDER BY clause. We could have used the relative position of the column. "ORDER BY 3" would have achieved the same result.

2. DB2 Compatibility: DB2 does not allow you to specify the expression in the ORDER BY clause. You may refer to a calculated value only by using its relative position number.

Summary

This chapter has introduced the use of arithmetic expressions to perform basic computations with data selected from a table. These expressions have a syntax similar to algebraic expressions described in a typical high-school algebra textbook.

The presence of an arithmetic expression in a SELECT clause will generate a column in the output display. We emphasize "column" because the next chapter introduces the group functions which perform calculations on the selected data to produce a row which summarizes the selected data.

The COLUMN command can be used to format results produced by arithmetic expressions. You simply specify the expression after the "COLUMN" keyword, followed by the FORMAT and/or HEADING specifications.

Summary Exercises

The following exercises refer to the STAFF table.

7E. Assume all staff members are given a hundred dollar raise. Display the name and adjusted salary of every staff member.

7F. Assume all staff members are given a 15 percent raise. Display the name, and old and new salary amounts for every staff member.

7G. Assume all salaries are decreased by one hundred dollars. Display the name and adjusted salary of every staff member whose adjusted salary is less than $25,000.

7H. Consider only staff members whose current salary is less than $25,000. Assume this group of staff members is given a thousand-dollar raise. Display their names and adjusted salaries in descending salary sequence.

II

ORACLE Built-in Functions

ORACLE provides a large number of built-in functions that perform many tasks you will find to be very useful. A built-in function is part of ("built into") SQL. Each function has a name (e.g., SUM) which usually indicates the purpose of the function. Each function will also accept one or more *"arguments"* which the function uses as input. Typically, a column name serves as an argument. For example, SUM(CLABFEE) is a function which accepts the CLABFEE column as an argument and produces the total of all labfees as a result.

Organization of Chapters

ORACLE provides three broad categories of functions. The three chapters in this part of the text correspond to each category. We describe most, but not all, functions available with the ORACLE product.

The first category of functions is called "group functions." We present the following functions in Chapter 8.

    SUM
    MAX
    MIN
    AVG
    COUNT
    VARIANCE
    STDDEV

The second category of functions is called "individual functions." These functions have four subcategories: Arithmetic, Character, Conversion, and Miscellaneous. We present the following functions in Chapter 9.

Arithmetic Functions	Character Functions
TRUNC	UPPER
ROUND	LOWER
FLOOR	INITCAP
CEIL	LPAD
ABS	RPAD
SIGN	LTRIM
SQRT	RTRIM
POWER	LENGTH
MOD	SUBSTR
	TRANSLATE
	INSTR

Conversion Functions	Miscellaneous
TO_NUMBER	GREATEST
TO_CHAR	LEAST
TO_DATE	DECODE
	NVL

We conclude Chapter 9 with a discussion of the concatenation operator (¦¦), which is not really a function, but is often used in conjunction with character functions.

The third category of functions is the "date functions." We present the following functions in Chapter 10.

```
LAST_DAY
NEXT_DAY
MONTHS_BETWEEN
ADD_MONTH
```

Chapter 10 presents a comprehensive overview of processing date/time information in addition to describing the above functions. We will see that ORACLE understands the semantics we normally associate with date/time information.

8

Group Functions

Chapter 7 presented arithmetic expressions that allow you to perform computations with selected data. This chapter continues the same theme. We introduce SQL's group functions which provide additional computational facilities.

A group function is used to scan a column of selected values and perform a computation based on those values. This chapter will present sample queries which illustrate all the group functions: AVG, MAX, MIN, SUM, COUNT, VARIANCE, and STDDEV.

Group functions operate on groups of rows and generate a single row for each group. At the outset we will simply consider the entire COURSE table as a single group. Sample Queries 8.1 through 8.8 will select rows from this group and then apply a group function to produce a calculated result. Thereafter, we introduce the GROUP BY clause. You will use the GROUP BY clause when you wish to decompose selected rows into multiple groups and then apply a function to each separate group.

AVG Function

The first sample query applies the AVG function to the entire COURSE table which is treated as a single group.

Sample Query 8.1:   What is the average labfee for all courses described in the COURSE table?

```
SELECT  AVG(CLABFEE)

FROM    COURSE
```

AVG(CLABFEE)
        110

Comments:

1.   A group function returns a result of the same data type as the argument to which it is applied. CLABFEE is defined as a numeric value; therefore, the result is also numeric. (Note that AVG can be applied only to numeric values.)

2.   The result is a calculated value. Therefore, SQL*Plus must generate a column heading. By default, this heading is simply the function and argument which generated the column. Sample Query 8.7.2 will show the use of the COLUMN command to override this default and generate any desired heading.

3.   ORACLE will display the calculated data with a decimal accuracy using the same rules described for arithmetic expressions. The COLUMN command can be used to format the result to any desired decimal accuracy.

4.   Note that the value returned by the AVG function is a single row. For this reason it makes no sense to include an ORDER BY clause to sort the result. However, it would not cause an error.

5.   In this example the group processed was the entire table. This does not have to be the case. A group function could be applied to a subset of rows by using a WHERE clause to form a smaller group. See the next sample query.

MIN and MAX Functions

The next sample query illustrates the MIN and MAX functions which accept both numeric and character string arguments. The example applies the functions to a group which is a subset of rows from the COURSE table.

Sample Query 8.2:   Consider only rows for the Philosophy Department. What are the lowest and highest labfees for these courses? Also, what are the lowest and highest values in the CNO column? (In other words, if the values in the CNO column were arranged in alphabetical sequence, what would be the first and last values?)

```
SELECT  MIN(CLABFEE), MAX(CLABFEE), MIN(CNO), MAX(CNO)

FROM    COURSE

WHERE   CDEPT = 'PHIL'
```

MIN(CLABFEE)	MAX(CLABFEE)	MIN	MAX
0	200	P11	P44

Comments:

1.   The present query demonstrates that column functions can be applied to a subset of the table by specifying selection criteria in a WHERE clause.

2.   The WHERE clause cannot reference any of the group functions. For example, "WHERE MAX(CLABFEE) > 50" is invalid. This restriction applies only to group functions. We will see in the next chapter that this does not apply to individual functions.

3.   Again, we note that a group function returns a result of the same data type as the column to which it is applied. MAX and MIN were applied to CLABFEE, a numeric column, and produced numeric results. When applied to CNO, a character string column, they generated character string results.

4.   Observe that the headings for MIN(CNO) and MAX(CNO) were truncated. This occurred because the column contains character data. As we indicated in Chapter 2, when a column contains character data, the width of the column heading is determined by the width of the character data in the column. This is not the case for numeric data. When the result contains numeric data, the column heading is not truncated.

SUM Function

Sample Query 8.3:   What is the sum of all the labfee values
for CIS courses?

```
SELECT  SUM(CLABFEE)

FROM    COURSE

WHERE   CDEPT = 'CIS'
```

SUM(CLABFEE)
       750

Comment:

This query demonstrates the SUM group function which
allows the values of a numeric column to be totaled. In
this query all six rows identifying the Computer and
Information Science Department courses were selected.
Their labfee values were added together and the total
presented as the result of the query.

Exercises:

8A.   Display the first course name which appears in
alphabetic sequence.

8B.   What is the total labfee for courses offered by the
Philosophy Department?

8C.   Display the average, maximum, and minimum course labfees
for those CIS courses which have nonzero labfees.

Use of DISTINCT

Each of the group functions allows the DISTINCT keyword to be used with the argument to the function, thus allowing only unique values to be considered. Any value which appears in more than one row in the identified column will be used only once to produce the function result. The next sample query demonstrates DISTINCT used with the SUM function.

Sample Query 8.4:   What is the total of the unique labfee values for CIS courses?

```
SELECT  SUM(DISTINCT CLABFEE)

FROM    COURSE

WHERE   CDEPT = 'CIS'
```

SUM(DISTINCTCLABFEE)
              650

Comments:

1.   The output value (650) is the result of applying the SUM function to all distinct CLABFEE values for rows corresponding to the CIS Department. Examination of the CIS rows shows that two CIS courses have the same labfee value of 100. The effect of specifying DISTINCT before CLABFEE in the function argument is to use only one occurrence of this value in the computation. This accounts for the difference between the 650 result shown above and the 750 result shown for the previous sample query.

2.   DISTINCT can be used with any group function. (However, when used with the MIN and MAX functions it serves no real purpose because the smallest and largest values will be the same even if duplicate maximum and minimum values exist.) Sample Query 8.6 will demonstrate DISTINCT used with the COUNT function.

COUNT Functions

There are three variations of the COUNT function.

1. COUNT(*) - a count of selected rows

2. COUNT(column) - a count of non-null values in a selected column

3. COUNT(DISTINCT column) - a count of distinct non-null values in a selected column

There is no difference between the first and second variations unless null values are present. Therefore, we postpone discussion of the COUNT(column) function until Chapter 14. The next two sample queries illustrate the COUNT(*) and COUNT(DISTINCT) functions.

Sample Query 8.5:   How many theology courses are recorded in the COURSE table?

```
SELECT  COUNT(*)

FROM    COURSE

WHERE   CDEPT = 'THEO'
```

COUNT(*)
   4

Comments:

1.   COUNT(*) simply counts the number of rows which match the selection criteria. The result is always an integer.

2.   COUNT(*) is different from the other group functions in that it does not consider any values within the selected rows. It merely notes the presence of a row which matches the selection criteria.

Recall that Sample Query 1.9 used the keyword DISTINCT to display, without duplication, the departments which offered courses. What if we merely wanted to know the number of such departments? This number can be determined by using DISTINCT with the COUNT function which returns the number of unique values present in a column.

Sample Query 8.6:   How many different academic departments offer courses?

```
SELECT  COUNT(DISTINCT CDEPT)

FROM    COURSE
```

COUNT(DISTINCTCDEPT)
            3

Comments:

1.   The COUNT (DISTINCT) built-in function is used to determine the number of unique values that exist for a particular column. The result informs us that there are three different departments which offer courses. If a department offers more than one course, it is counted only once because of the DISTINCT keyword. Unlike COUNT(*), this form of the COUNT function must examine the column values.

2.   What if you wanted the name of each department and a count of the courses offered by each department? You will need to learn the GROUP BY clause to answer this query. (See Sample Query 8.9 and Exercise 8II.)

Exercises:

8D.   How many rows are in the COURSE table?

8E.   Do not consider zero labfees. How many distinct labfees are present in the COURSE table?

VARIANCE and STDDEV Functions

ORACLE provides two group functions not supported by DB2. These functions, VARIANCE and STDDEV, are somewhat specialized. Statisticians will appreciate them. Most other users will probably never use them. We illustrate these functions without explaining the underlying statistical computations.

Sample Query 8.7.1: Display the variance and standard deviation of all the course labfees in the COURSE table.

```
SELECT  VARIANCE(CLABFEE),  STDDEV(CLABFEE)

FROM    COURSE
```

VARIANCE(CLABFEE)	STDDEV(CLABFEE)
16157.1429	127.11075

Formatting Group Functions

You can use the COLUMN command to format a calculated result produced by a group function. There is nothing new to learn. We illustrate with the previous example.

Sample Query 8.7.2: Same as previous sample query. Show result as integers. Display the column headings as "VAR" and "STD".

```
COLUMN  VARIANCE(CLABFEE)  FORMAT 999999 HEADING VAR
COLUMN  STDDEV(CLABFEE)    FORMAT 999999 HEADING STD

SELECT  VARIANCE(CLABFEE),  STDDEV(CLABFEE)
FROM    COURSE
```

VAR	STD
16157	127

Using Group Functions with Arithmetic Expressions

Group functions can be used with arithmetic expressions to have the system perform more complex calculations. A function may be applied to an expression, or an expression can contain a function.

Sample Query 8.8: Display two values. The first is the sum of all labfees assuming each has been increased by $25. The second is the result of adding $25 to the sum of all the labfees.

```
SELECT  SUM(CLABFEE+25),  SUM(CLABFEE)+25

FROM    COURSE
```

SUM(CLABFEE+25)   SUM(CLABFEE)+25
       1890   1565

Comments:

1.   SUM(CLABFEE+25):

An expression may serve as an argument to a built-in function. Here the expression, CLABFEE+25, is the argument of the function, SUM. The system will first evaluate the expression (increment each CLABFEE by 25) and then apply SUM to these values to determine the result.

2.   SUM(CLABFEE)+25:

Here an expression contains a built-in function as an operand. Note the difference between this computation and the previous one. Here the SUM was first evaluated using just CLABFEE as its argument. This intermediate result (1540) was then increased by 25 to produce the displayed result.

Exercise:

8F.   Assume new labfees are to be calculated at $50 for each credit. What would be the average labfee for courses offered by the Theology Department?

GROUP BY Clause

SQL provides the capability of forming smaller groups from the selected rows and then having group functions applied to each group. The column that the rows are to be grouped by is identified in the GROUP BY clause. When a GROUP BY clause is included in a query, all the selected rows are grouped by a common value within the specified column. This process is performed automatically without the need to specify actual values that may be present in the grouping column. Then the group function is applied to each group.

Sample Query 8.9:   For each department which offers courses, determine the average labfee for courses offered by the department.

```
SELECT CDEPT, AVG(CLABFEE)

FROM    COURSE

GROUP BY CDEPT
```

CDEPT	AVG(CLABFEE)
CIS	125
PHIL	87.5
THEO	110

Comments:

1.   The GROUP BY clause resulted in all COURSE rows being effectively reorganized in an intermediate result where the rows are grouped by the CDEPT column. This intermediate result has all rows with the same value in the CDEPT column placed in separate groups.

   In the present example all rows were arranged by common CDEPT values. After the groups were formed, the AVG function was applied to the CLABFEE values in each group. Because there are three distinct CDEPT values (CIS, PHIL, THEO), three groups were formed and three averages returned, each in a separate row.

2. Note that the SELECT clause contains a column name, CDEPT, along with a group function. The CDEPT value can be displayed with the function results because of the presence of the GROUP BY CDEPT clause. This column value is a characteristic of the group. It is the same for every value in the group. Therefore, it may be displayed with the summary information produced by the function.

3. The database is not at all changed by the use of the GROUP BY clause. The rows of the table being selected from are not actually rearranged in the table.

4. A Common Error: Many users get careless and enter a statement like the following. (Presumably, the user forgot the GROUP BY clause.) This causes an *error*.

        SELECT CDEPT, AVG(CLABFEE)
        FROM   COURSE

    Notice that the SELECT clause contains both a column name and a group function. Whenever a SELECT clause contains a group function, any other column which is not referenced by a group function must be referenced in a GROUP BY clause.

5. Recall that the ORDER BY clause can reference a column by its relative position. However, the GROUP BY clause must explicitly reference a column by its name (i.e., "GROUP BY 1" is invalid).

6. Because multiple rows are displayed, it makes sense to consider sorting the result. Note, however, that the output is already sorted by the CDEPT column. This occurred because the system will establish an internal sequence to establish the groups. Hence, the displayed sequence is somewhat of an accidental side effect of the grouping. Future versions of ORACLE could perform the grouping operation by some other technique. Therefore, it is best to include an ORDER BY clause to explicitly indicate the desired sequence which may or may not be the same as any sort done for the purpose of grouping. See the next sample query.

The WHERE clause can be used to include or exclude certain rows from consideration *prior to* the formation of groups. The next query illustrates this point. It also explicitly specifies the sequence of the output display.

Sample Query 8.10:   For each department which offers courses, determine the average labfee of all three-credit courses offered by the department. Display the output in ascending sequence by department id.

```
SELECT  CDEPT, AVG(CLABFEE)

FROM    COURSE

WHERE   CRED = 3

GROUP BY CDEPT

ORDER BY CDEPT
```

CDEPT	AVG(CLABFEE)
CIS	125
PHIL	166.666667
THEO	80

Comments:

1. The example uses a WHERE clause to select just the three-credit courses for inclusion in the groups. We emphasize that this selection applied to individual rows (not the groups) and occurred *before* the formation of the groups.

    Compare the output with that of the previous example. The average labfee for the CIS Department is unchanged because all its courses are worth three credits. However, the six-credit courses offered by the Philosophy and Theology Departments were excluded from the groups. Hence their average labfee values differ from those in the previous example.

2.   The ORDER BY clause established the sort sequence. Again, because this sequence corresponds to that used by the system to establish the groups, the output would be the same if we omitted the ORDER BY clause. However, it is best to include it. We reiterate a point made in Chapter 3. The ORDER BY clause is always the last clause in a SELECT statement.

3.   You can sort by any column in the result table. In this example, we could have sorted the result by AVG(CLABFEE) using either of the ORDER BY clauses shown in the following examples.

```
SELECT CDEPT, AVG(CLABFEE)
FROM    COURSE
WHERE   CRED = 3
GROUP BY CDEPT
ORDER BY 2
```

```
SELECT CDEPT, AVG(CLABFEE)
FROM    COURSE
WHERE   CRED = 3
GROUP BY CDEPT
ORDER BY AVG(CLABFEE)
```

Exercises:

8G.   For each department which offers courses, display the department id followed by the total number of credits offered by the department.

8H.   For each department which offers courses, display its department id and the number of courses it offers. Sort the result by department id.

8I.   Do not consider six-credit courses. For each department which offers courses, display the department id followed by the total of the labfees for courses offered by the department. Sort the result by the total labfee in descending sequence.

Sometimes a particular group may consist of just one row. The next query illustrates this situation.

Sample Query 8.11:   For each distinct labfee value, determine the total number of credits for courses having this labfee value. Sort the result by labfee in descending order.

```
SELECT  CLABFEE,  SUM(CRED)

FROM    COURSE

GROUP BY CLABFEE

ORDER BY CLABFEE DESC
```

CLABFEE	SUM(CRED)
500.00	3
200.00	9
150.00	3
100.00	9
90.00	3
50.00	6
.00	15

Comments:

1.   There are seven distinct CLABFEE values recorded in the COURSE table. The system formed a group corresponding to each of the seven values. The CLABFEE values of 90.00, 150.00, and 500.00 occurred only once in the table. Therefore, the system formed a group consisting of one row for each of these values. The sum of the credits for such values is what you would expect, namely, just the credit value itself.

2.   The ORDER BY clause was used to establish a sort sequence different from the one done by the system for the purpose of grouping.

Sometimes the selection criteria specified in a WHERE clause will eliminate all rows from a potential group. Hence, some possible groups will never be formed and will not appear in the output.

Sample Query 8.12:   For each department which offers six-credit courses, display the average labfee of the six-credit courses.

```
SELECT  CDEPT, AVG(CLABFEE)

FROM    COURSE

WHERE   CRED = 6

GROUP BY CDEPT
```

CDEPT   AVG(CLABFEE)
PHIL   0
THEO   200

Comments:

1.   The WHERE clause eliminated any three-credit courses from consideration. Hence, the potential group for the CIS Department, which only offers three-credit courses, was not formed.

2.   Note that because the Philosophy and Theology Departments each offer just one six-credit course, the PHIL and THEO groups each contained just one row. If you wanted to know the number of rows for each group, you could apply the COUNT(*) function.

HAVING Clause

The absence of a CIS group in the previous example occurred because the WHERE clause "just happened" to exclude every CIS row from the group. Sometimes we want to explicitly include just certain identifiable groups in the output display. The HAVING clause is used for this purpose. *We emphasize that the HAVING clause applies only to groups, whereas the WHERE clause applies only to individual rows.*

Sample Query 8.13:   Display the department id and average labfee for any department where that average exceeds $100.

```
SELECT CDEPT, AVG(CLABFEE)

FROM    COURSE

GROUP BY CDEPT

HAVING AVG(CLABFEE) > 100
```

CDEPT	AVG(CLABFEE)
CIS	125
THEO	110

Comments:

1. The purpose of the HAVING clause is to specify conditions for groups similar to the way the WHERE clause specifies conditions for rows. In row-level processing the WHERE clause identifies conditions which must be met for a row to be retrieved. Any row which does not meet the conditions will not be retrieved, and is removed from any further processing. The HAVING clause works in a similar manner but with regard to groups rather than to rows. The GROUP BY clause is used to specify how groups are formed. After the groups have been formed, a group must match the condition specified by the HAVING clause in order to be displayed. In this example, the PHIL group was formed but not displayed because its average labfee was not greater than 100.

2.   Syntax: The HAVING clause can only be present if the
      statement contains a GROUP BY clause. The HAVING clause
      must immediately follow the GROUP BY clause.

3.   The condition specified on the HAVING clause contains a
      reference to the function value, AVG(CLABFEE). This is
      almost always the case. In the current example, the
      HAVING clause condition cannot reference a specific
      column at the row level. For example, "HAVING CLABFEE =
      0" would result in an error. This occurs because the
      CLABFEE value is not present in the group after the AVG
      function has been applied. The condition can reference
      a value which is present only after the group has been
      formed.

4.   As with WHERE conditions we can use NOT to exclude
      certain groups from the display. For example, the
      following HAVING clause would display those groups with
      an average labfee which is less than or equal to $100.

          HAVING NOT AVG(CLABFEE) > 100

      The other Boolean operators, AND, OR, IN, and BETWEEN,
      can also be used with the HAVING clause. (See Sample
      Query 8.17.)

Exercises:

8J.   Display the department id and maximum labfee for any
      department which offers a course where the labfee
      exceeds $300.

8K.   Display the department id and total number of credits
      offered by the department if that total exceeds 15.

A SELECT statement will often contain both a WHERE clause and a HAVING clause. The WHERE clause will initially select rows for inclusion into groups, and a HAVING clause will subsequently select just certain groups for display. The following query is a modification of the previous one, which excludes the Theology Department from consideration.

Sample Query 8.14:   For every department, except the Theology Department, which has an average labfee over $100, display its department id followed by its average labfee.

```
SELECT  CDEPT, AVG(CLABFEE)

FROM    COURSE

WHERE   NOT CDEPT = 'THEO'

GROUP BY CDEPT

HAVING AVG(CLABFEE) > 100
```

CDEPT	AVG(CLABFEE)
CIS	125

Comment:

It is important that you understand the logical sequence of the operations SQL follows in response to this statement. First the WHERE clause prohibits the formation of a group for the Theology Department (even though its average labfee does exceed $100). This means that the intermediate result consists of two groups corresponding to the Philosophy and Computer Science Departments. Thereafter the HAVING clause selects the CIS Department for display because, unlike the Philosophy Department, its average labfee exceeds $100. This process is outlined in Figure 8.1.

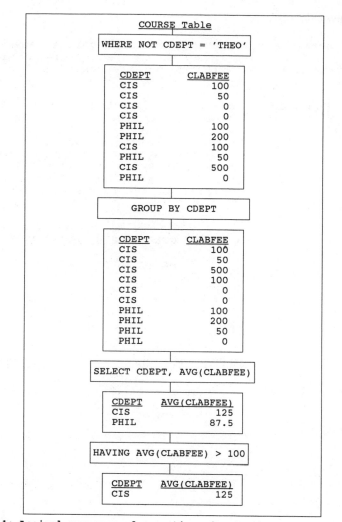

Figure 8.1: Logical sequence of operations for Sample Query 8.14.

Multilevel Groups

It is possible to reference multiple column names in the GROUP BY clause. The intent is to specify the formation of subgroups within groups. Consider the next example.

Sample Query 8.15: We are interested in finding the average, maximum, and minimum labfee values for all courses offered by each department. Within each department we need to have this information broken out for each distinct credit value. Display the department id and credit value followed by the requested statistics.

```
SELECT  CDEPT, CRED, AVG(CLABFEE),

        MAX(CLABFEE), MIN(CLABFEE)

FROM    COURSE

GROUP BY CDEPT, CRED
```

CDEPT	CRED	AVG(CLABFEE)	MAX(CLABFEE)	MIN(CLABFEE)
CIS	3	125	500	0
PHIL	3	116.666667	200	50
PHIL	6	0	0	0
THEO	3	80	150	0
THEO	6	200	200	200

Comments:

1. Logic: The sample query requested two levels of grouping to be applied. First, all courses had to be grouped by department. This was accomplished by specifying the CDEPT column in the GROUP BY clause. Second, within each of the department groups, smaller groups needed to be formed based on identical credit values. This was accomplished by specifying the CRED column after the CDEPT column in the GROUP BY clause. In the same way that we are able to specify different levels of ordering with the ORDER BY clause, we can also specify different levels of grouping with the GROUP BY clause.

2. Syntax: The "GROUP BY" is followed by one or more columns separated by commas. As a reminder, we observe that the SELECT clause contains some group functions and that two columns, CDEPT and CRED, are not arguments of grouping functions. This means that both columns must be referenced in the GROUP BY clause.

3. It can be observed in the output display that all of the CIS Department courses have the same CRED value of 3. This is apparent because there is only a single row produced with a CDEPT value of "CIS". Remember that a group function always produces a single row for each group of records to which it is applied. In the cases of the PHIL and THEO Departments, two rows were returned, indicating that these departments have courses with two different CRED values, 3 and 6.

Exercises:

8L. Consider only three-credit courses. Display the department id and total labfee for courses offered by each department if the total is less than or equal to $150.

8M. Do not consider courses with a labfee over $400. Display the department id and maximum labfee charged by the department if that maximum exceeds $175.

The HAVING clause can be used with multilevel grouping to select just certain groups for display.

Sample Query 8.16:   Extend the previous query by retrieving the average, maximum, and minimum labfee values by credit within a department only for those groups which have a maximum labfee value greater than zero.

```
SELECT CDEPT, CRED, AVG(CLABFEE),

        MAX(CLABFEE), MIN(CLABFEE)

FROM    COURSE

GROUP BY CDEPT, CRED

HAVING MAX(CLABFEE) > 0
```

CDEPT	CRED	AVG(CLABFEE)	MAX(CLABFEE)	MIN(CLABFEE)
CIS	3	125	500	0
PHIL	3	116.666667	200	50
THEO	3	80	150	0
THEO	6	200	200	200

Comment:

An examination of the previous query results reveal that the HAVING clause has eliminated one row from the output display. This is the row corresponding to the six-credit Philosophy group which consisted of one row having a zero labfee. Hence the maximum labfee of this group did not match the HAVING condition.

In Chapter 4 we learned that WHERE clause can contain multiple conditions connected with the Boolean operators (AND, OR, NOT, IN, and BETWEEN). Likewise a HAVING clause can have multiple conditions connected by Boolean operators. Again, the only difference is that the conditions pertain to group values.

Sample Query 8.17:   What is the average department labfee value for those departments where this average is greater than $100 and the department offers less than six courses?

```
SELECT  CDEPT, AVG(CLABFEE)

FROM    COURSE

GROUP BY CDEPT

HAVING AVG(CLABFEE) > 100

AND     COUNT(*) < 6
```

CDEPT   AVG(CLABFEE)
THEO   110

Comment:

This example illustrates that it is possible to specify more than one condition in a HAVING clause. Both conditions reference column functions which are applied to the groups formed by the GROUP BY clause. Both of these conditions must be met by any group if it is to be displayed because AND was used to connect the conditions. The same rules of logic and hierarchy of Boolean operators apply to the HAVING clause with multiple conditions as apply to the WHERE clause.

Nesting Group Functions

ORACLE allows the nesting of built-in functions. This is a
very useful feature which allows the result produced by one
function to serve as an argument to another function.

Sample Query 8.18:   Display   the   smallest   average
                          departmental labfee.

```
SELECT MIN(AVG(CLABFEE))

FROM    COURSE

GROUP BY CDEPT
```

MIN(AVG(CLABFEE))
            87.5

Comments:

1.   Consider the result of executing the above statement
      without the MIN function.

```
            SELECT AVG(CLABFEE)
            FROM    COURSE
            GROUP BY CDEPT
```

The result contains the values (125, 87.5, 110)
corresponding to the average labfees for the three
departments. These values form an intermediate result
which serves as the argument to the MIN function. MIN is
applied to this set of values and returns 87.5.

2.   DB2 Compatibility: DB2 has a restriction which prohibits
      the nesting of group functions within other group
      functions.

Exercise:

8N.   Consider the total labfees for each department. Display
       the largest of these values.

Final Comments on the Group Functions

HAVING Clause

The HAVING clause specifies a condition applied to groups which must be met in order for that group to be displayed. The HAVING condition must reflect a group-level value, something common to all rows in the group. We usually specify a group function in the HAVING clause. It is also possible, however, to specify the name of a grouping column and some condition which that column must meet for all rows in the group. Examples include statements like

```
SELECT CDEPT, CLABFEE          SELECT CDEPT, AVG(CLABFEE)
FROM    COURSE                 FROM    COURSE
GROUP BY CDEPT, CLABFEE        GROUP BY CDEPT
HAVING CLABFEE > 0             HAVING CDEPT LIKE '_ H _ _'
```

These queries are acceptable to the system because the column values are common to all rows in the group. However, we note these examples produce results which can be better realized by using WHERE clauses.

Null Values

A group function might return a questionable result if it is executed with any column argument which contains null values. Because the COURSE table has no null values, the previous sample queries avoided this complexity. This topic will be discussed in detail in Chapter 16.

Limitations of Grouping

When the group functions are applied to groups, the values of the individual rows are no longer available for display. Many reports show both detail lines (corresponding to rows in the table) and summary lines (corresponding to the group statistics). For example, we might like to see the following output.

CDEPT	CLABFEE
CIS	50
CIS	100
CIS	100
CIS	500
	750

Because the group functions "compress" the individual row values, such reports cannot be directly generated by SQL. However, you can use SQL to retrieve the raw data. Then you can utilize the report formatting facilities of SQL*Plus to produce the summary line. We will present this technique in Chapter 11.

Summary

This chapter introduced ORACLE's group built-in functions. These functions can operate over a group of values in a column of a table, a group of values produced by an arithmetic expression, or a group of values produced by another built-in function.

The GROUP BY clause was introduced. This clause forms separate groups based on some column value. When this clause is present in a SELECT statement, each group function performs its calculations on each separate group. Finally, the HAVING clause was presented. Its purpose is to identify specific groups for display. If the HAVING clause is not present, all groups are displayed.

DB2 Compatibility: DB2 refers to the group functions as "column functions." All the ORACLE group functions presented in this chapter, except VARIANCE and STDDEV, are compatible with DB2.

Summary Exercises

The following exercises refer to the STAFF table. Recall that the column names are ENAME, ETITLE, ESALARY, and DEPT.

8O.   Display the sum and average of all staff member salaries. Also display the largest and smallest individual salary.

8P.   How many staff members are employed by the Theology Department?

8Q.   How many different kinds of job titles apply to staff members?

8R.   Assume a total of $5000.00 is allocated for staff member raises. What is the new total salary for all staff members?

8S.   For all DEPT values found in the STAFF table, display the department id followed by the average salary for that department.

8T.   Consider only staff members whose salary exceeds $600.00. For each department which has such a staff member, display the department id followed by the total amount paid to these staff members. Sort the result by the total salary amounts.

9

Individual Functions

This chapter introduces ORACLE's individual functions. Like a group function, an individual function will accept an entire column of values as an argument. Unlike a group function, an individual function will not compress the values into a single result. Instead, an individual function will return a value for each column value.

Individual functions fall into five categories.

1. Arithmetic functions

2. Character functions

3. Data conversion functions

4. Date functions

5. Miscellaneous functions

This chapter will describe each category except the date functions, which will be described in Chapter 10. We note that many of the individual functions are almost self-explanatory. For this reason many of the sample queries will be presented without extensive comments. Most of the individual functions are specific to ORACLE. (LENGTH and SUBSTR are two exceptions; they work in DB2.) Therefore, most of the examples presented in this chapter will be enclosed by a double box.

We introduce a new table, FNTEST, which has two numeric columns, N1 and N2, and two character string columns, C1 and C2. These columns contain a variety of different data values which will be used to demonstrate the behavior of individual functions.

Arithmetic Functions

This section describes ORACLE's arithmetic functions. As you would expect, these functions can be applied only to numeric arguments. Figure 9.1 summarizes these functions.

```
TRUNC(N)      - Truncate the decimal digits of N.
TRUNC(N,M)    - Truncate N to M decimal places.

ROUND(N)      - Round N to integer.
ROUND(N,M)    - Round N to M decimal places.

FLOOR(N)      - Largest integer <= N.
CEIL(N)       - Smallest integer >= N.

ABS(N)        - Absolute value of N.

SIGN(N)       - +1 if N > 0, 0 if N = 0, -1 if N < 0.

SQRT(N)       - Square root of N.
POWER(N,M)    - N raised to Mth power.

MOD(N,M)      - Remainder of division: N/M
```

Figure 9.1: Arithmetic functions.

TRUNC and ROUND

Sample Query 9.1:   Display   (a) N1,
                               (b) N1 truncated to an integer,
                               (c) N1 truncated at the hundredths position,
                               (d) N1 rounded to the nearest integer, and
                               (e) N1 rounded to the hundredths position.

```
SELECT N1, TRUNC(N1), TRUNC(N1,2),

       ROUND(N1), ROUND(N1,2)

FROM FNTEST
```

N1	TRUNC(N1)	TRUNC(N1,2)	ROUND(N1)	ROUND(N1,2)
0	0	0	0	0
4	4	4	4	4
4.222	4	4.22	4	4.22
4.7777	4	4.77	5	4.78
-4	-4	-4	-4	-4
-4.222	-4	-4.22	-4	-4.22
-4.7777	-4	-4.77	-5	-4.78

ABS, FLOOR, and CEIL

Sample Query 9.2: Display   (a) N1,
                                   (b) the absolute value of N1,
                                   (c) the greatest integer <= N1, and
                                   (d) the least integer >= N1.

```
SELECT N1, ABS(N1), FLOOR(N1), CEIL(N1)

FROM    FNTEST
```

N1	ABS(N1)	FLOOR(N1)	CEIL(N1)
0	0	0	0
4	4	4	4
4.222	4.222	4	5
4.777	4.777	4	5
-4	4	-4	-4
-4.222	4.222	-5	-4
-4.7777	4.7777	-5	-4

SIGN, SQRT, POWER, and MOD

Sample Query 9.3: Display   (a) N1,
                                   (b) the sign of N1,
                                   (c) the square root of N1,
                                   (d) N1 raised to the third power, and
                                   (e) the remainder of N1 divided by 3.

```
SELECT N1, SIGN(N1), SQRT(N1), POWER(N1,3), MOD(N1,3)

FROM    FNTEST
```

N1	SIGN(N1)	SQRT(N1)	POWER(N1,3)	MOD(N1,3)
0	0	0	0	0
4	1	2	64	1
4.222	1	2.05475059	75.258349	1.222
4.7777	1	2.18579505	109.057774	1.7777
-4	-1		-64	-1
-4.222	-1		-75.258349	-1.222
-4.7777	-1		-109.05777	-1.7777

Comment:

ORACLE returns a null value (represented here by spaces) whenever the SQRT function is applied to a negative number. See Chapter 16 for a discussion of null values.

Character Functions

This section describes ORACLE's character functions. As you would expect, these functions can be applied only to character string arguments. Figure 9.2 summarizes most of these functions.

```
UPPER(C) - characters of C in uppercase

LOWER(C) - characters of C in lowercase

INITCAP(C) - the first letter of each word in C is capitalized

LPAD(C,L)     - C is left-padded with spaces to length of L
LPAD(C,L,'c') - C is left-padded with 'c' to length of L

RPAD(C,L)     - C is right-padded with spaces to length of L
RPAD(C,L,'c') - C is right-padded with 'c' to length of L

LTRIM(C,'S') - initial characters of C are trimmed if they are
               in set S

RTRIM(C,'S') - trailing characters of C are trimmed if they are
               in set S

LENGTH(C) - length of C

SUBSTR(C,N)   - substring of C: start at Nth position, stop at
                end of C
SUBSTR(C,N,L) - substring of C: start at Nth position, for
                length of L characters

TRANSLATE(C,'S1','S2') - returns C having replaced each character
                         from the set S1 with the corresponding
                         character in set S2

INSTR(C,'S')     - begin scan at first position of C: return index
                   of first occurrence of string S in C
INSTR(C,'S',N)   - begin scan at Nth position of C: return index
                   of first occurrence of string S in C
INSTR(C,'S',N,M) - begin scan at Nth position of C: return index
                   of Mth occurrence of string S in C
```

Figure 9.2: Some character functions.

The next five sample queries reference column C1 in FNTEST table. The C1 column is shown below. Note the mixture of lowercase and uppercase characters in column C1. Also, recognize that digits are stored as characters, not numbers.

```
C1
Julie Martyn
JESSIE MARTYN
jan martyn
ABC123456XYZ
abc de fghij kl m
0001234.67
$12,999.99 CR
```

UPPER, LOWER, and INITCAP

Sample Query 9.4:   Display   (a) C1 in uppercase,
(b) C1 in lowercase, and
(c) C1 with only the first letter of each "word" capitalized. Other letters should be displayed in lowercase.

```
SELECT UPPER(C1), LOWER(C1), INITCAP(C1)

FROM    FNTEST
```

UPPER(C1)	LOWER(C1)	INITCAP(C1)
JULIE MARTYN	julie martyn	Julie Martyn
JESSIE MARTYN	jessie martyn	Jessie Martyn
JAN MARTYN	jan martyn	Jan Martyn
ABC123456XYZ	abc123456xyz	Abc123456xyz
ABC DE FGHIJ KL M	abc de fghij kl m	Abc De Fghij Kl M
0001234.67	0001234.67	0001234.67
$12,999.99 CR	$12,999.99 cr	$12,999.99 Cr

Comment:

Observe the "Abc123456xyz" in the fourth row of the INITCAP(C1) column. Although the letters "Abc" and "xyz" are separated by nonletters, the "x" appears in lowercase. This is because ORACLE considers the beginning of a new "word" to be the first letter which follows a space.

In Version 5 the INITCAP function behaves differently. The system considers digits and other special symbols as separator characters. Hence, the "x" in "xyz" would mark the beginning of a new word and be capitalized.

LPAD and RPAD

Sample Query 9.5: Display (a) C1 left-padded with spaces in a column which is 30 characters wide, and
(b) C1 right-padded with spaces in a column which is 30 characters wide.

```
SELECT  LPAD(C1,30),  RPAD(C1,30)

FROM    FNTEST
```

LPAD(C1,30)	RPAD(C1,30)
Julie Martyn	Julie Martyn
JESSIE MARTYN	JESSIE MARTYN
jan martyn	jan martyn
ABC123456XYZ	ABC123456XYZ
abc de fghij kl m	abc de fghij kl m
0001234.67	0001234.67
$12,999.99 CR	$12,999.99 CR

Sample Query 9.6: Display (a) C1 left-padded with zeros in a column which is 30 characters wide, and
(b) C1 right-padded with "X"s in a column which is 30 characters wide.

```
SELECT  LPAD(C1,30,'0'),  RPAD(C1,30,'X')

FROM    FNTEST
```

LPAD(C1,30,'0')	RPAD(C1,30,'X')
00000000000000000Julie Martyn	Julie MartynXXXXXXXXXXXXXXXXXX
00000000000000000JESSIE MARTYN	JESSIE MARTYNXXXXXXXXXXXXXXXXX
000000000000000000jan martyn	jan martynXXXXXXXXXXXXXXXXXXXX
00000000000000000ABC123456XYZ	ABC123456XYZXXXXXXXXXXXXXXXXXX
0000000000000abc de fghij kl m	abc de fghij kl mXXXXXXXXXXXXX
00000000000000000000001234.67	0001234.67XXXXXXXXXXXXXXXXXXXX
0000000000000000$12,999.99 CR	$12,999.99 CRXXXXXXXXXXXXXXXXX

LTRIM and RTRIM

Sample Query 9.7:   Display   (a) C1 values with the initial
characters trimmed if they
are in the set {J,U,L,E,S,$}
(b) C1 values with the trailing
characters trimmed if they
are in the set:
{T,Y,N,Z,n,y,t}

```
SELECT  LTRIM(C1,'JULES$'),  RTRIM(C1,'TYNZnyt')

FROM    FNTEST
```

LTRIM(C1,'JULES$')	RTRIM(C1,'TYNZNYT')
ulie Martyn	Julie Mar
IE MARTYN	JESSIE MAR
jan martyn	jan mar
ABC123456XYZ	ABC123456X
abc de fghij kl m	abc de fghij kl m
0001234.67	0001234.67
12,999.99 CR	$12,999.99 CR

Functions in the WHERE Clause

Unlike the group functions, individual functions can be
referenced in a WHERE clause. This facility can be very
useful, as the following sample query illustrates.

Sample Query 9.8:   Display C1 values which end with the
letters "MARTYN" regardless of whether
the characters are stored in uppercase or
lowercase.

```
SELECT  C1

FROM    FNTEST

WHERE   UPPER(C1) LIKE '%MARTYN'
```

C1
Julie Martyn
JESSIE MARTYN
jan martyn

LENGTH and SUBSTR

We return to the COURSE table to illustrate the LENGTH, SUBSTR, INSTR, and TRANSLATE functions.

Sample Query 9.9: For each course with a labfee equal to or greater than $200, display its name, and the number of characters, including embedded spaces, in the name.

```
SELECT  CNAME, LENGTH(CNAME)

FROM    COURSE

WHERE   CLABFEE >= 200
```

CNAME	LENGTH(CNAME)
COMMUNISM	9
RELATIONAL DATABASE	19
EXISTENTIALISM	14

Sample Query 9.10: For each course with a labfee equal to or greater than $200, display
(a)   the course name,
(b)   the third character of its name,
(c)   the third through sixth characters of its name, and
(d)   the third through the last characters of its name.

```
SELECT  CNAME, SUBSTR(CNAME,3,1),
               SUBSTR(CNAME,3,4),
               SUBSTR(CNAME,3)

FROM    COURSE

WHERE   CLABFEE >= 200
```

CNAME	S	SUBS	SUBSTR(CNAME,3)
COMMUNISM	M	MMUN	MMUNISM
RELATIONAL DATABASE	L	LATI	LATIONAL DATABASE
EXISTENTIALISM	I	ISTE	ISTENTIALISM

TRANSLATE and INSTR

Sample Query 9.11: For each course with a labfee equal to or greater than $200, display the course name followed by a "translated" course name. The "translation" is realized by making the following character substitutions.

"A" is replaced by "W"
"E" is replaced by "X"
"I" is replaced by "Y"
"O" is replaced by "Z"
"U" is replaced by "Z"

```
SELECT  CNAME, TRANSLATE(CNAME, 'AEIOU', 'WXYZZ')

FROM    COURSE

WHERE   CLABFEE >= 200
```

CNAME	TRANSLATE(CNAME,'AEIOU','
COMMUNISM	CZMMZNYSM
RELATIONAL DATABASE	RXLWTYZNWL DWTWBWSX
EXISTENTIALISM	XXYSTXNTYWLYSM

Sample Query 9.12: For each course with a labfee greater than or equal to $200, display
(a) the course name,
(b) the position of the first occurrence of the letter "E" in the course name, and
(c) the position of the first occurrence of the string "ISM" in the course name.
Display a "0" for a position value if the specified string is not present.

```
SELECT  CNAME, INSTR(CNAME, 'E'),
               INSTR(CNAME, 'ISM')

FROM    COURSE

WHERE   CLABFEE >= 200
```

CNAME	INSTR(CNAME,'E')	INSTR(CNAME,'ISM')
COMMUNISM	0	7
RELATIONAL DATABASE	2	0
EXISTENTIALISM	1	12

Sample Query 9.13:   For each course with a labfee greater than or equal to $200, display
    (a)   the course name,
    (b)   the position of the first "E" at or after the sixth character in the course name, and
    (c)   the position of the first "E" at or after the seventh character in the course name.
Display a "0" for "no hit."

```
SELECT  CNAME,  INSTR(CNAME,  'E',  6),

                INSTR(CNAME,  'E',  7)

FROM    COURSE

WHERE   CLABFEE >= 200
```

CNAME	INSTR(CNAME,'E',6)	INSTR(CNAME,'E',7)
COMMUNISM	0	0
RELATIONAL DATABASE	19	19
EXISTENTIALISM	6	0

Sample Query 9.14:   For each course with a labfee greater than or equal to $200, display
    (a)   the course name,
    (b)   the position of the second "E" at or after the first character in the course name, and
    (c)   the position of the third "A" at or after the fifth character in the course name.
Display a "0" for "no hit."

```
SELECT  CNAME,  INSTR(CNAME,  'E',  1,  2),

                INSTR(CNAME,  'A',  5,  3)

FROM    COURSE

WHERE   CLABFEE >= 200
```

CNAME	INSTR(CNAME,'E',1,2)	INSTR(CNAME,'A',5,3)
COMMUNISM	0	0
RELATIONAL DATABASE	19	15
EXISTENTIALISM	6	0

Nesting Individual Functions

In the previous chapter we showed the nesting of group functions. Individual functions can also be nested. The next sample illustrates the nesting of the INSTR function within the SUBSTR function. Observe that the result of the "inner" function, INSTR, is incremented by 1 before it is used as an argument with the "outer" function, SUBSTR.

Sample Query 9.15:   For each course which has a "multiple word" course name, display
(a)   the course name, and
(b)   the course name without the first word. Define "NO-WORD-1" as the heading for this column.

```
SELECT  CNAME,

        SUBSTR(CNAME,INSTR(CNAME, ' ')+1) 'NO-WORD-1'

FROM    COURSE

WHERE   INSTR(CNAME,' ') <> 0
```

CNAME	NO-WORD-1
RELATIONAL DATABASE	DATABASE
INTRO TO CS	TO CS
DATA STRUCTURES	STRUCTURES
DISCRETE MATHEMATICS	MATHEMATICS
DIGITAL CIRCUITS	CIRCUITS
COMPUTER ARCH.	ARCH.

Exercises:

9A.   Display all course labfees as integers.

9B.   Display the course number and the labfee per credit for all courses. Round the calculated result to two decimal places.

9C.   For each philosophy course, display the last two digits of its course number, the first five characters of its name, and the fourth and fifth characters of its description.

9D.   For each course with "FOR" in its description, find the index of the first occurrence of "FOR".

9E.   For each course, display the length of each course name.

9F.   Display the course name for all courses. Capitalize the first letter in each word of the course name. Other characters should be displayed in lowercase.

Conversion Functions

We have just seen a number of very useful functions for performing arithmetic with numeric data and character string manipulation with character data. What if you wanted to utilize one of the character functions with a column containing numeric values? Or, conversely, what if you wanted to do arithmetic with a column of character string data which happened to consist of digits? These objectives can be realized by utilizing ORACLE's data conversion functions.

Before describing the data conversion functions, we note that ORACLE has an automatic data conversion facility which allows you to process numeric data with character string functions and vice versa. However, this presumes your objectives are reasonable and ORACLE can correctly deduce your intentions. In general, it is *not good practice to rely on automatic data conversion*. The recommended approach is to explicitly convert a data item from one data type to another type using the appropriate data conversion function.

Figure 9.3 outlines some of the more useful data conversion functions. We present examples of TO_NUMBER and TO_CHAR below. We postpone discussion of TO_DATE until the next chapter. There we will also show the TO_CHAR function with a date as an argument.

```
TO_NUMBER(C) - Returns C, a string of digits, as a
               numeric value.

TO_CHAR(X)   - If X is a number, returns X as a
               character string value long enough to
               hold the significant digits of the number.

             - If X is a date, returns X as a character
               string value in ORACLE's default date
               format (to be described in Chapter 10).

TO_CHAR(X,'fmt') - If X is a number, returns X as a
                   string value in the format specified
                   by "fmt"; fmt must be a legitimate
                   numeric format as described in
                   Chapter 2.

                 - If X is a date, returns X as a
                   character string in the format
                   specified by "fmt"; fmt must be a
                   legitimate date format as described
                   in Chapter 10.

TO_DATE(X)       ─────────┐
                          ├─ See Chapter 10
TO_DATE(X,'fmt') ─────────┘
```

Figure 9.3: Some conversion functions.

TO_NUMBER and TO_CHAR

Sample Query 9.16:   For each philosophy course, display its CNO value and the sum of 10 plus the number represented by the digits in the second and third positions of CNO.

```
SELECT  CNO,  TO_NUMBER(SUBSTR(CNO,2,2))+10

FROM     COURSE

WHERE    CDEPT = 'PHIL'
```

CNO	TO_NUMBER(SUBSTR(CNO,2,2))+10
P11	21
P22	32
P33	43
P44	54

Comment:

The SUBSTR function extracted two digits from the second and third positions of CNO. These digits became the argument for TO_NUMBER which converted them to a numeric value. The numeric value was then added to 10.

Sample Query 9.17:   For each course with a labfee equal to or greater than $200, display
(a)   the labfee as a number,
(b)   the labfee as a character string, and
(c)   the digit corresponding to the hundredths position in the numeric value.

```
SELECT  CLABFEE,  TO_CHAR(CLABFEE),

         SUBSTR(TO_CHAR(CLABFEE),1,1)

FROM     COURSE

WHERE    CLABFEE >= 200
```

CLABFEE	TO_CHAR(CLABFEE)	S
200.00	200	2
200.00	200	2
500.00	500	5

Comment:

Note that the third column heading is only one character. (Review the COLUMN command in Chapter 2.)

The following sample query uses the TO_CHAR function with a "fmt" argument to format numeric data. The same results can be achieved by using the COLUMN command with the FORMAT specification as described in Chapter 2.

Why use TO_CHAR if the COLUMN command will suffice? If you are using SQL*Plus, there is no big difference. However, the professional programmer, when writing embedded SQL, will not be using SQL*Plus to execute the application program. Therefore, the programmer cannot utilize the COLUMN command. (Remember, COLUMN is a SQL*Plus command, not a SQL statement.) The programmer must utilize TO_CHAR to have the numeric data returned to the program in a specified format.

Sample Query 9.18:   For each course offered by the CIS Department, display
(a)   the course labfee,
(b)   the labfee formatted to show a dollar sign and two digits after the decimal point, and
(c)   the labfee formatted with five digits with two digits after the decimal point; also show leading zeros.

```
SELECT  CLABFEE,  TO_CHAR(CLABFEE, '$999.99'),

                  TO_CHAR(CLABFEE, '099.99')

FROM     COURSE

WHERE    CDEPT = 'CIS'
```

CLABFEE	TO_CHAR(	TO_CHAR
100.00	$100.00	100.00
50.00	$50.00	050.00
.00	$.00	000.00
.00	$.00	000.00
100.00	$100.00	100.00
500.00	$500.00	500.00

Comment:

The symbols used in the "fmt" arguments ("$999.99" and "099.99") are described in Chapter 2.

Miscellaneous Functions

Some of ORACLE's individual functions do not fall into the previously described categories. Figure 9.4 outlines the functions we describe in this section. We will give special attention to the DECODE function because it provides a simple form of the "IF-THEN" statement found in most conventional third-generation programming languages. To illustrate these functions, we use the numeric columns of the FNTEST table.

```
GREATEST(N1,N2,...) - Determine the largest value of
                      the arguments and return this
                      value. There can be two or more
                      arguments.

LEAST(N1,N2,...) - Determine the smallest value of the
                   arguments and return this value.
                   There can be two or more arguments.

DECODE - Use conditional (IF-THEN) logic to display a
         value based on the value in a column. There
         may be many arguments (see Sample Query 9.21).

NVL(X) - Process null values (see Sample Query 16.13).
```

Figure 9.4: Some miscellaneous functions.

The next two sample queries illustrate the GREATEST and LEAST functions. These functions can accept an arbitrary number of arguments. The data types of the arguments can be numeric, character, or date. Usually a single invocation of a function has all arguments of the same type. The following examples use numeric arguments. As a reminder, note that if you use character string data you must be sensitive to the appropriate (ASCII vs. EBCDIC) collating sequence.

GREATEST and LEAST

Sample Query 9.19:   For every row in FNTEST display
(a) N1,
(b) N2,
(c) the larger of N1 and N2, and
(d) the smaller of N1 and N2.

```
SELECT N1, N2, GREATEST(N1,N2), LEAST(N1,N2)

FROM    FNTEST
```

N1	N2	GREATEST(N1,N2)	LEAST(N1,N2)
0	100	100	0
4	9	9	4
4.222	9	9	4.222
4.7777	-9	4.7777	-9
-4	0	0	-4
-4.222	100	100	-4.222
-4.7777	100	100	-4.7777

Sample Query 9.20:   For every row in FNTEST display
(a)   the largest of the values N1, N2, and 50, and
(b)   the smallest of the values N1, N2, and 50.

```
SELECT GREATEST(N1,N2,50), LEAST(N1,N2,50)

FROM    FNTEST
```

GREATEST(N1,N2,50)	LEAST(N1,N2,50)
100	0
50	4
50	4.222
50	-9
50	-4
100	-4.222
100	-4.7777

DECODE

We highlight the DECODE function because it allows you to define "IF-THEN" logic applicable to the display of a column value. Using the DECODE function, you can request ORACLE to examine a column value to see if it matches a particular value. If there is a match, then a corresponding (presumably different) value is displayed. The general syntax of the DECODE function is

    DECODE (C, s1, r1, s2, r2, ..., d)

where
* C is a column or an expression,
* s1 is the first comparison value or expression and r1 is the value returned if C equals s1, and
* s2 is the second comparison value or expression and r2 is the value returned if C equals s2, etc., and
* d is the default value displayed if C does not match s1, s2, etc. This argument is optional. If it is not specified and no match occurs, then a null value is returned.

Sample Query 9.21:   Display N1 in the FNTEST table. Also display a second column which contains
  (a)   0.01 if the N1 value equals 0,
  (b)   4.01 if the N1 value equals 4,
  (c)   3.99 if the N1 value equals -4, and
  (d)   1000 if the N1 value is something other than 0, 4, or -4.

```
SELECT  N1, DECODE(N1, 0, 0.01, 4, 4.01, -4, 3.99, 1000)

FROM    FNTEST
```

N1	DECODE(N1,0,0.01.,4,4.01,-4,3.99,1000)
0	.01
4	4.01
4.222	1000
4.7777	1000
-4	3.99
-4.222	1000
-4.7777	1000

Comments:

1.   Figure 9.5 presents a number of other examples of the DECODE function.

2.   DB2 compatibility: DB2 does not support any function comparable to ORACLE's DECODE function.

```
DECODE (N1, 0, -.999)
```

  If N1 = 0 then display -.999; otherwise display null
  symbol.

```
DECODE (N1, 0, 'ZERO')
```

  If N1 = 0 then display "ZERO"; otherwise display null
  symbol.

```
DECODE (N1, 0, 'ZERO', N1)
```

  If N1 = 0 then display "ZERO"; otherwise display N1.

```
DECODE (N1, 0, 'ZERO', 'NOT ZERO')
```

  If N1 = 0 then display "ZERO"; otherwise display
  "NOT ZERO".

```
DECODE (N1, 0, 'ZERO', 100, 'BIG')
```

  If N1 = 0 then display "ZERO";
  if N1 = 100 then display "BIG";
  otherwise display null symbol.

```
DECODE (N1, 0, 'ZERO', 100, 'BIG', 'NOT BIG OR ZERO')
```

  If N1 = 0 then display "ZERO";
  if N1 = 100 then display "BIG";
  otherwise display "NOT BIG OR ZERO".

```
DECODE (SIGN(N1), -1, 'NEG', 0, 'ZERO', +1, 'POS')
```

  If N1 < 0 then display "NEG";
  if N1 = 0 then display "ZERO";
  if N1 > 0 then display "POS".

```
DECODE (SIGN(N1-4)), 0, 'EQUAL 4', 'NOT EQUAL 4')
```

  If N1 = 4 then display "EQUAL 4";
  otherwise display "NOT EQUAL 4".

```
DECODE(SIGN(N1-N2), 0, 'N1=N2', -1, 'N1<N2', +1, 'N1>N2')
```

  If N1 = N2 then display "N1=N2";
  if N1 < N2 then display "N1<N2";
  if N1 > N2 then display "N1>N2".

```
DECODE (SUBSTR(UPPER(C1),1,1), 'J', 'Begins with J/j')
```

  If the first character of C1 is a "J" or a "j" then
  display "Begins with J/j"; otherwise, display null.

Figure 9.5: Examples of DECODE function.

Concatenation Operator (||)

The SUBSTR function is used to extract a portion of a string, a kind of string subtraction. SQL also provides a method for putting two strings together, a kind of string addition. This operation is called "concatenation" and is specified by placing two vertical bars (||) between the strings to be connected. We note that the concatenation operator is an operator, similar to the arithmetic operators that we had (+, -, *, /). It is not a built-in function.

Sample Query 9.22:   Display the concatenation of the CDEPT and CNAME columns for all six-credit courses.

```
SELECT  CDEPT || CNAME

FROM    COURSE

WHERE   CRED = 6
```

CDEPT||CNAME
PHILCOMMUNISM
THEOSOLIPSISM

Comments:

1.   ORACLE will allow you to concatenate columns of any data type. It will perform an automatic data type conversion. (Again, it is better to use the TO_CHAR conversion function.) The result is always a character string.

2.   Very often data are stored in separate columns which are merged in a report. For example, an employee table might have a last name column (LNAME) and a first name (FNAME). You would probably use concatenation to merge the name with an embedded blank or other separator as shown below.

FNAME||' '||LNAME

LNAME||', '||FNAME

Summary

In this chapter we presented the ORACLE individual functions. An individual function receives a column value as an argument and returns a single value for each row on which it operates. We examined individual functions which operate on arithmetic values and allow a variety of general arithmetic operations to be performed. Character strings can be examined or modified through the character functions. Values of one data type can be converted to another data type by the conversion functions. Finally, we showed that a limited form of conditional logic is possible with the DECODE function.

   DB2 Compatibility: DB2 refers to the individual functions as "scalar functions." Unlike the column functions, most of ORACLE's individual functions are not compatible with DB2's scalar functions.

Summary Exercises

9G.   For each department which offers courses, display the department id and the length of the department id. Display each department only once.

9H.   For each course, determine the ratio of the labfee per credit. Display this amount as an integer using the FLOOR and CEIL functions.

9I.   For each course, display only the rightmost digit of the course number.

9J.   Assume there is a 10-fold increase in each labfee. For each course, display the course number and adjusted labfee. Format the labfee as currency, using a dollar sign, comma for thousands, and a decimal point to separate dollars and cents.

9K.   For each course having a description which is less than 15 characters, display the course number and description.

9L.   Display the course number and name of every course. In the output display, replace each digit in the course number by a zero, and replace each space in the course name by a hyphen (-).

9M.   For each course, display the course number and number of credits. Also display the number of credits as a word. For example, display "two" if the number of credits is 2.

9N.   For each nonzero labfee, display the labfee and the number of significant digits in the labfee.

9O.   Concatenate the CDESCP and CNO columns.

10

Processing Date and Time Information

This chapter introduces ORACLE's special facilities for processing data which represent date and time information. Previous chapters introduced and emphasized the differences between two major "standard" data types, numeric and character. Traditional data processing systems use some form of numeric or character data to encode date and time information. This requires the user or some application program to go through extra effort to decode this data. This approach is aggravated by the multitude of different formats for date and time information. ORACLE has special facilities to simplify the storage and manipulation of date/time information. Most of these facilities involve the use of special built-in functions. While these functions will reduce the effort required for programming tasks involving date/time information, the logic of such tasks can be inherently complex. For this reason, this book will only introduce some of the more basic concepts and facilities of handling date/time information. This chapter will restrict its attention to displaying date/time information.

DATE Data Type

Chapter 14 will introduce the CREATE TABLE statement where you will see how each column in a newly created table is assigned a specific data type. There you will learn that, in addition to specifying the different variations of numeric and character data, it is possible to specify that a given column can contain only date and time values. To be specific, ORACLE supports a "primitive" date/time data type, called DATE. Any date between January 1, 4712 BC and December 31, 4712 AD can be represented in a DATE column. A column defined with the DATE data type can also contain time information.

We emphasize the fact that ORACLE has its own internal representation for the DATE data type which need not concern us because this code will automatically be converted to a character string representation when displayed. The sample queries of this chapter will describe a variety of formats for these character strings. We note that the default format for date information is DD-MON-YY (e.g., 04-JUL-85).

The availability of a primitive data type for date/time information means that such information does not need to be represented as some form of numeric or character string value. It also means that the system recognizes a column as containing date/time data and supports certain useful operations which are applicable to this data. In effect, date/time data represents a third category of data distinct from numeric and character string data. Many of the special built-in functions introduced in this chapter can only reference columns which contain date/time data.

The COURSE table does not have any columns with date/time information. For this reason we introduce the REGISTRATION table, which has a column, REG_DATE, which is declared as a DATE data type.

The REGISTRATION Table

In our mythical educational database we represent a course as
a row in the COURSE table. We now assume that a student, who
is identified by a student number (SNO), can take any of
these courses.

Because a department chairperson may choose to offer
multiple sections of the same course, each class is
identified by a combination of its course number (CNO) and a
section number (SEC). Students can register for one or more
classes by executing an application program which asks the
student to enter his student number and the course and
section numbers of the classes he wants to attend. The
program will use this information to update the REGISTRATION
table. It will insert one row for each class the student
wants to attend.

The REGISTRATION table contains the following columns.

CNO: Course Number (character string, length = 3)

SEC: Section Number (character string, length = 2)

SNO: Student Number (character string, length = 3)

REG_DATE: Registration Date (DATE data type)

This table contains a row for each class the student hopes
to attend. Because some classes have a limited class size, a
first-come first-served acceptance policy applies. Therefore,
the application program must store the date and time of the
student's registration in the table. This is the purpose of
the REG_DATE column. The process by which the application
program uses embedded SQL to insert rows in the REGISTRATION
table is beyond the scope of this text. We assume that the
program has been executed a number of times and that the
REGISTRATION table now contains some number of rows that you
would like to examine. The following sample queries
illustrate some of the SQL facilities that you might use.

Displaying Date/Time Data

We stated above that date/time information has a special internal data representation. However, whenever such information is displayed, you will observe the date/time values displayed as simple character strings. This is because the system will automatically convert the internal date/time code to a character string prior to display. The first sample query will display the REG_DATE values as simple character strings using the default date format (DD-MON-YY).

Sample Query 10.1: Display all information in the REGISTRATION table.

```
SELECT  *

FROM    REGISTRATION
```

CNO	SEC	SNO	REG_DATE
C11	01	325	04-JAN-88
C11	01	800	15-DEC-87
C11	02	100	17-DEC-87
C11	02	150	17-DEC-87
P33	01	100	23-DEC-87
P33	01	800	23-DEC-87
T11	01	100	23-DEC-87
T11	01	150	15-DEC-87
T11	01	800	15-DEC-87

Comments:

1.   Observe the REG_DATE column. The displayed values appear as character string data formatted according to the ORACLE default format. Again, we note that the internal representation of the date/time values is a special notation which is different from the displayed character string.

It is possible to display date/time values using other formats. The next sample query will illustrate this facility.

2.   It is also possible to display only parts of a date or time, such as the year, month, etc. Figure 10.1 will show some of these options.

Alternative Date Formats: TO_CHAR Function

You are not restricted to ORACLE's default date format. The
TO_CHAR function (one of the data conversion functions
introduced in the previous chapter) can be used to display a
date/time value in a variety of different formats. When its
first argument is a date value, it expects its second
argument to be a valid "date format model." A number of the
date format models are illustrated in Figure 10.1. The next
sample query illustrates the use of TO_CHAR with a typical
date format model ('MM/DD/YYYY').

Sample Query 10.2: Display the REGISTRATION table. Show the
REG_DATE values in the conventional
format of "month/day/year" (e.g.,
"12/25/1989"). Also show "REG_DATE" as
the column heading for the date values.

```
COLUMN DTFMT1 FORMAT A10 HEADING 'REG_DATE'

SELECT CNO, SEC, SNO,

       TO_CHAR (REG_DATE, 'MM/DD/YYYY') DTFMT1

FROM    REGISTRATION
```

CNO	SEC	SNO	REG_DATE
C11	01	325	01/04/1988
C11	01	800	12/15/1987
C11	02	100	12/17/1987
C11	02	150	12/17/1987
P33	01	100	12/23/1987
P33	01	800	12/23/1987
T11	01	100	12/23/1987
T11	01	150	12/15/1987
T11	01	800	12/15/1987

Comments:

1. TO-CHAR accepts a date value (REG_DATE) as its input and
    returns a character string value formatted according to
    the date format model ('MM/DD/YYYY'). The format model
    must be enclosed by apostrophes.

2. This example utilizes the COLUMN command to specify the
    column width and heading for the date values. If the
    COLUMN command was not specified, the heading for this
    column would default to "TO_CHAR(REG_DATE,'MM/DD/YYYY')"
    and the column width would be very long, forcing a line
    wrap. We will use similar COLUMN commands in the
    following sample queries for the same reason.

ORACLE provides a wide variety of date format models which can be specified as the second argument of the TO_CHAR function. The meaning of each model is illustrated by the examples shown in Figure 10.1. We assume the REG_DATE value is "07-MAR-82". In Figure 10.1, the Format-Model column shows some of the valid models which could be specified as the second argument. The second column shows the result returned by TO_CHAR, and the third column presents pertinent comments.

```
                   TO_CHAR (REG_DATE, 'Format-Model')

Format-Model        Result              Comment
'MM/DD/YYYY'        03/07/1982          leading zeros present
'MM/DD/YY'          03/07/82            last two digits of year
'YYYY/MM/DD'        1982/03/07          arbitrary sequence
'YYYY-MM-DD'        1982-03-07          hyphen as punctuation
'MONTH DD, YYYY'    MARCH     07, 1982  month in uppercase
'Month DD, YYYY'    March     07, 1982  capitalize month
'YYYY'              1982                year only
'MM'                03                  month only
'Month'             March               name of month
'Mon'               Mar                 three-letter abbreviation
'DD'                07                  day of month
'DDD'               066                 day of year
'DAY'               SUNDAY              name of day
'J'                 2445036             Julian day
'W'                 1                   week of month
'WW'                10                  week of year
'Q'                 1                   quarter of year
'YYYY BC'           1982 AD             show BC or AD
```

Figure 10.1: Examples of date format models.

The examples shown Figure 10.1 illustrate dates only. TO_CHAR can also be used to display information about time which may be present in a column defined with a DATE data type. Sample Query 10.4 and Figure 10.2 will present additional format models that serve this purpose.

Exercise:

10A. Display the REGISTRATION table. For each REG_DATE value, show the name of day followed by the name of the month, day of the month, and four-digit year (e.g., Sunday, March 07, 1982). Also show "FORMATTED_DATE" as the column heading for the date values.

Displaying Current Date: SYSDATE Pseudo-Column

A typical report will usually display the date (and maybe the time) that the report was generated. In ORACLE, the "current" date/time (the date/time that the statement is executed) can be displayed by referring to SYSDATE in any SELECT clause. SYSDATE is referred to as a "pseudo-column." It is "pseudo" because you can refer to the SYSDATE "column" in any table even though it is not actually a column in the table. The next sample query illustrates this point.

Sample Query 10.3:   Display the name of each theology course. Also display the current date in each row of the result.

```
COLUMN SYSDATE FORMAT A12 HEADING 'CURRENT DATE'

SELECT  CNAME, SYSDATE

FROM    COURSE

WHERE   CDEPT = 'THEO'
```

CNAME	CURRENT DATE
FUNDAMENTALISM	27-JUN-91
HEDONISM	27-JUN-91
COMMUNISM	27-JUN-91
SCHOLASTICISM	27-JUN-91

Comments:

1.   The syntax of the statement implies that SYSDATE is a column in the COURSE table. You know this is not the case. However, the special status of SYSDATE as a pseudo-column allows it to be displayed with the columns of any table.

2.   This example shows the current date displayed (redundantly) in each row of the result table. Usually the current date is shown in a report heading. This objective can be realized by storing the SYSDATE value in a variable and referencing the variable in a TTITLE or BTITLE command. This technique will be described in Chapter 11.

3.   SYSDATE also contains the "current time." However, you need to use the TO_CHAR function to display this time. See the next sample query.

Displaying Time Information

SYSDATE also contains the current time. However, as the previous sample query shows, the time is not automatically displayed when you reference SYSDATE in a SELECT clause. To display the current time, you must use the TO_CHAR function with special time format models which can be specified with the previously described date format models. The following sample query shows the use of one such model (HH24:MI). Figure 10.2 presents examples and brief explanatory comments about other time format models.

Sample Query 10.4:   Display the current date (MM/DD/YY format) and time (hours and minutes only using military format). Show "CURRENT DATE and TIME" as a column heading. (Assume the current date/time is 15 seconds after 6:55 PM on June 27, 1991.)

```
COLUMN DTFMT2 FORMAT A21 HEADING 'CURRENT DATE and TIME'

SELECT TO_CHAR (SYSDATE, 'MM/DD/YY HH24:MI') DTFMT2

FROM    COURSE

WHERE   CNO = 'C11'
```

CURRENT DATE and TIME
06/27/91 18:55

Comments:

1.   Because SYSDATE is a pseudo-column we need to select it from some table. Any table can be referenced. We chose the COURSE table and used a WHERE clause to select just one row. In Version 6, a special table called DUAL is available to all users to serve this purpose. (In Version 5 it was common practice for the DBA to create a table called DUMMY to serve this purpose.) The DUAL table always has exactly one row and one column. Any user can reference the DUAL table to access SYSDATE by entering the following statement, which does not require a WHERE clause.

           SELECT SYSDATE FROM DUAL

2.   Use of the time format models is not restricted to SYSDATE. Recall that time information is stored in any column, like REG_DATE, defined as a DATE data type. (The default time is 12:00 AM, midnight.) Such time values can be displayed by specifying a time format model with TO_CHAR.

Format-Model	Result	Comment
HH24	18	hour (0-23) only
HH12	06	hour (1-12) only
HH12 AM	06 PM	show appropriate "AM" or "PM" indicator
HH12 PM	06 PM	show appropriate "AM" or "PM" indicator
HH12 A.M.	06 P.M.	show "A.M." or "P.M." indicator
HH12 P.M.	06 P.M.	show "A.M." or "P.M." indicator
HH24:MI	18:55	hours and minutes, colon separator
HH24-MI	18-55	hours and minutes, hyphen separator
HH24MI	1855	hours and minutes, no separator
HH12:MI AM	06:55 PM	conventional USA format
HH24:MI:SS	18:55:15	hours, minutes, and seconds
MI	55	minutes only
SS	15	seconds only
SSSSS	65841	seconds past midnight

Figure 10.2: Examples of time format models.

Exercises:

10B. Display the current date in the "MM/DD/YYYY" format, and the current time (hours, minutes, and seconds) using conventional USA format. Also have the system append the appropriate A.M. or P.M. indicator. Show "TODAY'S DATE and TIME" as a column heading.

10C. In three separate columns, display just the hours, minutes, and seconds of the current time. Show "CURRENT HOUR," "CURRENT MINUTE," and "CURRENT SECOND" as column headings.

Comparing and Calculating Date Values

ORACLE allows date/time values to be compared using the standard comparison operators (=, <, etc.) in a WHERE clause. Comparison is based on your intuitive semantics of date/time sequence where a preceding date/time is less than (i.e., historically prior to) a subsequent date/time. For example,

        WHERE '17-MAY-78' < '07-MAR-82'

evaluates to "true."

ORACLE also permits a limited kind of date/time arithmetic. The following expressions, which reference date/time values, can be specified in SQL statements.

DATE + N   Result is a date/time equal to N days after DATE.

DATE - N   Result is a date/time equal to N days prior to DATE.

DATE1 - DATE2   Result is a number which represents the number of days between DATE1 and DATE2.

Care must be taken with date/time arithmetic, especially when the calculation can involve time information. We describe some of these concerns in our comments on the next sample query, which illustrates both the comparison and calculation of date/time values.

Sample Query 10.5:   For each row in the REGISTRATION table with a REG_DATE value indicating a date after December 20, 1987, display the following. Remove any duplicate dates.

    (a)   The REG_DATE value. Use the same heading specified in Sample Query 10.2.

    (b)   The date 30 days after REG_DATE. Show "Plus 30 Days" as a heading.

    (c)   The date 30 days prior to REG_DATE. Show "Less 30 Days" as a heading.

    (d)   The number of days, as a whole number, between REG_DATE and the current date. (Assume the current date is June 27, 1991.) Show "Days After Today" as a heading.

```
COLUMN DTFMT3 FORMAT A14    HEADING 'Plus 30 Days'
COLUMN DTFMT4 FORMAT A14    HEADING 'Less 30 Days'
COLUMN DTFMT5 FORMAT 9999   HEADING 'Days After Today'

SELECT DISTINCT REG_DATE DTFMT1, REG_DATE+30 DTFMT3,
       REG_DATE-30 DTFMT4,
       TRUNC (SYSDATE)-REG_DATE DTFMT5
FROM   REGISTRATION
WHERE  REG_DATE > '20-DEC-87'
```

REG_DATE	Plus 30 Days	Less 30 Days	Days After Today
04-JAN-88	03-FEB-88	05-DEC-87	1270
23-DEC-87	22-JAN-88	23-NOV-87	1282

Comments:

1. When you add or subtract a number and a date/time, ORACLE assumes the unit of measurement is days. Note that ORACLE considers the variations in days per month when performing the calculations. It will also consider leap years when determining the number of days for February.

2. The TRUNC function was used with SYSDATE before we performed the subtraction. This was necessary because we want an integer result, and we want the result to be the same regardless of the time of day that we execute the statement. When TRUNC is applied to a date/time argument, the result is the same date with a time value of 12:00 AM.

    Recall that each value in the REG_DATE column has the default time value of 12:00 AM. However, this is not so for SYSDATE (unless you execute the statement at 12:00 AM). Consider what happens without the TRUNC function. "SYSDATE - REG_DATE" would usually show a decimal result. The whole number component of this value would vary according to the time the statement was executed. For example, if REG_DATE contained yesterday's date, and the statement was executed at 6:00 AM today, the result would be 1.25. However, if the statement was executed at 6:00 PM today, the result would be 1.75. TRUNC(SYSDATE) establishes the time value to be 12:00 AM, the same as the REG_DATE values. Hence, the result is always a whole number.

3. REG_DATE is compared to "20-DEC-87", which is a character string. ORACLE will automatically convert the character string to a date to facilitate the date comparison. To avoid this automatic data type conversion, use the TO_DATE function which is described on the next page.

TO_DATE Function

Thus far we have made extensive use of the TO_CHAR function to convert a date value to a character string in some specified format. The inverse of this function is the TO_DATE function, which can be used to convert a character string into a date value. This can be useful because you may wish to perform "date arithmetic" with a character string which is formatted as a date. Another reason is to compare a date with a character string.

Sample Query 10.6:   For any row in the REGISTRATION table having a REG_DATE value after December 20, 1987, display the SNO and REG_DATE values followed by the number of days between the REG_DATE value and December 20, 1987. Do not display duplicate rows.

```
COLUMN DTFMT6 FORMAT 999 HEADING 'Days After 20-DEC-87'

SELECT DISTINCT SNO, REG_DATE,

      REG_DATE - TO_DATE('20-DEC-87') DTFMT6

FROM REGISTRATION

WHERE REG_DATE > TO_DATE('12/20/87', 'MM/DD/YY')
```

SNO	REG_DATE	Days After 20-DEC-87
325	04-JAN-88	15
100	23-DEC-87	3
800	23-DEC-87	3

Comments:

1.   Recall that ORACLE will attempt to automatically convert data types to support operations and comparisons between operands of different data types. However, note that the following statement, without the TO_DATE function, will not work.

```
SELECT SNO, REG_DATE, '20-DEC-87' - REG_DATE
FROM REGISTRATION
```

Again, we recommend the use of automatic data conversion be minimized. It is safer to use data conversion functions.

2.   The date can be specified using date format model in the TO_DATE function. For example, the WHERE clause for the sample query could have been specified as

```
WHERE REG_DATE > TO_DATE ('87-20-12', 'YY-MM-DD')
```

More DATE Built-In Functions

The two previous sample queries described the TO_DATE and TRUNC functions applied to date/time arguments. Figure 10.3 presents an overview of other ORACLE functions which facilitate date/time processing.

```
LAST_DAY (D)   Returns a date corresponding to the last day of the
               month containing D.

NEXT_DAY (D, 'DAY')  "DAY" must equal "MONDAY", or "TUESDAY" or
                     "WEDNESDAY" etc. Function returns a date
                     corresponding to the next "DAY" that is the
                     same as or later than D.

MONTHS_BETWEEN (D1, D2) Returns the number of months between D1
                        and D2.

GREATEST (D1, D2, ... ) Returns the greatest date from D1, D2, ...

LEAST (D1, D2, ... ) Returns the  least date from D1, D2, ...

ADD_MONTHS(D, N) Returns date derived by adding N months to date D.
```

Figure 10.3: Date/time functions.

The next sample queries will demonstrate the use of the date/time functions presented in Figure 10.3. We present these examples without comment as the descriptions provided in the figure should be sufficient to understand these functions. We encourage you to work through these examples to confirm your understanding of the date/time functions. Again, assume the current date is 27-JUN-91.

Sample Query 10.7:   For each row in the REGISTRATION table, display
    (a)   unique REG_DATE values,
    (b)   last day of the month containing REG_DATE,
    (c)   next Friday equal to or after REG_DATE, and
    (d)   number of months between the current date and REG_DATE. Ignore time, but show decimal component of the month.

```
COLUMN DTFMT7  FORMAT A10  HEADING 'Last Day'
COLUMN DTFMT8  FORMAT A10  HEADING 'Next Fri.'
COLUMN DTFMT9  FORMAT 99.9 HEADING 'Months Back'

SELECT DISTINCT REG_DATE DTFMT1,
       LAST_DAY(REG_DATE) DTFMT7,
       NEXT_DAY(REG_DATE, 'FRIDAY') DTFMT8,
       MONTHS_BETWEEN(TRUNC(SYSDATE), REG_DATE) DTFMT9
FROM   REGISTRATION
```

REG_DATE	Last Day	Next Fri.	Months Back
04-JAN-88	31-JAN-88	08-JAN-88	41.7
15-DEC-87	31-DEC-87	18-DEC-87	42.1
17-DEC-87	31-DEC-87	18-DEC-87	42.3
23-DEC-87	31-DEC-87	25-DEC-87	42.4

Sample Query 10.8:   For each row in the REGISTRATION table, display
    (a)   unique REG_DATE values,
    (b)   lesser of REG_DATE and December 20, 1987, and
    (c)   greater of REG_DATE and December 20, 1987.

```
COLUMN DTFMT10 FORMAT A20 HEADING '12/20/87 or Later'
COLUMN DTFMT11 FORMAT A20 HEADING '12/20/87 or Earlier'

SELECT DISTINCT REG_DATE,
       GREATEST(REG_DATE,TO_DATE('20-DEC-87')) DTFMT10
       LEAST(REG_DATE,TO_DATE('20-DEC-87'))    DTFMT11
FROM   REGISTRATION
```

REG_DATE	12/20/87 or Larger	12/20/87 or Smaller
04-JAN-88	04-JAN-88	20-DEC-87
15-DEC-87	20-DEC-87	15-DEC-87
17-DEC-87	20-DEC-87	17-DEC-87
23-DEC-87	23-DEC-87	20-DEC-87

Adding Months and Years to a Date

The last sample query of this chapter illustrates the distinction between two techniques for adding years to a date. The first technique is to add some multiple of 365 days to the date. The second technique is to use ADD_MONTHS to add some multiple of 12 months to the date. The example shows the second technique is preferred because ADD_MONTHS will account for 366 days in a leap year.

Sample Query 10.9:   For each registration which occurred during 1988, display
   (a)   the REG_DATE value,
   (b)   the date 730 days beyond the REG_DATE value, and
   (c)   the date 2 years beyond the REG_DATE value.
   Display appropriate headers in the result.

```
COLUMN DTFMT12 FORMAT A15 HEADING 'Plus 730 Days'
COLUMN DTFMT13 FORMAT A15 HEADING 'Plus 24 Months'

SELECT  REG_DATE DTFMT1, REG_DATE + 365*2 DTFMT12,
        ADD_MONTHS (REG_DATE, 12*2) DTFMT13
FROM    REGISTRATION
WHERE   TO_CHAR(REG_DATE, 'YY') = '88'
```

REG_DATE	Plus 730 Days	Plus 24 Months
04-JAN-88	03-JAN-90	04-JAN-90

Comments:

1.   ADD_MONTHS can also be used to perform subtraction of months by specifying a negative number of months. For example, to determine the date exactly 2 years prior to the current date, you would specify

        ADD_MONTHS (SYSDATE, -24)

2.   Observe that we can add both months and days to the current date as follows

        ADD_MONTHS (SYSDATE, 3) + 15

Summary

This chapter introduced the DATE data type, which is used to inform ORACLE that we wish to store date/time information in a column. This is different than numeric or character data and a special set of built-in functions are provided for processing date/time information. We noted that ORACLE has a default format for date values, but that the TO_CHAR function allows you to reformat these values in a variety of different ways. Finally, we saw that comparison and arithmetic operations can be performed with date/time values.

The significance of the DATE data type is that the system provides a consistent way of representing and processing date and time values. It is not necessary for the programmer or system designer to concoct some method of dealing with date/time values.

Summary Exercises

10D. Display the day of the week and week of the year for the date of July 4, 1776.

10E. Display the next Saturday from today's date.

10F. What is the date which occurs 3 months after the registration date(s) for student 325?

10G. Display the registration date, course number, section number, and student number for each student who registered for a course after December 31, 1987.

10H. Which students registered for courses during the month of December?

III

SQL*Plus

Parts I and II of this book focused on the ORACLE version of SQL. Only Chapter 2 made explicit reference to SQL*Plus commands. We reiterate the fact that SQL*Plus is a front-end to the ORACLE database engine and has its own set of commands which are distinct from SQL statements. This part of the book explicitly covers the concepts and facilities of SQL*Plus.

You can skip all three chapters in this part of the book if your primary objective is to learn SQL. If you choose this option, you can continue reading at Part IV without any loss of continuity. This might be appropriate for application programmers who are learning SQL with the objective of embedding SQL statements in application programs. However, we expect that most users will want to utilize the facilities provided by SQL*Plus. In fact, we expect many application programmers will use SQL*Plus to prototype the SQL statements to be embedded in their programs.

The two major topics to be presented in this part of the text are report formatting (Chapter 11) and command files (Chapter 12). In addition, we present a variety of miscellaneous commands which you will find to be quite useful.

This book teaches SQL and SQL*Plus. Its coverage of SQL data manipulation statements (SELECT, INSERT, UPDATE, and DELETE) is comprehensive. Space limitations do not permit a comprehensive discussion of all SQL*Plus concepts and facilities. However, we believe the following chapters substantially cover the important features of SQL*Plus. After reading these chapters, you should be able to explore the other features described in the ORACLE reference manual.

Organization of Chapters

Chapter 11 describes the SQL*Plus commands which allow you to display selected data in a variety of different report formats. We discuss the SET and SHOW commands for looking at system variables and the BREAK and COMPUTE commands for establishing report control breaks and generating summary totals at the control breaks. We emphasize that SQL*Plus provides only basic report formatting facilities. You cannot produce a report in *any* desired format. ORACLE Corporation provides another product, SQL*Report, which provides greater versatility in formatting reports.

Chapter 12 describes command files. These are files which allow you to save and subsequently retrieve SQL statements and SQL*Plus commands. Most users of SQL*Plus make considerable use of the convenience provided by command files. This chapter will discuss the GET, SAVE, and START commands.

Chapter 13 is an overview of a variety of SQL*Plus commands that serve a variety of purposes. These include printing a hard copy of your report, interfacing with your host system, describing tables, and getting on-line help.

11

Report Formatting

In Chapter 2 we introduced the basic idea of using SQL*Plus commands to format a report. There we presented the TTITLE and BTITLE commands to produce report titles and the COLUMN command with the HEADING and FORMAT specifications to format column data and headings. This chapter presents more information on this topic by introducing more advanced SQL*Plus concepts and commands relevant to report formatting. The following concepts and commands are introduced.

* System variables (SET and SHOW commands)

* Control breaks (BREAK command)

* Control break arithmetic (COMPUTE command)

* Other COLUMN specifications

* Variable data in report titles

System Variables

SQL*Plus makes a number of assumptions when it formats a report for display. For example, it assumes that the maximum number of characters it will display on a line is 80. This value is stored in an internal memory location called LINESIZE. LINESIZE is one of many system variables which SQL*Plus will use for report formatting purposes. You can display the current value of a system variable by executing the SHOW command. The SET command can be used to change the default value of a system variable.

In this section we examine some system variables which relate to report formatting. (There are other system variables which are not related to report formatting. These will be described in Chapter 13.) We begin by presenting the SHOW command followed by a discussion of the SET command.

SHOW Command

A variation of the SHOW command is

    SHOW system-variable

The following examples illustrate this command. The next section presents a more detailed list of the system variables which pertain to report formatting.

Example 11.1:   What is the number of characters SQL*Plus will display on a print line before it forces a line wrap?

```
SQL> SHOW LINESIZE
linesize 80
```

Example 11.2:   How many spaces will SQL*Plus display between columns of data?

```
SQL> SHOW SPACE
space 1
```

Example 11.3:   Execute one command to display all the system variables.

```
SQL> SHOW ALL
heading ON
linesize 80
       .
       .
       .
```

SET Command

The general form of the SET command is

    SET system-variable value

There are many system variables and each will accept specific values. We illustrate a simple example.

Example 11.4:   Establish 40 lines as the maximum number of lines to be displayed on a page of a report.

                SQL> SET PAGESIZE 40

   When setting a system variable only certain legitimate values can be specified. You should consult the ORACLE documentation to determine these values. We introduce some of the more useful system variables which affect report formatting.

LINESIZE {80|n}   Specifies the maximum number of characters which will be displayed before a line wrap occurs.

PAGESIZE {14|n}   Specifies the maximum number of lines which will be displayed on a single page.

SPACE {1|n}   Specifies the number of spaces between columns in a report. The maximum value is 10.

PAUSE {OFF|ON|text}   ON will cause the system to pause after displaying a page of a report. You will have to press the Enter key to see the next page. This is useful to avoid the rapid scrolling of pages for a multiple-page report.

                            "text" specifies the text to be displayed when a pause occurs. Usually the text is something like "Press the Enter key to see next page."

                            OFF inhibits the pause action.

HEADING {<u>ON</u>¦OFF}	ON causes the (normal) display of column headings.
	OFF will suppress the display of column headings in a report.
WRAP {<u>ON</u>¦OFF}	ON causes the wrapping of a character string value if it is too long to fit within the defined width of the column.
	OFF suppresses column wrapping and causes a truncation of the character string.
NUMWIDTH {<u>10</u>¦n}	Specifies the default column width for numeric values.
NUMFORMAT {model}	"model" is a numeric format model as described in Chapter 2. This model becomes the default for numeric columns.
FEEDBACK {<u>6</u>¦n¦<u>ON</u>¦OFF}	The default value of 6 means that selecting more than six rows causes the system to display a "number of records selected" message. You can change this number by substituting the desired number for "n".
	OFF will suppress this message
	ON will activate this message

Exercises:

Experiment with the system variables.

1.   Display some of the system variables using the SHOW command.

2.   Change some system variables with the SET command, and use SHOW to verify the changes.

3.   Execute some SELECT statements to observe the effects on the format of the report.

4.   Reset the system variables to their original values using the SET command. Or you could exit ORACLE and then sign on again. The system variables will be reset to their default values for those values established by the SET command placed in the LOGIN.SQL file. (See Appendix A.)

Report Control Breaks

In Chapter 8 we introduced the GROUP BY clause in the SELECT statement. Recall that group functions are used to perform summary arithmetic on each group. For example, consider the following SELECT statement.

```
SQL> SELECT CDEPT, SUM(CRED), SUM(CLABFEE)
  1   FROM    COURSE
  2   GROUP BY CDEPT

CDEPT SUM(CRED) SUM(CLABFEE)
----- --------- ------------
CIS          18       750.00
PHIL         15       350.00
THEO         15       440.00
```

Observe that the output display shows summary data (only) for each group of distinct CDEPT values. This statement does not display the selected rows within each group which were used to produce the summary data. What if you wanted to see the raw data in addition to the summary totals? Your objective might be to produce the following report.

```
CDEPT CNAME                  CRED CLABFEE
----- -------------------- ----- -------
CIS   INTRO TO CIS             3  100.00
      DATA STRUCTURES          3   50.00
      DIGITAL CIRCUITS         3     .00
      RELATIONAL DATABASE      3  500.00
      COMPUTER ARCH.           3  100.00
      DISCRETE STRUCTURES      3     .00
                           ----- -------
                              18  750.00

PHIL  EMPIRICISM               3  100.00
      RATIONALISM              3   50.00
      SOLIPSISM                6     .00
      EXISTENTIALISM           3  200.00
                           ----- -------
                              15  350.00
```

                        etc.

To display raw data along with summary totals you would not use the GROUP BY clause. Instead, you would use a SELECT statement to retrieve the rows containing the raw data in the appropriate sequence. Then you would use SQL*Plus commands (BREAK and COMPUTE) for establishing a control break and performing calculations at the control break. These commands are described in the following sections.

BREAK Command

The BREAK command defines a control break. A control break is simply a point in a report where a specified column value on one line is different from the corresponding value on the previous line. (We note that it makes sense to define a control break only on a report which is sorted by the specified column.) The BREAK command is used to identify a control break column. It can also specify the number of lines to skip at each control break. The simple form of the BREAK command is

        BREAK ON column SKIP number-of-lines

The following example illustrates the BREAK command. Here the BREAK command is used to produce a "single-level" control break report.

Example 11.5:   For each department, display its department identifier followed by the course name and corresponding credits for each course offered by the department. Sort the report by department identifier. Skip two lines between each group of departments.

```
SQL> BREAK ON CDEPT SKIP 2
SQL> SELECT CDEPT, CNAME, CRED
  2  FROM    COURSE
  3  ORDER BY CDEPT;
```

```
CDEPT CNAME                   CRED
----- -------------------- -----
CIS   INTRO TO CIS             3
      DATA STRUCTURES          3
      DIGITAL CIRCUITS         3
      RELATIONAL DATABASE      3
      COMPUTER ARCH.           3
      DISCRETE MATHEMATICS     3


PHIL  EMPIRICISM               3
      RATIONALISM              3
      SOLIPSISM                6
      EXISTENTIALISM           3


THEO  FUNDAMENTALISM           3
      COMMUNISM                6
      SCHOLASTICISM            3
      HEDONISM                 3
```

Comments:

1. Syntax: The general syntax for the BREAK command (shown
    in Figure 11.1) has many options. We will describe only
    some of these options. Refer to the ORACLE documentation
    for details on the other options.

2. The BREAK command uses the "ON CDEPT" clause to identify
    the CDEPT column as a control break column. This clause
    is followed by "SKIP 2", which directs the system to
    skip two lines after each change in a CDEPT value. This
    command *must be entered before* the SELECT statement.

3. Normally we do not wish to display the same value many
    times within the same group. The output display shows
    the CDEPT value only once (in the first line) for each
    control break group. Using the "DUPLICATES" option in
    the BREAK command would show the CDEPT value on each
    detail report line.

4. The SELECT statement is used to select the rows which
    form the detail lines of the report. The ORDER BY clause
    is used to establish a row sequence for the column
    (CDEPT) which is referenced by the BREAK command.

5. As mentioned above, we can use the COMPUTE command to
    perform calculations at a control break. This example
    shows that such calculations are optional. The next
    example will illustrate the COMPUTE command used with
    the BREAK command.

6. Only one BREAK command can be in effect at any time.
    (However, a single command can establish multiple
    control breaks. See Example 11.7.) It is easy to display
    the current breaks in effect. Simply enter

                        BREAK

7. The current BREAK command stays in effect until another
    BREAK command is executed. You can disable all breaks by
    entering the following CLEAR command.

                     CLEAR BREAKS

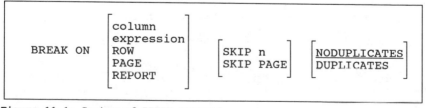

Figure 11.1: Syntax of BREAK command.

COMPUTE Command

The COMPUTE command is used to perform calculations at a specified control break. Hence, the COMPUTE command is meaningless unless an appropriate BREAK is in effect. The simple form of this command is

    COMPUTE calculation OF column ON break-column

The next example uses BREAK to establish a control break on the CDEPT column, followed by two COMPUTE commands to display the sums of CRED and CLABFEE values at each control break.

Example 11.6: For each department, display its department identifier followed by the course name and corresponding credits and labfee for each course offered by the department. Sort the report by department identifier. Show the sum of the credit and labfee values for each group of departments.

```
SQL> BREAK ON CDEPT SKIP 1
SQL> COMPUTE SUM OF CRED ON CDEPT
SQL> COMPUTE SUM OF CLABFEE ON CDEPT
SQL> SELECT CDEPT, CNAME, CRED, CLABFEE
  2    FROM    COURSE
  3    ORDER   BY CDEPT;
```

CDEPT	CNAME	CRED	CLABFEE
CIS	INTRO TO CIS	3	100.00
	DATA STRUCTURES	3	50.00
	DIGITAL CIRCUITS	3	.00
	RELATIONAL DATABASE	3	500.00
	COMPUTER ARCH.	3	100.00
	DISCRETE STRUCTURES	3	.00
*****			
sum		18	750.00
PHIL	EMPIRICISM	3	100.00
	RATIONALISM	3	50.00
	SOLIPSISM	6	.00
	EXISTENTIALISM	3	200.00
*****			
sum		15	350.00
THEO	FUNDAMENTALISM	3	90.00
	COMMUNISM	6	200.00
	SCHOLASTICISM	3	150.00
	HEDONISM	3	.00
*****			
sum		15	440.00

Comments:

1. Syntax: The general syntax for the COMPUTE command (shown in Figure 11.2) has many options. We will only comment on some of these options. Refer to the ORACLE documentation for details on the other options.

2. Examine the first COMPUTE command:

    COMPUTE SUM OF CRED ON CDEPT

    - SUM indicates "what calculation" is to be performed;

    - OF CRED indicates "what column" is summarized;

    - ON CDEPT indicates at "what control break" the calculation occurs.

3. Two separate COMPUTE commands are necessary because the calculations are based on different columns. Example 11.8 will illustrate a single COMPUTE command which specifies multiple different calculations for the same column at the same control break.

4. Observe that no final grand total line appears as a last line to summarize all control group totals. Example 11.9 will illustrate how to realize this objective.

5. You can ask the system to display the compute operations in effect by entering

    COMPUTE

6. The COMPUTE commands stay in effect until explicitly cleared by entering

    CLEAR COMPUTES

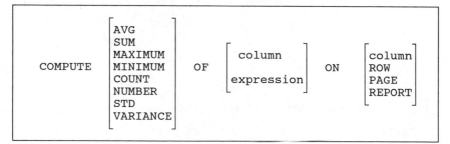

Figure 11.2: Syntax of COMPUTE command.

Multiple Control Breaks

The following example shows a "two-level" control break report. The selected data are sorted on two columns and a BREAK command references both of these columns. This single BREAK command establishes two distinct control breaks with a different line skipping action specified for each break.

Example 11.7:   For each department, display its department identifier followed by the credit values, course names, and labfees of the courses offered by the department. Sort the report by credits within department identifier. Establish a primary control break on department identifier and a secondary control break on credit value. No control break arithmetic is required. Skip two lines between each group of departments and one line between each subgroup of credit values.

```
SQL> CLEAR COMPUTES
SQL> BREAK   ON CDEPT SKIP 2  ON CRED SKIP 1
SQL> SELECT CDEPT, CRED, CNAME, CLABFEE
  2  FROM    COURSE
  3  ORDER   BY CDEPT, CRED;
```

CDEPT	CRED	CNAME	CLABFEE
CIS	3	INTRO TO CIS	100.00
		DATA STRUCTURES	50.00
		DIGITAL CIRCUITS	.00
		RELATIONAL DATABASE	500.00
		COMPUTER ARCH.	100.00
		DISCRETE STRUCTURES	.00
PHIL	3	EMPIRICISM	100.00
		RATIONALISM	50.00
		EXISTENTIALISM	200.00
	6	SOLIPSISM	0.00
THEO	3	FUNDAMENTALISM	90.00
		HEDONISM	0.00
		SCHOLASTICISM	150.00
	6	COMMUNISM	200.00

Comment:

CLEAR COMPUTES was necessary to clear the two COMPUTE commands specified in the previous example. CLEAR BREAKS is unnecessary because the new BREAK command redefines the previous one.

Reformatting Previous Query

You may often want to reexecute the previous SELECT statement with different report formatting requirements.

Example 11.8:   Same as previous example. Clear any previous BREAK or COMPUTE commands. Then establish a single-level control break on department id, skipping just one line between each group of departments. Compute the maximum and minimum labfee values for each group of departments.

```
SQL> CLEAR BREAKS
SQL> CLEAR COMPUTES
SQL> BREAK ON CDEPT SKIP 1
SQL> COMPUTE MAX MIN OF CLABFEE ON CDEPT
SQL> RUN
```

CDEPT	CRED	CNAME	CLABFEE
CIS	3	INTRO TO CIS	100.00
	3	DATA STRUCTURES	50.00
	3	DIGITAL CIRCUITS	.00
	3	RELATIONAL DATABASE	500.00
	3	COMPUTER ARCH.	100.00
	3	DISCRETE STRUCTURES	.00
*****			------
minim			.00
maxim			500.00
PHIL	3	EMPIRICISM	100.00
	3	RATIONALISM	50.00
	6	SOLIPSISM	.00
	3	EXISTENTIALISM	200.00
*****			------
minim			.00
maxim			200.00
THEO	3	FUNDAMENTALISM	90.00
	6	COMMUNISM	200.00
	3	SCHOLASTICISM	150.00
	3	HEDONISM	.00
*****			------
minim			.00
maxim			200.00

Comment:

Only one COMPUTE command was needed to specify multiple calculations (MAX and MIN) because they are based on the same column (CLABFEE) at the same control break (CDEPT).

Different Calculations at Different Control Breaks

The next example requires the specification of multiple control breaks with different calculations at each break. The BREAK command identifies two control breaks. One is a special control break at the end of the report (ON REPORT). The second COMPUTE command below identifies what calculation (SUM) is to be performed using all the detail rows for the report. This is the standard technique to produce a final summary line containing any grand totals.

Example 11.9:   Retrieve every row in the COURSE table. Display the CDEPT, CNAME, CRED, and CLABFEE values. Sort the result by CDEPT. Format the report using the following specifications.

   (a)   Define a control break on the CDEPT column and another at the end of the report.

   (b)   Calculate the sum, average, maximum, and minimum CLABFEE values at each CDEPT control break. The CLABFEE values and summary statistics should be edited to show up to six digits with two-digit decimal accuracy, a leading dollar sign and comma if necessary.

   (c)   Calculate and display on the last line of the report (at the REPORT control break) a sum representing a grand total of all the CLABFEE values.

   (d)   Display a left-justified report title of "LABFEE STATISTICS". Skip a line after the title.

```
SQL> CLEAR BREAKS
SQL> CLEAR COMPUTES
SQL> TTITLE LEFT 'LABFEE STATISTICS' SKIP 2
SQL> COLUMN CLABFEE FORMAT $9,999.99
SQL> BREAK   ON CDEPT SKIP 1   ON REPORT
SQL> COMPUTE SUM AVG MAX MIN OF CLABFEE ON CDEPT
SQL> COMPUTE SUM OF CLABFEE ON REPORT
SQL> SELECT CDEPT, CNAME, CRED, CLABFEE
  2  FROM    COURSE
  3  ORDER   BY CDEPT;
```

LABFEE STATISTICS

CDEPT	CNAME	CRED	CLABFEE
CIS	INTRO TO CIS	3	$100.00
	DATA STRUCTURES	3	$50.00
	DIGITAL CIRCUITS	3	$.00
	RELATIONAL DATABASE	3	$500.00
	COMPUTER ARCH.	3	$100.00
	DISCRETE STRUCTURES	3	$.00
*****			
avg			$125.00
minim			$.00
maxim			$500.00
sum			$750.00
PHIL	EMPIRICISM	3	$100.00
	RATIONALISM	3	$50.00
	SOLIPSISM	6	$.00
	EXISTENTIALISM	3	$200.00
*****			
avg			$87.50
minim			$.00
maxim			$200.00
sum			$350.00
THEO	FUNDAMENTALISM	3	$90.00
	COMMUNISM	6	$200.00
	SCHOLASTICISM	3	$150.00
	HEDONISM	3	$.00
*****			
avg			$110.00
minim			$.00
maxim			$200.00
sum			$440.00
			$1,540.00

Comment:

Observe that the format for the CLABFEE showed a six-digit number. We know that each individual labfee contains just five digits. However, the final summary total of all labfees is a six-digit number. Hence, the format specification must take this into account.

Exercise:

11A. Modify this example to include a second-level control break on the CRED column. (Review Example 11.7.) Perform the same calculations (AVG, MAX, MIN, and SUM) at the second control break.

More COLUMN Specifications

In Chapter 2 we introduced the COLUMN command with the FORMAT and HEADING specifications. The general format of this command is

$$\text{COLUMN} \quad \begin{bmatrix} \text{column} \\ \text{expression} \end{bmatrix} \quad \text{specification}$$

Below we introduce in outline form other specifications which can be used with the COLUMN command.

COLUMN Specifications:

$$\text{JUSTIFY} \quad \begin{bmatrix} \text{LEFT} \\ \text{CENTER} \\ \text{RIGHT} \end{bmatrix}$$

Column heading is aligned according to specification. The default is LEFT for character data and RIGHT for numeric data. Specify an option to override the default.

WRAPPED
WORD_WRAPPED
TRUNCATED

Headings and character string data may be too wide to fit in a column. If so, the heading or data is WRAPPED (default). Specify WORD_WRAPPED to have wrapping occur only at a word boundary. Specify TRUNCATED to truncate data at the end of a column.

NEWLINE

A new line is started (a line wrap occurs) before the column is displayed. NEWLINE is useful when the number of displayed columns cannot fit onto one line of the report.

NOPRINT
PRINT

It is possible to display a column value (usually a control break value) or SYSDATE in a heading using TTITLE or BTITLE. Under such circumstances you would often specify NOPRINT to avoid a duplicate display of the value in a column. (See the next example.)

ALIAS alias

Aliases can be referenced in BREAK and other COLUMN commands which can be useful for abbreviations, especially when referring to a long expression.

$$\text{LIKE} \quad \begin{bmatrix} \text{column} \\ \text{expression} \end{bmatrix}$$

If you have already designated a fairly long set of COLUMN specifications for one column/expression, you can use this specification to define the same specifications for a second column/expression. [e.g., COLUMN COL2 LIKE COL1]

OLD_VALUE variable
NEW_VALUE variable

Used to specify a variable to contain the value of a column which can be referenced by the TTITLE and BTITLE commands. This technique allows the display of a column value in a title. (See the next example.)

ON
OFF

Allows the enabling and disabling of a column's output format specification without modifying its definition. Default is ON.

HEADING text
(See Chapter 2)

FORMAT format-model
(See Chapter 2)

NULL char
(See Chapter 16)

Displaying Column Values and Dates in Report Headings

Variable data can be displayed in report titles. The TTITLE
and BTITLE commands can refer to a "variable" declared in a
COLUMN command using the NEW_VALUE and/or OLD_VALUE option.
We present an example and comment on the relevant commands.

Example 11.10:   For every row in the COURSE table, display
the CNO and CLABFEE values. Sort the result
by CNO within CDEPT. Format the report as
follows:
(a) Define control breaks on the CDEPT
column and at the end of the report.
(b) Calculate the sum of CLABFEE values at
control breaks and at the report break.
(c) Start a new page at each CDEPT control
break. Display the CDEPT value (left-
justified) followed by the current date
(right-justified) in the report title.

```
SQL> CLEAR BREAKS
SQL> CLEAR COMPUTES
SQL> SET LINESIZE 40
SQL> TTITLE LEFT DEPTVAR RIGHT DATEVAR
SQL> COLUMN CLABFEE FORMAT 9,999.99
SQL> COLUMN CDEPT NEW_VALUE DEPTVAR NOPRINT
SQL> COLUMN DTFMT FORMAT A8 NEW_VALUE DATEVAR NOPRINT
SQL> BREAK ON CDEPT SKIP PAGE ON REPORT
SQL> COMPUTE SUM OF CLABFEE ON CDEPT
SQL> COMPUTE SUM OF CLABFEE ON REPORT
SQL> SELECT CDEPT, CNO, CLABFEE,
  2    TO_CHAR(SYSDATE, 'MM/DD/YY') DTFMT
  3    FROM    COURSE
  4    ORDER BY CDEPT, CNO;
```

```
CIS                          07/18/91          {new page}
CNO     CLABFEE
---  ----------
C11     100.00
C22      50.00
C33        .00
C44        .00
C55     100.00
C66     500.00
     ----------
        750.00


PHIL                         07/18/91          {new page}
CNO     CLABFEE
---  ----------
P11     100.00
P22      50.00
P33     200.00
P44        .00
     ----------
        350.00
```

```
THEO                          07/18/91        {new page}
CNO     CLABFEE
---     ----------
T11      150.00
T12       90.00
T33         .00
T44      200.00
         ----------
         440.00


THEO                          07/18/91        {new page}
CNO     CLABFEE
---     ----------
         ----------
        1,540.00
```

Comments:

1. COLUMN CDEPT NEW_VALUE DEPTVAR NOPRINT

   The COLUMN command uses the NEW_VALUE specification to identify a variable (DEPTVAR) which will be set to the "new" value of the column (CDEPT) whenever the column value changes. Because the rows are sorted by the CDEPT column, a change in the CDEPT value occurs at each CDEPT control break. Because we intend to display the CDEPT value in the page title, it would be redundant to display it in a report column. Hence, the NOPRINT specification is used to suppress displaying of the selected CDEPT column.

2. COLUMN DTFMT FORMAT A8 NEW_VALUE DATEVAR NOPRINT

   This command is similar to the previous COLUMN command. It references a column alias (DTFMT) instead of the column (SYSDATE). Here the variable (DATEVAR) will contain the value of SYSDATE after it has been processed by the TO_CHAR function.

3. TTITLE LEFT DEPTVAR RIGHT DATEVAR

   The TTITLE command references the two variables, DEPTVAR and DATEVAR. The values of these variables will be displayed in the report title.

4. The OLD_VALUE specification is similar to the NEW_VALUE specification; however, it will set the variable to the "old" or previous column value when it changes. Usually, the variable is referenced in a BTITLE command.

5. The next chapter will show additional applications of variables.

Summary

This chapter expanded on the ideas initially presented in Chapter 2 about report formatting using the facilities of SQL*Plus. This chapter has presented the basic ideas of control breaks and control break arithmetic and introduced the use of system variables and user variables.

We have yet to show how a displayed report can be printed as a "hard copy." This is a very simple task which can be accomplished using the SPOOL command, which will be presented in Chapter 13.

Summary Exercise

11B. Construct a single-level control break report. For each staff member, display department, employee name, and salary values, in this order. Sort the report by the DEPT value. Establish a control break at the DEPT column. Show the maximum and minimum salaries for staff in each department. Skip three lines between each department. Display a final summary total for all salaries across all departments. Use conventional dollars and cents notation for the salaries. Show "SALARY REPORT" as a centered title at the top of the report.

12

Command Files

This chapter introduces "command files", which are simply regular host operating system files used by SQL*Plus to save SQL statements and SQL*Plus commands for future execution. These files are called "command" files because they save commands instead of data.

You will find command files to be very useful in a production environment. During the testing stage of application development you do a lot of work: typing, editing, and validating SQL statements and SQL*Plus commands. Command files save the fruits of your effort for execution during future terminal sessions in a production environment.

The following topics are presented:

*   The SAVE command, which is used to copy the content of a buffer to a command file

*   The GET command, which is used to retrieve a previously saved SQL statement and place it into the SQL Buffer

*   The START command, which is used to execute a command file containing SQL statements and SQL*Plus commands

*   The use of parameters with command files

*   Other options to the SET command (BUFFER and ECHO) which are often used in conjunction with command files

SAVE Command

In Chapter 2 we mentioned that SQL*Plus keeps the "current" SQL statement in the SQL Buffer. This feature allows you to use commands like LIST and CHANGE to examine and edit the current SQL statement. We also mentioned that only SQL statements, not SQL*Plus commands, are stored in the SQL Buffer. The SQL Buffer is "temporary" in that it contains only the current SQL statement. Each new statement becomes the new current statement replacing the previous statement in this buffer. Hence, the previous statement is lost. To reexecute any SQL statement, except the current statement residing in the SQL Buffer, you have to retype the entire statement. This is an inconvenience which can be avoided by using the SAVE command.

The SAVE command can be used to "permanently" save the current SQL statement by copying the contents of the SQL Buffer to a command file. A simple version of this command is

        SAVE file-name

The "file-name" is the name of the file which will be referenced in subsequent execution of the GET and START commands. We emphasize that the syntax of the file-name must conform to the rules for naming files in your host operating system. We assume that you are familiar with these rules. Some of the following examples will comment on this topic.

We present a simple example. Assume you have just entered the following COLUMN command and SELECT statement and the display screen appears as shown below

```
SQL> COLUMN CNAME HEADING "SIX-CREDIT COURSES"
SQL> SELECT CNAME, CRED, CLABFEE
     FROM    COURSE
     WHERE   CRED = 6;

SIX-CREDIT COURSES    CRED CLABFEE
-------------------- ----- -------
COMMUNISM                6  200.00
SOLIPSISM                6     .00
```

Assuming that you are satisfied with the result, the following example shows you how to save the SELECT statement for future execution.

Example 12.1: Save the current SELECT statement for future execution in a command file called "SIXCRED.SQL".

```
SQL> SAVE SIXCRED
Wrote file SIXCRED
```

Comments:

1.   The file-name in this example shows a name (SIXCRED) which will be valid on most (probably all) host operating systems. Specifying a file extension is optional. The system will automatically attach a file extension of "SQL" such that the complete file-name is "SIXCRED.SQL". Some host operating systems are case-sensitive. This is the case with UNIX, which would save the file as "SIXCRED.sql".

2.   The system responded with "Wrote file SIXCRED." What if a file by the name of "SIXCRED.SQL" already exists? This command would replace the existing file. Refer to Figure 12.1, which shows the general syntax of the SAVE command. Notice that REPLACE is the default option. This means you have to be careful when using this command. Using the CREATE option announces to the system that you intend to save a new file, and it will prohibit the replacement of any existing file. APPEND will cause the system to place the contents of the buffer at the end of an existing file.

3.   We emphasize that the result table is not saved; only the SELECT statement per se is saved in the file.

4.   This example saved the contents of the SQL Buffer. Because the SQL Buffer does not contain SQL*Plus commands, the COLUMN command was not saved in the command file with the SELECT statement. However, it is possible to save SQL*Plus commands with related SQL statements. This topic will be discussed in the section on saving SQL*Plus commands.

```
                      ┌─────────┐
                      │ CREATE  │
   SAVE file-name     │ REPLACE │
                      │ APPEND  │
                      └─────────┘
```

Figure 12.1: Syntax of the SAVE command.

GET Command

Assume you have saved the SIXCRED.SQL file and exited SQL*Plus. Then, after signing back onto SQL*Plus, you can now use the GET command to place the previously saved SIXCRED command file in the SQL Buffer. (Recall that when you sign onto SQL*Plus, you reset the standard COLUMN HEADING specification for the CNAME column.)

Example 12.2: Bring the SQL statement saved in SIXCRED.SQL into the SQL Buffer and run it.

```
SQL> GET SIXCRED
  1   SELECT CNAME, CRED, CLABFEE
  2   FROM    COURSE
  3*  WHERE   CRED = 6
SQL> RUN
  1   SELECT CNAME, CRED, CLABFEE
  2   FROM    COURSE
  3*  WHERE   CRED = 6


CNAME                    CRED CLABFEE
-------------------- ----- -------
COMMUNISM                   6  200.00
SOLIPSISM                   6     .00
```

Comments:

1.   Syntax: Figure 12.2 shows the general syntax for the GET command. This example shows the simple use of GET followed by just the name of the file, without the "SQL" file extension. The system assumes SQL as the default file extension. Observe that the SELECT statement is listed for verification purposes. Figure 12.2 shows LIST as the default parameter. The NOLIST parameter would suppress the listing.

      You can also edit a statement before entering RUN. This is useful if you want to execute a statement which is similar, but not identical, to a previously saved statement.

2.   The output shows the default column heading for the CNAME column. This is because the COLUMN command was not saved in the SIXCRED.SQL file.

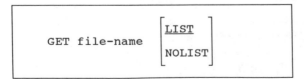

Figure 12.2: Syntax of the GET command.

START Command

The previous example involved multiple steps.

(1) Use GET to bring the statement into the SQL Buffer.
(2) Examine the listing for verification purposes.
(3) RUN the statement in the SQL Buffer.

If you are certain that you don't want to verify or edit the statement in the command file, you can use the START command to directly start the file. The syntax of the START command is

```
START file-name [options]
```

The following example illustrates START without any options. Certain options will be described in Example 12.6.

Example 12.3: Use the START command to execute the previously saved SIXCRED command file.

```
SQL> START SIXCRED
  1  SELECT CNAME, CRED, CLABFEE
  2  FROM    COURSE
  3  WHERE   CRED = 6

CNAME                  CRED CLABFEE
-------------------- ----- -------
COMMUNISM                6  200.00
SOLIPSISM                6     .00
```

Comment:

We will see that START can be used to execute a command file which contains both SQL statements and SQL*Plus commands. Such a command file is not defined by using the SQL Buffer as was the case with Example 12.1.

Restrictions on the SQL Buffer

We have already mentioned one restriction on the SQL Buffer. It cannot contain SQL*Plus commands. There is another restriction. The SQL Buffer can contain only one SQL statement. Thus we cannot use the SQL Buffer to save and subsequently execute multiple statements with a single START command.

Fortunately, we can circumvent both restrictions by not using the SQL Buffer. The general idea is to bypass the SQL Buffer and directly store SQL statements and related SQL*Plus commands in a command file. Then use the START command to execute this file. We demonstrate this process in the next section.

Saving SQL*Plus Commands

There are two techniques for saving SQL*Plus commands in a command file with related SQL statements. The first technique assumes you are familiar with the file editor on your host operating system; the second does not. Both techniques are described below.

1.   Use the file editor which is part of your host operating system to build and save a file which contains the desired SQL statements and SQL*Plus commands. An example of such a file (SAMPCF1.SQL) is shown in Figure 12.3.

     You can build this file before you sign onto SQL*Plus. Or, if you have already entered SQL*Plus, you can use the EDIT command (described in Chapter 2) or the HOST command (described in Chapter 13) to build the file.

2.   Within SQL*PLUS, use the SET BUFFER command to define another buffer. This buffer will not be subject to the aforementioned restrictions applicable to the SQL Buffer. Example 12.4 illustrates this technique.

   Regardless of which technique you use to build the command file, you will use the same START command to execute the statements and commands stored in the file. Example 12.5 will illustrate starting the command file shown in Figure 12.3.

```
CLEAR BREAKS
CLEAR COMPUTES
SET PAGESIZE 50
TTITLE LEFT 'REPORT VIA SAMPLE COMMAND FILE' SKIP 2
COLUMN CA FORMAT $990 HEADING 'LAB FEE'
COLUMN CB FORMAT $990 HEADING 'COST PER CREDIT'
BREAK   ON CDEPT SKIP   ON REPORT
COMPUTE AVG OF CA ON CDEPT
COMPUTE AVG OF CA ON REPORT
SELECT CDEPT, CNAME, CRED, CLABFEE CA, CLABFEE/CRED CB
FROM    COURSE
WHERE   CDEPT <> 'CIS'
ORDER BY CDEPT;
TTITLE OFF
COLUMN CA CLEAR
COLUMN CB CLEAR
CLEAR BREAKS
CLEAR COMPUTES
```

Figure 12.3: SAMPCF1.SQL command file.

SET BUFFER Command

The SET command with the BUFFER option is used to define another buffer which can contain both SQL statements and SQL*Plus commands. The syntax of this command is

        SET BUFFER buffer

   After executing this command, the named "buffer" becomes the current buffer. This means that all subsequent SQL statements and SQL*Plus commands are stored in it. As mentioned above, this buffer is not subject to the restrictions applicable to the SQL Buffer. The following example illustrates this command.

Example 12.4:   Assume the SAMPCF1.SQL command file does not exist. Build this file by establishing a buffer called "JJJ" as the current buffer and entering the contents of Figure 12.3 into this buffer. Then save the contents of JJJ in SAMPCF1. Finally, reset the SQL Buffer as the current buffer.

```
SQL> SET BUFFER JJJ
SQL> INPUT
  1    CLEAR BREAKS
  2    CLEAR COMPUTES
  3    SET PAGESIZE 50
  4    TTITLE LEFT 'REPORT VIA SAMPLE COMMAND FILE' SKIP 2
  5    COLUMN CA FORMAT $990 HEADING 'LAB FEE'
  6    COLUMN CB FORMAT $990 HEADING 'COST PER CREDIT'
  7    BREAK   ON CDEPT SKIP   ON REPORT
  8    COMPUTE AVG OF CA ON CDEPT
  9    COMPUTE AVG OF CA ON REPORT
 10    SELECT CDEPT, CNAME, CRED, CLABFEE CA, CLABFEE/CRED CB
 11    FROM    COURSE
 12    WHERE   CDEPT <> 'CIS'
 13    ORDER BY CDEPT;
 14    TTITLE OFF
 15    COLUMN CA CLEAR
 16    COLUMN CB CLEAR
 17    CLEAR BREAKS
 18    CLEAR COMPUTES
 19           (press Enter key to terminate INPUT command)
SQL> SAVE SAMPCF1
SQL> SET BUFFER SQL
```

Starting a Command File

Regardless of which technique you used to save the command
file, you must use the START command to execute the command
file.

Example 12.5:   Execute the previously saved SAMPCF1 command
                    file.

```
SQL> START SAMPCF1
SQL> CLEAR BREAKS
SQL> CLEAR COMPUTES
SQL> SET PAGESIZE 50
SQL> TTITLE LEFT 'REPORT VIA SAMPLE FILE' SKIP 2
SQL> COLUMN CA FORMAT $990 HEADING 'LAB FEE'
SQL> COLUMN CB FORMAT $990 HEADING 'COST PER CREDIT'
SQL> BREAK ON CDEPT SKIP  ON REPORT
SQL> COMPUTE AVG OF CA ON CDEPT
SQL> COMPUTE AVG OF CA ON REPORT
SQL> SELECT CDEPT, CNAME, CLABFEE CA, CLABFEE/CRED CB
  2    FROM    COURSE
  3    WHERE   CDEPT <> 'CIS'
  4    ORDER BY CDEPT;
```

```
REPORT VIA SAMPLE FILE

CDEPT SIX-CREDIT COURSES   LAB FEE COST PER CREDIT
----- -------------------- ------- ---------------
PHIL  RATIONALISM              $50             $17
      EMPIRICISM              $100             $33
      SOLIPSISM                 $0              $0
      EXISTENTIALISM          $200             $67
*****                        -------
avg                             $88

THEO  FUNDAMENTALISM           $90             $30
      SCHOLASTICISM           $150             $50
      COMMUNISM               $200             $33
      HEDONISM                  $0              $0
*****                        -------
avg                            $110

                             -------
                                $99
```

```
SQL> TTITLE OFF
SQL> COLUMN CA CLEAR
SQL> COLUMN CB CLEAR
SQL> CLEAR BREAKS
SQL> CLEAR COMPUTES
```

Comments:

1. After you enter "START SAMPCF1" the system will bring the first line of this file into the SQL Buffer for execution. This line contains the "CLEAR BREAKS" command. The system responds just as though you had typed this command from the terminal. Then the system brings in the second line of the file and executes it. And so on. You will see each line of the file and the corresponding system response displayed at the terminal.

2. There is one important difference between Example 12.3, which executed the SIXCRED command file, and this example. Because SIXCRED does not contain any SQL*Plus commands, it is possible to use GET to bring it into the SQL Buffer and then use RUN to execute it. (This was done in Exercise 12.2.) You cannot use GET and RUN with SAMPCF1 because it contains SQL*Plus commands. You must use START to execute this file.

3. What if you want to see only the displayed report? You do not want to see all of the commands and statements from the command file. You can realize this objective by entering the following command just before the START command.

    SET ECHO OFF

    This command will suppress the display of commands entered from a command file. You can reset the "echo" behavior by entering

    SET ECHO ON

4. The last command shown in Example 12.4 is "SET BUFFER SQL", which resets the SQL Buffer as the current buffer. Even if we had not reset SQL Buffer, START would have automatically reset it.

Exercises:

12A. Execute any SQL statement. Save the statement in a command file called "ROVER". Execute a second SQL statement. Use GET to place the first SQL statement in the SQL Buffer. Now run this statement.

12B. Create a command file called "FIDO" using any of the previously described techniques. Store two SELECT statements and related TTITLE statements in this file. Use the START command to execute the content of FIDO. Also, it is usually a good idea to place CLEAR BREAKS and CLEAR COMPUTES in a command file to avoid any unwanted formatting which might be in effect at the time you execute the command file.

Parameters in Command Files

The previous example showed command files which contain constant data values. A more flexible approach is to use parameters in command files. Consider a query to select the course number and name from each row in the COURSE table where the CDEPT value is 'CIS' and the CLABFEE value is between 50 and 100. The following statement would do the job.

```
SELECT CNO, CNAME
FROM    COURSE
WHERE   CDEPT = 'CIS'
AND     CLABFEE BETWEEN 50 and 100
```

You might consider saving this statement in a command file. But what if you wanted to execute the same query with a simple modification? You might what to specify "PHIL" instead of "CIS"; or you might want to change the ranges for the CLABFEE values. Saving the above statement would not allow for these changes (unless you chose to edit the file before each execution). Saving a command file containing parameters instead of constants is a more convenient way to provide the desired flexibility. Figure 12.4 shows a command file (SAMPCF2) which contains three parameters (&1, &2, and &3). Assume SAMPCF2 has been saved using previously described techniques. Comparing this file to the above SELECT statement, notice that we have substituted

```
&1 for CIS,
&2 for 50, and
&3 for 100
```

Up to nine parameters (&1, &2,..., &9) can be placed in a command file. Observe that &1 in the command file is enclosed within apostrophes. This is necessary because its value will be compared to a character string value (CDEPT).

Because SAMPCF2 has parameters, the specification of values is done in the START statement. The START command will specify the values to be substituted for the parameters.

```
START SAMPCF2 CIS 50 100
```

The values specified in the START command must correspond to the same sequence and data type as the parameters. The next example illustrates the versatility of this feature.

```
SELECT CNO, CNAME
FROM    COURSE
WHERE   CDEPT = '&1'
AND     CLABFEE BETWEEN &2 AND &3
```

Figure 12.4: SAMPCF2 command file with parameters.

Example 12.6:   Execute the SAMPCF2 command file to display the course number and name for each CIS course with a labfee between 50 and 100 dollars. Then reexecute the same command file to display the course number and name of each philosophy course with a labfee between 75 and 200 dollars. Do not "echo" the statements in the command file.

```
SQL> SET ECHO OFF
SQL> START SAMPCF2 CIS 50 100
old    3: WHERE CDEPT = '&1'
new    3: WHERE CDEPT = 'CIS'
old    4: AND CLABFEE BETWEEN &2 AND &3
new    4: AND CLABFEE BETWEEN 50 AND 100
```

```
CNO CNAME                  CLABFEE
--- -------------------- -------
C11 INTRO TO CIS           100.00
C22 DATA STRUCTURES         50.00
C55 COMPUTER ARCH.         100.00
```

```
SQL> START SAMPCF2 PHIL 75 200
old    3: WHERE CDEPT = '&1'
new    3: WHERE CDEPT = 'PHIL'
old    4: AND CLABFEE BETWEEN &2 AND &3
new    4: AND CLABFEE BETWEEN 75 AND 200
```

```
CNO CNAME                  CLABFEE
--- -------------------- -------
P33 EXISTENTIALISM         200.00
P11 EMPIRICISM             100.00
```

```
SQL> SET ECHO ON
```

Comments:

1.   Even though ECHO was set to OFF, the system displayed the "old" and "new" lines to allow verification of the parameter values. We could have executed the following command to suppress the display of these lines.

        SET VERIFY OFF

    You can reactivate verification by entering

        SET VERIFY ON

2.   You cannot use RUN to execute a command file which contains statements with parameters; you must use START.

3.   "Substitution" variables will be described in the next chapter. These variables serve a purpose similar to parameters and provide additional flexibility.

Summary

This chapter introduced command files which are used to save SQL statements for future execution. There are three ways to build a command file.

1.   You can use the SAVE command to save the contents of the SQL Buffer. Two restrictions apply in this case. Only one SQL statement can be saved. Furthermore, related SQL*Plus commands cannot be saved with the SQL statement. There are two ways to execute this kind of command file. You can execute the command file by using GET to bring it into the SQL Buffer and then using RUN. Or, you can use the START command.

2.   You can use the file editor available on your host operating system to build the command file.

3.   You can use the SET BUFFER command to establish some other buffer as the current buffer.

   The second and third approaches to building a command file allow multiple SQL statements and related SQL*Plus commands to be saved. However, you must use START (not GET and RUN) to execute these command files.

   A command file may contain parameters (&1, &2, ..., &9) which represent variable data. The actual values will be specified at execution time as options in the START command. Again, if the command file contains parameters, you must use START to execute it because RUN does not allow the specification of values for the parameters.

Summary Exercise

12C. Create a command file called "SPOT.SQL". Place a SELECT statement in this file which will retrieve all rows from the STAFF table where the ESALARY value is greater than or equal to some amount. Represent this amount by a parameter (&1). Store an arbitrary TTITLE command in this file. After creating the file, use START to execute the file twice. For the first execution, retrieve all rows where ESALARY exceeds $100. For the second execution, retrieve all rows where ESALARY exceeds $1000.

13

More About SQL*Plus

This chapter concludes our discussion of SQL*Plus facilities and commands by presenting a potpourri of topics which we expect you will find useful. We present the following topics.

* Printing a "hard copy" of your report (SPOOL command)

* Utilizing the facilities of your host operating system (HOST command)

* Learning the names of columns in a table (DESCRIBE command)

* Performance estimation (SET TIMING command)

* On-line help (HELP command)

* User variables (DEFINE and UNDEFINE commands)

* Documentation (REMARK command)

SPOOL Command

Thus far, all of the "reports" we have generated have been displayed on the terminal. What if you want a "hard copy?" The SPOOL command can be used to realize this objective. However, we note that the SPOOL command serves the more general purpose of sending a copy of terminal output to a designated file. Subsequently, you may or may not choose to print the spool file.

The three different options for the SPOOL command are shown in Figure 13.1. Specifying "SPOOL file-name" will initiate the spooling process by sending a copy of all terminal output to the designated file. Unless a file extension is explicitly designated in the file-name, the system will assume a file extension of "LST" or "lst". This spooling process will continue until it is terminated by entering "SPOOL OFF". Specifying "OUT" instead of "OFF" will also terminate the spooling and automatically generate a hard copy by printing the spool file on your system printer.

Example 13.1:   Start spooling a copy of the terminal output to a file called "HAR1.LST"; execute any two SELECT statements; then terminate spooling and print the spool file.

```
SQL> SPOOL HAR1
SQL> SELECT CNO, CNAME
  2    FROM    COURSE
  3    WHERE   CRED = 6;

CNO CNAME
--- --------------------
T44 COMMUNISM
P44 SOLIPSISM

SQL> SELECT CDESCP
  2    FROM    COURSE
  3    WHERE   CNO = 'C11';

CDESCP
--------------------
FOR ROOKIES

SQL> SPOOL OFF
```

Figure 13.1: Syntax of SPOOL command.

Comments:

1. Everything displayed on the terminal (even typos and
    errors) after the "SPOOL HAR1" command and up to and
    including the "SPOOL OFF" command is written to the
    HAR1.LST file. This is shown in Figure 13.2.

2. Typically, we only want the report per se to appear in
    the spool file. Usually we do not want the SQL
    statements and SQL*Plus commands which produce the
    report to appear in the hard copy. This objective can be
    realized by creating and executing a command file which
    contains the SPOOL commands. Execution of command file
    Q1, shown in Figure 13.3, will produce the spool file
    R1, shown in Figure 13.4.

3. Very often, especially when spooling long reports, we do
    not want the contents of the spool file to be displayed
    on the terminal screen. Entering "SET TERMOUT OFF"
    prohibits the display of output generated by commands in
    a command file from appearing on the screen. Entering
    "SET TERMOUT ON" restores the screen display.

```
SQL> SELECT CNO, CNAME
  2  FROM    COURSE
  3  WHERE   CRED = 6;

CNO CNAME
--- --------------------
T44 COMMUNISM
P44 SOLIPSISM

SQL> SELECT CDESCP
  2  FROM    COURSE
  3  WHERE CNO = 'C11';

CDESCP
--------------------
FOR ROOKIES

SQL> SPOOL OFF
```

Figure 13.2: HAR1.LST file.

```
SET ECHO OFF
TTITLE LEFT "REPORT Q1" SKIP 2
SPOOL R1
SELECT CNO, CNAME, CDEPT
FROM COURSE
WHERE CRED = 6;
SPOOL OFF
SET ECHO ON
```

Figure 13.3: Q1.SQL command file.

```
REPORT Q1

CNO CNAME                CDEPT
--- -------------------- -----
T44 COMMUNISM            THEO
P44 SOLIPSISM            PHIL
```

Figure 13.4: R1.LST spool file.

HOST Command

The HOST command is used to execute commands which are understood by the host operating system. (Not all versions of ORACLE support this command. Also, some versions allow "$" as an abbreviation for "HOST".) The syntax for this command is

        HOST [os-command]

Entering "HOST" followed by the appropriate "os-command" will cause SQL*Plus to pass the os-command to the host system for execution. If you simply enter "HOST" without specifying an os-command, you may enter any number of os-commands and then enter "exit" to return to the SQL*Plus environment.

Example 13.2.1:   Assume the operating system is DOS. Execute the "dir" command to display all the command files (file extension is "SQL").

```
SQL> HOST dir *.SQL /w
LOGIN.SQL SAMPCF1.SQL  SAMPCF2.SQL   SIXCRED.SQL
```


Example 13.2.2:   Assume the operating system is UNIX. Execute the "ls" command to display all the command files (file extension is "sql").

```
SQL> HOST ls *.sql
login.sql SAMPCF1.sql  SAMPCF2.sql   SIXCRED.sql
```


Example 13.2.3:   Assume the operating system is UNIX. Execute two "ls" commands to display files with an extension of "sql" or "lst".

```
SQL> HOST
xxx% ls *.SQL
login.sql SAMPCF1.sql  SAMPCF2.sql   SIXCRED.sql
xxx% ls *.lst
HAR1.lst
xxx% exit
```


Comment:

        Some versions of SQL*Plus allow the symbol "!" to be used as an abbreviation for "HOST."

DESCRIBE Command

Very often you will remember the name of a table but forget the precise name of each column in the table. The DESCRIBE command can be used to display the name of each column in a table along with other related information. The syntax for this command is

        DESCRIBE table-name

Example 13.3: What columns are in the COURSE table?

SQL> DESCRIBE COURSE

Name	Null?	Type
CNO	NOT NULL	CHAR(3)
CNAME	NOT NULL	CHAR(22)
CDESCP	NOT NULL	CHAR(25)
CRED		NUMBER
CLABFEE		NUMBER(5,2)
CDEPT	NOT NULL	CHAR(4)

Comments:

1. When you run this command on your system, you might observe other columns in addition to the ones shown above. Exactly what you will see will vary with different versions of ORACLE.

2. Chapter 23 will present a special type of table called a "view." DESCRIBE can also be used to display information about the columns in a view.

3. Chapter 26 will describe the ORACLE Data Dictionary. After reading this chapter you will understand how the DESCRIBE command extracts information from this dictionary.

4. The "Null?" column reflects whether the column was defined to allow null values. The topic of null values will be touched on in Chapter 14 and discussed in detail in Chapter 16.

SET TIMING Command

As mentioned in the introduction, this text does not address
the issue of machine performance in any detail. However, as
we progress through future chapters, we will encounter many
tasks which have more than one SQL solution. If two SQL
statements are logically equivalent, which one do you choose
to save in a command file for future execution in a
production environment? Most often, you will choose the more
efficient solution. You can determine the execution time of
a SQL statement by using the SET TIMING command illustrated
in Figure 13.5.

Example 13.4: Set the timer on. Execute an arbitrary select
statement. Set the timer off.


```
SQL> SET TIMING ON
SQL> SELECT CNO, CNAME
  2  FROM COURSE
  3  WHERE   CRED = 6;

CNO CNAME
--- --------------------
T44 COMMUNISM
P44 SOLIPSISM

 Elapsed: 00.00.00.20

SQL> SET TIMING OFF
```

Comment:

>   The example shows "SET TIMING ON" being entered before
>   a SELECT statement. Observe that "real: 0.3833" is shown
>   after the query result. When comparing SQL statements,
>   a smaller value implies a more efficient SQL statement.


```
+------------------------------+
|                    [ ON  ]   |
|   SET TIMING       [      ]   |
|                    [ OFF ]   |
+------------------------------+
```

Figure 13.5: Syntax of SET TIMING command.

HELP Command

Someday you will find yourself sitting at a terminal without easy access to this text or the ORACLE reference manual (the real "bible"). Fortunately, ORACLE provides an on-line help facility. There are two ways to use the help facility. One way is to seek help on a specific topic. This is illustrated below.

Example 13.5:   Obtain help on the ECHO command.

SQL> HELP ECHO

```
 E  C  H  O
+----------------------------------
| Syntax 1 |
+----------+
| SET ECHO { ON | OFF }
+----------------------------------
| Examples |
+----------+
| SET ECHO ON
| START TEST JOB
| SET ECHO OFF
+----------------------------------
```

(detailed description)

   This example illustrated obtaining help on a particular topic. How do you determine which topics you can obtain help on? This is simple. Simply entering "HELP" provides a list of help topics.

User Variables: DEFINE and UNDEFINE Commands

The DEFINE command can be used to define a user variable. A user variable is simply a named location which can contain any text which you choose to store in the location. The ability to define a user variable is convenient because it allows you to store a character string in a variable for future reference in some SQL*Plus commands. Figure 13.6 presents three variations of the DEFINE and UNDEFINE commands. The following examples illustrate these commands.

Example 13.6.1:   Define a variable called X and store the string "HELLO AND GOODBYE" in it. Define another variable called NAME and store "HEESOOK" in it.

```
SQL> DEFINE X = 'HELLO AND GOODBYE'
SQL> DEFINE NAME = HEESOOK
```

Comment:

The text string for X is enclosed with apostrophes because it contains embedded spaces. This was not the case for the string stored in NAME.

Example 13.6.2:   Display the value of the variable X.

```
SQL> DEFINE X
DEFINE X              = "HELLO AND GOODBYE"
```

Example 13.6.3:   Display the value of all user variables.

```
SQL> DEFINE
DEFINE X              = "HELLO AND GOODBYE"
DEFINE NAME           = "HEESOOK"
```

Example 13.6.4:   Remove the definition of X.

```
SQL> UNDEFINE X
```

```
DEFINE variable = text

DEFINE variable

DEFINE
```

```
UNDEFINE variable
```

Figure 13.6a: DEFINE command.   FIGURE 13.6b: UNDEFINE command.

User variables stay in effect until they are undefined. The following example illustrates a user variable (MYT) which is defined once and then used in multiple queries.

Example 13.7:   Define user variables MYT and YOURT as
(1) MYT: "MY FAVORITE TITLE"
(2) YOURT: "YOUR FAVORITE TITLE"
Run two queries. The first should display MYT using the TTITLE and BTITLE commands. The second should display the MYT using TTITLE and the YOURT using BTITLE. Undefine the user variables after executing the queries.

```
SQL> DEFINE MYT = 'MY FAVORITE TITLE'
SQL> TTITLE LEFT MYT
SQL> BTITLE LEFT MYT
SQL> SELECT CNAME, CRED
  2  FROM   COURSE
  3  WHERE  CNO = 'C11';
```

```
MY FAVORITE TITLE
CNAME                         CRED
-------------------- -----
INTRO TO CS                    3
```

```
MY FAVORITE TITLE
```

```
SQL> DEFINE YOURT = 'YOUR FAVORITE TITLE'
SQL> TTITLE LEFT MYT
SQL> BTITLE LEFT YOURT
SQL> SELECT CNAME, CRED
  2  FROM   COURSE
  3  WHERE  CNO = 'C11';
```

```
MY FAVORITE TITLE
CNAME                         CRED
-------------------- -----
INTRO TO CS                    3
```

```
YOUR FAVORITE TITLE
```

```
SQL> UNDEFINE MYT
SQL> UNDEFINE YOURT
SQL> TTITLE OFF
SQL> BTITLE OFF
```

Comment:

This example placed user variables in TTITLE and BTITLE commands. The next example will show the application of user variables as substitution variables.

Substitution Variables

In the previous chapter, we introduced the idea of using
parameters (&1, &2, ..., &9) in command files. A substitution
variable serves a similar purpose. A substitution variable is
a user variable name preceded by one or two ampersand (&)
characters. We usually place substitution variables in
command files. Figure 13.7 shows two command files with the
same user variable, D, which is referenced as a substitution
variable in the SELECT statements as &D. (Notice that the
ampersand is not followed by a digit. Hence, &D is a
substitution variable, not a parameter.)

The following example will show the definition of a value
for a user variable (D) which is referenced as a substitution
variable in both command files shown in Figure 13.7. The
example shows a single definition of the variable which will
stay in effect during the execution of both command files.

Example 13.8:   Execute the SAMPCF3 and SAMPCF4 command files
to display information pertaining to the
Philosophy Department.

```
SQL> SET ECHO OFF
SQL> SET VERIFY OFF
SQL> DEFINE D = PHIL
SQL> START SAMPCF3

PHIL
CNO CNAME
--- --------------------
P22 RATIONALISM
P33 EXISTENTIALISM
P44 SOLIPSISM
T11 EMPIRICISM

SQL> START SAMPCF4

ENAME      ETITLE
---------- ----------
HANK KISS  JESTER
DICK NIX   CROOK

SQL> UNDEFINE D
SQL> SET ECHO ON
SQL> SET VERIFY ON
```

```
TTITLE LEFT D              TTITLE LEFT D
SELECT CNO, CNAME          SELECT ENAME, ETITLE
FROM   COURSE              FROM   STAFF
WHERE  CDEPT = '&D';       WHERE  DEPT = '&D';
```

Figure 13.7: SAMPCF3 and SAMPCF4 command files.

Comments:

1. We set the ECHO and VERIFY system variables OFF to suppress display of extraneous information.

2. "DEFINE D = PHIL" set the value of the substitution variable &D. This remained in effect for execution of both queries. It is good practice to UNDEFINE the variable when you complete the task.

3. Notice the START command was not followed by any argument values as was the case when we specified values for parameters. (See Example 12.6.)

4. What if you did not execute the DEFINE statement? Assuming D was undefined, the system would prompt you for its value. The system would display

    Enter value for d:

    In this situation, you would see the above display twice. Even though you would enter "PHIL" after the first prompt in response to "START SAMPCF3", you would still be prompted again in response to the "START SAMPCF4" command. This is because the system does not permanently define D when it substitutes "PHIL" for &D.

    What if you did not want to be repeatedly prompted because you intend to enter the same value? If this were the case, you would place two ampersands in front of the variable name (&&D) in the command files. When a variable is preceded by two ampersands, the substitution process "permanently" defines the value of the variable until it is explicitly undefined or redefined.

Documenting Command Files: REMARK Command

By now you realize that some command files can be large and relatively complex. When this occurs, it is always good practice to provide documentation about the logic of the application. The REMARK command serves this purpose.

   REMARK, abbreviated REM, can be placed in a command file and followed by any text. The LOGIN.SQL file shown in Appendix A makes considerable use of REMARK.

Summary

This chapter introduced a miscellaneous collection of SQL*Plus commands and techniques which served a variety of purposes. You will find these commands to be useful in real-world application systems as you move from a testing to a production environment.

   After completing this chapter, it may be enlightening for you to examine any command files that your organization is already using for production purposes. You will probably find that you understand many of the commands and statements contained in these files.

Summary Exercises

13A. Execute some SELECT statement and spool the output to a file called "SPIKE.SQL".

13B. Use the HOST command to issue an operating system command to print "SPIKE.LST".

13C. Describe the STAFF table.

13D. Write a SELECT statement to display all information about courses with a labfee of 0, 50, or 100. Write the statement two ways. The first version should use IN. The second version should use multiple ORs. Use SET TIMING to determine which is the more efficient statement.

13E. Get help about on the ORDER BY clause.

13F. Define a user variable called "ZERO" and reference it as a substitution variable in a command file. The file should contain a SELECT statement which displays all information about courses with a labfee of 0.

IV

Data Definition and Manipulation

This part of the text introduces the SQL database definition and update statements. We could have completed our discussion of the SELECT statement prior to introducing these topics. However, many subtle points associated with complex data retrieval pertain to decisions which are made during database design and subsequently implemented using SQL's data definition and update statements. Potentially embarrassing data retrieval errors can be avoided by understanding the key concepts of database definition and update. This is especially true for SELECT statements which must reference multiple tables or process columns which contain null values. For this reason, the fundamental concepts of data definition and update are presented in this part of the text before describing the more complex variations of the SELECT statement in Part V.

We recommend that you scan Appendix B, which displays all the tables in the educational database design. This is important because the remainder of the text will address issues which pertain to the relationships between multiple tables within a relational database design. In the next two chapters we will be referring to all the tables in the educational database.

Organization of Chapters

Chapter 14 introduces two important SQL data definition statements: CREATE TABLE and CREATE INDEX. Typically the database administrator executes these statements (among others) to initially establish the database. Unless you plan to use ORACLE as a personal system, you will probably never have to execute either of these statements. If this is the case, you can skim over the details of syntax. However, you should understand the conceptual substance of this chapter. The CREATE TABLE statement, in addition to defining the structure of a table, can also declare certain integrity constraints.

In subsequent chapters we will see that a query which references multiple tables usually is premised on a semantic relationship corresponding to the definition on some foreign key. From a conceptual point of view, this is a very important chapter because it shows how an application design using ORACLE is more than just a collection of tables. **We emphasize that the design is actually a semantically meaningful collection of interrelated tables which should adhere to specified integrity constraints. The semantic relationships are always the basis of a multitable query.**

Chapter 15 is a comprehensive presentation of SQL's data manipulation statements: INSERT, UPDATE, and DELETE. You will find the syntax for these statements to be quite straightforward. However, these statements are potentially dangerous because erroneous execution can cause the loss of valuable data. The examples illustrate interactive execution of the statements. However, for a corporate (vs. personal) database, these statements are usually embedded within application programs. Therefore, professional programmers should master the subject matter of this chapter. Those users who will not modify data can skip this chapter.

Chapter 16, which returns to the SELECT statement, is presented in this part of the text for a very important reason. Our intention is to emphasize the potential problems which can occur when a column is allowed to contain null values. If the CREATE TABLE statement does not prohibit null values, and subsequent INSERT or UPDATE statements actually store such values in a table, then special consideration must be given to the proper formulation of SELECT statements and to the interpretation of the result. The sample queries will show that the presence of null values increases the possibility of error. Therefore, both users and professional programmers should understand the content of this chapter. Hopefully it will also encourage the prohibition of null values where appropriate.

14

Data Definition

The primary focus of this chapter is the CREATE TABLE statement. This statement is used to establish an "empty" table. Thereafter, you can store rows in the table by executing the INSERT statement. We postpone discussion of the INSERT statement and other update statements (UPDATE and DELETE) until the next chapter.

The CREATE TABLE statement creates an "object" (the table) within the system. We will also discuss another system object, an index, which is established by executing the CREATE INDEX statement. Finally, we shall introduce a statement which allows us to change previously defined objects, the ALTER statement.

This chapter will present simplified versions of the CREATE TABLE and CREATE INDEX statements. These simplified versions avoid a discussion of other objects which exist within the system. Fortunately, users and application programmers rarely need to be familiar with these objects. For this reason, a comprehensive discussion of the complete versions of these statements is beyond the scope of this text.

An important concern which arises in the definition of tables is that of database integrity. There is a significant difference between Version 5 (V5) and Version 6 (V6) pertaining to the declaration of integrity constraints. A major enhancement to V6 is the support for the declaration (but, unfortunately, not the enforcement of) integrity constraints. We give considerable attention to this topic on the following pages. However, we note that our discussion of integrity constraints is not comprehensive.

CREATE TABLE Statement

We begin our discussion by presenting the CREATE TABLE statement, which was used to create the COURSE table. The following comments will elaborate on the SQL keywords and related concepts.

Sample Statement 14.1:   Create a table called COURSE which has six columns with the following names and descriptions.

1. CNO: Character string of length = 3 (nonnull).

2. CNAME: Character string of length = 22 (nonnull).

3. CDESCP: Character string of length = 25 (nonnull).

4. CRED: An integer (nulls allowed).

5. CLABFEE: A decimal value with a precision of 5 and a scale of 2 (nulls allowed).

6. CDEPT: Character string of length = 4 (nonnull).

7. Furthermore, if you are using V6, then you should declare the following integrity constraints

   a. CNO should be specified as the primary key, and

   b. CDEPT should be specified as a non-null foreign key referencing the DEPARTMENT table.

(V5 solution)

```
CREATE TABLE COURSE

      (CNO        CHAR(3)      NOT NULL,

       CNAME      CHAR(22)     NOT NULL,

       CDESCP     CHAR(25)     NOT NULL,

       CRED       NUMBER,

       CLABFEE    NUMBER(5,2),

       CDEPT      CHAR(4)      NOT NULL)
```

(V6 solution)

```
CREATE TABLE COURSE

     (CNO          CHAR(3)   NOT NULL,

      CNAME        CHAR(22)  NOT NULL,

      CDESCP       CHAR(25)  NOT NULL,

      CRED         NUMBER,

      CLABFEE      NUMBER(5,2),

      CDEPT        CHAR(4)   NOT NULL,

PRIMARY KEY (CNO),

FOREIGN KEY (CDEPT) REFERENCES DEPARTMENT)
```

System Response:

The CREATE TABLE statement is not a query. Hence, there is no explicit display of data as happens with a SELECT statement. You should receive a system-generated message which states that the table was successfully created. An error message would imply that you violated one of the rules to be described below.

Comments:

1. The V5 solution, which is upward compatible with V6, only defines the column names, related types, and NOT NULL specification where appropriate. We describe data types later in this chapter.

2. The V6 solution is merely an extension of the V5 solution. The additional PRIMARY KEY and FOREIGN KEY clauses are used to declare database integrity constraints. The syntax is easy. The related concepts are important and will be described in detail below.

3. A simple version of the general syntax for the CREATE TABLE statement is outlined in Figure 14.1. (This figure does not include other clauses which reference internal system objects.) Before addressing the details of syntax we enumerate the objectives of the CREATE TABLE statement.

Objectives of CREATE TABLE Statement:

1.   Establish a new table and give it a name.

2.   Give a name to all the columns in the table.

3.   Specify the data type of each column.

4.   Specify the default column sequence.

5.   Update the Data Dictionary.

6.   Specify which columns cannot accept null values.

7.   Define database integrity constraints.

The following pages elaborate on each of these seven points.

```
CREATE TABLE [username.]name-of-table

(column1-name   data-type   [column-constraint],

 column2-name   data-type   [column-constraint],
                     .
                     .
                     .
 columnN-name   data-type   [column-constraint],

[table-constraint])
```

Some *column-constraints* are:

- NOT NULL
- NULL
- PRIMARY KEY

Some *table-constraints* are:

- PRIMARY KEY (column1 [, column2, ..., columnN])

- FOREIGN KEY (column1 [, column2, ..., columnN])
  REFERENCES (table-name)

Figure 14.1: CREATE TABLE statement.

1. Table Names:

A table name may be 1 to 30 characters long. It must begin with a letter. This letter may be followed by other letters, digits, or the special characters of underscore (_), dollar sign ($), or pound sign (#). The table name is specified immediately after "CREATE TABLE" in the statement. The example shows "COURSE" as the specified table name.

The CREATE TABLE statement and previous SELECT statements referenced this table as "COURSE." However, "COURSE" is not the complete name. This is because ORACLE is a multiuser system and it is possible for different users to specify "COURSE" in different CREATE TABLE statements used to create different tables. To handle this situation, the system will automatically attach each user's "username" as a prefix to the table name. This means that the complete name of any table consists of two parts.

1. Username: This is the sign-on id used when you signed onto the ORACLE system (e.g., U48989).

2. Table-name: This is the name specified in the CREATE TABLE statement (e.g., COURSE).

Therefore, assuming your username is "U48989", the complete table name is "U48989.COURSE". Notice this scheme of naming tables allows many different users to give the same name to a table. For example, assume another user with a username of "U99999" issued the following statement.

```
CREATE TABLE COURSE
(XXX CHAR(100),
 YYY NUMBER(8,1))
```

If user U99999 inserted rows into this table and subsequently entered the statement "SELECT * FROM COURSE", ORACLE would automatically attach his username as a prefix to the table name and execute "SELECT * FROM U99999.COURSE". Likewise, whenever you enter "SELECT * FROM COURSE", the system converts this to "SELECT * FROM U48989.COURSE".

There are occasions where you would be required to explicitly specify a complete table name in a statement. For example, it is possible for user U99999 to grant you permission to access his COURSE table. (Chapter 24 will describe how this permission is granted.) You could then enter the following statement to examine his COURSE table.

```
SELECT YYY, XXX
FROM   U99999.COURSE
ORDER BY YYY
```

Observe that the complete table name is specified and column names refer to those contained within the U99999.COURSE table.

2. Column Names:

Column names are formulated according to the same syntax rules as table names. Column names must be unique within a given table; but it is possible to have the same column name specified within multiple tables. For example, both the COURSE table and the REGISTRATION table contain a column named "CNO". There is no ambiguity when a SELECT statement refers to CNO because the FROM clause indicates the appropriate table.

Chapter 17 will introduce the join operation, which references multiple tables in the same SELECT statement. If two tables have a column with the same name, then a column name must be qualified by specifying a table name as a prefix. For example, you would specify "COURSE.CNO" to reference the CNO column of the COURSE table and "REGISTRATION.CNO" to reference the CNO column of the REGISTRATION table. Chapter 17 will present sample queries where table name qualification of columns is required.

3. Data Types:

The data type of each column is specified after the column name. We have seen that the type of data in a column can affect how conditions are formulated in a WHERE clause. For example, we saw that character strings, unlike numeric constants, must be enclosed in apostrophes. Serious consideration should be given to the choice of data type. We shall present a comprehensive overview of available data types below.

4. Default Column Sequence:

The example shows the column definitions specified in a certain order. CNO is defined first, CNAME second, etc. This order establishes the default left-to-right column sequence to be displayed when a SELECT statement uses an asterisk to indicate the display of all columns (SELECT * FROM ...).

5. Data Dictionary:

ORACLE maintains a catalog of information about the existence of database tables, columns, and integrity constraints. This catalog is referred to as the Data Dictionary. When CREATE TABLE is executed, ORACLE stores information about the table, column, and the constraints in its Data Dictionary. When the system processes a query, it examines the Data Dictionary to validate the presence of any referenced table and column names. A comprehensive knowledge of the structure of the Data Dictionary is required by database designers. However, users of interactive SQL and most application programmers can function very well with a limited knowledge of the Data Dictionary. Throughout this text we may make an occasional reference to the Data Dictionary. An overview of this dictionary will be presented in Chapter 26.

6. NULL Values:

The next chapter will present examples of the INSERT statement, where values are not specified for some columns. When a row is inserted into a table, and a column value is not specified, the system interprets the missing information as a special "null" value. This value is interpreted as "value unknown."

There are circumstances where null values may be unreasonable. For example, CNO serves as a unique identifier (the primary key) for a course. Also, it is academic policy that every course should be assigned a name and description and be sponsored by some academic department. For these reasons the NOT NULL clause entered with the CNO, CNAME, CDESCP, and CDEPT column definitions. In effect, specifying NOT NULL helps maintain database integrity. The presence of this clause will instruct the system to reject any update to the COURSE table which would produce a null value anywhere in these columns.

The other columns (CRED and CLABFEE) will accept null values. We could have specified the keyword NULL in the declaration of these columns. Our example illustrates that NULL is the default.

The presence of null values may cause some confusion. They require that greater attention be given to query formulation. (These issues will be discussed in Chapter 16.) Attaching NOT NULL to a column definition can eliminate these potential problems. It is strongly suggested that NOT NULL be specified wherever appropriate.

7. Database Integrity Constraints:

A database serves to represent real world data and to capture relationships which exist between these data. These relationships give rise to the notions of "entity integrity" and "referential integrity." Such integrity constraints are defined by the PRIMARY KEY and FOREIGN KEY clauses in V6. (These clauses are not supported in V5.)

The following comments of primary keys and foreign keys pertain to the general topics of entity and referential integrity which are described later in this chapter. We introduce these topics with a few comments about the PRIMARY KEY clause in the current example. *We note that Version 6 of ORACLE introduced the syntax for defining primary and foreign keys. However, the system does not yet enforce referential integrity.*

Primary Key:

It is recommended, but not required, that every table have some column or group of columns specified as the primary key of the table. The primary key is a value which should always be (1) nonnull and (2) unique. The current example shows CNO as the primary key of the COURSE table. The "PRIMARY KEY" clause is followed by "CNO" within parentheses. Also, the NOT NULL clause is specified with the CNO column definition. You can enforce uniqueness by creating a unique index. This will be described in Sample Statement 14.3.

Foreign Key:

Foreign keys, like primary keys, enhance database integrity. In the previous discussion of null values we noted that a school policy of each course being sponsored by some academic department means that NOT NULL should be specified for the CDEPT column. However, the NOT NULL clause only keeps null values out of the CDEPT column. It would not prohibit any "garbage" character string values like "WXYZ" or "ART" from being stored in this column. A more desirable objective is to restrict CDEPT values to those found in the DEPT column of the DEPARTMENT table. This objective can be declared by specifying CDEPT as a foreign key which references the DEPARTMENT table.

A foreign key is a column or group of columns where each column value equals some primary key value in a specified table. The current example shows "FOREIGN KEY (CDEPT) REFERENCES DEPARTMENT" in the CREATE TABLE statement. This means that CDEPT, as a foreign key within the COURSE table, references the DEPARTMENT table because any value in the CDEPT column must equal some existing primary key value in the DEPARTMENT table. Assuming that the CREATE TABLE statement for DEPARTMENT designates DEPT as its primary key, then all CDEPT values must equal some existing DEPT value in the DEPARTMENT table. (Examination of the DEPARTMENT and COURSE tables in Appendix B will verify this fact.)

Additional Form of CREATE TABLE:

We note that there is a second form of the CREATE TABLE statement which allows you to create a table and load it with data from some other existing table. This version of the statement is discussed in Comment 4 of Sample Statement 15.5.

ORACLE Data Types

ORACLE supports a variety of data types. Each data type can be placed in one of three categories: (1) character string data, (2) numeric data, and (3) date/time data. We describe each category and its associated data types below.

Character String Data:

The different character string data types are enumerated in Figure 14.2. Each string data type is used to represent alphanumeric characters using the ASCII or EBCDIC codes. Related to the character string data type is the RAW data type. This is used to describe byte-oriented data that are not interpreted by ORACLE, but may be used to store graphics. Its processing is similar to that for CHAR, but the values may not have any meaning as characters. A discussion of this data type and graphical character codes is beyond the scope of this text.

You will find the greatest use for the CHAR data type which is specified for character strings up to 240 bytes long. Earlier in the text, we classified data with the more general terms "character data" and "numeric data." The CHAR data type is used to define a column which contains character data. We can use any of the string functions and perform comparisons on this data type. The LONG data type is used to store long (up to 65,535 bytes) character strings. These strings have many limitations with respect to comparison and function reference. They are primarily used to store and subsequently display long text strings. Finally, recall that arithmetic cannot be done with any of the string data types.

As mentioned above, LONG strings have many limitations with respect to comparison and function reference. In particular, only one column of type LONG may be declared for a table. Such columns cannot be referenced in a WHERE clause, nor can they be used in a subquery, function, or expression. In addition, they cannot be used in an index.

Date/Time Data:

Character and numeric data types are found in traditional high-level programming languages (COBOL, FORTRAN, etc.). Programmers often use one of the traditional data types to encode a value which represents a date or a time. However, SQL has a "primitive" date/time data type, which can help avoid the complexity of the encoding process and can be used as arguments to the date/time functions presented in Chapter 10. Values are stored in a special internal format (not described here) which can be converted to or from a variety of display formats. This data type simplifies the storing of chronological information which can be operated on for comparisons and computations.

Name	Description
CHAR(n)	Column contains character strings represented using ASCII or EBCDIC. n is in the range of 1 to 240 and is the maximum number of characters allowed in the column.
VARCHAR(n)	Same as CHAR.
LONG	The values in the column may have different lengths not to exceed a maximum of 65635. There may be only one column of this type for a table. There are other processing restrictions on a column defined as LONG.
LONG VARCHAR	Same as LONG.
RAW(n)	Raw binary data of n bytes. n may be up to 240.
DATE	Contains a date and a time of day. Dates can range between January 1, 4712 BC and December 31, 4712 AD.

Figure 14.2: SQL character and date data types.

Numeric Data:

Numeric data types are defined for data items which will be
used in arithmetic operations. Figure 14.3 presents the
numeric data types.

Name	Description
NUMBER	Column can contain up to 40 digits. Numbers may be expressed as digits with a decimal point, and a possible sign +/-, or in scientific notation.
NUMBER(n)	Numeric data with n (up to 105) digits. The precision of the number is based on only 40 digits.
NUMBER(p,s)	p is total number of digits, the precision, and s is the number of those digits after the decimal point, the scale. If p is not specified, the column may have all of its digits after the decimal point.
DECIMAL	Same as NUMBER.
FLOAT	Same as NUMBER.
INTEGER	Same as NUMBER.
SMALLINT	Same as NUMBER.

Figure 14.3: SQL numeric data types.

Exercises:

14A. Examine the CREATE TABLE statements for the educational
database shown in Appendix B.

14B. Create a table called JUNK. It has three columns.
  C1: character string of length = 10 (nonnull)
  C2: a number (nulls allowed)
  C3: a decimal value with a precision of 7 and a
        scale of 2 (nonnull)
  Designate C1 as the primary key.

Entity Integrity and Referential Integrity

Sample Statement 14.1 introduced the PRIMARY KEY and FOREIGN KEY clauses which are used to achieve entity and referential integrity. The purpose of this section is to elaborate on these concepts. The identification of primary and foreign keys occurs during database design when the semantic issues of entities, relationships, and database integrity are explicitly considered. A comprehensive discussion of database design is beyond the scope of this text. This is a very complex topic which requires attention to many issues which transcend SQL. But it is impossible to present the CREATE TABLE or CREATE INDEX statements without touching on design issues. The following discussion offers some insight into the notions of entity and referential integrity. This is necessary to provide a context for a more detailed discussion of the PRIMARY KEY and FOREIGN KEY clauses.

Entity Integrity:

A row in a table usually corresponds to an instance of an entity type which the database is modeling. An entity may be described as any identifiable object. For example, the COURSE table represents a type of entity, "course," and each row in the COURSE table corresponds a particular course offered by the college. Because each real-world course entity is uniquely identifiable, it is desirable that each corresponding row in the COURSE table also be uniquely identifiable by some column or group of columns. This is the purpose of defining a primary key. Consider the ambiguity which occurs when a table contains two or more rows which cannot be distinguished from each other. There would be a loss of entity integrity because the one-to-one correspondence between a course entity and its corresponding row would be destroyed. By identifying CNO as the primary key we are stating that a course number can always be used to uniquely identify a course. Also, there are circumstances where the proper formulation of an SQL statement requires that the WHERE condition select only one row. If you write the statement such that multiple rows are actually selected, an error will occur. (Future sample queries will show such examples. Also, this is an especially important consideration when embedding SQL code in an application program.) The specification of CNO in the PRIMARY KEY clause means that no update operation should insert a null or duplicate value in the CNO column. Therefore any statement containing "WHERE CNO = value" can never select more than one row.

Sometimes it is necessary to specify more than one column value in order to uniquely identify a row in a table. For example, because multiple sections of a course may be offered during a given semester, the CLASS table can have multiple rows with the same CNO value. For this reason, a composite primary key would be specified to include the CNO and SEC columns. In this case the PRIMARY KEY clause would be written as "PRIMARY KEY (CNO, SEC)".

Occasionally you will find that you have more than one choice for a primary key. For example, assume it is school policy that every course has a unique name. Then you could choose either CNO or CNAME as the primary key. But only one primary key is specified. How would you choose? A choice of CNO could be based on the fact the school established course numbers for the purpose of uniquely identifying courses. However, choosing CNAME would not be wrong. And it would even be a better choice if there were significantly more queries which selected rows based on CNAME values than CNO values. This is because you enforce uniqueness on a column by creating a unique index on that column. The same index will help the system perform more efficient retrieval of rows. We will return to this issue in our discussion of the CREATE INDEX statement.

Referential Integrity:

Sample Statement 14.1 used the FOREIGN KEY clause to specify the CDEPT column in the COURSE table as a foreign key which references the DEPARTMENT table. We continue with this example to introduce terminology relevant to referential integrity. This terminology is borrowed from the DB2 community and is becoming generic in the context of referential integrity.

Parent Table: A table which is referenced by some foreign key. DEPARTMENT is a parent table because it is referenced by the CDEPT foreign key. A primary key, such as DEPT in DEPARTMENT, must be specified for the parent table. This is because any nonnull foreign key (CDEPT) value must be equal to some existing primary key (DEPT) value. We say that a foreign key references the parent table. It does so by identifying some primary key value in the parent table.

Dependent Table: A table which contains a foreign key. COURSE, which contains CDEPT as a foreign key, is a dependent table. It is dependent on DEPARTMENT, the parent table. The academic policy requiring every course to be sponsored by some department means that courses are dependent on departments. At the database level this means every dependent (COURSE) row is dependent on some parent (DEPARTMENT) row. A dependent row cannot exist with a foreign key (CDEPT) value unless that value exists as some primary key (DEPT) value in the parent table. Many people refer to a dependent table as a "child" table.

Descendant Table: It is possible for a table which is dependent on one table to be the parent of another table. For example, assume it is school policy that every class correspond to some course. This means that every CNO value in the CLASS table must equal some existing CNO value in the COURSE table. Therefore CNO in the CLASS table would be defined as a foreign key referencing COURSE. [In this example the foreign key (CNO) happens to be part of the primary key (CNO,SEC) for CLASS. This will occur often in practice.] This relationship means that COURSE becomes a parent table for CLASS in addition to being a dependent for DEPARTMENT. It also means that CLASS is dependent on COURSE, which is in turn dependent on DEPARTMENT. Under this circumstance we say that CLASS is a descendant of DEPARTMENT. Figure 14.4 illustrates the relationship between these three tables.

Independent Table: A table without any foreign keys. The CREATE TABLE for the STAFF table will not have a FOREIGN KEY clause specified for any column. (Note that the DEPT column in the STAFF table will contain department id values. However, this column is not specified as a foreign key because it may contain values not found in the primary key column of the DEPARTMENT table.)

A table may have multiple parent and/or dependent tables. Consider the REGISTRATION table originally introduced in Chapter 10. The key of this table is a composition of three columns (CNO,SEC,SNO). To ensure referential integrity we would specify two foreign keys in this table. The compound foreign key (CNO,SEC) would reference the CLASS table. And the SNO foreign key would reference the student table. Hence, REGISTRATION is dependent on two tables, CLASS and STUDENT. Also, assume that all students must major in a subject corresponding to some existing academic department. This means the CREATE TABLE statement for STUDENT would specify SMAJ as a foreign key referencing DEPARTMENT. Hence, DEPARTMENT is the parent of two tables, COURSE and STUDENT. Figure 14.5 reflects this expanded view of the design.

Cycle: Foreign keys can be defined such that a cyclic relationship is established. Assume it is school policy that each faculty member is assigned to some academic department. Then the FDEPT column in the FACULTY table would be specified as a foreign key referencing DEPARTMENT. (DEPARTMENT is the parent table and FACULTY is the dependent table.) Also assume that the chairperson of each academic department is some faculty member. Then the DCHFNO value in the DEPARTMENT is specified as a foreign key referencing FACULTY. (Here, FACULTY is the parent table and DEPARTMENT is the dependent table.) Figure 14.6 illustrates this relationship.

Sometimes a cycle involves more than two tables. TABLE1 could be the parent of TABLE2, which could be the parent of TABLE3, which could be the parent of TABLE1. In general, a cycle is formed if the descendant of any table becomes the parent of that table. In effect, every table in a cyclic relationship becomes the descendant of itself.

Self-Referencing Cycle: It is possible for a table to be the parent and dependent of itself. In other words, the table contains a foreign key which references itself. For example, assume that some courses have at most one prerequisite course which students must take before registering for a class on the course. We could denote the prerequisite course in the COURSE table by altering this table to include a new column,

PCNO, which contains the course number of the prerequisite course. Then the CREATE TABLE statement for COURSE would contain an additional FOREIGN KEY clause specifying PCNO as a foreign key referencing COURSE. Figure 14.7 illustrates this relationship. This self-referencing cycle is sometimes called a "recursive" relationship.

The data type and length of each component of a foreign key must be the same as the primary key. This is true for all the previous examples. But a foreign key, unlike a primary key, may be allowed to contain null values. (Thus, it is not necessary to specify NOT NULL for a foreign key column.) For example, there are many introductory courses which do not have a prerequisite course. Rows for such courses could have a null value in the PCNO column. Another example is the SMAJ column in the STUDENT table. If we assume that some students do not have to declare a major, then corresponding SMAJ values could be null.

Thus far only the structural aspect of referential integrity has been considered. We now outline some of the processing rules which impose reasonable constraints on data manipulation statements which reference primary and/or foreign key values. These statements (INSERT, UPDATE, and DELETE) will be described in the next chapter. When executing these statements you should verify that the update operation does not violate any of the integrity constraints.

Insert of Primary Key: The primary key value should be unique. If it is not, the insert should be rejected.

Insert of Foreign Key: Any nonnull foreign key should equal some existing primary key in the parent table. If it does not, the insert should be rejected.

Update of Primary key: Updating the primary key should be rejected if there exists any dependent rows referencing the current primary key value.

Update of Foreign Key: The new foreign key should equal some existing primary key in the referenced table (or be null, if allowed). Otherwise, the update should be rejected.

Delete of Primary Key: Do not delete a row if its primary key value is referenced by any foreign key value. (You could delete the corresponding foreign key rows and then retry the deletion of the primary key row.)

Delete of Foreign Key: No restrictions (unless the foreign key is part of a primary key or some other foreign key where other restrictions apply.)

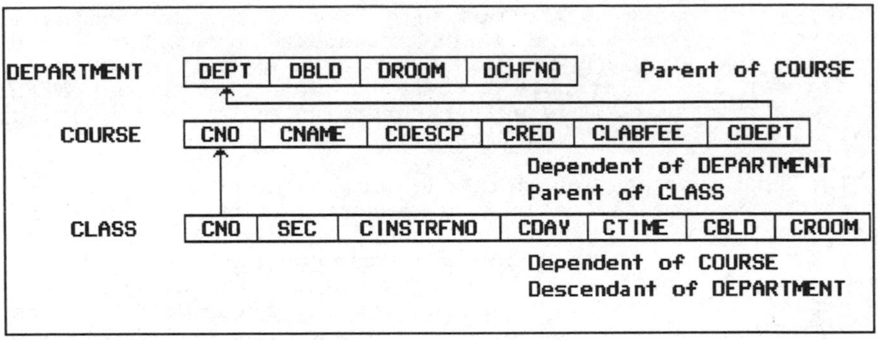

Figure 14.4: Parent, dependent, and descendant tables.

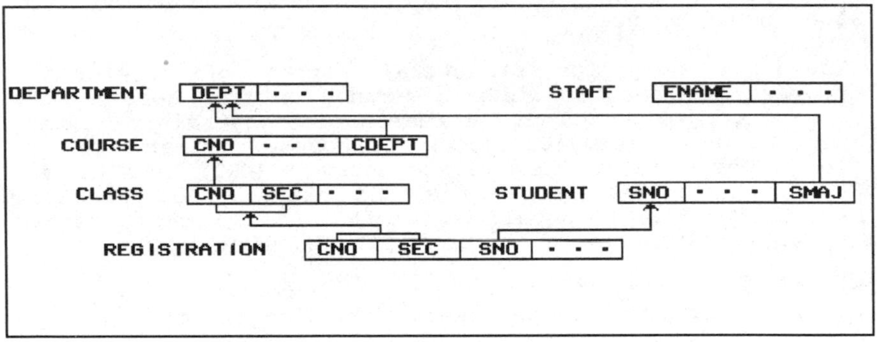

Figure 14.5: Expanded view of database design.

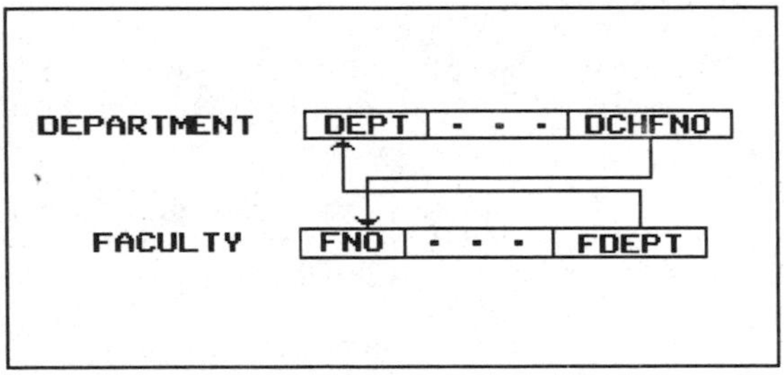

Figure 14.6: A cycle.

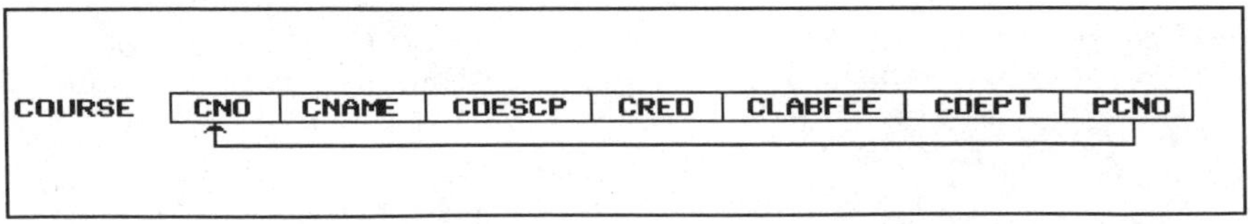

Figure 14.7: Self-referencing cycle.

CREATE INDEX Statement

The CREATE INDEX statement is used to create a database object called an index. Before introducing the CREATE INDEX statement, we present the fundamental objectives and concepts of database indexes.

What is an index?

An index is an internal structure which the system can use to find one or more rows in a table. Figure 14.8 presents the general idea of an index. In effect, a database index is conceptually similar to an index found at the end of this or any other textbook. In the same way that a reader of a book would refer to an index to determine the page locations of a specified topic, a database system would read an index to determine the disk locations of rows selected by a SQL query. Simply put, the presence of an index can help the system process some queries in a more efficient manner.

A database index is created for a column or group of columns. Figure 14.8 shows an index (XCNAME) for the CNAME values found in the COURSE table. Observe that the index, unlike the COURSE table, represents the CNAME values in sequence. Also, the index is small relative to the size of the table. Therefore, it is probably easier for the system to search the index to locate a row with a given CNAME value than to scan the entire table in search of that value. For example, the XCNAME index might be helpful to the system when it executes the following SELECT statement.

```
SELECT *
FROM    COURSE
WHERE   CNAME = 'EXISTENTIALISM'
```

Because the WHERE clause references CNAME, the system would consider using the XCNAME index. Now consider the statement

```
SELECT *
FROM    COURSE
WHERE   CDESCP = 'FOR THE GREEDY'
```

The XCNAME index is of little use when searching for CDESCP values. Therefore, the system would probably not reference it. Of course, we might consider creating an index on CDESCP values.

There are many complex issues pertaining to database indexes. Some of these issues will be introduced below. However, we first present an example of the CREATE INDEX statement which is used to create the CNAME index.

XCNAME Index   **COURSE Table**

XCNAME Index	
COMMUNISM	◉
COMPUTER ARCH.	◉
DATA STRUCTURES	◉
DIGITAL CIRCUITS	◉
DISCRETE MATHEMATICS	◉
EMPIRICISM	◉
EXISTENTIALISM	◉
FUNDAMENTALISM	◉
HEDONISM	◉
INTRO TO CS	◉
RATIONALISM	◉
RELATIONAL DATABASE	◉
SCHOLASTICISM	◉
SOLIPSISM	◉

CNO	CNAME	...
C22	DATA STRUCTURES	...
T44	COMMUNISM	...
C55	COMPUTER ARCH.	...
C33	DISCRETE MATHEMATICS	...
P11	EMPIRICISM	...
T33	HEDONISM	...
P33	EXISTENTIALISM	...
C44	DIGITAL CIRCUITS	...
T12	FUNDAMENTALISM	...
C11	INTRO TO CS	...
P22	RATIONALISM	...
P44	SOLIPSISM	...
T11	SCHOLASTICISM	...
C66	RELATIONAL DATABASE	...

Figure 14.8: Index (XCNAME) based on CNAME column in COURSE table.

Sample Statement 14.2: Create an index on the CNAME column of the COURSE table. Call this index XCNAME.

```
CREATE INDEX XCNAME

ON COURSE (CNAME)
```

System Response:

Like the CREATE TABLE statement, the CREATE INDEX statement is not a query and, hence, there is no output display. Instead the system returns a diagnostic which (presumably) indicates the successful creation of the XCNAME index. This index will be conceptually like that shown in Figure 14.8. Its actual internal structure, like that of the database tables, is considerably more complex.

Comments:

1.   Syntax: A simplified version of the general syntax is

         CREATE INDEX index-name
         ON table-name (column-name)

An index is given a name (XCNAME in our example) according to the same rules as apply to table names. The ON clause must reference a valid table name. The column name must be enclosed within parentheses and refer to a valid column name within the specified table.

2.   In this example the COURSE table already has rows stored in it. The system will scan this table to obtain the CNAME values and corresponding row locations to construct the index. In practice it is better to issue the CREATE INDEX statement before any rows are actually inserted into the table. However, the index can be created at any time.

3.   Once the index is created, the system will automatically maintain it. For example, if you issue an INSERT statement to place a new row in the COURSE table, the system will automatically determine the CNAME value and location of the new row and place a new entry in the XCNAME index. Simply put, once you create the index, the system does the rest.

4.   Like the CREATE TABLE statement, the CREATE INDEX statement will cause the system to update the Data Dictionary. In this case the system will record the presence of a new index (XCNAME) and its dependence on the COURSE table.

Do indexes force a change to the SELECT statement?

There is absolutely no change to the coding of a SELECT statement due to the presence of an index. The SELECT statements for all previous sample queries would remain the same. This means that many users of the system can remain ignorant of the presence or absence of any database indexes.

Whenever a SELECT statement is submitted by a user, the system uses a special internal module, the "optimizer," to analyze the statement to determine if using an index would be beneficial. If this is the case, the system consults the Data Dictionary to determine if an index is available. If it is, the system will consider using the index. If it is not, the system simply scans the table to search for the desired rows.

The use of an optimizer to determine the most efficient access path means that ORACLE possesses the desirable characteristic of physical data independence. The database administrator can modify internal data structures without forcing changes to previously written applications. In particular, indexes can be created and dropped without affecting the validity of any existing or future SELECT statements.

What are the advantages of indexes?

The system can use an index to enhance machine efficiency in a number of circumstances. Some of these are described below.

1.   **Direct access to a specified row:** This assumes the index is defined on the appropriate column. The previous discussion illustrated this point.

2.   **Sorting:** Note that Figure 14.8 showed the CNAME values in sequence. This means that the system can use the XCNAME index to retrieve the COURSE rows in CNAME sequence. If an index is not established on an appropriate column, the system must execute an internal sort routine which can be costly, especially for a large number of rows. The optimizer may consider using an index whenever the SELECT statement contains any of the following keywords or clauses: ORDER BY, DISTINCT, GROUP BY, or UNION.

3.   **Join Operation:** The join operation is presented in Chapter 17. Here we merely state that the join operation can be costly, and indexes can facilitate this process.

How many indexes can be created?

Any number of indexes can be created for a given table. However, there is a cost associated with each index which may offset its advantages.

What are the disadvantages of indexes?

There are two cost factors associated with database indexes which prohibit their unlimited use.

1. **Disk space used by the index:** An index, although it is smaller than the table, can occupy a considerable amount of disk storage. A table with many rows means that the index will have many entries. This means a large index is created. And, if the table has many indexes, it could cause the total disk space used by all the indexes to exceed the size of the table itself.

2. **Update costs:** While indexes expedite the retrieval process, they penalize the update process. Whenever a new row is inserted into or deleted from a table, the system must make the corresponding change to the indexes. If, for example, a table has five indexes then an insert or delete operation forces an update to the five indexes. This could severely impact response time.

Composite Indexes and Unique Indexes

The CREATE INDEX statement provides other advantages in addition to those specified above. By including special keywords in the statement (to be described below), either of the following special type indexes can be created.

1. **Composite Index:** An index can be created on a combination of column names. A simple example of such an index is a CNO-SEC composite index for the CLASS table. Note that a composite index is just a single index where the key is composed of data found in multiple columns. Also note that the order of the index components is significant. For example, the CNO-SEC index is different from the SEC-CNO index.

2. **Unique Index:** A unique index is an index which cannot contain any duplicate values. The presence of a unique index causes the system to reject any update to the table which will result in duplicate values in the column(s) specified by the index. A *unique index should be created for the primary key column(s)*. Although only one primary key can be specified for a table, any number of unique indexes can be specified for a table. For example, if you wanted the system to enforce uniqueness on CNAME values, you could have included the keyword "UNIQUE" in the CREATE INDEX statement shown in Sample Query 14.1.

These types of indexes are not mutually exclusive. It is possible for a single index to have both of the above characteristics. Figure 14.9 shows a more general syntax of the CREATE INDEX statement which can be used to establish the above special types of indexes. This figure shows the syntax and keywords necessary to establish a compound or unique index.

```
CREATE [UNIQUE] INDEX index-name

ON table-name

    (column1-name [ASC/DESC,]

    column2-name [ASC/DESC,]

        . . .

    columnN-name [ASC/DESC]
```

Figure 14.9: CREATE INDEX statement.

Guidelines for Creating Indexes

Choosing the right set of indexes is a challenging task. In fact, choosing the optimal set of indexes for a large design is practically impossible. In the absence of performance information (e.g., frequency of retrieval or update), the best that you can do is to follow some established guidelines.

- Create a unique index on the primary key.

- Create an index on each foreign key.

- Create an index on any column(s) which will be frequently referenced in a WHERE clause or an ORDER BY clause.

Sample Statement 14.3: Create a unique composite index for the CLASS table presented in Part IV. The composite key is based on the CNO and SEC columns.

```
CREATE UNIQUE INDEX U48989.XCNOSEC

ON U48989.CLASS (CNO, SEC)
```

Comments:

1. The keyword "UNIQUE" is specified prior to "INDEX." This causes the system to reject any update which would cause multiple rows to have the same CNO-SEC combination.

2. This index is a composite index because it is defined for more than one column (CNO, SEC). Note that the order specified is significant.

3. The sequence of each component of the composite key can be designated as ascending (ASC) or descending (DESC). The ON clause could have been written as

        ON CLASS (CNO ASC, SEC ASC)

    Because the example did not explicitly specify the ASC or DESC parameters, ORACLE will default to an ascending sequence for both CNO and SEC.

Exercise:

14C. Create a unique index for the SNO primary key of the STUDENT table. Also, create an index for the SMAJ foreign key in this table.

ALTER Statement

Assume that after you created the STUDENT table and inserted some rows, you decide that the database should include each student's height and weight. This means that two new columns containing student heights and weights need to be attached to the STUDENT table. This is the purpose of the ALTER statement. It can be used to add one or more new columns to an existing table.

Sample Statement 14.4:   Add two new columns to the STUDENT table. The first is called SHT, which represents student height in inches; the second is called SWT, which represents student weight in pounds. Represent both of these values as decimals with a precision of 4 and a scale of 1.

```
ALTER TABLE STUDENT ADD

    (SHT NUMBER(4,1) NULL,

     SWT NUMBER(4,1) NULL)
```

System Response:

Like the CREATE statements, the ALTER statement does not produce any output. However, the system should return a message which indicates that the table was successfully altered.

Comments:

1.   The SHT and SWT columns are appended to the right-hand side of the STUDENT table.

2.   A new column is specified in the same way as with the CREATE TABLE statement. The column name is followed by the data type of the column and a clause to indicate if the column will allow null values. Note that the example used NULL to indicate that the new columns would allow null values. This is the default specification when adding columns. NOT NULL is acceptable only if the table does not have any rows.

3.   The example showed the ADD feature, which allows a new column to be added to a table. The ALTER statement also has a MODIFY feature to allow changes to existing column characteristics. A more general format of the ALTER TABLE statement is presented in Figure 14.10.

4.   SQL has other ALTER statements to modify certain physical characteristics of indexes and other system objects. These statements are not covered in this text.

```
ALTER TABLE table-name ADD
      (column-name   data-type   [NULL|NOT NULL],
       column-name   data-type   [NULL|NOT NULL],
                         .
                         .
                         .
       column-name   data-type   [NULL|NOT NULL])

                     -  or  -

ALTER TABLE table-name MODIFY
      (column-name [data-type]   [NULL|NOT NULL],
       column-name [data-type]   [NULL|NOT NULL],
                         .
                         .
                         .
       column-name [data-type]   [NULL|NOT NULL])
```

Figure 14.10: Syntax of ALTER TABLE statement.

Other Database Objects

We have presented an overview of two types of database objects, tables and indexes. We will describe another type of object called a view in Chapter 23. ORACLE does have other database objects. ORACLE (V6) supports the following CREATE statements.

- CREATE DATABASE

- CREATE TABLESPACE

- CREATE CLUSTER

- CREATE SEQUENCE

These objects are generally created by the DBA. Therefore a discussion of these objects is beyond the scope of this text.

DROP Statement

All of the aforementioned database objects can be removed from the system by the DROP statement. This statement is the inverse of the CREATE statement. It is executed whenever the created object no longer serves any purpose in the application environment. We illustrate this statement with two examples.

Sample Query 14.5:   Remove the XCNOSEC index.

```
DROP INDEX XCNOSEC
```

System Response:

> The system will produce some message which should confirm that the specified index has been dropped.

Comments:

1.   The XCNOSEC index is based on the CLASS table. Note that the DROP statement does not need to specify the table name. This is because the system can determine this information from the Data Dictionary. If you wished to verify the table name, you could specify this name with the ON clause

     DROP INDEX XCNOSEC ON CLASS

2.   Again we note that the CLASS table still exists and any queries against this table will still work. The system optimizer will simply choose an access path which does not rely on the dropped index.

3.   Earlier it was noted that the CREATE INDEX statement causes the system to update the Data Dictionary to record the presence of a new index. Likewise, the DROP INDEX statement causes the system to delete information about the index from the Data Dictionary.

Sample Statement 14.6:   Drop the COURSE table. (Do not actually execute this statement if you are testing the examples shown in this text.)

```
DROP TABLE COURSE
```

System Response:

The system would display a message which confirms that the COURSE table has been dropped.

Comments:

1.   Execution of the DROP TABLE statement not only deletes all rows present from the table, it removes the very definition of the table from the system catalog. This means that a subsequent attempt to insert rows into the table would fail. The DELETE statement (described in the next chapter) is used to delete any or all rows in a table without removing the table definition. Obviously, the DROP TABLE statement is potentially dangerous, which is why we advised you not to actually execute the above statement. If you did, you would have to go through the effort of recreating the COURSE table and inserting its rows.

2.   Whenever a table is dropped, any indexes based on the table are also automatically dropped. If the COURSE table were dropped, the system would drop the previously described XCNAME index.

3.   SQL does not have any statement which can be used to remove specified columns from a table (i.e., there is no "drop column" statement). To realize this objective a new table must be created with just the desired columns. Chapter 15 will show a variation of the INSERT statement which can be used to copy data from selected columns in the original table to the new table.

Summary

This chapter has introduced some of ORACLE's most useful data definition statements, as follows.

* CREATE TABLE: To create a new table.

* ALTER TABLE: To add or modify columns for an existing table.

* CREATE INDEX: To create an index on an existing table.

* DROP INDEX: To remove an index.

* DROP TABLE: To remove a table.

In a production environment, where the database contains corporate data, these statements would only be executed by the database administrator. The database administrator would also execute other SQL statements not covered in this text because such statements would reference specific physical objects other than tables or indexes. However, some users and programmers may have permission to create tables for personal data or testing purposes. This chapter has covered the above data definition statements in enough detail to realize these objectives.

DB2 Compatibility: The general syntax of CREATE TABLE and CREATE INDEX statements is quite similar. However, there are differences in data types which can lead to compatibility problems.

Comment on forthcoming Version 7 of ORACLE: We emphasized that the integrity constraint clauses, with the exception of NULL/NOT NULL, can only be *declared* in V6. V6 does not automatically enforce these declarations. For this reason we did not discuss many of the other integrity constraint clauses (e.g., CHECK, UNIQUE, REFERENCES) which can also be declared. Full automatic implementation of all integrity constraint clauses is expected in the forthcoming Version 7 (V7) of ORACLE.

Summary Exercise

14D. Create a table called CISCOURSE. It should have four columns called CISCNO, CISCNAME, CISCRED, and CISCLABFEE which, respectively, have the same attributes as the CNO, CNAME, CRED, and CLABFEE columns in the COURSE table. CISCNO is the primary key. There are no foreign keys. Also create a unique index for the primary key.

Data Manipulation

The previous chapter introduced the CREATE TABLE statement which is used to create an empty table. We now turn our attention to SQL's data manipulation statements which are used to store rows in a table and subsequently modify these rows. These are the INSERT, UPDATE, and DELETE statements.

The INSERT statement is used to store rows in a table. This statement could be used to store rows into an empty table or a table which already contains some number of rows. Thereafter, if you wish to change the contents of any existing rows, you must use the UPDATE statement. The DELETE statement is used to remove one or more rows from the table. In this chapter we will discuss each of these statements. Again we emphasize that execution of these statements is potentially dangerous because errors could cause the loss of valuable data. If you are running the sample statements on a sample database, double-check each statement before execution.

INSERT Statement

There are two forms of the INSERT statement. The first allows for exactly one row to be inserted into a table. In this form data which currently do not exist in the database may be introduced to a table. The second form allows data from multiple rows already existing in some table to be inserted into another table. Both forms are shown in Figure 15.1. We introduce the first form of the INSERT statement by illustrating the addition of a new row into the COURSE table.

Sample Statement 15.1:   Assume the CIS department offers a new course with the name "INTRODUCTION TO SQL". The course number is "C77". This course is worth three credits, and its labfee is $150.00. The course description is "GOOD STUFF!". Insert a new row into the COURSE table corresponding to this course.

```
INSERT INTO COURSE

VALUES ('C77', 'INTRODUCTION TO SQL',

        'GOOD STUFF!', 3, 150.00, 'CIS')
```

System Response:

The system will display a message which indicates that the system (1) successfully inserted the new row or (2) rejected the insert operation due to an error (e.g., syntax, NOT NULL violation, unique value violation). Assuming that the insert operation is successful, you can further verify the presence of the new row by executing the following SELECT statement.

SELECT * FROM COURSE WHERE CNO = 'C77'

The system should display

CNO	CNAME	CDESCP	CRED	CLABFEE	CDEPT
C77	INTRODUCTION TO SQL	GOOD STUFF!	3	150	CIS

Comments:

1.   Syntax: INSERT Clause

      The name on the table, COURSE, immediately follows "INSERT INTO". The table name must correspond to some previously created table.

2.   Syntax: VALUES Clause

      The VALUES keyword is followed by a pair of parentheses enclosing the values to be placed in the fields of the newly inserted row. The example shows that the values are specified in the COURSE table's default left-to-right column sequence. Each value must comply with the data type of the corresponding column. Apostrophes must be used to enclose character string and date/time values. Numeric values must not be enclosed within apostrophes. Each value must be separated by a comma, which may or may not be followed by one or more spaces.

3.   Recall that the relational model makes no assumptions about the ordering of rows within a table. This simplifies the insertion process because it is not necessary (in fact, it is not possible) to specify where the row actually gets placed in the table. Recall that the ORDER BY clause can be used in a SELECT statement to display rows in any desired sequence.

4.   The previous chapter described the concept of entity integrity. If we assume that CNO is the primary key of the COURSE table and there is a unique index on the CNO column, then an error message indicating the violation of an integrity constraint could occur if the CNO value in the new row equals some existing CNO value.

Format 1:

```
INSERT INTO name-of-table [(col1, col2, ..., colN)]
VALUES (value1, value2, ..., valueN)
```

Format 2:

```
INSERT INTO name-of-table [(col1, col2, ...,colN)]
    subselect-statement
```

Figure 15.1: SQL INSERT statement.

5.   What if a certain value is unknown? For example, determination of a course labfee may require further financial analysis, but it still may be necessary to insert a row for a new course. Sample Statement 15.3 will illustrate the use of the NULL keyword to handle this situation.

6.   You must have permission (recognized by the system) to insert rows into the table. If you created the table, then you automatically have permission to insert rows into it. Otherwise, you must obtain INSERT privileges from the creator of the table. The process of granting privileges is described in Chapter 24.

7.   The current example does not explicitly specify the column names. Therefore, the VALUES clause must contain values for all columns specified in the default left-to-right column sequence. This requires that you know the data type and position of every column in the table. The next example will illustrate a variation of the INSERT statement which allows you to relate a value to a column by explicitly referencing the name of the column.

8.   Inserting date/time values: You need to be careful when inserting date/time information. If you are inserting a date using ORACLE's default date format, then you only need to enclose the date within apostrophes. You can also reference SYSDATE within a VALUES clause.

      INSERT INTO REGISTRATION VALUES
      ('T33', '01', '325', '19-SEP-81')

      INSERT INTO REGISTRATION VALUES
      ('T11', '01', '325', SYSDATE)

      If you want to insert the date using another date format model, or if you want to insert time information with the date, then you must use the TO_DATE function as shown in the following two examples.

      INSERT INTO REGISTRATION VALUES
      ('T33', '01', '150', TO_DATE('09/19/81', 'MM/DD/YY'))

      INSERT INTO REGISTRATION VALUES
      ('T33', '01', '100',
      TO_DATE('09/19/81 01:45', 'MM/DD/YY HH24:MI'))

      It is possible to insert only time information as shown below. However, ORACLE will automatically store the current date with the time information.

      INSERT INTO REGISTRATION VALUES
      ('C55', '01', '325', TO_DATE('01:45', 'HH24:MI'))

Sample Statement 15.2:   Same as previous example. This time specify the column names in the INSERT statement.

```
INSERT INTO COURSE

  (CNO, CNAME, CDESCP, CRED, CLABFEE, CDEPT)

VALUES ('C77', 'INTRODUCTION TO SQL',

      'GOOD STUFF!', 3, 150.00, 'CIS')
```

System Response:

Same as the previous example.

Comment:

The specification of the column names requires extra typing. However, it forces you to confirm your understanding of the columns in the table. The specification of column names also allows for some flexibility. The column names may be specified in any left-to-right sequence as long as the values in the VALUES clause match the same sequence. The following INSERT statements would produce the same result.

```
INSERT INTO COURSE
        (CNAME, CNO, CDESCP, CRED, CLABFEE, CDEPT)
VALUES  ('INTRODUCTION    TO    SQL',    'C77',
        'GOOD STUFF!', 3, 150.00, 'CIS')

INSERT  INTO COURSE
        (CRED, CNAME, CDEPT, CDESCP, CLABFEE, CNO)
VALUES  (3,    'INTRODUCTION   TO   SQL',   'CIS',
        'GOOD STUFF!', 150.00, 'C77')
```

Using this variation of INSERT eliminates the need to know the actual left-to-right sequence of the columns. However, it is still necessary to know the data types of the columns.

Inserting Rows with Unknown Values

The previous INSERT statements specified values for all columns. However, there may be circumstances where some data values are unknown, yet you would still like to insert the row using just the known values. The next two examples illustrate techniques where only some column values are entered for a row. The column for any unknown value will be set to the null value.

Sample Statement 15.3:   Insert a row into the COURSE table with the following information. (Assume the course description, credit, and labfee values are unknown.)

- Course Number: C78
- Course Name: EMBEDDED SQL
- Department: CIS

```
INSERT INTO COURSE VALUES

('C78', 'EMBEDDED SQL', ' ', NULL, NULL, 'CIS')
```

Comments:

1. This example does not specify column names. Therefore, the VALUES clause should indicate all column values in the proper left-to-right sequence. (The absence of explicit column names is the same as naming all the columns.) Because the CRED and CLABFEE values are unknown, their values are specified by using the keyword NULL. The CDESCP value is also unknown, but NULL cannot be specified because NOT NULL was declared in its definition. For this reason, a space (or some other default character) must be specified. Specifying NULL for a column defined with the "NOT NULL" parameter would cause an error.

2. NULL can be used for any data type, not just numeric values as in this example. Also, observe that NULL is not enclosed by apostrophes.

The next example illustrates another technique for inserting a row with just some known values.

Sample Statement 15.4:   Perform the same insert as in the previous example, but explicitly identify the columns for which you are providing information.

```
INSERT INTO COURSE (CNO, CNAME, CDEPT, CDESCP)

VALUES ('C78', 'EMBEDDED SQL', 'CIS', ' ')
```

Comments:

1.   This example specifies the column names and corresponding values of just those columns where the values are known. When column names are explicitly identified, it is not necessary to use the NULL keyword. This is because any unspecified column will be set to a null value, provided that the column has not been defined as NOT NULL. In this case the CRED and CLABFEE values are set to null.

2.   Again, note that the system will not let a column value default to the null value for any column which was defined as NOT NULL. For this reason the CDESCP must receive a value.

Exercises:

15A.   Insert a row into the STAFF table with the following values.

        ENAME: ALAN
        ETITLE: LAB ASSIST
        ESALARY: 3000
        DEPT: CIS

15B.   Insert a row into the STAFF table with the following values.

        ENAME: GEORGE
        DEPT: CIS

The ETITLE and ESALARY values are unknown.

The previous examples illustrated the first format of the INSERT statement which is used to insert exactly one row into a table. The next sample statement illustrates the second format of the INSERT statement which can be used to extract information from one or more rows in a table and use that information to insert one or more rows into another table.

The next sample statement assumes that the CISCOURSE table has been created. (See Exercise 14D.) This table contains columns CISCNO, CISCNAME, CISCRED, and CISCLABFEE, which have the same respective definitions as the CNO, CNAME, CRED, and CLABFEE columns in the COURSE table.

Sample Statement 15.5:   Copy the course number, course name, credits, and labfee for all CIS courses from the COURSE table into the CISCOURSE table.

```
INSERT INTO CISCOURSE

      SELECT CNO, CNAME, CRED, CLABFEE

      FROM    COURSE

      WHERE   CDEPT = 'CIS'
```

Comments:

1.   Syntax: Like previous examples, this example begins with an INSERT clause ("INSERT INTO CISCOURSE"). Unlike previous examples, it does not have a VALUES clause. Instead, the INSERT clause is followed by a "good old SELECT statement" which conforms to the syntax rules presented earlier in this text. Considered in isolation, this SELECT statement is

```
SELECT CNO, CNAME, CRED, CLABFEE
FROM    COURSE
WHERE   CDEPT = 'CIS'
```

A SELECT statement which follows an INSERT clause is called a "subselect" or a "subquery." (Chapters 20 and 21 will examine subqueries placed within other SELECT statements.)

The sequence in which the rows are to be inserted cannot be specified. This means that the ORDER BY clause cannot be used in the subselect.

2. Behavior: The subquery behaves like previous queries. It extracts the CNO, CNAME, CRED, and CLABFEE columns for rows corresponding to the CIS Department. However, this time it does not display the selected data. Instead, the system inserts these data into the CISCOURSE table. The columns of rows selected by the subselect must be compatible with the columns of the CISCOURSE table. Observe that the left-to-right column sequence of the subselect is the same as the columns of the CISCOURSE table. The data types of corresponding columns are the same. If these conditions are not met, the system will reject the insert.

3. This example did not explicitly name the columns of the receiving table. The following INSERT statement is equivalent to the current example.

```
INSERT INTO CISCOURSE
     (CISCNO, CISCNAME, CISCRED, CISCLABFEE)
     SELECT CNO, CNAME, CRED, CLABFEE
     FROM    COURSE
     WHERE   CDEPT = 'CIS'
```

4. ORACLE supports another version of CREATE TABLE which can be used to create a table and load rows from another table in a single statement. If we had not previously created the CISCOURSE table, we could have executed the following statement to achieve this task.

```
CREATE TABLE CISCOURSE
(CISCNO, CISCNAME, CISCRED, CISCLABFEE)
AS SELECT CNO, CNAME, CRED, CLABFEE
    FROM    COURSE
    WHERE   CDEPT = 'CIS'
```

The general syntax for this statement is

```
CREATE TABLE table-name (col1, col2, ..., colN)
AS sub-select-statement
```

5. The COURSE table is unchanged. After execution of the INSERT statement some duplication of data exists in the COURSE and CISCOURSE tables. This is potentially dangerous from a database integrity point of view because any changes to CIS rows in the COURSE table do not automatically carry over into the CISCOURSE table. (If data consistency is desirable, then the view mechanism should be used. Chapter 23 will present the CREATE VIEW statement, which can realize this goal.)

6. Although the CISCOURSE table was empty prior to this insert operation, this is not necessary. If the table already contained rows, the new rows would simply have been appended to the table.

The UPDATE Statement

The UPDATE statement can be used to change any value in a table. It will contain a SET clause to identify which columns are to be changed. And it may include a WHERE clause to identify the rows to be modified. The next sample statement simply changes one value in one row. Sample Statement 15.7 will illustrate how many row and column values can be changed by executing a single UPDATE statement.

Sample Statement 15.6:   Change the labfee for the course with course number "C77" to $175.00.

```
UPDATE COURSE

SET CLABFEE = 175

WHERE CNO = 'C77'
```

System Response:

The system will display a message which indicates (1) a successful update or (2) failure of the update operation due to an error. (Assuming that the update operation is successful, you can further verify the change by displaying the COURSE table.)

Comments:

1.   The keyword "UPDATE" is followed by the name of the table (COURSE) to be changed.

2.   The SET clause, which follows the UPDATE clause, specifies the column(s) to be changed. "SET CLABFEE = 175" means CLABFEE will be set to 175 in the row(s) identified by the WHERE clause. The previous CLABFEE value is lost. It is overlaid by the value of 175. All other column values remain unchanged.

3.   The WHERE clause, which follows the SET clause, identifies the row(s) to be changed. Knowing that CNO is the primary key (and presumably has a unique index) gives us assurance that only the C77 row will be changed.

The previous example simply changed one value in a table. Figure 15.2 outlines the general syntax of the UPDATE statement which shows that the SET clause can reference many columns and the WHERE clause can specify any search condition. Both the SET and WHERE clauses are described below.

SET Clause

The SET clause identifies each column to be changed and specifies the value to be used in making the change. This value can be an expression which is evaluated. The expression can also be a simple constant value, the NULL keyword, or it may involve a subselect. (This last variation of SET will be illustrated in Sample Statement 15.8.) More than one column can be changed in a single UPDATE statement by ending the first expression with a comma and following it with another column and expression.

WHERE Clause

The WHERE clause identifies the row(s) to be changed. The changes made by the SET clause will apply only to the rows which match the condition specified by the WHERE clause. If the WHERE clause identifies multiple rows, then all such rows are updated. The WHERE clause is coded just like a WHERE clause in the SELECT statement. Its syntax is the same and can contain any of the Boolean operators. The WHERE clause can also contain a subselect statement.

The WHERE clause is optional. *However, we emphasize that the absence of a WHERE clause will cause every row in the table to be changed.* For example, if we wanted to change all CISCRED values to 9, we would execute

```
UPDATE CISCOURSE
SET    CISCRED = 9
```

This behavior parallels that of the SELECT statement. The absence of a WHERE clause means that all rows are selected for display. The UPDATE statement without a WHERE clause is used to make a global change to every row in the table.

```
UPDATE name-of-table
   SET name-of-column-1 = expression-1,
       name-of-column-2 = expression-2,
                       .
                       .
                       .
       name-of-column-n = expression-n,
   [WHERE search-condition]
```

Figure 15.2: SQL UPDATE statement.

The next example illustrates the set-level processing of SQL which allows many rows to be updated by execution of a single UPDATE statement.

Sample Statement 15.7:   Make the following changes to any course with a course number beginning with "C7".

- Set the credit value equal to 6
- Increase the labfee by 10%
- Change the description to "THE LANGUAGE OF ORACLE"

```
UPDATE COURSE

SET CRED = 6,

    CLABFEE = CLABFEE * 1.10,

    CDESCP = 'THE LANGUAGE OF ORACLE'

WHERE CNO LIKE 'C7%'
```

Comments:

1.   Previous examples inserted two rows into the COURSE table with course numbers C77 and C78. These are the only courses which match the WHERE condition. Hence, two rows will be changed by the UPDATE statement.

2.   This example changes three columns in each target row. All changes are expressed in a SET clause. Each expression except the final expression is terminated by a comma. If the comma is omitted, an error occurs.

Both the CRED and CDESCP columns are assigned new values in the same manner as in the previous example. The new value assigned to the CLABFEE column is based on the value presently existing in the column. The result of the calculation replaces the existing value.

The next example uses a subselect to obtain the new value to be used in the update operation.

Sample Query 15.8:   Change the labfee value for any course listed in the CISCOURSE table having a course number that begins with "C7". Make the labfee equal to the largest CIS labfee value found in the COURSE table.

```
UPDATE CISCOURSE

SET CLABFEE = (SELECT MAX(CLABFEE)

                FROM    COURSE

                WHERE   CDEPT = 'CIS')

WHERE CNO LIKE 'C7%'
```

Comments:

1.   The expression in the SET clause included a subselect to information stored in the database. When a subselect is used in a SET clause, it must return exactly one row and one column.

2.   The WHERE clause can contain a subselect. The following example will change the credits for any course having a labfee greater than the smallest salary recorded in the STAFF table. There are a number of issues pertaining to subselect statements. These will be described in detail in Chapter 20.

```
        UPDATE CISCOURSE
        SET CRED = 4
        WHERE CLABFEE >
            (SELECT MIN(ESALARY)
             FROM   STAFF)
```

Exercise:

15C. Update the ESALARY value for any staff member assigned to the CIS Department. The new salary for all such individuals is $4000.

The DELETE Statement

The DELETE statement is used to remove an entire row or group of rows from a table. You cannot delete a column or just part of a row.

Sample Statement 15.9:   Delete all rows from the COURSE table which have a course number beginning with "C7". (Remove the two rows previously inserted into the COURSE table.)

```
DELETE

FROM COURSE

WHERE CNO LIKE 'C7%'
```

System Response:

The system responds with a message which (1) confirms successful deletion or (2) rejects the deletion due to an error.

Comments:

1.   Given the current status of the COURSE table, the WHERE clause identifies the C77 and C78 courses for deletion. After deletion of these rows, the contents of the COURSE table becomes the same as it was prior to the execution of the data manipulation examples shown in this chapter.

2.   The general format of the DELETE statement is shown in Figure 15.3. The syntax is simple, but you should be careful to accurately specify the correct rows for deletion.

   The DELETE keyword identifies the operation. The FROM clause is followed by the name of the target table.

The WHERE clause is used to identify the row(s) to be deleted. The search condition has the same structure as that of the SELECT and UPDATE statements. (It can also reference a subselect.) The WHERE clause can be used to identify many rows and is therefore subject to the same accuracy considerations. (The previous example illustrated the set-level processing capabilities of the DELETE by selecting multiple rows for deletion.) Therefore, we again recommend caution in the coding of the WHERE clause to avoid the erroneous deletion of rows. If you want to delete just one row, make certain the WHERE clause identifies the row by the primary key or some other column which has a unique index defined for it.

The WHERE clause is optional. *However, we emphasize that failure to include it will cause every row in the table to be deleted.* For example, the following statement will delete every row in the CISCOURSE table.

        DELETE
        FROM CISCOURSE

Because the WHERE clause is omitted, all rows are deleted from the table. The table will still exist, but will not contain any rows. A subsequent reference to the CISCOURSE table in a SELECT statement would not cause an error, but would not return any rows.

Exercise:

15D. Delete all rows in the STAFF table corresponding to employees assigned to the CIS Department.


```
DELETE
FROM name-of-table
[WHERE search-condition]
```

Figure 15.3: SQL DELETE statement.

Summary

In this chapter we introduced the data manipulation statements of SQL which allow

- The insertion of new rows into a table using the INSERT statement
- The modification of data in existing rows of a table using the UPDATE statement
- The deletion of existing rows from a table using the DELETE statement

These statements may be executed in the interactive environment as demonstrated in this chapter. However, operations which affect the content of the database will usually be performed from within an application program using embedded SQL to ensure greater control and reduce the change of error. In the event that database changes must be made interactively, there are precautionary measures which can be used to prevent a permanent change from being applied to the database until such changes are confirmed. This topic will be addressed in Chapter 24, which presents the concept of transaction processing as implemented by the COMMIT and ROLLBACK statements.

Summary Exercises

15E. Create a table called EXPENSIVE with the columns EXPCNO, EXPCNAME, EXPCLABFEE, and EXPDEPT, which, respectively, have the same data types and lengths as the CNO, CNAME, CLABFEE, and CDEPT columns in the COURSE table. (Do not specify any primary or foreign keys for this table.) Then, for every COURSE table row with a CLABFEE value over $100, copy the column information into the corresponding columns of the EXPENSIVE table.

15F. Update the EXPENSIVE table by subtracting $50 from the EXPCLABFEE column if its current value exceeds $400.

15G. Delete all rows in the EXPENSIVE table which correspond to courses offered by the Theology Department.

15H. Insert a new row into the EXPENSIVE table. The EXPCNO value is "X99", and the EXPDEPT value is "XXX". The EXPCNAME and EXPCLABFEE values are unknown.

15I. Change every EXPCNAME value in the EXPENSIVE table to "JUNK".

15J. Delete all rows from the EXPENSIVE table.

15K. Drop the EXPENSIVE table.

16

Processing Null Values

When we first encountered the STAFF table we observed that the DEPT value for the row describing Da Vinci contained a null value. This value implies that Da Vinci's department is unknown. All the previous sample queries and exercises involving the STAFF table were designed to avoid any potential problems which can result from the presence of null values. This chapter will describe these potential problems and present techniques for handling such problems.

In Chapter 14 we emphasized that the creator of a table should consider using the NOT NULL option to prohibit any database operation from storing null values in a specified column. However, there will be circumstances when values are unknown. Chapter 15 described how the INSERT statement allows a column to be assigned or default to a null value. Unless the designer uses the traditional default approach of using a specific value, typically blank or zero, to represent an unknown value, null values may be present in database tables. When this occurs, the results produced by a SELECT statement may not be what you expect. This is because of the semantic subtleties associated with unknown values. This chapter presents sample queries which illustrate the behavior of the SELECT statement when it encounters null values. You may think that this behavior is unnecessarily complex and may conclude, as others have, that null values are just not worth the trouble. However, null values can occur in ORACLE tables. Therefore, you should understand how to code SELECT statements which process them correctly.

NULLTAB Table

To present sample queries on this topic we digress from our educational database design and introduce a special table which contains a spectrum of null values. The table's name is NULLTAB, and its content is shown in Figure 16.1. We use a hyphen (-) to represent a null value. (A space is the usual default to represent a null value. Using a hyphen to represent a null value presumes we have executed the SET NULL command to change the null value symbol.) In particular, note that NULLTAB has some rows where every value is null. This is most unusual, but is nonetheless valid.

PKEY	COLA	COLB	COLC
1	10	20	5
2	30	30	5
3	160	-	10
4	-	170	5
5	-	-	10
6	10	40	5
7	30	60	5
8	-	-	-
-	-	-	-
-	-	-	-
-	-	-	-

Figure 16.1: **NULLTAB** table.

SET NULL Command

SQL*Plus offers two useful commands when dealing with the display of null values, SHOW NULL and SET NULL. The SHOW NULL command reveals how SQL*Plus will display a null value.

```
SQL> SHOW NULL;
null   "           -"
```

SET NULL allows you to specify a string of characters to represent a null in an output display. If the string contains spaces, you must enclose it in apostrophes. Below are some possible strings and how they affect the display of a null.

```
SET NULL XXXX          Display XXXX for null value
SET NULL '*  *  *'     Display spaces & asterisks for null
SET NULL ''            Display spaces for null
SET NULL '          -' Display hyphen preceded by blanks
                       for null (see Figure 16.1)
```

Calculating with Null Values

Assume you were asked to add 10 to the winning number of tomorrow's Connecticut Million-Dollar Lottery. Unfortunately, today you cannot guarantee to calculate the correct answer. Because the calculation involves at least one unknown value, the result of the calculation is unknown. SQL applies this logic when evaluating an arithmetic expression involving an unknown value. The result is a null value.

Sample Query 16.1:   Calculate the sum and the difference of the COLA and COLB values in NULLTAB.

```
SELECT PKEY, COLA, COLB, COLA+COLB, COLA-COLB

FROM    NULLTAB
```

PKEY	COLA	COLB	COLA+COLB	COLA-COLB
1	10	20	30	-10
2	30	30	60	0
3	160	-	-	-
4	-	170	-	-
5	-	-	-	-
6	10	40	50	-30
7	30	60	90	-30
8	-	-	-	-
-	-	-	-	-
-	-	-	-	-
-	-	-	-	-

Comments:

1.   This example shows that any arithmetic expression will produce a null value if one or more of its operands is a null value.

2.   A null value is shown as a hyphen with preceded by spaces. This is the result of having previously issued a SET NULL command. If you do not use this command to specify a value, ORACLE will be display spaces in place of a null value.

Sample Query 16.2: Find the sum, average, maximum, and minimum values of COLA in NULLTAB.

```
SELECT SUM(COLA), AVG(COLA), MAX(COLA), MIN(COLA)

FROM    NULLTAB
```

SUM(COLA)	AVG(COLA)	MAX(COLA)	MIN(COLA)
240	48	160	10

Comments:

1.   This example shows that group functions ignore nulls in their calculation. These functions do not simply treat an unknown value as zero. If this were the case, the average of column COLA would be 240/11 = 21.82. Instead, the AVG function only used the five known values to determine the result, 240/5 = 48.

2.   We stress the apparent lack of symmetry in the way SQL handles nulls. For group functions, it ignores the null values and produces a nonnull result based on the present known values. But, as Sample Query 16.1 illustrates, the presence of a null value causes an arithmetic expression to evaluate to null.

3.   What if all values passed to a column function are null? Then the result of the function is also null.

In Sample Query 8.5 we noted that the COUNT(*) function counts the number of rows selected without concern for the actual values that are stored in the rows. We now consider the COUNT(column) function.

Sample Query 16.3: How many non-null values are in COLA of the NULLTAB table? Also show the number of rows in the NULLTAB table.

```
SELECT COUNT(COLA), COUNT(*)

FROM    NULLTAB
```

COUNT(COLA)	COUNT(*)
5	11

Comments:

1.   COUNT(COLA) is quite different from COUNT(*). It requests the system to examine the values found in COLA and return the number of non-null values.

2.   How might you calculate the average of the values in COLA? Would you divide the sum of the values by COUNT(*) or by COUNT(COLA)? SUM(COLA) produces 240 (see Sample Query 16.2.), so 240/COUNT(*) = 21.82, while 240/COUNT(COLA) = 48. How is it done by ORACLE? Refer to Sample Query 16.2 to review the output of the AVG(COLA) function.

We stated above that null values are potentially dangerous. The next sample query demonstrates that the previous reasonable behavior of arithmetic expressions and built-in functions may generate confusing results when processing null values.

Sample Query 16.4:   Calculate the overall total of the values found in COLA and COLB. Use two approaches: (1) find the sum of COLA, then the sum of COLB, then add the results; (2) for each row, add the COLA and COLB values, then summarize these row totals.

```
SELECT  SUM(COLA)+SUM(COLB), SUM(COLA+COLB)

FROM    NULLTAB
```

SUM(COLA)+SUM(COLB)   SUM(COLA+COLB)
          560   230

Comment:

Note the different results to two apparently equivalent mathematical expressions. In effect they are only equivalent when all the COLA and COLB values are known. Review Sample Queries 16.1 and 16.2 to confirm your understanding of this example.

Comparing with Null Values

Assume you have $10 in your pocket and you pass a complete stranger on the street. If you were asked to compare your 10 dollars to the presumably unknown amount the stranger has, the result would be unknown. Again, SQL applies the same reasonable logic. When it does a comparison involving at least one null value, the result is null. And again, we will see that this reasonable behavior has potential pitfalls.

Sample Query 16.5:   Display all rows from NULLTAB where the COLA value equals the COLB value.

```
SELECT *

FROM    NULLTAB

WHERE   COLA = COLB
```

PKEY	COLA	COLB	COLC
2	30	30	5

Comments:

This query returned only one row. Consider why the WHERE clause resulted in a "no hit" for the other 10 rows.

1.   Rows corresponding to PKEY values of 1, 6, and 7 have known COLA and COLB values which are not equal to each other. Hence it is clear why they are not selected.

2.   Rows corresponding to PKEY values of 3 and 4 have one null value in either COLA or COLB. Because one value is unknown, the comparison results in a "no hit," and hence these rows are not selected. Note this is the case even though one of the unknown (null) values could possibly be equal to the known value. SQL only selects a row when it is certain that the WHERE condition evaluates to true.

3. Rows corresponding to PKEY values of 5, 8, and null have null values in both COLA and COLB. These rows are not selected. *SQL does not consider two null values to be equal to each other.* This is analogous to trying to deduce whether two complete strangers have the same amount of money in their pockets. The answer is "unknown," not "true." Again, SQL only selects a row when it is certain that the WHERE condition evaluates to "true." To emphasize the point, this means that SQL does not consider "null = null" to be true. (Likewise, "null <> null" is not considered to be true.)

4. The example uses the equals comparison operator. The same logic applies to the other comparison operators. A greater than (>), less-than (<), etc., comparison results in "unknown" if any operand is null. In particular, "null <> null" evaluates to "unknown."

Exercises:

16A. Refer to the FACULTY table for this exercise. Display the average number of dependents and the total number of dependents for all faculty members together with the number of faculty members.

16B. Assume that each faculty member was awarded a $250.00 tuition credit for each dependent. What would be the total remuneration for each faculty member if this amount were added to their salary? In other words, display the total of the salary and $250.00 for each dependent for all faculty members. (Consider Sample Query 16.4 when reviewing your solution.)

16C. Display any row in NULLTAB where the COLA value is not equal to the COLB value. (If you execute this query, observe that only three rows are selected for this display. These correspond to PKEY values 1, 6, and 7. Because Sample Query 16.6 selected only one row, and there are 11 rows in NULLTAB, it might seem that this exercise should produce 10 rows. Why not? See the following sample queries for a discussion of this point.)

The next two examples together show the potential problems with WHERE clauses involving null values.

Sample Query 16.6.1:   How many staff members are assigned to the Theology Department?

```
SELECT COUNT(*)   FROM   STAFF

WHERE   DEPT = 'THEO'
```

COUNT(*)
     4

Comment:

This query selected the four rows corresponding to Matthew, Mark, Luke, and John.

Sample Query 16.6.2:   How many staff members are not assigned to the Theology Department?

```
SELECT COUNT(*)   FROM   STAFF

WHERE   DEPT <> 'THEO'
```

COUNT(*)
     4

Comment:

This query selected the four rows corresponding to Dick Nix, Hank Kiss, Euclid, and Archimedes.

The previous two queries show four members assigned to the Theology Department and four members not assigned to the Theology Department. Can we deduce that we have a total of eight staff members? No! There are nine rows in the STAFF table. Neither of the above queries had a match on the row corresponding to Da Vinci, whose DEPT value is null. In particular, Sample Query 16.6.1 did not select Da Vinci's row because SQL could not conclude that Da Vinci is assigned to the Theology Department. Likewise, Sample Query 16.6.2 did not select Da Vinci's row because SQL concludes that he could be assigned to the Theology Department. The WHERE clause in both sample queries evaluates to "unknown" when considering Da Vinci's row. Again, SQL will select only those rows which evaluate to "true."

These sample queries illustrate the potential danger associated with using a WHERE clause to test for the presence or absence of a given value when a null value can occur. Sample Query 16.11 will introduce the use of "IS NULL" as a means of testing for the presence of a null value. Then, if we assume that a null DEPT value can be interpreted as "not assigned to any department, including the Theology Department," Sample Query 16.6.2 could be expressed as

```
SELECT COUNT (*)
FROM    STAFF
WHERE   DEPT <> 'THEO'
OR      DEPT IS NULL
```

The result of executing this statement is 5. Most users would consider this to be a better answer than 4. However, the choice of which answer is "correct" depends on how you interpret the query objective.

Three-Value Logic

Traditional database systems and traditional computing
languages which manipulate them are based on a system of
two-value logic. This simply means that any comparison will
always result in a "true" or "false" conclusion. The source
of the potential confusion in the aforementioned problems
lies in the fact that null values force the introduction of
a three-value logic system where a comparison reduces to a
"true," "false," or "unknown" result. A three-value logic
system is more complex and requires greater attention in
entering SELECT statements and interpreting the results of a
query.

In Chapter 4 we presented the Boolean operators (AND, OR,
NOT) in the context of the traditional two-value logic.
Figure 16.2 summarizes the behavior of these operators in a
three-value logic system. We do not explain the details of
each comparison except to note that the evaluations of "true"
(T), "false" (F), and "unknown" (U) are consistent with the
notions of AND, OR, and NOT as described earlier. The AND of
two conditions only evaluates to "true" if both conditions
are "true." The OR of two conditions evaluates to "true" if
either or both of the conditions are "true." The NOT of a
"true" condition is "false" and vice versa. The NOT of an
"unknown" condition is "unknown."

```
Logic of NOT:        condition    | T   F   U
                     NOT condition| F   T   U

Logic of AND:        AND | T    F    U
                      T  | T    F    U
                      F  | F    F    F
                      U  | U    F    U

Logic of OR:         OR  | T    F    U
                      T  | T    T    T
                      F  | T    F    U
                      U  | T    U    U
```

Figure 16.2: Boolean operators in a three-value logic system.

Sample Query 16.7:   Display any row from NULLTAB where COLA is equal to COLB, or where COLA is greater than COLC.

```
SELECT *

FROM    NULLTAB

WHERE   COLA = COLB

OR      COLA > COLC
```

PKEY	COLA	COLB	COLC
2	30	30	5
1	10	20	5
7	30	60	5
6	10	40	5
3	160	–	10

Comment:

You should work through the logic of this query to confirm your understanding of the three-way logic.

Sorting Null Values

We begin by noting that ORACLE will place null values at the low end of the sort sequence. The next sample query illustrates this point.

Sample Query 16.8:   Display all rows of NULLTAB in ascending sequence by COLA.

```
SELECT PKEY, COLA

FROM    NULLTAB

ORDER BY COLA
```

PKEY	COLA
6	10
1	10
2	30
7	30
3	160
–	–
–	–
5	–
4	–
8	–
–	–

Comments:

1.   Null values appear at the bottom of the output display because they sort higher than any known value.

2.   This raises another subtle semantic issue. Earlier we emphasized that a comparison involving a null value evaluates to "unknown." However, sorting a collection of values involves comparing them, and, if the system doesn't know a value (because it's null), how does it know where to put it in sequence? This is an apparent contradiction. It is resolved by noting that the displayed row must go somewhere. ORACLE decides to put it at the high end of the sequence. This is an arbitrary decision.

3.   Prior to Version 6, ORACLE placed null values at the low end of the sequence. Users of these earlier versions should take note.

SQL also treats null values like known values when it does internal sorting for the sake of removing duplicate values or forming groups. The next two examples illustrate this point.

Sample Query 16.9: Display the unique values (including null) found in COLA of NULLTAB.

```
SELECT DISTINCT COLA

FROM    NULLTAB
```

COLA
10
30
160
–

Comment:

We emphasize that DISTINCT considers null values equal to each other. Hence only one null value is shown in the result.

Exercise:

16D. Display the name, faculty number, and number of dependents for all faculty members. Arrange the result in descending sequence by the number of dependents.

Sample Query 16.10:   Using the NULLTAB table, form groups of COLC values and display the sum of the COLA values for each group.

```
SELECT COLC, SUM(COLA)

FROM    NULLTAB

GROUP BY COLC
```

COLC	SUM(COLA)
5	80
10	160
–	–

Comment:

We emphasize that SQL treats null values as equal for the purpose of grouping. Hence only one group is formed for the nulls found in COLC. The sum of the COLA values shown in SUM(COLA) for this group is null because all the corresponding COLA values are null and the sum of null values is null.

Exercise:

16E. Display the average salary of faculty members who have the same number of dependents.

Summary of Problems with Null Values

The previous examples presented a number of situations where an unsophisticated user could easily misinterpret the contents of an output display. The general source of the problem is the more complex semantics of a three-value logic. So again we encounter complexity which transcends SQL. To briefly consider the semantics, note that the "null value" is not really a "value" since its purpose is to designate the absence of a value. Sometimes, when performing calculations and comparisons, SQL behaves in a way which is consistent with this "absence of a value" concept. Under other circumstances, for example, when you use ORDER BY, DISTINCT, and GROUP BY features, SQL ends up treating nulls as though they were values.

Avoiding the Complexity of Null Values

The easiest way to avoid the complexity described above is to simply keep nulls out of the database by using the NOT NULL option for every column of every table in the database. Many database designers adopt this approach. However, others say that this is just sweeping the problem under the carpet. The real world presents situations where data are unknown, and our database should reflect this reality. In this case, nulls should be allowed to appear in some columns of some tables. The remaining examples present some SQL techniques for handling null values when they are necessary.

IS NULL

It is possible to explicitly test for the presence of a null value in a row by using "IS NULL" in a WHERE clause.

Sample Query 16.11:   Display any row in NULLTAB which has a null value in COLA.

```
SELECT *

FROM    NULLTAB

WHERE   COLA IS NULL
```

PKEY	COLA	COLB	COLC
-	-	-	-
8	-	-	-
-	-	-	-
5	-	-	10
4	-	170	5
-	-	-	-

Comments:

1.   Only those rows with a null value in COLA are displayed.

2.   You cannot use an equal sign with the NULL predicate. (That is, "WHERE COLA = NULL" does not make any sense. ORACLE will produce the message "no records selected".) You must specify "IS NULL".

Exercise:

16F. Display the names, number of dependents, and department numbers of all faculty members for whom it is not known whether they have any dependents.

IS NOT NULL

The NOT keyword can be used with the NULL predicate. The "IS NOT NULL" phrase is probably more useful than "IS NULL" because it allows you to bypass some of the aforementioned problems by explicitly excluding null values from consideration. The next sample query is a modification of Sample Query 16.4, where null values caused two different summary totals to be displayed.

Sample Query 16.12:   Calculate the overall total of the values found in COLA and COLB. Use two approaches: (1) find the sum of COLA, then the sum of COLB, then add the results; (2) for each row, add the COLA and COLB values, then summarize these row totals. Exclude those rows which have null values in COLA or COLB.

```
SELECT SUM(COLA+COLB),  SUM(COLA)+SUM(COLB)

FROM   NULLTAB

WHERE COLA IS NOT NULL

   AND COLB IS NOT NULL
```

SUM(COLA+COLB)	SUM(COLA)+SUM(COLB)
230	230

Comments:

1.   The WHERE clause eliminated any rows having a null value in COLA or COLB. Hence only five rows were selected and the average was calculated as 240/5 = 48. Most of the time it is a good idea to explicitly exclude null values from mathematical calculations.

2.   Again, the not equal sign cannot be used with the NULL predicate (i.e., "WHERE COLA <> NULL" makes no sense and will not produce a match in ORACLE).

NVL Built-in Function

The SET NULL command can be used to define a value to represent a null value in an output display. In this chapter we used this command to display a hyphen to represent a null value. ORACLE provides a special function, the NVL function, which can be used to designate a specific (presumably more meaningful) value to be displayed for a given SELECT statement. The first argument of the NVL function is a column or an expression which could possibly evaluate to null. The second argument is a (presumably nonnull) value to be substituted in the output display whenever the first argument is actually null.

Sample Query 16.13:   Display NULLTAB as described below.
1.   Display COLC. Substitute 999.99 for any null values.
2.   Display COLB. Substitute the value of COLC whenever the COLB value is null.
3.   Display COLA. Whenever COLA is null, substitute the COLB value. If it is also null, substitute the COLC value.

```
SELECT PKEY, NVL(COLC,999.99),

       NVL(COLB,COLC),

       NVL(COLA,NVL(COLB,COLC))

FROM    NULLTAB
```

PKEY	NVL(COLC,999.99)	NVL(COLB,COLC)	NVL(COLA,NVL(COLB,COLC))
1	5	20	10
2	5	30	30
3	10	10	160
4	5	170	170
5	10	10	10
6	5	40	10
7	5	60	30
8	999.99	-	-
-	999.99	-	-
-	999.99	-	-
-	999.99	-	-

Comments:

1. You are advised to examine the NULLTAB table to verify the value substitutions shown in the output display.

2. The NULLTAB table contains all numeric values. Hence all the substituted values were numeric. Character strings and date values can also be used as arguments in the NVL function. For example, if the CDESCP column in the COURSE table could contain nulls, we could specify

    NVL(CDESCP,'DESCRIPTION UNKNOWN')

    The character string "DESCRIPTION UNKNOWN" would be displayed whenever CDESCP is null.

3. As we saw in Chapter 8, a group function might evaluate to null. For example, applying the SUM function to a column of null values produces a null result. Assume the sum of some COLX could be null. Then you could specify

    NVL(SUM(COLX),0)

    to display a 0 whenever the sum is actually null.

    If only some of the column values were null and we wanted to include these in the function calculation, we could substitute a value such as 0 for each null value. For example

    AVG(NVL(CLABFEE,0))

    would substitute a value of 0 for each null labfee. To understand the effect, we suggest that you review Sample Query 16.3.

NULL Pseudo-column

We conclude this chapter by introducing another ORACLE-specific pseudo-column, NULL, which can be referenced in a SELECT clause. Although it might not appear to be a very useful feature, the following SELECT statement is correct and would produce a column of null values in the output display.

```
SELECT CNO, NULL

FROM COURSE
```

An application of this feature will be shown in Chapter 21.

Summary

This chapter introduced null values. We examined the complexities of dealing with a three-value logic system incorporating the notion of an unknown value. The following major points were discussed:

1. A null "value" does not represent 0 or spaces, but indicates that the value is not known. This results in a three-value logic system. We note that the null value is essentially typeless, and, hence, can represent "unknown value" for any data type.

2. Because we do not have any knowledge about unknown values, two such values can be said to be neither equal nor unequal. The same approach to handling null values is used by ORACLE. This means that one null value is neither equal nor unequal to another. A special syntax is used to examine a column for null values. Rather than using "=" as the comparison operator, we must use "IS NULL" and in the negative sense, "IS NOT NULL".

3. Null values affect the results of computations in both calculated expressions and group built-in functions. Null values do not participate in these operations and therefore may distort the results if you are not aware of their presence.

4. Null values sort higher than any other value when the system is required to order the result.

5. The SET NULL command may be used to specify a string value to be displayed wherever a null value is encountered in the query result. ORACLE will display spaces if you do not use this command to define a value to represent a null value.

6. The NVL function is used in a SELECT statement to identify a specific value to represent a null value.

Summary Exercises

16G. Display the name and department of any staff member who is not assigned to a known department.

16H. For each department, display its department id and the number of all staff members in the department.

V

Accessing Multiple Tables

In this part of the text we return to the task of data retrieval. The following chapters complete our exhaustive examination of the SELECT statement. As you progress through these chapters you will notice a shift in perspective. The logical considerations for most examples presented in Part I of the text were relatively simple. Our primary focus was on the syntax of the SELECT statement. In this part of the text you will find it easy to learn the new syntactical constructs. However, the sample queries and exercises become more complex because you will be required to give more thought to the logical dimension of the query objective. The complexity of these examples will pertain to the "conceptual navigation" required when multiple tables need to be referenced.

Organization of Chapters

Chapter 17 presents the "inner join operation," which is probably the most important topic covered in this part of the book. The join operation is the most useful technique for referencing multiple tables. Many of the sample queries presented in subsequent chapters can also be solved using the join operation.

Chapter 18 presents a powerful and useful feature of ORACLE called the "outer join operation." We shall see that an outer join may reveal more information than an inner join using the same join condition. An appreciation of the power of the outer join operation requires a deeper understanding of the semantics of the data stored in the database.

Chapter 19 introduces the union (UNION), intersection (INTERSECT), and difference (MINUS) operations. These simple operations are very useful. Many reasonable queries could not be expressed if the UNION keyword were missing from SQL. This topic is covered before correlated subqueries because some of the more interesting correlated subquery examples also utilize the union operation.

Chapter 20 introduces subqueries. Most of the sample queries and exercises presented in this chapter can be solved using the inner join operation.

Chapter 21 presents correlated subqueries. These subqueries are important because, unlike those described in Chapter 20, they allow us to solve certain problems which could not be solved using the join operation. The logic of correlated subqueries is different from that of the subqueries presented earlier. This is our rationale for discussing them in a separate chapter.

Chapter 22 presents recursive processing. We introduce ORACLE's special facility for processing tree-structured data. This is a special topic which most users can skip on their first reading or skip entirely.

17

Join Operation

This chapter introduces the join operation, which allows a single SELECT statement to reference columns from more than one table. The join operation allows a query to specify the merging of columns from two or more tables by matching values found in columns from each table. The precise definition of this "merging" and "matching" will be described below. We begin by presenting three queries which could utilize the join operation. This is followed by a detailed explanation of the join operation and a number of sample queries which demonstrate its use.

Query 1:   For every employee who is assigned to some
            existing department, select that person's name,
            title, salary, and department id, along with the
            department building, room location, and department
            chairperson faculty number.

   This query requires that the system display
   1. All columns from the STAFF table
   2. All columns from the DEPARTMENT table (with the possible
      exception of the DEPT column because each value would be
      identical to the DEPT column from the STAFF table)

   This query is based on the fact that some of the DEPT
values in the STAFF table match the DEPT values in the
DEPARTMENT table. Note this query is phrased to exclude
Archimedes and Euclid, who are assigned to nonexistent
departments; and Da Vinci, whose department assignment is
unknown.

Query 2:   For every course with a labfee over $175, display
            the course name and labfee, along with the faculty
            number of the chairperson responsible for the
            course.

   This query requires that the system display
   1. CNAME and CLABFEE from the COURSE table
   2. DCHFNO from the DEPARTMENT table.

   This query presumes that every CDEPT value in the COURSE
table matches some DEPT value in the DEPARTMENT table.

   Observe that neither of the above queries could be
satisfied using the previously described SQL techniques. A
join operation is necessary because the result of each query
contains data from more than one table. However, there are
other reasons for using the join operation. For example, we
might want to display columns from one table, but specify row
selection criteria relative to some other table. Consider the
third query.

Query 3:   Display the name and title of every staff member
           who is known to work in the Humanities Building.

This query displays the ENAME and ETITLE columns, which are
both found in the STAFF table. However, the system must
examine the DEPARTMENT table to determine which departments
are located in the Humanities Building. Only staff members
assigned to these departments will be selected. (Again, the
query is phrased to exclude Archimedes, Euclid, and Da Vinci,
whose DEPT values do not match any DEPT value in the
DEPARTMENT table.)

You could satisfy this query with your current knowledge of
SQL. However, the process would be awkward because you must
execute two independent SELECT statements. The first
statement would determine which departments are located in
the Humanities Building. This is

```
SELECT  DEPT
FROM    DEPARTMENT
WHERE   DBLD = 'HU'
```

The output would identify the "THEO" and "PHIL" values. You
would then use this information to construct the following
SELECT statement.

```
SELECT  ENAME, ETITLE
FROM    STAFF
WHERE   DEPT = 'THEO'
OR      DEPT = 'PHIL'
```

While this approach will work, it is not desirable for a
couple of reasons. The first is that the user must memorize
or write down the intermediate result (THEO and PHIL). This
requires some effort, especially if the intermediate is
large. A second reason why this approach is undesirable is
machine inefficiency. The execution of two separate SELECT
statements is usually more costly than executing a single
equivalent statement.

Each of the previous queries can be satisfied by issuing a
single SELECT statement which implements a join operation.
The following pages explain the important concepts pertaining
to the join operation. After you understand these concepts,
the sample queries will demonstrate that the SQL syntax for
expressing the join operation is relatively straightforward.

Joining Two Tables

From a conceptual point of view, the join of two tables is
the concatenation of rows from the two tables where values
from a column in the first table match values from a column
in the second table. The result of the join operation is a
new table which has a row for each match which occurred
between the original two tables. The original tables remain
unchanged. This is best illustrated by an example.

Figure 17.1 shows two tables, TABLE1 and TABLE2, which will
be joined to form a third table, shown in Figure 17.2. The
first step is to specify the "join column" (match column) for
each table. Column C3 of TABLE1 and column CA of TABLE2 are
specified as the join columns. This means that whenever the
C3 value of a row in TABLE1 is equal to the CA value of a row
in TABLE2, a new row is established in the resulting join
table. This row is formed by concatenating the rows where the
match occurred. We make the following observations about the
join result.

* In TABLE1, the rows with C3 values of 45, 55, and 15 did
  not match any values in column CA of TABLE2. Hence, they do
  not appear in the join result.

* Likewise, in TABLE2, the rows with CA values of 35, 65, and
  75 did not match any values in column C3 of TABLE1. Hence,
  they do not appear in the join result.

* There was one match on the value 10. This produced the
  first row of the join result.

	TABLE1				TABLE2	
C1	C2	C3			CA	CB
A	AAA	10			35	R
B	BBB	45			10	S
C	CCC	55			65	T
D	DDD	20			20	U
E	EEE	20			90	V
F	FFF	90			90	W
G	GGG	15			75	X
H	HHH	90			90	Y
					35	Z

Figure 17.1: Tables to be joined.

* Both of the TABLE1 rows with a C3 value of 20 matched the CA value of 20 in TABLE2. These two matches produced the second and third rows in the join result.

* In TABLE1 there are two rows with a C3 value of 90. Each of these two rows matched the three rows in TABLE2 with CA values of 90. This is a total of six matches for the value of 90. It produced the last six rows of the join result.

Observe that neither of the join columns, CA and C3, is a primary key or a foreign key. Usually a foreign key in one table and its corresponding primary key in another table are specified as the join columns. However, as the example shows, this is not necessary. That is, the system is not bound by the semantics of the data stored in the database. Any columns with comparable data types can be specified as join columns.

Subsequent sample queries will illustrate the syntax of a SELECT statement which implements a join operation. These will show both tables referenced in the FROM clause and the join columns specified in the WHERE clause. The SELECT statement to produce the join result of Figure 17.2 is

```
SELECT *
FROM    TABLE1, TABLE2
WHERE   C3 = CA
```

We will postpone further discussion of syntax until the presentation of this chapter's sample queries. For the moment we return to the more important conceptual considerations.

C1	C2	C3	CA	CB
A	AAA	10	10	S
D	DDD	20	20	U
E	EEE	20	20	U
F	FFF	90	90	V
F	FFF	90	90	W
F	FFF	90	90	Y
H	HHH	90	90	V
H	HHH	90	90	W
H	HHH	90	90	Y

MATCHING
COLUMNS

Figure 17.2: Join result.

To reiterate a previously mentioned point, it is necessary to specify the join columns. We could have joined TABLE1 and TABLE2 on *any* two columns. For example, we could have requested the system to join the tables by matching columns C1 and CB. In this case, no matches would occur, and the result would be an empty table. In most realistic situations we join tables only by matching columns which contain values based on some common set of values. For example, in the COURSE, DEPARTMENT, and STAFF tables of our sample database, we will be matching those columns which contain department id values.

Observe that two extreme results can occur when joining any two tables.

1.   "Empty-Table" Result: This is the case mentioned above where no matches occur.

2.   "Worst-Case" Result: This occurs when every column of the first table matches every column of the second table. Figure 17.3 illustrates this situation. TABLE3 is joined with TABLE4 on columns C2 and CB. Every "X" value in column C2 matches every "X" value in column CB. Because TABLE3 has three rows and TABLE4 has four rows, the join result has 3 * 4 = 12 rows. This is the largest number of rows which could be generated. We call this the "worst case" because it takes more computer time to process a large join result than a small one.

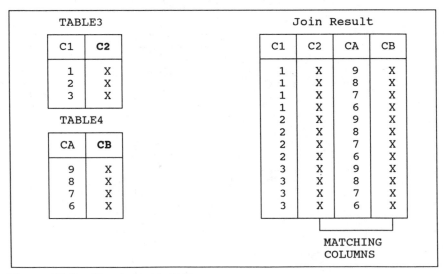

Figure 17.3: "Worst-case" join.

Nulls in the Join Columns

The preceding examples referenced tables which did not contain null values. Recall that null means "value unknown." Therefore, a null cannot match with any other value; it does not even match another null value. Figure 17.4 shows TABLE1A and TABLE2A. These tables are similar to TABLE1 and TABLE2 except that nulls have replaced some values. The result of joining TABLE1A and TABLE2A on columns C3 and CA is shown in Figure 17.5. We make the following observations.

* The non-null values match (or didn't match) in the same way as occurred in the join of the original TABLE1 and TABLE2.
* The null values in the join columns did not match with any other values. In particular, note that the null values in the last row of each table did not match with each other.
* The only null value which appears in the join result is the null which is present in column CB. This is not a join column; hence, it is treated like any other data value.

A final comment before turning to the sample queries. The term "match" is not very precise. In this chapter it means "equal to." From a formal point of view, the join operation described thus far is called "equi-join." This is the most common join operation used in practice. The SQL language allows for other types of joins where the join condition can include any of the comparison operators. These other join operations will be introduced in Sample Query 17.13.

TABLE1A				TABLE2A	
C1	C2	C3	<—⊤—>	CA	CB
A	AAA	10	Join	35	R
B	BBB	45	Columns	10	–
C	CCC	55		65	T
D	DDD	20		20	U
E	EEE	20		90	V
F	FFF	90		90	W
G	GGG	15		75	X
H	HHH	–		90	Y
				–	Z

Figure 17.4: Nulls in join columns.

C1	C2	C3	CA	CB
A	AAA	10	10	–
D	DDD	20	20	U
E	EEE	20	20	U
F	FFF	90	90	V
F	FFF	90	90	W
F	FFF	90	90	Y

MATCHING COLUMNS

Figure 17.5: Join of TABLE1A and TABLE2A.

Join STAFF and DEPARTMENT Tables

The first sample query involving a join operation will join
the STAFF and DEPARTMENT tables. The semantic relationship
which justifies this join is the "employee works in
department" relationship. The match is based on join columns
which happen to have the same name (DEPT). Although this
query itself is not very realistic, it serves the purpose of
illustrating a pure equi-join.

Sample Query 17.1:   For all staff members assigned to
existing departments, select all
information about the staff members and
their respective departments.

```
SELECT *

FROM    STAFF, DEPARTMENT

WHERE   STAFF.DEPT = DEPARTMENT.DEPT
```

ENAME	ETITLE	ESALARY	DEPT	DEPT	DBLD	DROOM	DCHFNO
HANK KISS	JESTER	25000	PHIL	PHIL	HU	100	60
DICK NIX	CROOK	25001	PHIL	PHIL	HU	100	60
MATTHEW	EVANGLIST1	51	THEO	THEO	HU	200	10
MARK	EVANGLIST2	52	THEO	THEO	HU	200	10
LUKE	EVANGLIST3	53	THEO	THEO	HU	200	10
JOHN	EVANGLIST4	54	THEO	THEO	HU	200	10

Comments:

1.   Logic:

Confirm your understanding of the join operation by
observing that both DEPT columns have equal values. Also
note that the STAFF and DEPARTMENT rows do not appear in
the join result. STAFF rows corresponding to EUCLID,
ARCHIMEDES, and DA VINCI did not match on DEPT values;
likewise, the MGT row from the DEPARTMENT table is
absent for the same reason.

2.   Syntax:

FROM clause:

The logic of the query requires that data be extracted
from two tables. Therefore, both tables are referenced
in the FROM clause. The table names must be separated by
a comma. The table names can be specified in any order.
A complex query could involve more than two tables. The
general rule is simple: If the query references any
column of a table, the name of the table must be
included in the FROM clause. (See Sample Query 17.9,
which illustrates the join of three tables.)

WHERE clause:

The join columns are specified in the WHERE clause. The
match is effected by specifying that the two join
columns are equal. Our sample query illustrates

       WHERE STAFF.DEPT = DEPARTMENT.DEPT

This condition is called a "join condition." Note that
the column names are qualified. Qualification is
required in this statement because both the join columns
have the same name (DEPT). An error would occur if the
join column names were not qualified.

SELECT clause:

The "SELECT *" means the same as in previous queries. In
this example, the system will display all columns in the
join result. Since the FROM clause references STAFF
before DEPARTMENT, the columns of the STAFF table are
displayed first (to the left of the DEPARTMENT table
columns).

Observe that the result displays both DEPT columns which
have the same values. In practice, we would not display
redundant columns. We would identify just those columns
we want displayed. See the next sample query.

Displaying a Subset of the Join Result

We rarely want to see all rows and columns of a join result. For example, the previous equi-join result showed duplicate DEPT columns which are completely redundant. Usually our intention is to display only some of the row and column data present in the join result. This objective is achieved by applying previously described row and column selection techniques to the intermediate table produced as the result of the join operation. The next sample query shows that the syntax is the same as with previous queries that referenced just one table. The only difference is conceptual. The row and column selection criteria apply to the intermediate table produced as a result of the join operation.

Sample Query 17.2:   Display the name, salary, department identifier, and building and room location for every staff member assigned to an existing department whose yearly salary exceeds $1000.

```
SELECT  ENAME, ESALARY, STAFF.DEPT,

        DBLD, DROOM

FROM    STAFF, DEPARTMENT

WHERE   STAFF.DEPT = DEPARTMENT.DEPT

AND     ESALARY > 1000
```

ENAME	ESALARY	DEPT	DBLD	DROOM
HANK KISS	25000	PHIL	HU	100
DICK NIX	25001	PHIL	HU	100

Comments:

1. Logic:

    Any query which involves a join requires that the user really understand the meaning of the data items. This is especially true of the relationships between the tables as reflected by the join columns. Consider the following semantic assumptions implicit in the SQL code for the current sample query.

    * Staff members always work in the same building and room where their department is located. (Is it possible for a staff member to work in a building other than the department's location?) We must confirm that department location and staff work location are the same thing.

    * We are not interested in information about staff members who are not assigned to existing departments. Rows corresponding to these staff members are "flushed out" by the join operation.

    These issues are logical. They transcend the SQL language. They must be addressed by the database administrator during the process of database analysis and design. This is beyond the scope of this text. However, it is mandatory that users properly interpret the meaning of the data and relationships implicit in the database design.

    The current sample query illustrates that there are potential pitfalls even with a simple database. Throughout the remainder of this text we will assume that the semantics of the sample queries are correct. This is necessary to focus on the SQL code and to avoid a long digression into issues of database analysis and design.

2. Syntax:

    (1) The FROM clause and join condition are identical to the previous sample query. This is

        FROM STAFF, DEPARTMENT
        WHERE STAFF.DEPT = DEPARTMENT.DEPT

(2)   As mentioned above, there is no syntax change just because we are working with an intermediate join result.

*   We want only some rows. These rows correspond to staff members whose salary exceeds $1000. This implies that another condition should be appended to the join condition. This is

AND ESALARY > 1000

*   We want only some columns. These are explicitly named in the SELECT clause. Columns from different tables can be specified because the columns are selected from the join result. Thus, we have

SELECT ENAME, ESALARY, STAFF.DEPT, DBLD, DROOM

Qualification of the DEPT column is necessary. We may understand that both DEPT columns in the join result are identical, but ORACLE does not. If DEPT is not qualified, an error will occur. Either table name may be used as the qualifier. The following SELECT clause will produce the same result.

SELECT ENAME, ESALARY, DEPARTMENT.DEPT, DBLD, DROOM

3.   Physical Efficiency:

Earlier we identified the "worst-case" situation where all the join columns match with each other. When we consider that we usually want just some subset of rows and columns from the join result, it seems that the system could incur the cost of generating a large intermediate join result. This is not necessarily the case. ORACLE has an internal software module called an "optimizer" which can usually avoid this effort. In fact, the "AND ESALARY > 1000" clause will help the optimizer. From a user's point of view, only two comments are necessary.

a.   Don't worry about efficiency. That is the job of the optimizer. It is intelligent enough to avoid the unnecessary generation of a large intermediate join result.

b.   Even though the system may not generate the actual join table, it is helpful for you to think that it does. This can simplify your thought process as described below.

4.   Mental Steps:

There are three basic steps which you can follow when you need to reference multiple tables.

a.   Join the Tables:

Determine the tables to be joined and their respective join columns. Then construct the FROM clause and the join condition. In the current example, this leads to

```
FROM  STAFF, DEPARTMENT
WHERE STAFF.DEPT = DEPARTMENT.DEPT
```

b.   Specify the Desired Columns:

Construct the SELECT clause which identifies the columns that you want displayed. Don't forget any necessary qualification. In the current example, this yields

```
SELECT ENAME, ESALARY, STAFF.DEPT, DBLD, DROOM
```

c.   Specify the Desired Rows:

Use the AND connector to append other selection criteria to extract the desired rows from the join result. In the current example, this is

```
AND ESALARY > 1000
```

These pieces of code are put together in the standard order of

```
SELECT  ---------
FROM    ---------
WHERE   ---------
AND     ---------
```

You are encouraged to apply these mental steps to future workshop exercises.

Join Based on Primary Key and Foreign Key Values

The next sample query joins the COURSE and DEPARTMENT tables. The semantic relationship which justifies this join is the "course is offered by department" relationship. This example reflects a typical situation where the join operation matches the *foreign key* of the referencing table (CDEPT in COURSE) with the *primary key* of the referenced table (DEPT in DEPARTMENT). The notion of referential integrity tells us that *because every CDEPT value will be equal to some DEPT value, we can expect every row of the COURSE table to be present in the intermediate join result.*

Sample Query 17.3:   For every course with a labfee over 175 dollars, display the course name, labfee, and faculty number of the chairperson responsible for the course. Display the output by course name in ascending sequence.

```
SELECT CNAME, CLABFEE, DCHFNO

FROM    COURSE, DEPARTMENT

WHERE   CDEPT = DEPT

AND     CLABFEE > 175

ORDER BY CNAME
```

CNAME	CLABFEE	DCHFNO
COMMUNISM	200.00	10
EXISTENTIALISM	200.00	60
RELATIONAL DATABASE	500.00	80

Comments:

1. The course name and labfee are stored in the COURSE
    table, and the chairperson's faculty number is stored in
    the DEPARTMENT table. The join columns are CDEPT in the
    COURSE table and the DEPT column in the DEPARTMENT
    table. Hence, the example shows

        FROM   COURSE, DEPARTMENT
        WHERE CDEPT = DEPT

    Note that, unlike the previous two examples,
    qualification of column names is unnecessary. The join
    columns have distinct names, so there is no possible
    ambiguity. We could have used qualified names for the
    purpose of documentation. Then the WHERE clause would be

        WHERE COURSE.CDEPT = DEPARTMENT.DEPT

2. Unlike previous sample queries, neither of the two join
    columns, CDEPT and DEPT, is referenced in the SELECT
    clause. It is not necessary to display join columns.

3. Sorting the result implies use of the ORDER BY clause.
    Any column(s) from either table can be specified. All
    the variations of the ORDER BY clause, described in
    Chapter 3, apply.

The next sample query displays columns from just one table (STAFF). This is not unusual. The purpose of the join is to permit row selection based on information found in a second table (DEPARTMENT).

Sample Query 17.4:   Display the name and title of every staff member who works in the Humanities Building.

```
SELECT ENAME, ETITLE

FROM    STAFF, DEPARTMENT

WHERE   STAFF.DEPT = DEPARTMENT.DEPT

AND     DBLD = 'HU'
```

ENAME	ETITLE
HANK KISS	JESTER
DICK NIX	CROOK
MATTHEW	EVANGLIST1
MARK	EVANGLIST2
LUKE	EVANGLIST3
JOHN	EVANGLIST4

Comments:

1.   Observe that both of the displayed columns are located in the STAFF table. The join operation is necessary to determine which departments are located in the Humanities Building.

2.   Sample Query 20.8 will illustrate an alternative solution to this problem. It will show a "nested subquery" solution which can be applied only because all the displayed columns come from a single table. This point will be emphasized in Chapter 20 when we introduce nested subqueries.

Recall that displaying just some columns of a table can produce an output display with duplicate rows. (The DISTINCT keyword was used to remove this duplication.) The next example shows that duplicate rows can occur in a result produced by a join operation.

Sample Query 17.5:   Where can I find an evangelist? More precisely, display the building and room of any academic department which employs a staff member whose title begins with "EVANGLIST".

```
SELECT DBLD, DROOM

FROM    DEPARTMENT, STAFF

WHERE   DEPARTMENT.DEPT = STAFF.DEPT

AND     ETITLE LIKE 'EVANGLIST_'
```

DBLD	DROOM
HU	200
HU	200
HU	200
HU	200

Comment:

Because all four evangelists reside in the same room of the same building, the output display contains four duplicate rows. Duplicate rows can be removed from the output display by including DISTINCT in the SELECT clause. We rewrite the example including the DISTINCT keyword.

```
SELECT DISTINCT DBLD, DROOM
FROM    DEPARTMENT, STAFF
WHERE   DEPARTMENT.DEPT = STAFF.DEPT
AND     ETITLE LIKE 'EVANGLIST_'
```

Exercises:

17A. Display the equi-join of the COURSE and DEPARTMENT tables where the join operation matches the CDEPT values in COURSE with the DEPT values in DEPARTMENT.

17B. The "natural join" of the two tables is the same as the equi-join except that one of the duplicate columns present in the equi-join is not displayed. Modify the previous exercise so that it produces the natural join of the COURSE and DEPARTMENT tables based on the CDEPT and DEPT columns. (You can display either the CDEPT column or the DEPT column from the join result, but not both columns.)

17C. For each course with a labfee over $100, display the course name and its labfee along with the faculty number of the chairperson of the department which offers the course.

17D. Display the course number and name of any course which is offered by a department chaired by the person having the faculty number of 60. Display the output result in descending sequence by course number.

17E. Display the name and salary of any staff member assigned to a department which is located in the Science Building.

17F. For any staff member who is assigned to an existing department and whose salary exceeds $200, display the building and room location of the staff member. The output should not display any duplicate rows.

Previous sample queries illustrated the use of familiar techniques to display a given row-column subset of a join result. We also saw that the DISTINCT keyword and ORDER BY clause apply. In fact, there do not exist any special display restrictions specific to a join result. You can treat a join result like any other table. In particular, you can perform calculations with a join result. The next three sample queries illustrate some of the computational techniques originally presented in Chapters 7 and 8. This time the techniques are applied to intermediate join results.

Sample Query 17.6:   What is the total salary of staff members who work in Room 100 of the Humanities Building?

```
SELECT  SUM (ESALARY)

FROM    DEPARTMENT, STAFF

WHERE   DEPARTMENT.DEPT = STAFF.DEPT

AND     DBLD = 'HU'

AND     DROOM = '100'
```

SUM(ESALARY)
       50001

Comments:

1.   There is really nothing new in this example. The FROM and WHERE clauses identify the join operation and row selection criteria. The SUM function is then applied to the ESALARY column. As usual, a group built-in function compresses the displayed output to a single row.

2.   All the SQL built-in functions described in Part III of this text apply. The function arguments may be any of the columns in the intermediate join result.

The next sample query joins the COURSE and STAFF tables. The semantic relationship which justifies this join is the "employee works in the department which offers the course" relationship. The join columns are CDEPT and DEPT, both of which contain department id values.

Note that the semantics of this relationship is more complex than the previously described "employee works in department" and "course is offered by department" relationships. This is because courses and employees are only indirectly related via the aforementioned direct relationships with a department. Proper understanding of the next sample query requires that you comprehend these relationships and further assumptions specified below.

Assume that any staff member employed by an existing department is available and qualified to serve as tutor for any course offered by the department. Staff members not assigned to existing departments are not required to tutor. If a given department does not offer courses or does not have any staff members assigned to it, then that department does not offer tutoring services. Some of the following sample queries are based on these assumptions.

Sample Query 17.7:   Display the name and salary for every staff member who has tutoring responsibilities, along with the course number and credits of any course he can tutor. Also, display the ratio of salary to credits for each staff member and course combination. Sort the output by course number within staff member name.

```
SELECT ENAME, ESALARY, CNO, CRED, ESALARY/CRED

FROM    STAFF, COURSE

WHERE   DEPT = CDEPT

ORDER BY ENAME, CNO
```

ENAME	ESALARY	CNO	CRED	ESALARY/CRED
DICK NIX	25001	P11	3	8333.66667
DICK NIX	25001	P22	3	8333.66667
DICK NIX	25001	P33	3	8333.66667
DICK NIX	25001	P44	6	4166.83333
HANK KISS	25000	P11	3	8333.33333
HANK KISS	25000	P22	3	8333.33333
HANK KISS	25000	P33	3	8333.33333
HANK KISS	25000	P44	6	4166.66667
JOHN	54	T11	3	18
JOHN	54	T12	3	18
JOHN	54	T33	3	18
JOHN	54	T44	6	9
LUKE	53	T11	3	17.6666667
LUKE	53	T12	3	17.6666667
LUKE	53	T33	3	17.6666667
LUKE	53	T44	6	8.83333333
MARK	52	T11	3	17.3333333
MARK	52	T12	3	17.3333333
MARK	52	T33	3	17.3333333
MARK	52	T44	6	8.66666667
MATTHEW	51	T11	3	17
MATTHEW	51	T12	3	17
MATTHEW	51	T33	3	17
MATTHEW	51	T44	6	8.5

Comments:

1. This example illustrates the generation of a column containing calculated values. This is the rightmost column produced by dividing ESALARY by CRED. The fact that these two columns come from different tables is incidental. They are both present in the intermediate join result and hence can be referenced in the expression to calculate the ratio.

2. The column showing the calculated result is processed and displayed according to the rules for arithmetic expressions presented in Chapter 7.

The next sample query demonstrates grouping within the context of a join operation.

Sample Query 17.8:   For every department which offers tutoring services, display the department id along with the average labfee of the courses it offers and the average salary of staff members who can tutor such courses. Sort the output by department id.

```
SELECT DEPT, AVG(CLABFEE), AVG(ESALARY)

FROM    STAFF, COURSE

WHERE   DEPT = CDEPT

GROUP BY DEPT

ORDER BY DEPT
```

DEPT	AVG(CLABFEE)	AVG(ESALARY)
PHIL	87.5	25000.5
THEO	110	52.5

Comments:

1.   Again, there is nothing new in this example. The example merely demonstrates the GROUP BY clause with values present in an intermediate join result. All previously specified rules pertaining to grouping must apply. (See Chapter 8.)

2.   The summary output of this example confirms our earlier observations regarding the content of the sample tables. Only the Philosophy and Theology Departments offer courses and have staff members assigned to them. Hence, only these departments appear in the output display.

Exercises:

17G. Display the smallest and largest labfees associated with any course offered by a department located in the Science Building.

17H. How many staff members are assigned to existing departments (i.e., those departments described in the DEPARTMENT table)?

17I. If a staff member can tutor a course, and the labfee for the course exceeds his salary by at least $52, then display the staff member's name and salary along with the course labfee and the difference between the labfee and the salary.

17J. For each department which employs staff members, display the department id followed by the total staff salary and average staff salary for the department.

17K. For those courses which have staff members available as tutors, display the course name followed by the number of available tutors for the course.

17L. Display the department id of any department described in the DEPARTMENT table which employs at least three staff members.

17M. For each department described in the DEPARTMENT table which employs at least one staff member, display the department id followed by the number of staff members assigned to the department.

Join of Three Tables

The next sample query requires the join of three tables.
Again, we rely on the previous assumptions about staff
members tutoring courses offered by their departments.

Sample Query 17.9:   For any course which has a staff member
available to tutor students, display its
number, the names and titles of the
staff members who can serve as a tutor
for the course, and their respective
building and room locations. Sort the
output by staff member name within
course number.

```
SELECT CNO, ENAME, ETITLE, DBLD, DROOM

FROM    COURSE, STAFF, DEPARTMENT

WHERE   CDEPT = STAFF.DEPT

AND     CDEPT = DEPARTMENT.DEPT

ORDER BY CNO, ENAME
```

CNO	ENAME	ETITLE	DBLD	DROOM
P11	DICK NIX	CROOK	HU	100
P11	HANK KISS	JESTER	HU	100
P22	DICK NIX	CROOK	HU	100
P22	HANK KISS	JESTER	HU	100
P33	DICK NIX	CROOK	HU	100
P33	HANK KISS	JESTER	HU	100
P44	DICK NIX	CROOK	HU	100
P44	HANK KISS	JESTER	HU	100
T11	JOHN	EVANGLIST4	HU	200
T11	LUKE	EVANGLIST3	HU	200
T11	MARK	EVANGLIST2	HU	200
T11	MATTHEW	EVANGLIST1	HU	200
T12	JOHN	EVANGLIST4	HU	200
T12	LUKE	EVANGLIST3	HU	200
T12	MARK	EVANGLIST2	HU	200
T12	MATTHEW	EVANGLIST1	HU	200
T33	JOHN	EVANGLIST4	HU	200
T33	LUKE	EVANGLIST3	HU	200
T33	MARK	EVANGLIST2	HU	200
T33	MATTHEW	EVANGLIST1	HU	200
T44	JOHN	EVANGLIST4	HU	200
T44	LUKE	EVANGLIST3	HU	200
T44	MARK	EVANGLIST2	HU	200
T44	MATTHEW	EVANGLIST1	HU	200

Comments:

1. It is necessary to display CNO (from the COURSE table), ENAME and ETITLE (from the STAFF table), and DBLD and DROOM (from the DEPARTMENT table). This requires the join of three tables based on columns containing the department identifiers.

2. A join of three tables requires two join conditions. The COURSE and STAFF tables are joined by

    WHERE CDEPT = STAFF.DEPT

    and the COURSE and DEPARTMENT tables are joined by

    AND CDEPT = DEPARTMENT.DEPT

3. The system behaves as follows.

    a. It joins two tables to establish an intermediate join result. If the first two tables are the COURSE and STAFF tables, COURSE rows corresponding to the CIS courses, and STAFF rows for staff with "ENG," "MATH" and null values in the DEPT column will not match. They will not be part of the intermediate join result. Hence, they will not appear in the final result.

    b. If the next join operation is based on the condition "CDEPT = DEPARTMENT.DEPT", the system will join the DEPARTMENT table with the previous intermediate result (not just the COURSE table as the code might indicate). Here the row for the MGT department will not match any value in the intermediate result. Hence it will not appear in the final result.

    Item a above stated, "If the first two tables are the COURSE and STAFF tables." We said "If" because the system may, for reasons of efficiency, initially choose to join the COURSE and DEPARTMENT tables to establish an intermediate join result. Then it would join the STAFF table to the intermediate result. The result would be the same.

Cross Product

The next example has a FROM clause which refers to two tables, but there is no WHERE clause specifying a join condition. Usually someone writes such a statement by accident. They intend to perform a regular join operation, but forget to include the join condition. Then they are surprised by the large number of rows displayed. What they get is known as the "cross product" or the "Cartesian product" where every row of the first table is paired with every row of the second table. This occurs because the join condition, which restricts the join result to matching values, is not present.

Sample Query 17.10:   Form the Cross Product of the STAFF table and the DEPARTMENT table.

```
SELECT *

FROM STAFF, DEPARTMENT
```

Comments:

1.   Observe that the columns of the STAFF table are displayed to the left of the columns of the DEPARTMENT table. This is because "STAFF" was referenced before "DEPARTMENT" in the FROM clause. The following statement would result in the DEPARTMENT columns being displayed to the left of STAFF columns.

```
SELECT *
FROM   DEPARTMENT, STAFF
```

2.   The cross product coincides with the "worst-case" join situation described earlier. The number of rows generated could be very large. For example, if two tables each had one thousand rows, their cross product would have one million rows. As indicated above, users rarely need a cross product. However, there are occasions when this operation is useful.

3.   We presume that the following SQL*Plus SET command has been previously executed, resulting in a null value being displayed as a hyphen.

```
SET NULL "-"
```

ENAME	ETITLE	ESALARY	DEPT	DEPT	DBLD	DROOM	DCHFNO
HANK KISS	JESTER	25000	PHIL	THEO	HU	200	10
DICK NIX	CROOK	25001	PHIL	THEO	HU	200	10
MATTHEW	EVANGLIST1	51	THEO	THEO	HU	200	10
MARK	EVANGLIST2	52	THEO	THEO	HU	200	10
LUKE	EVANGLIST3	53	THEO	THEO	HU	200	10
JOHN	EVANGLIST4	54	THEO	THEO	HU	200	10
DA VINCI	LAB ASSIST	500	-	THEO	HU	200	10
EUCLID	LAB ASSIST	1000	MATH	THEO	HU	200	10
ARCHIMEDES	LAB ASSIST	200	ENG	THEO	HU	200	10
HANK KISS	JESTER	25000	PHIL	MGT	SC	100	-
DICK NIX	CROOK	25001	PHIL	MGT	SC	100	-
MATTHEW	EVANGLIST1	51	THEO	MGT	SC	100	-
MARK	EVANGLIST2	52	THEO	MGT	SC	100	-
LUKE	EVANGLIST3	53	THEO	MGT	SC	100	-
JOHN	EVANGLIST4	54	THEO	MGT	SC	100	-
DA VINCI	LAB ASSIST	500	-	MGT	HU	100	-
EUCLID	LAB ASSIST	1000	MATH	MGT	HU	100	-
ARCHIMEDES	LAB ASSIST	200	ENG	MGT	HU	100	-
HANK KISS	JESTER	25000	PHIL	CIS	SC	300	80
DICK NIX	CROOK	25001	PHIL	CIS	SC	300	80
MATTHEW	EVANGLIST1	51	THEO	CIS	SC	300	80
MARK	EVANGLIST2	52	THEO	CIS	SC	300	80
LUKE	EVANGLIST3	53	THEO	CIS	SC	300	80
JOHN	EVANGLIST4	54	THEO	CIS	SC	300	80
DA VINCI	LAB ASSIST	500	-	CIS	SC	300	80
EUCLID	LAB ASSIST	1000	MATH	CIS	SC	300	80
ARCHIMEDES	LAB ASSIST	200	ENG	CIS	SC	300	80
HANK KISS	JESTER	25000	PHIL	PHIL	HU	100	60
DICK NIX	CROOK	25001	PHIL	PHIL	HU	100	60
MATTHEW	EVANGLIST1	51	THEO	PHIL	HU	100	60
MARK	EVANGLIST2	52	THEO	PHIL	HU	100	60
LUKE	EVANGLIST3	53	THEO	PHIL	HU	100	60
JOHN	EVANGLIST4	54	THEO	PHIL	HU	100	60
DA VINCI	LAB ASSIST	500	-	PHIL	HU	100	60
EUCLID	LAB ASSIST	1000	MATH	PHIL	HU	100	60
ARCHIMEDES	LAB ASSIST	200	ENG	PHIL	HU	100	60

Joining a Table with Itself

All previous join operations involved two or more *different*
tables. The next example illustrates that a table can be
joined with itself. The SQL technique involves the use of a
"table alias" for a table name. In this case, we assign the
STAFF table two distinct aliases, which allows us to think of
and reference this single table as two distinct tables. An
alias is assigned to a table by placing it after the table
name in the FROM clause. The following example assigns two
aliases, ST1 and ST2, to the STAFF table. Then all reference
to columns of the conceptually distinct STAFF tables is done
by using the alias names for qualification.

   *The solution to this sample query is intentionally
incomplete.* There is a considerable amount of redundant
information in the output. Our intention is to show the
matching of values which occurs when a table is joined with
itself. Sample Query 17.12 will present a more precise
solution which does not display redundant information.

Sample Query 17.11:   For each department referenced in the
STAFF table, we would like to form a
committee composed of two staff members
from the department. For each possible
pair of staff members, display the
department id followed by the names of
two staff members. The result should
contain a row for every possible pair
of staff members.

```
SELECT ST1.DEPT, ST1.ENAME, ST2.ENAME

FROM    STAFF ST1, STAFF ST2

WHERE   ST1.DEPT = ST2.DEPT
```

DEPT	ENAME	ENAME
ENG	ARCHIMEDES	ARCHIMEDES
MATH	EUCLID	EUCLID
PHIL	DICK NIX	DICK NIX
PHIL	DICK NIX	HANK KISS
PHIL	HANK KISS	DICK NIX
PHIL	HANK KISS	HANK KISS
THEO	JOHN	JOHN
THEO	JOHN	LUKE
THEO	JOHN	MARK
THEO	JOHN	MATTHEW
THEO	LUKE	JOHN
THEO	LUKE	LUKE
THEO	LUKE	MARK
THEO	LUKE	MATTHEW
THEO	MARK	JOHN
THEO	MARK	LUKE
THEO	MARK	MARK
THEO	MARK	MATTHEW
THEO	MATTHEW	JOHN
THEO	MATTHEW	LUKE
THEO	MATTHEW	MARK
THEO	MATTHEW	MATTHEW

Comments:

1.   Syntax:

   A table alias is placed after the table name in the FROM
   clause. One or more spaces must separate the table name
   from its alias. (Note that a comma should not be used to
   separate a table name from its alias. The separator
   comma follows the alias.)

   A "table alias" is sometimes called a "correlation
   variable." We will have more to say about correlation
   variables in Chapter 21.

2.   Logic:

   After defining aliases in the FROM clause, we can
   conceptually operate under the assumption that there are
   two distinct tables with the names of ST1 and ST2, both
   of which happen to have the same data as the STAFF
   table. (The system does not actually make two copies of
   the STAFF table. Our discussion of correlation variables
   in Chapter 21 will provide more insight into the actual
   process.) The WHERE clause specifies a join condition
   which joins the ST1 and ST2 "tables" by matching each of
   their DEPT columns.

   Observe the duplication of information present in the
   result. This is less than desirable. Because every staff
   member's name and department id is in both ST1 and ST2,
   each row in ST1 matches with its corresponding row in
   ST2. Therefore, every staff member appears on the same
   committee with himself. In particular, ARCHIMEDES, who
   is the only staff member with "ENG" as a department id,
   can be on a committee with only himself. (Likewise for
   EUCLID.) Also, if MARK is in the same department as
   JOHN, then JOHN is in the same department as MARK. This
   means that the result table will show two rows for each
   match of different staff members assigned to the same
   department. The joining of a table with itself produces
   these matches. The solution to the next sample query
   presents a trick to eliminate these undesirable rows
   from the result.

3.   Do not confuse a table alias (correlation variable) with
   a synonym. Synonyms are established with the CREATE
   SYNONYM statement and remain in effect until explicitly
   dropped. A table alias is temporary. It is in effect
   only while the query is being executed.

Sample Query 17.12:   Refine the previous sample query. For each department id referenced at least twice in the STAFF table, display a row for each possible combination of *distinct* staff member names. The row should contain the department id followed by staff member names.

```
SELECT  ST1.DEPT, ST1.ENAME, ST2.ENAME

FROM    STAFF ST1, STAFF ST2

WHERE   ST1.DEPT = ST2.DEPT

AND     ST1.ENAME < ST2.ENAME
```

DEPT	ENAME	ENAME
PHIL	DICK NIX	HANK KISS
THEO	JOHN	LUKE
THEO	JOHN	MARK
THEO	JOHN	MATTHEW
THEO	LUKE	MARK
THEO	LUKE	MATTHEW
THEO	MARK	MATTHEW

Comment:

The additional condition (ST1.ENAME < ST2.ENAME) removes redundant rows from the output. It also prohibits any staff member with a unique department id (e.g., ENG or MATH) from appearing in the result. Because this clause compares two columns from (conceptually) different tables, it could be considered as defining a second join condition where the comparison operator is "less than" instead of "equals" as in previous examples. This leads us into a discussion of the more general concept of "theta join," which is described in the following sample queries.

Theta-Join

SQL permits a join condition to be formulated with any of the standard comparison operators. The term "theta-join" is used to indicate this more general capability where "theta" represents a given comparison operator. The next sample query illustrates use of the "less-than" operator to define the join condition.

Sample Query 17.13: Assume we would like to compare the salary of every staff member with every course labfee. Whenever the salary is less than the labfee, display the staff member name and salary followed by the corresponding course name and labfee.

```
SELECT ENAME, ESALARY, CNAME, CLABFEE

FROM    COURSE, STAFF

WHERE   ESALARY < CLABFEE
```

Comments:

1.   Syntax:

The syntax is consistent with all previous rules pertaining to the syntax of a join operation. The FROM clause identifies the names of the tables, and a WHERE clause specifies the join condition. The join condition can use any of the comparison operators. This example used the "<" operator.

2.   Logic:

The process is similar to previous join examples. The only difference in this example is that comparison is based on the "less than" operator. Examination of each row in the output shows the ESALARY value is less than the corresponding CLABFEE value. The definition of what we mean by a "match" has to be expanded to incorporate all the comparison operations.

3.   Equi-join is just a special case of the theta-join where
      theta represents the "equals" operator. Because equi-
      join has greatest application, the term "join" usually
      implies "equi-join." However, to be precise, "join" in
      the general sense is really "theta-join" and therefore
      encompasses all the comparison operators.

ENAME	ESALARY	CNAME	CLABFEE
MATTHEW	51	SCHOLASTICISM	150.00
MATTHEW	51	FUNDAMENTALISM	90.00
MATTHEW	51	COMMUNISM	200.00
MATTHEW	51	EMPIRICISM	100.00
MATTHEW	51	EXISTENTIALISM	200.00
MATTHEW	51	INTRO TO CS	100.00
MATTHEW	51	COMPUTER ARCH.	100.00
MATTHEW	51	RELATIONAL DATABASE	500.00
MARK	52	SCHOLASTICISM	150.00
MARK	52	FUNDAMENTALISM	90.00
MARK	52	COMMUNISM	200.00
MARK	52	EMPIRICISM	100.00
MARK	52	EXISTENTIALISM	200.00
MARK	52	INTRO TO CS	100.00
MARK	52	COMPUTER ARCH.	100.00
MARK	52	RELATIONAL DATABASE	500.00
LUKE	53	SCHOLASTICISM	150.00
LUKE	53	FUNDAMENTALISM	90.00
LUKE	53	COMMUNISM	200.00
LUKE	53	EMPIRICISM	100.00
LUKE	53	EXISTENTIALISM	200.00
LUKE	53	INTRO TO CS	100.00
LUKE	53	COMPUTER ARCH.	100.00
LUKE	53	RELATIONAL DATABASE	500.00
JOHN	54	SCHOLASTICISM	150.00
JOHN	54	FUNDAMENTALISM	90.00
JOHN	54	COMMUNISM	200.00
JOHN	54	EMPIRICISM	100.00
JOHN	54	EXISTENTIALISM	200.00
JOHN	54	INTRO TO CS	100.00
JOHN	54	COMPUTER ARCH.	100.00
JOHN	54	RELATIONAL DATABASE	500.00
ARCHIMEDES	200	RELATIONAL DATABASE	500.00

Multiple Join Conditions

It is possible to facilitate a join operation where multiple
columns from each table are matched to determine the join
result. All that is required is the specification of multiple
join conditions. Consider the next example, which is a
refinement of the previous example.

Sample Query 17.14:   We want to compare the salary of every
staff member with the labfee of every
course offered by their respective
departments. Whenever a staff member
has a salary which is less than the
labfee of a course offered by his
department, display the department id,
followed by the staff member name and
salary, and the corresponding course
name and labfee.

```
SELECT DEPT, ENAME, ESALARY, CNAME, CLABFEE

FROM    STAFF, COURSE

WHERE   ESALARY < CLABFEE

AND     DEPT = CDEPT
```

DEPT	ENAME	ESALARY	CNAME	CLABFEE
THEO	MATTHEW	51	SCHOLASTICISM	150.00
THEO	MARK	52	SCHOLASTICISM	150.00
THEO	LUKE	53	SCHOLASTICISM	150.00
THEO	JOHN	54	SCHOLASTICISM	150.00
THEO	MATTHEW	51	FUNDAMENTALISM	90.00
THEO	MARK	52	FUNDAMENTALISM	90.00
THEO	LUKE	53	FUNDAMENTALISM	90.00
THEO	JOHN	54	FUNDAMENTALISM	90.00
THEO	MATTHEW	51	COMMUNISM	200.00
THEO	MARK	52	COMMUNISM	200.00
THEO	LUKE	53	COMMUNISM	200.00
THEO	JOHN	54	COMMUNISM	200.00

The final sample query in this chapter utilizes the techniques introduced in the previous four sample queries. It joins a table with itself based on a comparison of multiple join conditions.

Sample Query 17.15:   Assume the dean is considering moving the administrative office of the Management Department. The intention is to combine its administrative facilities with those of another department which is located in the same building (which is unknown to the dean). To evaluate all possible options, display all information about the Management Department followed by all information about any other department which is located in the same building.

```
SELECT *

FROM    DEPARTMENT D1, DEPARTMENT D2

WHERE   D1.DBLD  =  D2.DBLD

AND     D1.DEPT <> D2.DEPT

AND     D1.DEPT  =  'MGT'
```

DEPT	DBLD	DROOM	DCHFNO	DEPT	DBLD	DROOM	DCHFNO
MGT	SC	100	-	CIS	SC	300	80

Comment:

Again, we have not introduced any new SQL techniques. Previous techniques were applied to solve this problem. Any complexity pertains to the logical dimension of the query. This is dealt with in the WHERE clause as explained below.

(1)   "D1.DBLD = D2.DBLD" satisfies the requirement that the two departments be located in the same building.

(2)   "D1.DEPT = 'MGT'" indicates that we are specifically concerned with the Management Department.

(3)   "D1.DEPT <> D2.DEPT" eliminates any nonsense combinations of the same department.

Summary

The basic structure of a SELECT statement which joins two or more tables is essentially the same as one which references just one table. For two tables this is

```
SELECT col1, col2, col3, ...
FROM   table1, table2
WHERE  table1.joincol1 = table2.joincol2
AND    (other row selection conditions)
ORDER BY (any columns)
```

The logic of a join condition is another matter. You must understand the relationship between the tables as reflected in the join columns. Sometimes the database design can simplify the situation. For example, every CDEPT value in the COURSE table matches some DEPT value in the DEPARTMENT table. Also, there were no null values in the CDEPT column. Therefore, every COURSE row will be present in a join of these two tables. There is no chance of an undetected COURSE row missing from an output display. Desired rows are explicitly selected (or undesired rows explicitly rejected) by coding conditions in the SELECT statement. It is possible for a designer to establish this simplified situation by (1) using the NOT NULL option for the CDEPT column when creating the COURSE table and (2) editing all INSERT and UPDATE commands for the COURSE table to verify that CDEPT values match some existing DEPT value in the DEPARTMENT table. This second step usually involves the writing of an application program using embedded SQL.

Very often the application environment does not permit the designer to incorporate the above procedures. We mirrored this complexity in the STAFF and DEPARTMENT tables. Some departments might not have chairpersons, staff, or courses. Some staff members might not have department assignments or might be assigned to nonexisting departments. This creates a situation where the join of the DEPARTMENT and STAFF tables causes "no match" situations, which remove certain rows from the join result. The key point is that users of SQL must be sensitive to this situation. Otherwise, incorrect output displays could be generated. Once again we emphasize that this issue transcends SQL. *Simply, users must understand the semantic structure of their database.*

Summary Exercises

17N. Display the faculty number of any faculty member who chairs a department which offers six-credit courses.

17O. Display the course number, name, and section of every class which is offered on a Monday.

17P. Display the course number and name of every course that student 800 is registered for.

17Q. Display all information about any scheduled class which has a labfee less than $100 and is not offered on a Friday.

17R. Display the student number and date of registration from all students who registered for at least one course offered by the Theology Department.

17S. How many students are registered for all sections of the EXISTENTIALISM course?

17T. How many students have registered for classes offered by the Philosophy Department?

17U. Display the name and number of every faculty member who teaches a class which meets on a Monday or a Friday. Do not display duplicate rows.

The following exercises are more of a challenge. They require that you use techniques presented toward the end of this chapter.

17V. Display the name of any faculty member who chairs a department which offers a six-credit course.

17Wa. Produce a class list for the first section of the EXISTENTIALISM course. Display the course number, section number, course name, and faculty number of the instructor followed by the student number of every student registered for the class.

17Wb. Modify the previous "class list" query. For each student, display the student's name followed by the student's number.

17Wc. Make another modification to the "class list" query. Display the faculty name instead of faculty number.

17X.   This is a "paper and pencil" exercise. Verify that any
        of the following join sequences involving three tables
        will produce the same result.

   a.   Join the COURSE and STAFF tables to get an
         intermediate result. Then join this with the
         DEPARTMENT table.

   b.   Join the COURSE and DEPARTMENT tables to get an
         intermediate result. Then join this with the STAFF
         table.

   c.   Join the STAFF and DEPARTMENT tables to get an
         intermediate result. Then join this with the
         COURSE table.

17Y.   Display the cross product of the COURSE and FACULTY
        tables.

17Za.   Display the department identifiers of each pair of
        departments which are located in the same building.

17Zb.   Compare the salaries for each pair of staff members.
        Whenever the salary of the first staff member exceeds
        the salary of the second staff member by more than
        $1000, display the name and salary of both staff
        members followed by the difference in salaries.

17Zc.   Modify the previous "salary comparison" query. Compare
        only the salaries of staff members who have the same
        department id value specified in the STAFF.DEPT column.

17Zd.   Make another modification to the "salary comparison"
        query. This time, compare just the salaries of staff
        members who are assigned to existing departments which
        are located in the Humanities Building.

18

Outer Join

In Chapter 17 we emphasized that the result of joining two tables will contain rows only where a match occurred on the join condition. The precise label for this kind of join operation is the "inner join." This term distinguishes it from a different kind of join operation, called the "outer join," which is the subject of this chapter.

There is a potential loss of information through an inner join because only those rows which match on the join condition will appear in the final result. The result of an outer join operation, however, will contain the same rows as an inner join operation plus a row corresponding to each row from the original tables which did not match on the join condition.

You will find the outer join to be a very useful operation. One desirable feature of the ORACLE version of SQL is that, unlike many other database products (including DB2), it provides direct support for this important operation.

Definition of Outer Join

There are three variations of the outer join operation. Figure 18.1 illustrates each variation of an outer equi-join of TABLE1 and TABLE2 using columns C2 and CA as the join columns.

Full Outer Join:

The result of a full outer join is shown in table FULLOJ. Note that the first three rows of FULLOJ correspond to the inner equi-join of TABLE1 and TABLE2. The fourth and fifth rows correspond to rows in TABLE1 (the "left" table) which did not match in the join operation. The last row of table FULLOJ corresponds to the row in TABLE2 (the "right" table) which did not match. The "no match" rows from the left table have null values appended to the right. And the "no match" rows from the right table have null values appended to the left. Obviously the terms "left" and "right" are relative. We could visualize TABLE1 as the right table and TABLE2 as the left table. ORACLE does not directly support the full outer join. (However, the left outer join can be used with the UNION operation to form a full outer join. The UNION operation will be presented in the next chapter.)

Left Outer Join:

The LEFTOJ outer join result in Figure 18.1 is the "left outer join" of TABLE1 and TABLE2. This result excludes the "no match" rows of TABLE2, the right table, from the result of FULLOJ. It includes the "no match" rows of only TABLE1, the left table. *It is important to note that ORACLE provides direct support only for the left outer join.* In practice you will find greater application for the left outer join operation than the full outer join operation.

Right Outer Join:

The RIGHTOJ outer join result in Figure 18.1 is the "right outer join" of TABLE1 and TABLE2. This result excludes the "no match" rows of TABLE1, the left table, from the result of FULLOJ. It includes the "no match" rows of only TABLE2, the right table. Because left and right are relative terms, there is no difference in principle between the left and right outer joins. It is simply a matter of which table you visualize as the left table. This means we can say that ORACLE provides direct support for both the left and right outer join.

Recall that SQL permits an inner join condition to be formulated with any of the standard comparison operators. The term "theta-join" is used to indicate this more general capability where "theta" represents a given comparison operator. The same operators may be used with an outer join. Hence, a more general term which describes an outer join is "outer theta-join."

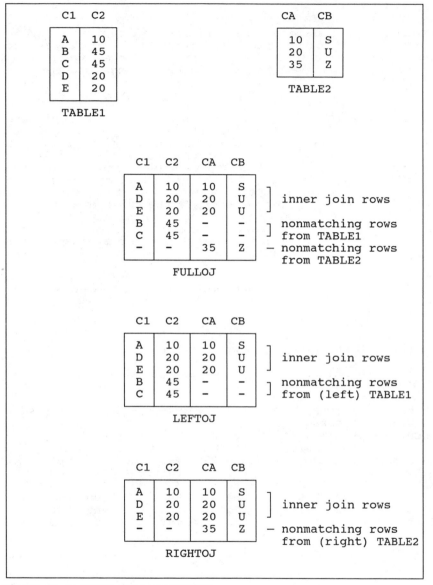

Figure 18.1: Outer join operations.

Left Outer Join

ORACLE provides a special operator "(+)" which can be used to specify a left outer join. This operator is placed in the WHERE clause following the join column of the right table. (The nonmatching rows in this table will be excluded from the result.)

Sample Query 18.1:   Display the name, title, salary, and department id for every staff member recorded in the STAFF table along with all information about the department to which that person is assigned (i.e., the department's id, building, room, and faculty number of the department chairperson). If the staff member is not assigned to an existing department, or if the assignment is unknown (null), display null values for the department information.

```
SELECT *

FROM    STAFF, DEPARTMENT

WHERE   STAFF.DEPT = DEPARTMENT.DEPT (+)
```

ENAME	ETITLE	ESALARY	DEPT	DEPT	DBLD	DROOM	DCHFNO
DA VINCI	LAB ASSIST	500	-	-	-	-	-
ARCHIMEDES	LAB ASSIST	200	ENG	-	-	-	-
EUCLID	LAB ASSIST	1000	MATH	-	-	-	-
HANK KISS	JESTER	25000	PHIL	PHIL	HU	100	60
DICK NIX	CROOK	25001	PHIL	PHIL	HU	100	60
MATTHEW	EVANGLIST1	51	THEO	THEO	HU	200	10
JOHN	EVANGLIST4	54	THEO	THEO	HU	200	10
LUKE	EVANGLIST3	53	THEO	THEO	HU	200	10
MARK	EVANGLIST2	52	THEO	THEO	HU	200	10

Comments:

1. Syntax: The left outer join is formed by placing the outer join operator "(+)" after the column name of the "right" table in the join condition. This syntax can be slightly confusing. (The table to which this column belongs is sometimes called the *outer-joined table*.) The placement of the "(+)" determines which table will have its nonmatching rows excluded from the result.

   The ORACLE reference manual states that the outer join symbol tells SQL*Plus to treat the table as though it contained an extra row with a null value in every column. This null row will be joined to any row of the "left" table that does not match a real row in the "right" table.

   Again, left and right are relative terms. The key point is that the outer join symbol is placed after the appropriate column name. For example, the WHERE clause could have been written as

   WHERE DEPARTMENT.DEPT (+) = STAFF.DEPT

   and the query would have produced the same result.

2. Compare this example to Sample Query 17.1, which showed the inner join of the STAFF and DEPARTMENT tables. The result of that query was "all staff members assigned to existing departments." That query produced six rows in the result. Observe that the last six rows of this result correspond to the rows returned by the inner join operation. The first three rows are missing from the inner join result. These rows correspond to the "no match" rows from the STAFF table and pertain to those employees who are not assigned to an existing department.

3. The operator may be placed after the other table to form a right outer join. (See the next sample query.) The placement of the operator determines whether the join will be a left outer join or a right outer join. Only one table may be designated as the outer-joined table.

Exercise:

18A. Display the left outer join of the COURSE table and the STAFF table using the CDEPT and DEPT columns as the join columns. Let COURSE be the left table. This would provide a listing of every course and corresponding staff members that can tutor the course. Courses which do not have tutors will appear in the result with null values in the columns corresponding to the STAFF table.

Right Outer Join

Obviously the terms "left" and "right" are relative. In the last example we designated the table named to the right of the join condition (DEPARTMENT.DEPT) as the right or outer-joined table and formed the left outer join. In the next example we specify the other table (STAFF.DEPT) as the outerjoin table and form a right outer join. Note that not only are the column values different in the result, but the number of rows has changed. Notice the only difference between this statement and the previous statement is the placement of the outer join operator after "STAFF.DEPT".

Sample Query 18.2: For every department with staff members, display the staff member's name, title, salary, and department together with all information about the department to which that person is assigned (i.e., the department's id, building, room, and faculty number of the department chairperson). If the department has no staff members, display the department information along with null values for staff information.

```
SELECT *

FROM    STAFF, DEPARTMENT

WHERE   STAFF.DEPT (+) = DEPARTMENT.DEPT
```

ENAME	ETITLE	ESALARY	DEPT	DEPT	DBLD	DROOM	DCHFNO
-	-	-	-	CIS	SC	300	80
-	-	-	-	MGT	SC	100	-
HANK KISS	JESTER	25000	PHIL	PHIL	HU	100	60
DICK NIX	CROOK	25001	PHIL	PHIL	HU	100	60
MATTHEW	EVANGLIST1	51	THEO	THEO	HU	200	10
JOHN	EVANGLIST4	54	THEO	THEO	HU	200	10
LUKE	EVANGLIST3	53	THEO	THEO	HU	200	10
MARK	EVANGLIST2	52	THEO	THEO	HU	200	10

Comments:

1. The right outer join was formed by using the outer join operator "(+)" after the column name which appears to the left of the join condition. In this example, the "(+)" was placed after the STAFF table. This allowed every row in the DEPARTMENT table to find a match on the join condition. For those departments without staff members, the department row was "matched" with null values.

2.   The first two rows in the result correspond to the two departments which do not have staff members, CIS and MGT. The remaining rows in the result correspond to the result produced by an inner join.

3.   A suggestion: Always think in terms of left outer join. If you would like all of the rows of a specific table to appear in the result, designate that table as the left table (LT). Designate the other table as the right table (RT). Then formulate your outer join statement as shown below

```
SELECT ...
FROM    LT, RT
WHERE   LT.C = RT.C (+)
```

4.   It is important to note that there is no primary key - foreign key relationship between the STAFF and DEPARTMENT tables. This means that a left outer join, a right outer join and a full outer join can produce different results. This is the case with the data shown in Figure 18.1.

5.   Observations regarding primary key - foreign key relationship:

a. If the left table contains a primary key which is referred to by a foreign key in the right table, then the left outer join and full outer join are equivalent. Examine exercise 18B.

b. If the left table contains a foreign key which references the primary key of the right table, then the left outer join is equivalent to an inner join.

Exercise:

18B. Display the left outer join of the DEPARTMENT table and the COURSE table using the DEPT and CDEPT columns as the join columns. Let DEPARTMENT be the left table. This would provide a listing of every department and corresponding courses offered by that department. Departments which do not offer courses will appear in the result with null values in the columns corresponding to the COURSE table. Execution of this example will illustrate comment 5a above.

Three-Table Outer Join

Just as with the inner join operation, you are not limited to joining two tables in an outer join. The next example illustrates a three-table outer join.

Sample Query 18.3:   Display the department id and building for each department. In addition, for each department which offers courses, display the course number, credits, and name of these courses. If a course has one or more class offerings, also display the section number and the faculty number of the instructor teaching the course.

```
SELECT  DEPT, DBLD, COURSE.CNO, CRED, CNAME, SEC,

        CINSTRFNO

FROM    DEPARTMENT, COURSE, CLASS

WHERE   DEPT = CDEPT (+)

AND     COURSE.CNO = CLASS.CNO (+)
```

DEPT	DBLD	CNO	CRED	CNAME	SEC	CINSTRFNO
MGT	SC	-	-	-	-	-
CIS	SC	C11	3	INTRO TO CIS	01	08
CIS	SC	C11	3	INTRO TO CIS	02	08
CIS	SC	C22	3	DATA STRUCTURES	-	-
CIS	SC	C33	3	DISCRETE MATHEMATICS	01	80
CIS	SC	C44	3	DIGITAL CIRCUITS	-	-
CIS	SC	C55	3	COMPUTER ARCH.	01	85
CIS	SC	C66	3	RELATIONAL DATABASE	-	-
PHIL	HU	P11	3	EMPIRICISM	01	06
PHIL	HU	P22	3	RATIONALISM	-	-
PHIL	HU	P33	3	EXISTENTIALISM	01	06
PHIL	HU	P44	6	SOLIPSISM	-	-
THEO	HU	T11	3	SCHOLASTICISM	01	10
THEO	HU	T11	3	SCHOLASTICISM	02	65
THEO	HU	T12	3	FUNDAMENTALISM	-	-
THEO	HU	T33	3	HEDONISM	01	65
THEO	HU	T44	6	COMMUNISM	-	-

Comments:

1. This sample query formed the left outer join of the
    DEPARTMENT, COURSE, and CLASS tables, in that order.

    When forming an outer join with three or more tables,
    special care must be given in designating the outer-
    joined tables. Again, it is necessary to understand the
    meaning of the data stored in the database and the
    relationships between rows stored in different tables.
    First, we consider the relationships between the tables
    in the current example.

    DEPARTMENT-COURSE: Departments offer courses. A course
    cannot exist unless it is associated with a particular
    department. In our database design this is captured
    through the designation of DEPT as the primary key of
    the DEPARTMENT table and the CDEPT as a foreign key in
    the COURSE table. It is possible, however, for a
    DEPARTMENT to exist and not offer any courses. Hence,
    the DEPARTMENT table is designated as the outer-joined
    table in the join condition of these two tables.

    COURSE-CLASS: Classes are offered on courses. A class
    section is a particular offering of an existing course.
    A course must be defined in the COURSE table before a
    class may be offered on it. This relationship was
    captured in our design by specifying CNO as the primary
    key of the COURSE table and CNO as the foreign key in
    the CLASS table. It is possible, however, for a COURSE
    to exist and have any class offerings. Hence, the
    designation of the COURSE table as the outer-joined
    table in the join condition of these two tables.

    Note well: Review Figure 14.4. The primary key - foreign
    key relationships between these three tables form a
    dependency hierarchy where each dependent child must
    have a parent. The left-to-right ordering of the tables
    (DEPARTMENT, COURSE, CLASS) in the three-way left outer
    join operation corresponds to the top-to-bottom sequence
    of tables in the hierarchy. This sequence is important.
    If the sequence were different, the result would be
    different and the query objective would not have been
    satisfied. For example, specifying "DEPT (+) = CDEPT"
    instead of "DEPT = CDEPT (+)" would have resulted in the
    display of only those departments which offer courses.
    Hence, the MGT row would not appear in the result.

Summary

In this chapter we presented a powerful and useful feature of ORACLE, the left outer join operation. We saw that an outer join may reveal more information than an inner join using the same join condition. With an inner join, a row from one table must find an exact match in the other table as specified in the join condition. This is because every row in the left table achieves a "match" condition. The row either matches a value in the other table, as with the inner join, or it is "matched" with a row of null values. This is the reason for additional information being returned from an outer join.

Thus far, using your current knowledge of SQL, it is impossible to produce a full outer join. You are not allowed to use the outer join operator more than once in a condition. Hence, the following statement is *invalid*.

    SELECT * FROM T1, T2 WHERE T1.CA (+) = T2.CA (+)

The UNION operation (presented in the next chapter) is necessary to generate a full outer join.

Summary Exercises

18C. For every department, display all information about the department. Also, if the department has faculty members, display the information from the FACULTY table for these faculty members. If a department does not have any faculty members, display nulls for faculty information.

18D. For every faculty member, display all information about the faculty member. Also, if the faculty member is assigned to an existing department, display the information from the DEPARTMENT table for this faculty member. If a faculty member is not assigned to an existing department, display nulls for the department information. (This exercise is hypothetical because the FDEPT column is a foreign key referencing the DEPARTMENT table. Would an inner join satisfy this query? See comment 5b for Sample Query 18.2.)

18E. Display the department identifier and building for each department. In addition, for each department which has faculty members, display the faculty number and faculty name of these members. If a faculty member is the instructor for a class, then also display the course number and section number of the class. If a department does not currently have any faculty members, then display nulls for the faculty and class information. If a faculty member is not teaching this semester, then display nulls for the class information.

UNION-INTERSECT-MINUS

This chapter describes simple but very useful SQL operations. These are union, intersection, and difference. All of these operations combine the results of separate SELECT statements. However, the union operation is perhaps the most powerful and most interesting of the three operations. In Chapter 21 we will see that intersection and difference can be implemented using alternative operations.

The purpose of the union operation is introduced by means of a simple example. Assume you were asked to display the names of all faculty and staff members. This simple request could be satisfied by executing two separate SELECT statements.

    1.   Display all the faculty names.

```
SELECT      FNAME
FROM        FACULTY
```

    2.   Display all the staff member names.

```
SELECT      ENAME
FROM        STAFF
```

These are two *separate* SELECT statements which are executed independently of each other and which generate two *separate* result tables. This approach is not satisfactory if we want all the faculty and staff member names to be merged into a single result table. The union operation must be used to achieve this objective.

UNION Keyword

The union operation allows execution of multiple SELECT statements as a single statement. The result of each statement is merged into and subsequently displayed as a single result table.

Sample Query 19.1:   Display the names of all faculty and staff members (in a single result table).

```
SELECT FNAME

FROM    FACULTY

UNION

SELECT ENAME

FROM    STAFF
```

```
FNAME
AL HARTLEY
ARCHIMEDES
BARB HLAVATY
DA VINCI
DICK NIX
EUCLID
FRANK MARTYN
HANK KISS
JOE COHN
JOHN
JULIE MARTYN
KATHY PEPE
LISA BOBAK
LUKE
MARK
MATTHEW
```

Comments:

1. Syntax: The keyword UNION is placed between the two SELECT statements separated by one or more spaces. As with other SQL statements, the format is free form and can be written on any number of lines.

2. Logic: The UNION keyword tells the system to execute each SELECT statement and then merge the intermediate results into a single result table.

   Question: What if duplicate rows occur in the intermediate results?

   Answer: Duplicate rows selected by individual SELECT statements are not displayed. This is because the UNION keyword corresponds to the union operation as defined in classical set theory. This theory defines the union of two sets as the set of all values taken from both sets. Because a mathematical set must contain distinct values, the result of the union operation, which is a set, will not contain duplicate values.

   For example, given set $A = \{2,4,6,8\}$ and set $B = \{1,4,5,6\}$, the union of sets A and B is $\{1,2,4,5,6,8\}$. Observe that the values common to both sets, 4 and 6, occur only once in the union result. The same principle applies to the formation of a result table, which is the union of two or more intermediate tables generated by independent SELECT statements. We emphasize that duplicate rows are not displayed, even though the DISTINCT keyword is not specified in either SELECT statement.

   Notice that all the FNAME values in the FACULTY table are distinct from all ENAME values in the STAFF table. Hence, in this example it just so happens that duplicate rows do not occur in the intermediate results.

3. We cannot arbitrarily form the union of any two SELECT statements. The intermediate tables produced by the individual SELECT statements must be "union-compatible." This means that

    a. Each intermediate result table must have the same number of columns.

    b. Corresponding columns must have comparable data types. If a given column contains numeric, character, or date/time data, then its corresponding column must respectively contain numeric, character, and date/time data. (However, ORACLE is forgiving with respect to this rule because of its automatic data conversion. Again, we discourage reliance on this conversion.)

    In the current example each SELECT statement produces a table with just one column. The first contains FNAME values which are defined as character. The second contains ENAME values which are also defined as character.

4. Observe that the corresponding column names in the SELECT statements do not need to be identical. However, only one such name can occur as the column heading for the displayed result. ORACLE will use the first SELECT statement to determine the column headings for the output display. Hence the output column heading shows FNAME. Because the column values actually represent both faculty and staff names, it is recommended that you use the SQL*Plus COLUMN command to change the heading to a more representative title (e.g., "EMPLOYEE NAME"). Sample Query 19.4 will illustrate this technique.

5. It is not possible by mere examination of the output display to determine which rows were selected from which table. Sample 19.4 will illustrate a technique to realize this objective.

6. Observe that the result is sorted even though the ORDER BY clause is not specified. This is because the current version of ORACLE automatically performs an internal sort to facilitate the identification of duplicate values. Again, we state that you should not rely on this sort. Sample 19.3 will illustrate use of the ORDER BY clause with the union operation.

The next example illustrates a situation where the union operation causes duplicate rows to be removed from the displayed result.

Sample Query 19.2:   Display every department id referenced in the STAFF and FACULTY tables.

```
SELECT DEPT

FROM STAFF

UNION

SELECT FDEPT

FROM FACULTY
```

DEPT
CIS
ENG
MATH
PHIL
THEO
–

Comments:

1.   This example illustrates how the union operation removes duplicate rows from the intermediate results. For example, THEO occurs many times in both the FACULTY and STAFF tables, but it appears only once in the output display. Also, multiple null values are considered duplicates so that only one null value appears in the output.

2.   Again note that an internal sort was done to facilitate the removal of duplicate rows. The null value appears at the low end of the sequence. The next example will show use of the ORDER BY clause, which should be used to specify a desired row sequence.

Exercise:

19A. Display the salaries of all staff and faculty as a single result table.

The next example illustrates union-compatible SELECT statements which display multiple columns. The SELECT statements contain WHERE clauses, and the result is sorted in a specified row sequence.

Sample Query 19.3: Display the name, department id, and title (in that order) of all staff members assigned to the Theology Department. Include the name, department id, and address (in that order) of all faculty members assigned to that department. Sort the output by name in descending sequence.

```
SELECT  ENAME, DEPT, ETITLE

FROM    STAFF

WHERE   DEPT = 'THEO'

UNION

SELECT  FNAME, FDEPT, FADDR

FROM    FACULTY

WHERE   FDEPT = 'THEO'

ORDER BY 1 DESC
```

ENAME	DEPT	ETITLE
MATTHEW	THEO	EVANGLIST1
MARK	THEO	EVANGLIST2
LUKE	THEO	EVANGLIST3
LISA BOBAK	THEO	77 LAUGHING LANE
JOHN	THEO	EVANGLIST4
JESSIE MARTYN	THEO	2135 EASTON DRIVE

Comments:

1.   The SELECT statements fit the definition of "union-compatible" even though the content of the third column, which is a mixture of titles and addresses, is probably confusing. The point is that the system has no insight into the fact that the ETITLE and FADDR columns contain semantically different kinds of data.

2.   Both WHERE clauses happen to reference columns containing the same type of data (department ids). This is typical, but it is not necessary. In general, each individual SELECT statement may contain any valid WHERE clause.

3.   Special rules apply to the ORDER by clause when used with the union operation.

   a.   The ORDER BY clause can appear only once, and it must be the last clause of the entire statement.

   b.   The ORDER BY clause must reference a column by its relative column number, not by a column name.

Exercise:

19B. Display the department id, number of credits, and the description of all philosophy courses together with the department id, number of dependents, and the address of each faculty member from that same department.

In the last sample query demonstrating UNION, the individual SELECT statements associate constant data with the computed values. This provides a means of attaching identification labels to rows displayed in the final result.

Sample Query 19.4: Assume the second character of a course's CNO value represents the level of the course. Lower-level courses have a "1" or "2". Intermediate-level courses have a "3" or "4". Upper-level courses have a "5" or "6". Calculate the average labfee for each of the three levels of courses. Also, tag a self-identifying label to each row.

```
COLUMN LFMT FORMAT A15 HEADING LEVEL

SELECT 'LOWER' LFMT, AVG(CLABFEE)

FROM    COURSE

WHERE   CNO LIKE '_1%'

OR      CNO LIKE '_2%'

UNION

SELECT 'INTERMEDIATE', AVG(CLABFEE)

FROM    COURSE

WHERE   CNO LIKE '_3%'

OR      CNO LIKE '_4%'

UNION

SELECT 'UPPER', AVG(CLABFEE)

FROM    COURSE

WHERE   CNO LIKE '_5%'

OR      CNO LIKE '_6%'
```

LEVEL	AVG(CLABFEE)
INTERMEDIATE	66.6666667
LOWER	90
UPPER	300

Comments:

1.   The specification of a constant identifier in each
     SELECT statement is most helpful in this example. The
     preceding examples did not include any self-identifying
     constants, but such constants would have made the output
     more readable.

2.   Unlike the previous sample queries, the individual
     SELECT statements in this example refer to the same
     table (COURSE) and utilize a group function (AVG). In
     effect, the three individual SELECT statements perform
     a calculation with rows from the COURSE table to produce
     three summary rows which are subsequently merged into
     the final result by UNION.

     This example shows the utility of the union operation.
     Note that it allows for a type of grouping which cannot
     be done with the GROUP BY clause. The GROUP BY clause
     will form a group for each individual value found in a
     specified column. The current example illustrates the
     formation of groups where each group corresponds to a
     set of multiple values.

3.   This example used the SQL*Plus COLUMN command to
     generate the first column heading. If this technique had
     not been used, the heading would have been 'LOWER'
     corresponding to the first SELECT statement. Also, this
     query would be DB2-compatible if LFMT were not present
     in the first SELECT statement.

Intersection and Difference Operations

As with the union operation, intersection and difference allow the execution of multiple SELECT statements which are treated as a single statement. Figure 19.1 shows the previously described union operation and the intersection and difference operations, which will be illustrated in the next sample queries. The intersection operation (INTERSECT) produces a result which contains only the rows which are common to TABLE1 and TABLE2. Difference (MINUS) produces a result which contains the rows of one table which are not found in the second table.

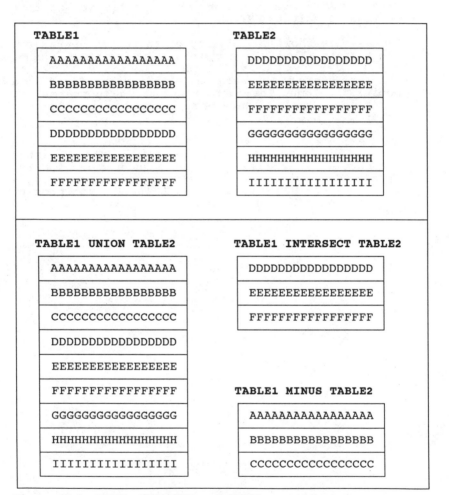

Figure 19.1: UNION, INTERSECT, and MINUS operations.

INTERSECT Keyword

The keyword INTERSECT, like UNION, is positioned between two SELECT statements.

Sample Query 19.5:   Display the department ids of all staff members who belong to existing departments.

```
SELECT  DEPT

FROM     DEPARTMENT

INTERSECT

SELECT  DEPT

FROM     STAFF
```

<u>DEPT</u>
PHIL
THEO

Comments:

1.   The DEPARTMENT and STAFF tables both contain department ids other than those shown in the result. However, only those department ids common to both tables appear in the result.

2.   The notion of "union" compatibility applies to intersection.

3.   We note that INTERSECT, unlike UNION, is superfluous in SQL. Other DBMS products (e.g., DB2) do not support this keyword. This is because the intersection operation can be achieved using a subquery. Chapters 20 and 21 will discuss subqueries.

Exercise:

19C. Display the set of values common to those found in the CLABFEE column of the COURSE table and the ESALARY column of the STAFF table.

MINUS Keyword

The difference operation, implemented in ORACLE through the MINUS keyword, allows you to identify rows present in one table but not in another.

Sample Query 19.6:   Display the department id of any staff member who does not have a matching department id in the COURSE table.

```
SELECT  DEPT

FROM    STAFF

MINUS

SELECT  CDEPT

FROM    COURSE
```

<u>DEPT</u>
-
ENG
MATH

Comments:

1.   The null, "ENG", and "MATH" values appear in the result because they are present only in the STAFF table but are not present in the COURSE table.

   Note that, unlike UNION and INTERSECTION, the order of the SELECT statements makes a difference with MINUS. Only rows which are present in the first table (STAFF) and *not* present in the second table (COURSE) appear in the result. If the two SELECT statements were reversed, then the result would be different.

2.   Union compatibility applies to difference.

3.   Like INTERSECT, MINUS is superfluous in SQL. Other DBMS products (e.g., DB2) do not support this keyword. This is because the intersection operation can be achieved using a subquery. Chapters 20 and 21 will discuss subqueries.

Exercise:

19D. What is the result of executing the following statement?

```
SELECT CDEPT FROM COURSE
MINUS
SELECT DEPT FROM STAFF
```

Summary

This chapter presented the UNION, INTERSECT, and MINUS keywords which allow for operations on different sets of rows selected by individual SELECT statements. We noted that the union operation was the most powerful and most useful of the three operations.

We conclude this chapter by listing constraints associated with UNION, INTERSECT, and MINUS. Some of these have been specified in the previous examples, while others are defined for the first time.

1. All intermediate result tables produced by the SELECT statements must be union-compatible. This means that they have the same number of columns and each corresponding column has a comparable data type. Whenever a given column is union compatible with its corresponding column, but the two columns do not have the exact same SQL data type, the data type conversion rules specified in Chapter 7 apply.

2. The ORDER BY clause may be specified only once. If used, it must be placed after the last SELECT statement. Furthermore, it must reference the sort column(s) by relative column number(s).

3. Sometimes you may want to use the NULL pseudo-column to force union compatibility. For example, to display the name and title of every staff member along with just the name of every faculty member, you would enter

```
SELECT FNAME, NULL
FROM FACULTY
UNION
SELECT ENAME, ETITLE
FROM STAFF
```

4. DB2 Compatibility: DB2 does not presently support either INTERSECT or MINUS operations. They may be executed in DB2 using alternative methods. (See Exercises 21H and 21I.) However, DB2 does provide a variation on the UNION operation which ORACLE does not support. This is the UNION ALL operation, which does not remove duplicate rows from either the intermediate or final result.

Summary Exercises

19E. Use the MINUS operation to display the faculty numbers of those faculty members who are not department chairpersons.

19F. What course credit values match the number of dependents for any of the faculty members? Provide two solutions.

19G. Display the labfee value and number of credits for each CIS course together with a label of "course." Also display rows which contain the salary and number of dependents for each faculty member from the CIS department. Identify the faculty rows with a tag of "faculty."

19H. Display the course name, department identifier, and the labfee value for all courses with a labfee value that is at least 200.00. Append a label of "expensive" on each row retrieved. Display the columns for those courses with a labfee value of 50.00 or less. Append to these rows the label of "cheap." Display all of the rows in a single result.

19I. Construct the full outer join of the STAFF table and the DEPARTMENT table.

20

Subqueries

This chapter introduces the technique of nesting a SELECT statement within another SELECT statement. Figure 20.1 shows the basic structure of a SELECT statement which contains another SELECT statement nested within it. The nested SELECT statement is called a "subquery," a "subselect," or an "inner SELECT." For discussion purposes we will reference the first SELECT as the "main query" or the "outer SELECT." Most of the sample queries presented in this chapter can be solved using the join operation. However, the use of a subquery is often considered to provide a simpler solution. There are some circumstances where the use of a subquery becomes necessary. Chapter 21, which describes correlated subqueries, will present examples of such queries.

Background

We first examine a deceptively simple query, which cannot be conveniently expressed in a single SELECT statement given the SQL techniques described thus far.

Query 1:   Display the course number and name of the course(s) with the highest labfee.

Recall that it is easy to display the highest labfee. This is achieved by executing the following statement

```
SELECT MAX(CLABFEE)
FROM   COURSE
```

The system would return 500.00, which enables us to enter the following statement.

```
SELECT CNO, CNAME
FROM   COURSE
WHERE  CLABFEE = 500.00
```

While this procedure will work, it requires the execution of two independent SELECT statements. This is less than desirable for the same reasons specified earlier in our discussion of the join operation. (See preliminary discussion in Chapter 17.)

Recall that the following statement will *not* work

```
SELECT CNO, CNAME, MAX(CLABFEE)
FROM   COURSE
```

Because the SELECT clause contains a group function, MAX(CLABFEE), the other columns, CNO and CNAME, must be referenced in a GROUP BY clause.

The basic problem is that we do not know what the largest CLABFEE value is. Essentially, we want to construct a WHERE clause for an unknown value. This represents a class of queries where a subquery can be used to determine the unknown value.

A second reason to use a subquery is to avoid explicit coding of a join operation for a query which requires examination of multiple tables, but displays only columns from a single table. The following query illustrates this situation.

Query 2:   Display the name and title of every staff member who works in the Humanities Building.

Sample Query 17.4 presented a solution to this query by joining the DEPARTMENT and STAFF tables. This was

```
SELECT  ENAME, ETITLE
FROM    STAFF, DEPARTMENT
WHERE   STAFF.DEPT = DEPARTMENT.DEPT
AND     DBLD = 'HU'
```

Because all the displayed columns, ENAME and ETITLE, are in a single table, the STAFF table, it is possible to code a subquery solution to this problem. Sample Query 20.8 will illustrate this solution. Many users will prefer the subquery solution because it circumvents some of the logical complexities associated with the join operation.

The sample queries presented in this chapter employ subquery solutions to a variety of problems. The first seven sample queries present subqueries which produce a single value. The remaining sample queries illustrate subqueries which can produce multiple values. We will see that you must be aware of whether a subquery can produce more than a single value.

```
SELECT  ---------
FROM    --------           ------- Main Query
WHERE   --------                   (Outer Select)
   (SELECT  --------
    FROM    --------           ------- Subquery
    WHERE   --------)                  (Subselect)
```

Figure 20.1: Subquery SELECT statement.

Subquery: WHERE Clause Examines Unknown Value

The first seven sample queries in this chapter have a WHERE clause which compares a column to a single unknown value. This unknown value is resolved by a nested subquery. After the subquery is evaluated, its result is returned to the WHERE clause of the main query which is then evaluated to determine which rows should be selected for display.

Sample Query 20.1:   Display the course number and name of the course(s) with the highest labfee.

```
SELECT CNO, CNAME

FROM    COURSE

WHERE   CLABFEE =

        (SELECT MAX(CLABFEE)

        FROM    COURSE)
```

CNO	CNAME
C66	RELATIONAL DATABASE

Comments:

1.   Logic:

The system will execute the subquery first. In this case it will find the maximum labfee value of 500.00 and substitute this value in the WHERE clause of the main query. The main query then becomes

```
SELECT CNO, CNAME
FROM    COURSE
WHERE   CLABFEE = 500.00
```

The main query is then executed and the result is displayed. Note that the subquery result of 500.00 is not displayed. It is just substituted in the WHERE clause of the main query. If you also wanted to display the maximum labfee value, you would reference CLABFEE in the main query SELECT clause. The entire statement would be

```
SELECT  CNO, CNAME, CLABFEE
FROM    COURSE
WHERE   CLABFEE =
    (SELECT  MAX(CLABFEE)
     FROM    COURSE)
```

2.   Syntax:

The subquery must be enclosed within parentheses.

The WHERE clause in the main query has an equals sign. Effectively, it is stating "where the CLABFEE is equal to some value" (not "values"). Because the WHERE clause is written to compare the CLABFEE with a single value, the subquery must be coded such that only a single value is returned by the subquery. In the current example the subquery returns the maximum labfee value, which is a single value (500.00). Note that this would be the case even if multiple COURSE rows contained the same maximum value.

Both the main query and the subquery happen to reference the COURSE table. This is not necessary. (See Sample Query 20.7.)

As with all previous SQL statements, the format is free form. Indentation is arbitrary.

Exercise:

20A. Display the course number, name, and department of the course(s) with the smallest labfee.

Subquery Contains a WHERE Clause

To further influence the result of the main query, the subquery could contain a WHERE clause to exclude certain rows. A subquery can contain any valid WHERE clause.

Sample Query 20.2:   Display the course number, name, and labfee of the course(s) with the smallest nonzero labfee.

```
SELECT CNO, CNAME, CLABFEE

FROM    COURSE

WHERE   CLABFEE =

   (SELECT MIN(CLABFEE)

    FROM    COURSE

    WHERE   NOT CLABFEE = 0)
```

CNO	CNAME	CLABFEE
C22	DATA STRUCTURES	50.00
P22	RATIONALISM	50.00

Comments:

1.   Logic:

The WHERE clause in the subquery will exclude zero as a
minimum value. Assuming there are no negative labfee
values, the subquery will return the smallest positive
labfee value to the WHERE clause of the main query. The
main query will select rows based on this value. The
output will display this value after the course number
and name of any courses which have this labfee value.

This WHERE clause is simple. It has only one condition.
In general, the WHERE clause can include any number of
conditions connected with Boolean operators.

2.   The subquery WHERE clause could have been written as

WHERE CLABFEE > 0

This would eliminate any concern about possible negative
labfee values.

3.   Syntax:

No special syntax requirements exist. The subquery is a
standard SELECT statement enclosed with parentheses.

Exercises:

20B.   Assume you know that the highest labfee is 500.00. Write
a SELECT statement which will display the course number,
name, department, and labfee of the course(s) having the
second highest labfee.

20C.   Assume that you know the lowest labfee is 0. Write a
SELECT statement which will display the course number,
name, department, and labfee of the course(s) having the
second lowest labfee.

The next sample query includes the same WHERE clause in both the main query and the subquery. The logic of the query forces us to code it this way. Once again we see that, although SQL is simple, the logic of a query can be subtle.

Sample Query 20.3:   Display the course number and name of the philosophy course(s) with the highest labfee.

```
SELECT CNO, CNAME

FROM    COURSE

WHERE   CDEPT = 'PHIL'

AND     CLABFEE =

    (SELECT MAX(CLABFEE)

     FROM    COURSE

     WHERE   CDEPT = 'PHIL')
```

CNO   CNAME
P33   EXISTENTIALISM

Comments:

1.   Logic:

The subquery determines the maximum labfee for any philosophy course. This value (200.00) is substituted in the WHERE clause of the main query. Thus, the statement reduces to

```
SELECT CNO, CNAME, CLABFEE
FROM    COURSE
WHERE   CDEPT = 'PHIL'
AND     CLABFEE = 200.00
```

Both the main query and the subquery must contain the same condition (WHERE CDEPT = 'PHIL') in order to restrict the displayed courses to those offered by the Philosophy Department. This might appear to be redundant, but it is not. Consider the effect of excluding this condition in either case.

```
SELECT CNO, CNAME, CLABFEE
FROM    COURSE
WHERE   CLABFEE =
   (SELECT MAX(CLABFEE)
    FROM    COURSE
    WHERE   CDEPT = 'PHIL')
```

This statement displays all courses with a 200.00 labfee value. In particular, it would display the row for the "T44" theology course. This is not consistent with the objective to display only philosophy courses. The following statement is also incorrect, but for a different reason.

```
SELECT CNO, CNAME
FROM    COURSE
WHERE   CDEPT = 'PHIL'
AND     CLABFEE =
   (SELECT MAX(CLABFEE)
    FROM    COURSE)
```

This statement results in a "no hit" because the subquery evaluates to 500.00 and the main query determines that no philosophy courses have a labfee equal to this value.

2.   Syntax:

The subquery is simply another condition which is AND-connected to the main query WHERE clause. Subqueries do not need to be written last. The following statement is valid.

```
SELECT CNO, CNAME, CLABFEE
FROM    COURSE
WHERE   CLABFEE =
        (SELECT MAX(CLABFEE)
         FROM    COURSE
         WHERE   CDEPT = 'PHIL')
AND     CDEPT = 'PHIL'
```

Exercise:

20D. Display the course number, name, department, and labfee of the six-credit course(s) with the most expensive labfee.

The logic of the preceding sample query required the same WHERE clause to be included in both the main query and subquery. This is not always the case. You need to be very sensitive to the objective of the query and the logic to achieve the objective. Again, this is an issue which transcends the relatively simple syntax rules of SQL (or that of any other computer language). The next two sample queries demonstrate this point. They have different objectives, but they are sufficiently similar that ambiguity can occur unless the objectives are precisely articulated and understood.

Sample Query 20.4:   Display the course number and name of any non-CIS course with the smallest labfee of all courses. (This is the smallest labfee recorded in the COURSE table, including rows for CIS courses.)

```
SELECT CNO, CNAME

FROM    COURSE

WHERE   NOT CDEPT = 'CIS'

AND     CLABFEE =

    (SELECT MIN(CLABFEE)

     FROM    COURSE)
```

CNO	CNAME
T33	HEDONISM
P44	SOLIPSISM

Comment:

The sample query examines courses offered by every department, including CIS, to determine the minimal CLABFEE value. However, because of the WHERE clause in the main query, the output will not contain any CIS courses with this minimal labfee. Note the difference between this example and Sample Query 20.5, which has a WHERE clause in both the main query and subquery.

Sample Query 20.5:   Do not consider CIS courses. Display the course number and name of the course(s) with the smallest labfee.

```
SELECT CNO, CNAME

FROM    COURSE

WHERE   NOT CDEPT = 'CIS'

AND     CLABFEE =

    (SELECT MIN(CLABFEE)

    FROM    COURSE

    WHERE   NOT CDEPT = 'CIS')
```

CNO   CNAME
T33   HEDONISM
P44   SOLIPSISM

Comment:

This result is the same as the previous query. However, it is important to note that this is just a coincidence. It happened because the current contents of the COURSE table has CIS rows and non-CIS rows with the same minimal CLABFEE value of zero.

Assume that the COURSE table was updated such that courses T33 and P44 have labfee values of 5.00. This means that neither the Philosophy nor the Theology Department had any courses with zero labfees. Under this circumstance, the difference between the two preceding queries would be observable in the displayed results. Sample Query 20.4 would result in a "no hit" situation because none of the non-CIS courses have the minimal labfee of zero. However, Sample Query 20.5 would display the same two rows for courses T33 and P44.

All previous subquery examples showed the WHERE clause of the main query with an "equals" comparison operator. In practice, any of the other comparison operators (<, >, <=, >=, <>) can be used. The next sample query uses the "less than" operator in comparing the intermediate result produced by the subquery.

Sample Query 20.6:   Display the course number, name, and labfee of any course with a labfee which is less than the overall average labfee.

```
SELECT CNO, CNAME, CLABFEE

FROM    COURSE

WHERE   CLABFEE <

    (SELECT AVG(CLABFEE)

    FROM    COURSE)
```

CNO	CNAME	CLABFEE
T12	FUNDAMENTALISM	90.00
C11	INTRO TO CS	100.00
T33	HEDONISM	.00
C22	DATA STRUCTURES	50.00
C33	DISCRETE MATHEMATICS	.00
C44	DIGITAL CIRCUITS	.00
C55	COMPUTER ARCH.	100.00
P22	RATIONALISM	50.00
P44	SOLIPSISM	.00
P11	EMPIRICISM	100.00

Comments:

1. The WHERE clause of the main query contains a "less than" comparison operator. Any valid comparison operator is permitted.

2. The subquery references the AVG built-in function. Like the previous subqueries, this returns a single value which is used as the comparison value in the WHERE clause of the main query. Because the average labfee value is 110.00, the main query reduces to

    ```
    SELECT CNO, CNAME, CLABFEE
    FROM    COURSE
    WHERE   CLABFEE < 110.00
    ```

Exercise:

20E. Display the course number, name, and labfee of any course with a labfee which is less than the average labfee of courses offered by the Theology Department.

20F. Display all information about any course with a labfee which exceeds the maximum labfee for any theology or philosophy course.

All the preceding examples illustrated subqueries which reference the same table as the main query. Although this is common, it is not a requirement. In the next example, the main query and subquery reference different tables.

To understand the basis of this query, we assume that it may be poor policy to have the labfee of any course greater than or equal to the salary of any staff member. The goal is to determine which courses, if any, have such labfees.

Sample Query 20.7:   Display the course number, name, and labfee of any course which has a labfee greater than or equal to the salary of any staff member.

```
SELECT CNO, CNAME, CLABFEE

FROM    COURSE

WHERE   CLABFEE >=

        (SELECT MIN(ESALARY)

         FROM    STAFF)
```

CNO	CNAME	CLABFEE
T12	FUNDAMENTALISM	90.00
C11	INTRO TO CS	100.00
T44	COMMUNISM	200.00
C55	COMPUTER ARCH.	100.00
C66	RELATIONAL DATABASE	500.00
T11	SCHOLASTICISM	150.00
P33	EXISTENTIALISM	200.00
P11	EMPIRICISM	100.00

Comments:

1. The logic determines the lowest salary paid to any staff member, and then which courses, if any, have labfees greater than or equal to this amount.

2. The main query references the COURSE table and the subquery references the STAFF table. The subquery returns the minimum salary which, as a legitimate numeric value, can be compared to labfee values in the main query. Because the minimum ESALARY value is 51, the main query reduces to

        SELECT CNO, CNAME, CLABFEE
        FROM   COURSE
        WHERE   CLABFEE >= 51

3. There exists an alternative solution to this problem. See Sample Query 17.13 for a discussion of the "theta-join."

Exercises:

20G. Display the employee name and salary of any staff member whose salary is less than or equal to the maximum course labfee.

20H. Display all information about any CIS course with a labfee which is less than the average salary of staff members assigned to the Theology Department.

Subquery: WHERE Clause Examines Multiple Unknown Values

All previous subquery examples and workshop exercises involved a subquery which returned a single value. The value was substituted in the WHERE clause of the main query. This basic format is

WHERE column comparison-operator single-value

Subsequent sample queries will illustrate subqueries which return multiple values to be referenced by the main query. In place of a single comparison operator, the WHERE clause uses the IN keyword.

WHERE column IN set-of-values

Allowing the subquery to return multiple values extends the use of the subquery technique to a broader class of problems. It also permits alternative SQL solutions to some problems which could be solved using the join operation.

Sample Query 20.8:   Display the name and title of every staff member who works in the Humanities Building. (Same as Sample Query 17.4.)

```
SELECT ENAME, ETITLE

FROM    STAFF

WHERE   DEPT IN

        (SELECT DEPT

        FROM    DEPARTMENT

        WHERE   DBLD = 'HU')
```

ENAME	ETITLE
HANK KISS	JESTER
DICK NIX	CROOK
MATTHEW	EVANGLIST1
JOHN	EVANGLIST4
LUKE	EVANGLIST3
MARK	EVANGLIST2

Comments:

1. The logic of this sample query is to have the subquery examine the DEPARTMENT table to determine which departments are located in the Humanities Building. Then the main query will examine the STAFF table to determine the name and title of staff members who work in those departments.

2. The subquery will return the department identifiers for the two departments located in the Humanities Building. These are "THEO" and "PHIL." These values will be substituted into the WHERE clause of the main query as follows:

    ```
    SELECT ENAME, ETITLE
    FROM   STAFF
    WHERE  DEPT IN ('THEO', 'PHIL')
    ```

3. Note that, unlike previous subqueries, multiple values are returned as an intermediate result. For this reason, the main query WHERE clause must use the IN keyword. If the WHERE clause contained an equals sign, an error would result. This is because, after substitution of the subquery values, the clause would be WHERE DEPT = ('THEO', 'PHIL'). This is invalid because the comparison operators can be applied only to a single value.

4. This same problem was solved using the join technique in Sample Query 17.4. The reason the subquery technique can be applied is that all the displayed columns come from a single table (STAFF). This is the only table referenced in the main query.

    Many users find the subquery approach easier to understand than the join technique. This is a matter of personal preference from a logical problem-solving point of view.

Exercise:

20I. Display the department name and the chairperson faculty number for all departments responsible for a six-credit course.

It was noted in our previous discussion of the join operation that sometimes many matches could occur and duplicate rows could be displayed. Sample Query 17.5 was such a case where the same row was displayed four times. You were instructed to use the DISTINCT keyword to avoid this duplication. The following shows a subquery solution to the same sample query. However, note that this solution does not contain DISTINCT, yet duplicate rows are not displayed. Our comments will address this point.

Sample Query 20.9: Where can I find an evangelist? Display the building and room of any academic department which employs a staff member whose title contains the character string "EVANGLIST".

```
SELECT DBLD, DROOM

FROM    DEPARTMENT

WHERE   DEPT IN

   (SELECT DEPT

    FROM    STAFF

    WHERE   ETITLE LIKE 'EVANGLIST%')
```

DBLD   DROOM
HU   200

Comments:

1. Why were duplicate rows not displayed?

    Consider the intermediate result returned by the subquery. If it were executed as an independent query, it would display the following table.

        THEO
        THEO
        THEO
        THEO

This table is interpreted by the system as a "set" of four department values. These same values are substituted into the WHERE clause of the main query, which would be is evaluated as

```
SELECT  DBLD, DROOM
FROM    DEPARTMENT
WHERE   DEPT IN ('THEO', 'THEO', 'THEO', 'THEO')
```

Execution of the above statement would display the same single row shown for the subquery solution. The precise explanation involves recognition of the fact that a mathematical set does not contain duplicate elements. SQL would interpret the four occurrences of "THEO" as one value. Hence, the main query effectively becomes

```
SELECT  DBLD, DROOM
FROM    DEPARTMENT
WHERE   DEPT IN ('THEO')
```

2. The following solution makes the logic explicit by using DISTINCT in the subquery.

```
SELECT  DBLD, DROOM
FROM    DEPARTMENT
WHERE   DEPT IN
        (SELECT DISTINCT DEPT
         FROM    STAFF
         WHERE   ETITLE LIKE 'EVANGLIST%')
```

The use of DISTINCT in a subquery is always superfluous. However, this is not the case with the main query. The next sample query describes a situation where DISTINCT must be present in the main query SELECT clause.

The next sample query uses DISTINCT in the main query. This is necessary if we assume that a faculty member could be the chairperson of more than one academic department.

Sample Query 20.10:   Display the faculty number of any faculty member who serves as chairperson of any department which offers a six-credit course. Do not display duplicate values.

```
SELECT DISTINCT DCHFNO

FROM    DEPARTMENT

WHERE   DEPT IN

  (SELECT CDEPT

   FROM    COURSE

   WHERE   CRED = 6)
```

DCHFNO
10
60

Comments:

1. In this example, the subquery returns the CDEPT values of rows in the COURSE table which have a CRED value of 6. Only two rows match this condition. Their CDEPT values are "THEO" and "PHIL". Hence, the main query is evaluated as

   ```
   SELECT DISTINCT DCHFNO
   FROM    DEPARTMENT
   WHERE   DEPT IN ('THEO', 'PHIL')
   ```

2. Examination of the current contents of the DEPARTMENT table reveals that DCHFNO values are unique. (At this point, it just happens to be the case that no faculty member is serving as chairperson for more than one department.) Hence, the displayed results would have been the same if you omitted DISTINCT in the main query. It is important to note that this is a matter of luck. Because school policy permits a faculty member to chair multiple departments, it is possible for the same DCHFNO to occur in multiple rows of the DEPARTMENT table. It is poor show to write SQL code which is correct only under special conditions. Therefore, DISTINCT should be included in the main query SELECT clause.

3. This query displayed faculty numbers. What if you wanted to display faculty names? Note that faculty names are not stored in the DEPARTMENT table. This problem can be solved by nesting the current example within another SELECT statement. Try to code this query before examining the next sample query, which describes the solution in detail.

Exercise:

20J. Display the course number, section number, and building of any class which is offered in the same building where staff member Dick Nix works.

Second Level of Nesting

The next sample query is an extension of the previous query. This extension requires that we nest the previous SELECT statement, which already contains a subquery, within another SELECT statement. This leads to multiple levels of nesting of SELECT statements. We will see that there is nothing new to learn relative to syntax. However, the logic of the query becomes slightly more complex.

Sample Query 20.11:   Display the faculty number and name of any faculty member who serves as chairperson of any department which offers a six-credit course.

```
SELECT DISTINCT FNO, FNAME

FROM    FACULTY

WHERE   FNO IN

    (SELECT  DCHFNO

     FROM    DEPARTMENT

     WHERE   DEPT IN

         (SELECT CDEPT

          FROM    COURSE

          WHERE   CRED = 6))
```

FNO	FNAME
10	JULIE MARTYN
60	FRANK MARTYN

Comments:

1.   The system will execute the innermost subquery first. In this example it will return the department identifiers of all six-credit courses. The COURSE table has two such courses. One is offered by the Theology Department, and the other is offered by the Philosophy Department. Hence the query reduces to

```
SELECT DISTINCT FNO, FNAME
FROM    FACULTY
WHERE   FNO IN
   (SELECT DCHFNO
    FROM    DEPARTMENT
    WHERE   DEPT IN ('THEO', 'PHIL'))
```

This intermediate result still contains a subquery which requires evaluation. This subquery will examine the DEPARTMENT table and return the faculty numbers of chairpersons of the Theology and Philosophy Departments. These values are 10 and 60, respectively. The query is now reduced to

```
SELECT DISTINCT FNO, FNAME
FROM    FACULTY
WHERE   FNO IN (10, 60)
```

2. The use of DISTINCT in the main query is unnecessary because FNO values are unique within the FACULTY table. From a logical point of view, it is simpler to always use DISTINCT to avoid displaying duplicate rows.

3. Note that if a single department offered multiple six-credit courses, or if any faculty member was chairperson of multiple departments where each department offered at least one six-credit course, duplicate values would have been produced by the subqueries. Recall that DISTINCT is always superfluous in a subquery. (See Sample Query 20.9 for discussion.)

4. This query could have been expressed as a three-way join operation.

```
SELECT FNO, FNAME
FROM    FACULTY, DEPARTMENT, COURSE
WHERE   FNO = DCHFNO
AND     DEPT = CDEPT
AND     CRED = 6
```

Using NOT IN with Subqueries

The intermediate result generated by a subquery can be compared using NOT IN. The next example illustrates this fact. The logic is simple enough. However, there is a subtle circumstance which occurs with this example that can lead to an erroneous interpretation of the result. Try to detect this circumstance prior to reading the comments.

Sample Query 20.12:   Display the name, title, and department id of every staff member with a department id not found in the DEPARTMENT table.

```
SELECT ENAME, ETITLE, DEPT

FROM    STAFF

WHERE   DEPT NOT IN

    (SELECT DEPT

      FROM    DEPARTMENT)
```

ENAME	ETITLE	DEPT
EUCLID	LAB ASSIST	MATH
ARCHIMEDES	LAB ASSIST	ENG

Comments:

1.   The subquery produces the set of DEPT values found in the DEPARTMENT table. These are "THEO", "PHIL", "CIS", and "MGT". Hence, the main query reduces to

```
SELECT ENAME, ETITLE
FROM    STAFF
WHERE   DEPT NOT IN ('THEO', 'PHIL', 'CIS', 'MGT')
```

2.   Note that "DA VINCI" does not occur in the output. This is the subtle circumstance which needs to be recognized. DA VINCI has a null DEPT value. It cannot evaluate to "true" on any comparison. Hence, it is not selected for display.

Sample Query 20.5 will show a solution which includes DA VINCI.

Exercise:

20K. Display the name and department of any faculty member who is not teaching a class this semester.

Subquery within HAVING Clause

The next sample query illustrates the use of a subquery to generate an intermediate result for subsequent comparison within a HAVING clause. Other than the fact that the subquery is located within a HAVING clause, there is really nothing new to learn.

Sample Query 20.13: For every department which offers courses, display the department identifier and the average labfee of courses offered by the department if that average is less than the overall average labfee for all courses.

```
SELECT CDEPT, AVG(CLABFEE)

FROM    COURSE

GROUP BY CDEPT

HAVING AVG(CLABFEE) <

     (SELECT AVG(CLABFEE)

     FROM    COURSE)
```

CDEPT   AVG(CLABFEE)
PHIL   87.5

Comment:

Because we want to display the average labfee by department, it is necessary to establish groups using the GROUP BY clause. Because we only want to display those groups where the average is less than the overall average, a HAVING clause is required to compare the group averages to the overall average. A subquery is necessary to calculate this overall average. The subquery will determine that the overall average is 110. The main query is then evaluated as

```
SELECT CDEPT, AVG(CLABFEE)
FROM    COURSE
GROUP BY CDEPT
HAVING AVG(CLABFEE) < 110
```

The next sample query includes many of the aforementioned subquery techniques and includes an ORDER BY clause to sort the final displayed result. Note, however, that the SQL statement is longer than previous examples because of the complexity of the query. No new concepts are introduced.

Sample Query 20.14:   For all departments recorded in the DEPARTMENT table which employ staff members, display the department id and the average salary of staff members in the department if that average is less than the largest labfee recorded in the COURSE table. Sort the displayed result by department id.

```
SELECT STAFF.DEPT, AVG(ESALARY)

FROM    STAFF, DEPARTMENT

WHERE   STAFF.DEPT = DEPARTMENT.DEPT

GROUP BY STAFF.DEPT

HAVING AVG(ESALARY) <

      (SELECT MAX(CLABFEE)    FROM COURSE)

ORDER BY STAFF.DEPT
```

DEPT   AVG(ESALARY)
THEO   52.5

Comment:

The query is processed as follows. The STAFF and DEPARTMENT tables are joined as prescribed by the condition in the WHERE clause. Only PHIL and THEO rows match. From these rows, logical groups are formed on the basis of a common DEPT value. The system then acts upon these logical groups to summarize the average salary for the comparison in the HAVING clause. (Each group is then represented by a single row containing the DEPT value together with the average salary of all staff members associated with that department.)

The subquery in the HAVING clause is evaluated to return the highest labfee value of any course recorded in the COURSE table (500). This value is compared with each average salary value in the summarized group records. If the average salary for a group is less than 500, the summary record for the group is selected for display.

The final step is to satisfy the ORDER BY clause and sequence the result by ascending DEPT values.

Subquery Returns More Than One Column

At times you may find a need to test more than a single column to determine if a row should be retrieved. The next sample query demonstrates how this can be done using a subquery.

Sample Query 20.15:   Display the department id, other than the Philosophy Department, of any department which offers a course with the same number of credits and labfee as any philosophy course.

```
SELECT DISTINCT CDEPT

FROM    COURSE

WHERE   CDEPT <> 'PHIL'

AND     (CRED, CLABFEE) IN

  (SELECT CRED, CLABFEE

   FROM    COURSE

   WHERE   CDEPT = 'PHIL')
```

CDEPT
CIS

Comments:

1.   The columns in the main query which we wish to test are enclosed in parentheses. Whenever more than one column is to be tested in the main query, the columns must be enclosed in parentheses.

2.   The order in which the columns are specified in the main query must match the order of the columns in the subquery. Consider what would happen if the columns were in different orders. We would be trying to match credits with labfees and labfees with credits. Note that if the values in the database were such, we could find a match. However, this would clearly not satisfy the requirement of the query.

3.   DB2 Compatibility: Current versions of DB2 allow for the return of only a single column from a subquery.

ANY and ALL

The keywords ANY and ALL can be used with WHERE conditions which reference subqueries. Before discussing these keywords, we emphasize two facts.

1.   Given a query which can be solved using ANY or ALL, it is always possible to specify an alternative SQL solution which does not contain these keywords.

2.   Under certain circumstances, it is easy to misinterpret the logical behavior of statements containing ANY or ALL.

For these reasons, some authorities have argued that ANY and ALL should not be part of the SQL language. However, this is wishful thinking. They are part of SQL. Hence, we discuss them with the preliminary recommendation that you should understand these keywords, but should also restrict your use of such.

We need to review an important point prior to discussing the use of ANY and ALL. When a subquery is executed, it can return one or more values. Sample Queries 20.8 through 20.12 were coded such that the subquery could produce multiple values. These queries used the IN keyword. Sample Queries 20.2 through 20.7 were coded so that the subquery always produced a single value. Therefore, the WHERE condition in the main query used the standard comparison operators (=, <, >, <>) when evaluating the subquery result. The following sample queries use the standard comparison operators in conjunction with ANY and ALL to evaluate an intermediate result produced by a subquery which can return multiple values.

The following sample query introduces the ANY keyword. The ANY keyword can be used with any of the standard comparison operators when the subquery can return one or many values. When ANY is used in a comparison, the condition evaluates to "true" if the expression is true for any of the values returned by the subquery.

Sample Query 20.16: Display the name and title of any staff member employed by an existing academic department.

```
SELECT ENAME, ETITLE

FROM    STAFF

WHERE   DEPT = ANY

   (SELECT DEPT

      FROM    DEPARTMENT)
```

ENAME	ETITLE
HANK KISS	JESTER
DICK NIX	CROOK
MATTHEW	EVANGLIST1
JOHN	EVANGLIST4
LUKE	EVANGLIST3
MARK	EVANGLIST2

Comments:

1. The subquery returns the name of existing departments: "CIS", "PHIL", "THEO", and "MGT". Hence, the query reduces to

    ```
    SELECT ENAME, ETITLE
    FROM    STAFF
    WHERE   DEPT = ANY ('CIS','PHIL','THEO','MGT')
    ```

    Only staff members with a DEPT value "equal to any" of the values returned by the subquery appear in the output display.

2. An alternative solution to the sample query is

    ```
    SELECT ENAME, ETITLE
    FROM    STAFF
    WHERE   DEPT IN (SELECT DEPT FROM DEPARTMENT)
    ```

    The only difference is that "IN" has replaced "= ANY" in the WHERE clause. In effect, "IN" and "= ANY" are synonymous.

3. Another solution involves use of the join operation.

    ```
    SELECT ENAME, ETITLE
    FROM    STAFF, DEPARTMENT
    WHERE   STAFF.DEPT = DEPARTMENT.DEPT
    ```

The ALL keyword, like ANY, can be used with any of the standard comparison operators when a subquery can return multiple values. When ALL is used, the condition evaluates to "true" if the expression is true for all of the values returned by the subquery.

Sample Query 20.17:   Display the course number, name, and labfee of any course having a labfee less than all the salaries of staff members.

```
SELECT CNO, CNAME, CLABFEE

FROM    COURSE

WHERE   CLABFEE < ALL

    (SELECT ESALARY

    FROM    STAFF)
```

CNO	CNAME	CLABFEE
T33	HEDONISM	.00
C22	DATA STRUCTURES	50.00
C33	DISCRETE MATHEMATICS	.00
C44	DIGITAL CIRCUITS	.00
P22	RATIONALISM	50.00
P44	SOLIPSISM	.00

Comments:

1.   The subquery returns every ESALARY value in the STAFF table. If a course has a CLABFEE value "less than all" of these ESALARY values, then its number, name, and labfee appear in the output.

2.   Note that if a CLABFEE value is less than all the ESALARY values, then it is less than the smallest ESALARY value. This observation motivates the following alternative solution.

```
SELECT CNO, CNAME, CLABFEE
FROM    COURSE
WHERE   CLABFEE < (SELECT MIN(ESALARY) FROM STAFF)
```

Sample Query 20.18: Display the name and salary of any staff member whose salary is greater than or equal to all the course labfees.

```
SELECT ENAME, ESALARY

FROM    STAFF

WHERE   ESALARY >= ALL

        (SELECT CLABFEE

        FROM    COURSE)
```

ENAME	ESALARY
HANK KISS	25000
DICK NIX	25001
DA VINCI	500
EUCLID	1000

Comments:

1. The subquery returns every CLABFEE value in the COURSE table. If a staff member has a labfee value "greater than or equal to all" of these values, then that person's name and salary appear in result.

2. Note that if an ESALARY value is greater than or equal to all the CLABFEE values, then it is greater than or equal to the largest CLABFEE value. This observation motivates the following alternative solution.

    ```
    SELECT ENAME, ESALARY
    FROM    STAFF
    WHERE   ESALARY = (SELECT MAX(CLABFEE) FROM COURSE)
    ```

3. We stated that all of the comparison operators can be used with ALL. Regardless of the operator, an alternative solution can be specified which is usually more direct. This especially applies to "= ALL", which can evaluate to "true" only if the subquery returns just one value which equals the comparison field value.

Logic of ANY and ALL

The following comments pertain to the logical behavior of ANY and ALL when used with certain comparison operators.

1. "= ANY" is equivalent to "IN". (But do not jump to the erroneous conclusion that "<> ANY" means the same thing as "NOT IN". See comment 4 below.)

2. "<> ANY" has little application. Consider the following examples.

    a. WHERE COLX <> ANY (2,4,6)
        This condition is always true. Even if the COLX value appears in the set of values, it will not be equal to some other value which is also in the set.

    b. WHERE COLX <> ANY (4)
        This condition is the same as WHERE COLX <> 4.

3. "= ALL" has little application. Consider the following examples.

    a. WHERE COLX = ALL (2,4,6)
        This condition is always false because COLX will always contain only a single value and, therefore, cannot match all of the values in the set.

    b. WHERE COLX = ALL (4)
        This condition is the same as WHERE COLX = 4.

4. "<> ALL" means the same thing as "NOT IN". (It is good mental exercise to think this through. It may be helpful to reexamine the previous discussion on NOT IN in Sample Query 4.14.)

    These comments reinforce the position that use of ANY and ALL should be restricted. Alternative solutions were presented to each sample query which used these keywords. From a formal point of view, both ANY and ALL are superfluous.

Exercises:

20L. Rewrite the following query without using "> ANY".

```
SELECT  CNO, CNAME, CLABFEE
FROM    COURSE
WHERE   CLABFEE > ANY
        (SELECT ESALARY
         FROM    STAFF)
```

20M. Display the name and number of dependents for faculty members who have as many dependents as the number of credits offered for any course. Give two solutions. The first should use the ANY keyword. The second should not.

The final sample query of this chapter illustrates the nesting of group functions inside a subquery.

Sample Query 20.19:   Display the department id and average labfee of the academic department(s) having the highest average course labfee.

```
SELECT CDEPT, AVG(CLABFEE)

FROM    COURSE

GROUP BY CDEPT

HAVING AVG(CLABFEE) =

    (SELECT MAX(AVG(CLABFEE))

    FROM    COURSE

    GROUP BY CDEPT)
```

CDEPT   AVG(CLABFEE)
CIS   125

Comments:

1.   The intermediate result produced by the subquery is a set of three values corresponding to the average labfees of the PHIL, THEO, and CIS departments. The largest, or maximum, of these three values is returned to complete the main query WHERE clause. Thus the main query is reduced to

```
SELECT CDEPT, AVG(CLABFEE)
FROM    COURSE
GROUP BY CDEPT
HAVING AVG(CLABFEE) = 125.00
```

2.   Note that the objective of the query is to determine the average labfee for each department and then display the maximum. What we want is a "maximum of averages." We accomplished this objective through the nesting of group functions.

3.   DB2 Compatibility: Current versions of DB2 do not allow group functions to be nested. Hence, this query would not work on a DB2 system. However, by using ALL, an acceptable query could be formulated with the following changes to the current query.

```
HAVING AVG(CLABFEE) >= ALL
(SELECT AVG(CLABFEE) FROM COURSE GROUP BY CDEPT)
```

Summary

This chapter has introduced the use of a subquery to generate an intermediate result for comparison purposes within a WHERE or HAVING clause. You must use this technique when you want to compare a field with an unknown value. The subquery serves the purpose of determining the unknown value. The subquery was also illustrated as an alternative to coding a join operation when the desired displayed results all come from one table.

A subquery is simply another SELECT statement which is most often used to produce a single column result which is compatible with the comparison operation to be performed within the WHERE or HAVING clause of another SELECT statement. ORACLE allows more than one column to be returned from a subquery.

We noted one significant restriction in the coding of a subquery. The subquery itself cannot contain an ORDER BY clause. Sorting applies only to the result table. The ORDER BY clause must be the last clause in the entire statement.

This chapter introduced the fundamental subquery techniques which are used most often. Chapter 20 will continue our discussion of subqueries by presenting alternatives to some of the techniques shown in this chapter and introducing some new keywords and techniques which can be applied to more challenging problems.

Summary Exercises

20N. Display the course number and name for every course that student 800 is registered for.

20O. Display all information about any scheduled class which has a labfee less than $100 and is not offered on a Friday.

20P. Display the student number and date of registration for all students who are registered for at least one course offered by a department located in the science (SC) building.

20Q. Assume that you do not know the highest labfee. Write a SELECT statement which will display the course number, name, department, and labfee of the course(s) having the second highest labfee.

20R. Display the name and number of dependents for faculty members who have fewer dependents than the number of credits offered for all courses.

20S. Real challenge: Solve Sample Query 20.1 using a join instead of a subquery.

21

Correlated Subqueries

This chapter expands on the subquery concept by introducing a variation known as a "correlated subquery." This is an important and powerful feature which allows you to solve certain data-retrieval problems which cannot be solved by the techniques described previously. There are significant differences between correlated subqueries and the subqueries introduced in Chapter 20. These differences introduce a new level of complexity which motivates the placement of this topic in a separate chapter.

Preliminary Comments

Before presenting correlated subquery problems and their solutions, it is important to make three preliminary observations about the subquery examples presented in Chapter 20. These observations are made to emphasize the unique features of correlated subqueries.

Observation 1:

Previous examples presented subqueries which were "self-contained." This is an informal term to describe the fact that the subquery constitutes a valid SELECT statement and could be independently executed if it were detached from the main query. For example, consider the following SELECT statement, which displays information about any course with a labfee equal to the maximum labfee of all theology courses.

```
SELECT  CDEPT, CNO, CNAME, CLABFEE
FROM    COURSE
WHERE   CLABFEE =
                (SELECT MAX(CLABFEE)
                 FROM COURSE
                 WHERE CDEPT = 'THEO')
```

The subquery, considered as an independent statement, is

```
SELECT  MAX(CLABFEE)
FROM    COURSE
WHERE   CDEPT = 'THEO'
```

This statement could be executed to return a result of 200.00. All previous subquery examples demonstrated this "self-contained" property. We emphasize this point because the correlated subqueries presented in this chapter do not have this property. Trying to execute these correlated subqueries as independent queries will cause errors. This is because the SELECT statement of a correlated subquery will contain a variable (a correlation variable) which references the outer query.

Observation 2:

The second observation is that ORACLE will execute a self-contained subquery just once. In the above example, the single execution of the subquery returned a value (200.00). This result is used to reformulate the outer query as

```
SELECT CDEPT
FROM    COURSE
WHERE   CLABFEE = 200.00
```

Even though the COURSE table contains 14 rows, the self-contained subquery is executed just once. This behavior differs from a correlated subquery which will usually be executed many times. This means that you will not be able to conceptualize the solution as a one-time execution on the subquery to obtain an intermediate result, followed by a one-time substitution of the result to reformulate the outer query as shown above. For correlated subqueries, each execution of the subquery presumably produces a different result which leads to a different reformulation of the outer query.

Observation 3:

The third observation pertains to syntax. None of the previously described self-contained subqueries contained a correlation variable. Correlation variables are usually used to reference values specified by the outer query. (This is why the subquery is not self-contained.) We will see that correlation variable can be explicitly specified in the FROM clause or, in some cases, implicitly specified by simple reference in the subquery. The following sample queries will illustrate both explicit and implicit specification of correlation variables.

Finally, for the sake of completeness, we comment (without explanation at this point) that correlation variables can be used in SELECT statements which do not contain subqueries.

The first sample query of this chapter shows a correlated subquery containing "CX" as the correlation variable. The ORACLE reference manual uses the term "table alias" instead of "correlation variable." Correlation variables are sometimes referred to as "correlation names" or "range variables." We choose to use the term "correlation variable."

We introduce the first sample query and its solution as the basis of a detail discussion on the special logic of correlated subqueries.

Sample Query 21.1:   For each department which offers courses, display the department's identifier followed by the number, name, and labfee of the department-sponsored course having the largest labfee.

```
SELECT CDEPT, CNO, CNAME, CLABFEE

FROM    COURSE CX

WHERE   CLABFEE =

        (SELECT MAX(CLABFEE)

        FROM COURSE

        WHERE CDEPT = CX.CDEPT)
```

CDEPT	CNO	CNAME	CLABFEE
THEO	T44	COMMUNISM	200.00
CIS	C66	RELATIONAL DATABASE	500.00
PHIL	P33	EXISTENTIALISM	200.00

Comments:

1.   Syntax: The FROM clause in the main query contains

FROM COURSE CX

The presence of CX after COURSE means that CX is defined as a correlation variable for the COURSE table. There must be one or more spaces between the table name and the corresponding correlated variable name. (Do not use a comma as a separator. If you do, the system will incorrectly interpret CX as the name of another table.)

Assuming the correlation variable CX has been defined in the outer SELECT statement, it can then be referenced in a subquery. In the current example, we see

    WHERE CDEPT = CX.CDEPT

We will describe the function of CX.CDEPT below. For the moment we ask you to consider just the subquery in isolation and note that it is not self-contained.

        SELECT MAX(CLABFEE)
        FROM   COURSE
        WHERE   CDEPT = CX.CDEPT

Independent execution of this statement would result in an error because the system has no knowledge of CX.CDEPT. However, it is valid as a correlated subquery where CX has been specified as a correlation variable in the FROM clause of an outer SELECT statement.

2. Logic: It is absolutely imperative that you understand the logic of this sample query in order to understand the purpose of the correlation variable. It is helpful to distinguish the objective of this example from the query mentioned in our preliminary comments which illustrated a self-contained subquery. That query used a subselect to determine that the maximum labfee value for any theology course was 200.00. Then the system compared the CLABFEE value in every row to 200.00. If the CLABFEE value equaled 200.00, it was selected for display. The key point is that every row, regardless of its CDEPT value, had its CLABFEE value compared to 200.00. This value remained constant throughout the execution of the statement.

The current sample query is quite different because the system needs to *compare the CLABFEE value in each row to the maximum CLABFEE value for the department identified by the CDEPT value in the row under consideration. This CDEPT value will vary from row to row. Hence, the maximum CLABFEE will vary from row to row.*

In effect, for each row in the COURSE table, the system must

* Examine the CDEPT value of the row.

* Execute the subquery to determine the maximum CLABFEE value for that department.

* Compare the CLABFEE value of the row under consideration to see if it equals the value returned by the subquery. If it does, the row is selected for display.

This is the essence of a correlated subquery. The execution of the subquery must be correlated with a particular value (CDEPT in this case) which will vary from row to row. Hence, the subquery must be executed for each row in the table. It also means that the system must keep track of the particular row being processed. This is the precise purpose of a correlation variable. It serves as a pointer to the row being considered for selection. These concepts will be illustrated below.

Because the COURSE table has 14 rows, the system will execute the subquery 14 times. On each execution the system will use CX to point to a row. In order to illustrate the overall process, we need to assume that the system encounters the COURSE table rows in some sequence. Assume the first three rows of this sequence are

CNO	CNAME	CDESCP	CRED	CLABFEE	CDEPT
T11	SCHOLASTICISM	FOR THE PIOUS	3	150.00	THEO
P33	EXISTENTIALISM	FOR CIS MAJORS	3	200.00	PHIL
C11	INTO TO CS	FOR ROOKIES	3	100.00	CIS
.	.	.	.	.	. .
.	.	.	.	.	. .
.	.	.	.	.	. .

We describe the system logic for processing the first three rows.

a. The system examines the first row shown below.

T11	SCHOLASTICISM	FOR THE PIOUS	3	150.00	THEO

This means that the correlation variable CX will initially point to this row. Hence, the CDEPT value of this row (THEO) is substituted for CX.CDEPT in the subquery. Thus, the subquery is evaluated as

```
SELECT MAX(CLABFEE)
FROM    COURSE
WHERE   CDEPT = 'THEO'
```

Execution of this query returns a value of 200.00. After substitution of this intermediate result, the main query is evaluated as

```
SELECT CDEPT, CNO, CNAME, CLABFEE
FROM    COURSE CX
WHERE   CLABFEE = 200.00
```

This query is effectively asking whether the current row under consideration (i.e., the row pointed to by CX, the T11 row) has a CLABFEE value of 200.00. It does not. Hence, this row is not selected and does not appear in the output display.

We emphasize that this behavior is considerably different from other main query SELECT statements which scanned the entire table and selected all rows which matched the selection criteria. This main query SELECT statement, which has a CX in its FROM clause, is only asking if the current row, the one referenced by the correlation variable, has a CLABFEE value of 200.00. The same logic will be described for the next two rows.

b. Next, the system examines the second row shown below.

P33	EXISTENTIALISM	FOR CIS MAJORS	3	200.00	PHIL

The CDEPT value of "PHIL" is substituted for CX.CDEPT in the subquery. Thus, the subquery is evaluated as

```
SELECT MAX(CLABFEE)
FROM    COURSE
WHERE   CDEPT = 'PHIL'
```

Execution of this query returns a value of 200.00. Then the main query is evaluated as

```
SELECT CDEPT, CNO, CNAME, CLABFEE
FROM    COURSE CX
WHERE   CLABFEE = 200.00
```

This statement is only asking if the current row (P33) has a CLABFEE value of 200.00. It does, so it appears in the output.

c. The system then examines the third row shown below.

C11	INTRO TO CS	FOR ROOKIES	3	100.00	CIS

Its CDEPT value of "CIS" is substituted for CX.CDEPT in the subquery. Thus, the subquery is evaluated as

```
SELECT MAX(CLABFEE)
FROM    COURSE
WHERE   CDEPT = 'CIS'
```

Execution of this query returns a value of 500.00. Then the main query is evaluated as

```
SELECT CDEPT, CNO, CNAME, CLABFEE
FROM    COURSE CX
WHERE   CLABFEE = 500.00
```

This statement is asking if the current row (C11) has a CLABFEE value of 500.00. It does not. Hence it does not appear in the output.

The same process continues for the remaining 11 rows. Each time the subquery determines the maximum departmental labfee value for the department corresponding to the CDEPT value for the row. If the CLABFEE value equals this maximum, then the row is selected for display.

3.   Efficiency: The execution of a correlated subquery for each row in a table will obviously use more computer time than the single execution of a self-contained subquery. This is especially true if the table has a large number of rows. However, for some problems, like the current example, there is no alternative way of expressing the query in a single SELECT statement.

4.   The current example shows the *explicit declaration* of the CX correlation variable by specifying it in the main query FROM clause. There are circumstances where a correlation variable can be *implicitly* declared. The next sample query will show the implicit declaration of a correlation variable.

The explicit declaration of a correlation variable is necessary in the current example because the main query and subquery both reference the same table. If CX were omitted, the statement would be *incorrectly* written as

```
SELECT CDEPT, CNO, CNAME, CLABFEE
FROM    COURSE
WHERE   CLABFEE =
           (SELECT MAX(CLABFEE)
            FROM    COURSE
            WHERE   CDEPT = CDEPT)
```

Note this subquery WHERE clause, "WHERE CDEPT = CDEPT", is always true and hence meaningless in this context.

Exercise:

21A. Display the name, department id, and salary for those faculty members who have a salary which is greater than the average faculty salary for their department.

The next sample query illustrates a correlated subquery which utilizes, but does not explicitly declare, a correlation variable.

Sample Query 21.2: For each department which offers courses, display the department id, number, name, and labfee of any department-sponsored course having a labfee which exceeds the salary of the highest-paid staff member employed by that department.

```
SELECT CDEPT, CNO, CNAME, CLABFEE

FROM    COURSE

WHERE   CLABFEE >

        (SELECT MAX(ESALARY)

        FROM STAFF

        WHERE DEPT = COURSE.CDEPT)
```

CDEPT	CNO	CNAME	CLABFEE
THEO	T12	FUNDAMENTALISM	90.00
THEO	T44	COMMUNISM	200.00
THEO	T11	SCHOLASTICISM	150.00

Comments:

1. Logic: The logic of this query requires a correlated query because we want to compare the labfee for each course with the maximum salary of a staff member employed by the same department which offers the course. The department is identified by the CDEPT value, which changes from row to row. Hence the need for a correlated subquery.

2. Syntax: As a self-contained statement the WHERE clause in the subquery is invalid because COURSE.CDEPT does not refer to a column in the STAFF table. However, this SELECT statement is meaningful as a subquery within an outer query which contains a "FROM COURSE" clause. Then, the system will interpret the subquery as a correlated subquery with COURSE.CDEPT as an implicitly declared correlation variable.

The explicit definition of a correlation variable (similar to CX in the previous example) is unnecessary because the main query and subquery reference different tables in their FROM clauses. However, it enhances readability and, therefore, it is better to explicitly define correlation variables whenever you need to write a correlated subquery. The current example is rewritten using C as a correlation variable.

```
SELECT  CDEPT, CNO, CNAME, CLABFEE
FROM    COURSE C
WHERE   CLABFEE >
                (SELECT MAX(ESALARY)
                 FROM    STAFF
                 WHERE   DEPT = C.CDEPT)
```

It is common practice to define a correlation variable for the all tables, including those identified in the FROM clause of the subquery. The following equivalent statement includes S as a correlation variable for STAFF.

```
SELECT  CDEPT, CNO, CNAME, CLABFEE
FROM    COURSE C
WHERE   CLABFEE >
                (SELECT MAX(ESALARY)
                 FROM    STAFF S
                 WHERE   S.DEPT = C.CDEPT)
```

3. If a subquery refers to a column (CDEPT) which is not in a table referenced by the subquery FROM clause (FROM STAFF), then ORACLE (but not DB2) assumes that the subquery is a correlated subquery. Using ORACLE, the following query is equivalent to the current example.

```
SELECT  CDEPT, CNO, CNAME, CLABFEE
FROM    COURSE
WHERE   CLABFEE >
                (SELECT MAX(ESALARY)
                 FROM    STAFF
                 WHERE   DEPT = CDEPT)
```

Exercise:

21B. Display the name and department id for those faculty members who have a number of dependents greater than the average number of credits for courses offered by their department.

EXISTS Keyword

In previous subquery examples the main query WHERE clause was used to perform an explicit comparison with the value returned by the subquery. Sometimes the logic of the problem implies that an explicit comparison is unnecessary. Instead, a subquery is used only to determine if there are any rows in a table which match some condition. In this case, the main query can use the EXISTS keyword to test whether any match on the condition occurred.

Sample Query 21.3: Display the name and title of any staff member assigned to an existing department. More precisely, display the ENAME and ETITLE values in those STAFF table rows which have a DEPT value equal to any DEPT value in the DEPARTMENT table.

```
SELECT  ENAME, ETITLE

FROM    STAFF

WHERE   EXISTS

   (SELECT *

   FROM    DEPARTMENT

   WHERE   DEPARTMENT.DEPT = STAFF.DEPT)
```

ENAME	ETITLE
HANK KISS	JESTER
DICK NIX	CROOK
MATTHEW	EVANGLIST1
MARK	EVANGLIST2
LUKE	EVANGLIST3
JOHN	EVANGLIST4

Comments:

1. Logic: The subquery is a correlated subquery where
    STAFF.DEPT is an implicitly defined correlation variable
    in the subquery. Therefore, the system will execute the
    subquery for each row in the STAFF table. Assume that
    the first STAFF table row encountered corresponds to
    "LUKE" which has a DEPT value of "THEO". Then the
    subquery (for the "LUKE" row) reduces to

    ```
    SELECT *
    FROM    DEPARTMENT
    WHERE   DEPARTMENT.DEPT = 'THEO'
    ```

    This statement results in a "hit" because there is at
    least one row in the DEPARTMENT table with a DEPT value
    of "THEO." This means that the EXISTS test of the main
    query results in a "true" condition and the "LUKE" row
    is selected for display.

    Next assume that the second STAFF table row corresponds
    to "EUCLID", which has a DEPT value of "MATH". Then the
    subquery reduces to

    ```
    SELECT *
    FROM    DEPARTMENT
    WHERE   DEPARTMENT.DEPT = 'MATH'
    ```

    This statement results in a "no hit" because there are
    no rows in the DEPARTMENT table with a DEPT value of
    "MATH." This means that the main query EXISTS test
    results in a "false" condition; hence the "EUCLID" row
    is not selected. Likewise, the row corresponding to
    "ARCHIMEDES" is not selected because its CDEPT value
    ("ENG") does not exist in the DEPARTMENT table. The "DA
    VINCI" row is not selected because its DEPT value is
    null. (Note that the "DA VINCI" row would not be
    selected even if a null value did exist in the DEPT
    column of DEPARTMENT. This is because the "null = null"
    compare results in "unknown," and cannot be considered
    "true.")

2.   Syntax: The subquery SELECT clause contains an asterisk
      even though column names could be specified. An asterisk
      is usually specified in the subquery when the main query
      performs an EXISTS test because the system does not
      return values from the subquery; rather, it confirms
      existence based on the test.

3.   The current example is presented for tutorial purposes
      only. The query could have been satisfied by equivalent
      SELECT statements without using EXISTS. The following
      statements would produce the same result.

```
SELECT ENAME, ETITLE
FROM   STAFF, DEPARTMENT
WHERE  STAFF.DEPT = DEPARTMENT.DEPT

SELECT ENAME, ETITLE
FROM   STAFF
WHERE  DEPT IN
          (SELECT DEPT
           FROM   DEPARTMENT)
```

However, there are problems which can be solved only by
using the EXISTS keyword; you should recognize that
EXISTS is an important keyword in the SQL language and
understand its behavior. See Sample Query 21.8.

Exercise:

21C. Display the name and department id of any faculty member
     assigned to a department which offers a six-credit
     course.

     For this exercise, write three SELECT statements which
     will satisfy the query. The first statement should be a
     correlated subquery which utilizes the EXISTS keyword.
     The second statement should be a self-contained
     subquery. The third statement should represent a join
     operation.

     Consider executing each solution with SET TIMING ON to
     determine which solution is most efficient.

The next example demonstrates the use of EXISTS with a correlated subquery where the correlation variables are explicitly specified.

Sample Query 21.4: Display the course number, name, and labfee of any course where there exists some staff member whose salary is less than that labfee.

```
SELECT  CNO, CNAME, CLABFEE

FROM    COURSE C

WHERE   EXISTS

    (SELECT *

    FROM    STAFF S

    WHERE   S.ESALARY < C.CLABFEE)
```

CNO	CNAME	CLABFEE
T12	FUNDAMENTALISM	90.00
C11	INTRO TO CS	100.00
T44	COMMUNISM	200.00
C55	COMPUTER ARCH.	100.00
C66	RELATIONAL DATABASE	500.00
T11	SCHOLASTICISM	150.00
P33	EXISTENTIALISM	200.00
P11	EMPIRICISM	100.00

Comment:

For each row in the COURSE table the subquery determines if any row in the STAFF table has an ESALARY value less than the CLABFEE value of the COURSE row. If such a row exists in the STAFF table, then the COURSE row is selected.

Exercise:

21D. Rewrite the current sample query using (a) a self-contained subquery and (b) a join operation.

NOT EXISTS

A correlated subquery can be formulated using NOT EXISTS, which, as you would expect, tests for a "does not exist" condition. It will select precisely those rows which would not be selected by the EXISTS condition. In fact, you will probably find that NOT EXISTS is more useful than EXISTS. This is because it can avoid a potentially problematic situation which can occur when a table contains null values. This sample query illustrates such a situation.

Sample Query 21.5: Display the name, title, and department id of any staff member who is not assigned to an existing department. More precisely, display the ENAME, ETITLE, and DEPT values of any row in the STAFF table with a DEPT value which does not match any value in the DEPT column of the DEPARTMENT table.

```
SELECT ENAME, ETITLE, DEPT

FROM    STAFF

WHERE   NOT EXISTS

    (SELECT *

      FROM    DEPARTMENT

      WHERE   DEPARTMENT.DEPT = STAFF.DEPT)
```

ENAME	ETITLE	DEPT
DA VINCI	LAB ASSIST	-
EUCLID	LAB ASSIST	MATH
ARCHIMEDES	LAB ASSIST	ENG

Comments:

1. The subquery is identical to that of Sample Query 21.3. Here the main query will select just those rows where a "no hit" occurs in the subquery.

2. Observe that the "DA VINCI" row, which has a null DEPT
    value, is shown in the output display. When the main
    query was considering the "DA VINCI" row for selection,
    the subquery did not select any rows because it is
    impossible for the STAFF.DEPT value, which is null, to
    equal any DEPARTMENT.DEPT, including another null value.
    This "no hit" situation in the subquery means that the
    "DA VINCI" row (or any other STAFF row with a null DEPT
    value) will be selected under the NOT EXISTS condition.

    We emphasize this aspect of the NOT EXISTS test to
    emphasize the following statement is *not equivalent* to
    the current example.

```
SELECT ENAME, ETITLE, DEPT
FROM    STAFF
WHERE   DEPT NOT IN
    (SELECT DEPT
     FROM    DEPARTMENT)
```

    This statement will not select the "DA VINCI" row
    because it has a null DEPT value. In effect, this
    difference in behavior means that EXIST always operates
    on a two-value logic unlike the other SQL operators,
    which operate on a three-value logic.

    It is possible to write a SELECT statement which is
    equivalent to the current example, but you must
    explicitly test for null values.

```
SELECT ENAME, ETITLE
FROM    STAFF
WHERE   DEPT NOT IN
    (SELECT DEPT
     FROM    DEPARTMENT)
OR DEPT IS NULL
```

3. The correlation variable STAFF.DEPT is implicitly
    specified in the subquery. There is no possible
    ambiguity because the main query and subquery reference
    different tables in their FROM clauses.

Exercise:

21E. Display the name and department id of any faculty member
     in a department which does not offer a six-credit
     course. Specify two SELECT statements which will satisfy
     the query. The first statement should be a correlated
     subquery which utilizes the NOT EXISTS keywords. The
     second statement can use any other technique.

The next sample query uses NOT EXISTS with a correlated subquery. Correlation variables are explicitly specified because the main query and subquery both reference the same table.

Sample Query 21.6:   Display the course number, name, and labfee of any course which has a unique labfee. This is a labfee which does not equal the labfee of any other course.

```
SELECT CNO, CNAME, CLABFEE

FROM    COURSE C1

WHERE   NOT EXISTS

    (SELECT *

    FROM    COURSE C2

    WHERE   C1.CLABFEE = C2.CLABFEE

    AND     C1.CNO <> C2.CNO)
```

CNO	CNAME	CLABFEE
T12	FUNDAMENTALISM	90.00
C66	RELATIONAL DATABASE	500.00
T11	SCHOLASTICISM	150.00

Comments:

1.   The correlated variable C1 is necessary. C2 is not necessary, but its use makes the statement more readable.

2.   Each row in the COURSE table is considered for selection with C1 serving as the correlation variable for referencing these rows. The corresponding course number and labfee value are substituted for C1.CNO and C1.CLABFEE for each execution of the subquery. If the subquery results in a "no hit," the row under consideration (the one pointed by C1) is selected.

Correlation Variables without Subqueries

It is possible to utilize correlation variables in SELECT statements which do not contain a subquery. Sample Queries 17.11 and 17.12 illustrated the joining of a table with itself. The SELECT statement for 17.12 is shown below.

```
SELECT  ST1.DEPT, ST1.ENAME, ST2.ENAME
FROM    STAFF ST1, STAFF ST2
WHERE   ST1.DEPT = ST2.DEPT
AND     ST1.ENAME < ST2.ENAME
```

In our previous discussion of this example we referred to ST1 and ST2 as "table aliases." They effectively gave two names to the same table so that we could write a SELECT statement which joined these tables. In fact, ST1 and ST2 are correlation variables. The system will use ST1 as a pointer to a given row. It will then execute the statement substituting that row's DEPT value for ST1.DEPT and that row's ENAME value for ST1.ENAME. Likewise, it will do the same for ST2. (The system does not produce a duplicate copy of this table.) If the WHERE condition is true after substituting the corresponding values referenced by ST1 and ST2, the ST1.DEPT, ST1.ENAME, and ST2.ENAME values are displayed. Both ST1 and ST2 range over the entire STAFF table to compare every possible pair of rows.

This discussion provides insight into an alternative, but less elegant, solution to Sample Query 21.6.

```
SELECT  CNO, CNAME, CLABFEE
FROM    COURSE
WHERE   CNO NOT IN
     (SELECT CA.CNO
      FROM   COURSE CA, COURSE CB
      WHERE  CA.CLABFEE = CB.CLABFEE
      AND    CA.CNO <> CB.CNO)
```

Observe that the subquery is self-contained; it is *not correlated with the main query*. However, the subquery does use correlation variables, CA and CB, to implement the join of the COURSE table with itself.

Outer Join Using Correlated Subquery

In Chapter 18 we introduced the outer join operation. We now
introduce an alternative way of accomplishing this operation
using a correlated subquery. In systems such as DB2, which do
not directly provide the outer join operation, we would have
to use this alternative approach.

Sample Query 21.7:   For every staff member recorded in the
STAFF table, display his name, title,
salary, and department id along with all
information about the department to
which he is assigned (i.e., the
department's identifier, building, room,
and faculty number of the department
chairperson). If the staff member is not
assigned to an existing department, or
if the assignment is unknown (null),
display blanks for department
information.

```
SELECT *

FROM    STAFF, DEPARTMENT

WHERE   STAFF.DEPT = DEPARTMENT.DEPT

UNION

SELECT ENAME, ETITLE, ESALARY,

       STAFF.DEPT, ' ', ' ', ' ', ' '

FROM    STAFF

WHERE   NOT EXISTS

    (SELECT *

     FROM   DEPARTMENT

     WHERE  DEPARTMENT.DEPT = STAFF.DEPT)
```

ENAME	ETITLE	ESALARY	DEPT	DEPT	DBLD	DROOM	DCHFNO
DICK NIX	CROOK	25001	PHIL	PHIL	HU	100	60
HANK KISS	JESTER	25000	PHIL	PHIL	HU	100	60
JOHN	EVANGLIST4	54	THEO	THEO	HU	200	10
LUKE	EVANGLIST3	53	THEO	THEO	HU	200	10
MARK	EVANGLIST2	52	THEO	THEO	HU	200	10
MATTHEW	EVANGLIST1	51	THEO	THEO	HU	200	10
EUCLID	LAB ASSIST	1000	MATH				
ARCHIMEDES	LAB ASSIST	200	ENG				
DA VINCI	LAB ASSIST	500	-				

Comments:

1. The sample query formed a left outer join by using UNION to merge two SELECT statements. The first SELECT statement generates those rows which correspond to the conventional (inner) equi-join of DEPARTMENT and STAFF along the DEPT columns. The second SELECT statement generates those rows which correspond to the "no match" rows from the STAFF table. These rows pertain to those employees who are not assigned to an existing department. This second SELECT uses NOT EXISTS in conjunction with a correlated subquery.

2. The example shows blanks instead of null values appended to the "no match" rows. What if you wanted to display null values instead of blanks? Recall that ORACLE provides the NULL keyword. The following SELECT clause is acceptable.

   SELECT ENAME, ETITLE, ESALARY, DEPT, NULL, NULL, NULL, NULL

   Note that not all relational products allow the use of the NULL keyword in the SELECT clause. In particular, current versions of DB2 do not allow its use.

3. We could form a full outer join of the STAFF and DEPARTMENT tables along the DEPT columns by appending the following code to the current example.

   ```
   UNION
   SELECT ' ', ' ', 0, ' ', DEPT, DBLD, DROOM, DCHFNO
   FROM    DEPARTMENT
   WHERE NOT EXISTS
           (SELECT *
            FROM    STAFF
            WHERE   STAFF.DEPT = DEPARTMENT.DEPT)
   ```

   Note that zero, or any other numeric value, instead of blanks must be displayed in the ESALARY column. This is necessary for reasons of union compatibility.

"FOR ALL"

The final sample query of this chapter illustrates the formulation of a SELECT statement which embodies the notion of "for all the values in a column, there exists ...." SQL has no keyword which directly supports "for all." However, it is possible to write an equivalent statement using NOT EXISTS twice. This is effectively a "double negative," which is poor grammar but logically correct. In fact, it is the only way to express "for all" within SQL.

   The complexity of the following example occurs for two reasons. The first is that SQL is far from a perfect language. In this case, the absence of a "for all" operator means that the query must be reformulated into an equivalent, but far less concise, expression of the problem. The second reason is that five different tables need to be referenced in order to satisfy the query objective. This means that you must have a good understanding of the semantic relationships reflected in the database design. Finally, the authors felt that it would be "good for the soul" to conclude this chapter with a problem which is deceptively nasty. This is a problem which is simple to articulate in everyday English, but can be considered a real challenge.

Sample Query 21.8:   Are there any students who are taking a course from every department which offers courses? If so, display the name of each student. To put it another way:

Display the name of any student who has registered for at least one class in a course offered by each department which offers courses. Or, to put it yet another way using the double negative articulation of the problem:

Display the name of any student where there does not exist a department (which offers courses) such that there does not exist a class on a course offered by that department where the student has registered for a class offered by that department.

```
SELECT  SNAME

FROM    STUDENT S

WHERE   NOT EXISTS

        (SELECT *

        FROM    DEPARTMENT D

        WHERE   D.DEPT IN

                (SELECT CDEPT FROM COURSE)

        AND NOT EXISTS

                (SELECT *

                FROM    REGISTRATION R, COURSE C,

                        CLASS CL

                WHERE   R.CNO = C.CNO

                AND     R.CNO = CL.CNO

                AND     R.SEC = CL.SEC

                AND     C.CDEPT = D.DEPT

                AND     R.SNO = S.SNO))
```

SNAME
MOE DUBAY
ROCKY BALBOA

Comments:

In the following comments we refer to the "second-level" and "third-level" queries. These references are correlated with the indentation used in the sample query.

1.   Syntax: The example shows a second-level subquery which contains two other third-level subqueries. (Nesting of subqueries was introduced in Sample Query 20.11.) The key difference here is that the second-level subquery and one of the third-level subqueries are correlated subqueries. This is no more than an extension of the idea of a correlated subquery to a lower-level subquery.

2. Logic: In this case the top-level SELECT statement of the main query references the STUDENT table. This means that the system will examine each row in the STUDENT table to determine if any rows are selected by the second-level SELECT statement. If no rows are selected, then the corresponding SNAME value is displayed. Assume the system encounters a row corresponding to a student who matches the selection criteria (i.e., the student has registered for at least one course offered by the Theology, Philosophy, and Computer and Information Science Departments). If this student has a SNO value "800", then the second-level SELECT statement, after making the substitution for S.SNO, reduces to

```
SELECT *
FROM    DEPARTMENT D
WHERE   D.DEPT IN (SELECT CDEPT FROM COURSE)
AND     NOT EXISTS
        (SELECT *
        FROM    REGISTRATION R, COURSE C, CLASS CL
        WHERE   R.CNO = C.CNO
        AND     R.CNO = CL.CNO
        AND     R.SEC = CL.SEC
        AND     C.CDEPT = D.DEPT
        AND     R.SNO = '800')
```

For the moment consider this statement as an independent SELECT statement. The first subquery, "SELECT CDEPT FROM COURSE", is a self-contained subquery which selects the department ids of those departments which offer courses. We can replace this subquery with the CDEPT values found in the COURSE table. This statement then becomes

```
SELECT *
FROM    DEPARTMENT D
WHERE   D.DEPT IN ('CIS', 'PHIL', 'THEO')
AND     NOT EXISTS
        (SELECT *
        FROM    REGISTRATION R, COURSE C, CLASS CL
        WHERE   R.CNO = C.CNO
        AND     R.CNO = CL.CNO
        AND     R.SEC = CL.SEC
        AND     C.CDEPT = D.DEPT
        AND     R.SNO = '800')
```

This statement contains the second correlated subquery which causes the system to examine each row of the DEPARTMENT table to determine if any rows are selected by the low-level subquery. If none are selected, and the department id is "CIS," "PHIL," or "THEO," the corresponding DEPARTMENT row is selected. Assume the system encounters the CIS Department row. Then the bottom-level subquery reduces to

```
SELECT *
FROM    REGISTRATION R, COURSE C, CLASS CL
WHERE   R.CNO = C.CNO
AND     R.CNO = CL.CNO
AND     R.SEC = CL.SEC
AND     C.CDEPT = 'CIS'
AND     R.SNO = '800'
```

The statement is a three-way join of the REGISTRATION, COURSE, and CLASS tables. (Sample Query 17.8 originally introduced a three-way join.) The objective of this statement is to determine if the student identified by SNO value "800" has registered for any class offered by the CIS Department. Assume there is a "hit" on this condition.

Returning to the second-level SELECT statement, a "hit" on student 800 registering for a CIS course means that the NOT EXISTS condition evaluates to false and hence the row for the CIS Department is not selected. For the same reason, the DEPARTMENT rows for the Theology and Philosophy Departments are not selected. Finally, the row for the Management Department is not selected because its id is not in the set ("CIS," "PHIL," "THEO"). This means that none of the four DEPARTMENT rows are selected by the second-level subquery.

Returning to the top-level SELECT statement, the NOT EXISTS condition is met because none of the DEPARTMENT rows were selected. Hence, the STUDENT row for student number 800 is selected and the SNAME value (ROCKY BALBOA) is displayed.

The same process begins all over again for the next
STUDENT row encountered by the system. The SNO value is
held constant during the iteration over the four
DEPARTMENT rows indicated by the second-level subquery.
The bottom-level correlated subquery then determines if
the student registered for a course offered by the
department. You are encouraged to work through the
example for a student who did not register for a course
offered by some department which offers courses. A "no
hit" on the bottom-level correlated subquery means that
the second-level NOT EXISTS condition is true for some
department, which in turn means that the top-level NOT
EXISTS condition is not met. Hence, the name of this
student would not be displayed.

Summary

This chapter introduced the notion of a correlated subquery,
a subselect which relates back to, and is dependent on, a
higher-level SELECT statement. The reference is made through
a correlation variable. The concept of existence testing was
introduced through the EXISTS keyword. We saw that the "for
all" operation could be implemented using NOT EXISTS.
Finally, it was demonstrated that the outer join operation
could also be implemented through the use of correlated
subqueries and EXISTS. All told, this chapter revealed some
very important aspects of relational database which are
supported (albeit not directly) in SQL.

Summary Exercises

21F. Display the course name, department id, and labfee for
each course which has the largest labfee of all courses
in that department.

21G. Display a list for each department of all classes
offered by the department. The list contains department
id and department building and room location, followed
by course number and name of courses offered by the
department, followed by section number and day of any
classes on those courses. If a department does not offer
any courses, or a course has no class offerings, display
spaces in the respective positions.

21H. Use EXISTS to construct an equivalent solution to Sample
Query 19.5 (the INTERSECT operation).

21I. Use NOT EXISTS to construct an equivalent solution to
Sample Query 19.6 (the MINUS operation).

22

Recursive Queries

This final chapter on the SELECT statement introduces recursive data structures and recursive queries against these structures. In Chapter 14 we briefly touched on the idea of a recursive data structure when we indicated that a table may contain a foreign key which happens to reference the primary key of that very same table. Recursion is a powerful but subtle concept which occurs in many areas of computer science. This chapter will examine some of the ideas associated with recursion and describe how ORACLE supports this process.

Recursive database processing is often referred to as the "bill-of-materials" or "parts-explosion" problem. The ORACLE reference manuals refer to this topic as "tree-structured information." We begin by describing the conceptual idea of recursion. We present the standard techniques for representing recursive data in a relational database table. Then we describe some typical recursive queries against such a table.

After discussing recursion from a conceptual viewpoint, we examine the special clauses used in a SELECT statement to support recursive queries. These clauses are the "CONNECT BY" clause and the "START WITH" clause.

Finally, we note that many real-world databases do not have any recursive data. This means that many users will never use ORACLE's recursive processing capabilities. For this reason you might consider skipping this chapter on your first reading.

An Example of Recursion

Before we present the essential characteristics of recursive structures and recursive processing, we consider a simple example. Assume that each course in the curriculum could have some other course as a prerequisite course. To keep the example simple, we further assume that a course will never have more than one prerequisite. However, it is possible for a single course to be the prerequisite for many courses. We say that this relationship between courses is "recursive" because the relationship ("is a prerequisite for") relates an entity (COURSE) to another entity of the same type (COURSE).

We can represent this recursive relationship, which happens to be a one-to-many relationship, by using the COURSEX table shown in Figure 22.1. This table includes the same information as the COURSE table. The only difference is the second column, PCNO, which contains the prerequisite course number. If a course does not have a prerequisite, then its PCNO value will be null. Figure 22.1 shows the COURSEX table with sample PCNO values. Confirm your understanding of the recursive relationship by verifying the following observations about this table.

- Most courses have some other course as a prerequisite. For example, course C33 has course C11 as a prerequisite.

- Some courses serve as the prerequisite for multiple courses. For example, C33 is the prerequisite for C22 and C44.

- Some (presumably introductory) courses do not have any course as a prerequisite. This is the case with C11, T11, P11, and P44. Each of these rows has a null PCNO value. We will use the hyphen (-) to represent a null value.

- The P44 course is independent of the other courses. It has no prerequisite, and it is not the prerequisite for any other course.

CNO	PCNO	CNAME	CDESCP	CRED	CLABFEE	CDEPT
C11	-	INTRO TO CS	FOR ROOKIES	3	100.00	CIS
C33	C11	DISCRETE MATHEMATICS	ABSOLUTELY NECESSARY	3	.00	CIS
C22	C33	DATA STRUCTURES	VERY USEFUL	3	50.00	CIS
C44	C33	DIGITAL CIRCUITS	AH HA!	3	.00	CIS
C66	C22	RELATIONAL DATABASE	THE ONLY WAY TO GO	3	500.00	CIS
C55	C44	COMPUTER ARCH.	VON NEUMANN'S MACH.	3	100.00	CIS
T11	-	SCHOLASTICISM	FOR THE PIOUS	3	150.00	THEO
T44	T11	COMMUNISM	FOR THE GREEDY	6	200.00	THEO
T33	T44	HEDONISM	FOR THE SANE	3	.00	THEO
T12	T11	FUNDAMENTALISM	FOR THE CAREFREE	3	90.00	THEO
P44	-	SOLIPSISM	ME MYSELF AND I	6	.00	PHIL
P11	-	EMPIRICISM	SEE IT-BELIEVE IT	3	100.00	PHIL
P22	P11	RATIONALISM	FOR CIS MAJORS	3	50.00	PHIL
P33	P11	EXISTENTIALISM	FOR CIS MAJORS	3	200.00	PHIL

Figure 22.1: COURSEX table with PCNO column.

Tree-Structured Information

The prerequisite course sequence shown in Figure 22.1 can be described as a collection of hierarchical or tree structures. This collection of trees is shown in Figure 22.2. Each course corresponds to a "node" in the tree. Only the primary key of each row is shown in the corresponding node.

Each course without a prerequisite course (having a null PCNO value) is positioned at the top of a tree. When a course (e.g., C33) serves as a prerequisite for another course (e.g., C44), then the first course is shown directly above the second course (C33 is directly above C44). Observe that P44, the independent course, defines a trivial tree consisting of just one node. You are advised to make the same observations you just made when examining Figure 22.1. (We believe the recursive prerequisite relationship between courses is much easier to visualize when examining the trees than when examining the table. This can be considered a criticism of the relational model. Nothing is perfect.)

An essential characteristic of a recursive relationship is that it can be represented as a tree-structured diagram. (For some database designs this structure might form a single tree; see Figures 22.3 and 22.4.) For this reason, a special terminology for describing trees is used to describe recursive relationships. We present this terminology below.

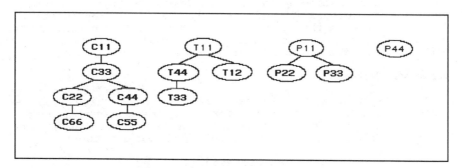

Figure 22.2: Tree representation of recursive relationship.

Terminology:

The terms "parent" and "child" are used to describe the relationship between the nodes of a tree. For example, C11 is the parent of C33; C33 is the child of C11. C33 is the parent of C22 and C44; C22 and C44 are the children of C33.

Some nodes (C11, T11, P11, and P44) have no parent. These nodes correspond to courses which do not have a prerequisite course. They are positioned at the top of a tree. Each is called the "root" of the tree.

Some nodes (C66, C55, T33, T12, P22, P33, and P44) have no children. Each of these nodes appears at the bottom of a tree and is referred to as a "terminal" node or a "leaf."

Node-1 is a "descendant" of Node-2 if Node-1 appears, directly or indirectly, under Node-2 in a tree. For example, C55 is a descendant of C44 (its parent) and C33 and C11.

Alternative Design:

Observe that the preceding design represented by COURSEX (Figure 22.1) corresponds to a collection of tables (Figure 22.2). Sometimes a special case occurs where the data in the table correspond to a single tree. In this case there is only one root node in the entire table. See the tree shown in Figure 22.4. Sometimes this situation naturally occurs in the application design. Other times the database designer will force this situation by inserting a special "dummy" row which serves this purpose. This is exactly what we did by inserting the "X00" row in the COURSEY table shown in Figure 22.3. The potential advantage to inserting a single "superroot" row will be illustrated in Sample Query 22.9.2.

Tree vs. Network:

A tree is just a special case of a network which will be described later in this chapter. For the moment we merely note that every non-root node in a tree has exactly one parent. This restriction will not apply to a network.

Recursive Structures and Processing:

The significant feature of the tables shown in Figures 22.1 and 22.3 is that PCNO is a foreign key which happens to reference the primary key (CNO) of the same table. *This "self-reference" is the defining characteristic of recursion.* The recursive relationship described by PCNO referencing CNO can be represented by a tree which is a recursive data structure.

Another classic data processing application of a recursive data structure which requires recursive processing is the parts-explosion problem. In this application, a part is composed of other parts; each of these parts is in turn composed of still more parts; etc. A simple relational database representation of this application is shown below.

    PART(PART_NO, PNAME, WGT, COLOR, SHAPE, PARENT_PART_NO)

The PARENT_PART_NO column in the PART table is a foreign key which references the primary key, PART_NO, in the same PART table.

The process of retrieving data from this recursive structure is called "recursive processing." The rest of this chapter will provide a detailed explanation of these concepts and describe ORACLE's facilities for recursive query processing.

CNO	PCNO	CNAME	CDESCP	CRED	CLABFEE	CDEPT
X00	-	DUMMY	TOP OF TREE	-	-	XXX
C11	X00	INTRO TO CS	FOR ROOKIES	3	100.00	CIS
C33	C11	DISCRETE MATHEMATICS	ABSOLUTELY NECESSARY	3	.00	CIS
C22	C33	DATA STRUCTURES	VERY USEFUL	3	50.00	CIS
C44	C33	DIGITAL CIRCUITS	AH HA!	3	.00	CIS
C66	C22	RELATIONAL DATABASE	THE ONLY WAY TO GO	3	500.00	CIS
C55	C44	COMPUTER ARCH.	VON NEUMANN'S MACH.	3	100.00	CIS
T11	X00	SCHOLASTICISM	FOR THE PIOUS	3	150.00	THEO
T44	T11	COMMUNISM	FOR THE GREEDY	6	200.00	THEO
T33	T44	HEDONISM	FOR THE SANE	3	.00	THEO
T12	T11	FUNDAMENTALISM	FOR THE CAREFREE	3	90.00	THEO
P44	X00	SOLIPSISM	ME MYSELF AND I	6	.00	PHIL
P11	X00	EMPIRICISM	SEE IT-BELIEVE IT	3	100.00	PHIL
P22	P11	RATIONALISM	FOR CIS MAJORS	3	50.00	PHIL
P33	P11	EXISTENTIALISM	FOR CIS MAJORS	3	200.00	PHIL

Figure 22.3: Single tree in COURSEY table.

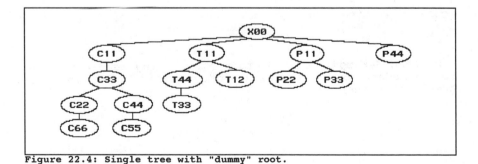

Figure 22.4: Single tree with "dummy" root.

Recursive Queries

There is a special challenge to recursive processing which entails "walking the tree" to display related rows. Before describing this process we note that some queries can be satisfied using your current knowledge of SQL. Consider the following sample queries (which do not require recursive processing) and their relatively simple SQL solutions.

Sample Query 22.1: What are the course number and name of any course which has course C11 as a prerequisite?

```
SELECT CNO, CNAME
FROM   COURSEX
WHERE  PCNO = 'C11'
```

CNO   CNAME
C33   DISCRETE MATHEMATICS

Sample Query 22.2: What is the course number of the prerequisite course for course C55?

```
SELECT PCNO
FROM   COURSEX
WHERE  CNO = 'C55'
```

PCNO
C44

We consider modifications to the preceding sample queries to introduce our discussion of recursive ("walking the tree")-type queries.

Modify Sample Query 22.1:

Sample Query 22.1 effectively asked for the display of information about the children of C11 in the tree structure. What if you were asked to display information about any course which is a descendant of C11? (That is, what courses, directly or indirectly, have C11 as a prerequisite?) To answer this query using your current knowledge of SQL requires considerable effort. (See Sample Query 22.3.) This task requires that you

(i) Enter the tree at a specified node (C11). This means retrieving the row corresponding to the specified node.

(ii) Then "walk down" the tree visiting every node (retrieving the row corresponding to every node) under the specified node.

Modify Sample Query 22.2:

Sample Query 22.2 identified a child (CNO = 'C55') and asked you to display just the key of its parent (C44). Fortunately, this value is stored as the PCNO value in the very same row. The following variations on this query require that you retrieve information stored in a node one or more levels above the child node.

1.   What if the sample query asked you to display the course number and name of the prerequisite course for C55? This query requires that you obtain information (course name of C44) stored one level higher than course C55 in the tree. (You can do this using a technique shown in Chapter 19. See Exercise 22D, below.)

2.   What if you wanted the course number of every course a student must take before taking course C55. (In other words, what are the direct and indirect prerequisite courses for C55?) To answer this query using your current knowledge of SQL also requires considerable effort. This task requires that you

   (i)   Enter the tree at a specified node (C55). This means retrieving the row corresponding to the specified node.

   (ii) Then "walk up" the tree visiting every node (retrieving the row corresponding to every node) above the specified node.

"Do-It-Yourself" Recursive Processing

The next two sample queries illustrate the process of walking down a tree. The problem is the same in both queries. However, the solutions are quite different. We begin by doing things the hard way. It is important that you understand the logic of this "hard way" solution because ORACLE's "easy way" solution (shown in Sample Query 22.4) provides a syntactic abbreviation for this process.

Sample Query 22.3: Display the course number and name of any course which has course C11 as a direct or indirect prerequisite course (i.e., enter the tree containing C11 and walk down it, retrieving information from every descendent node). Solve this problem using your current knowledge of SQL.

In order to satisfy this query without using the recursive processing facilities provided by ORACLE, you need to execute six separate SELECT statements.

1. Execute the statement shown in Sample Query 22.1.

   ```
   SELECT CNO, CNAME
   FROM   COURSEX
   WHERE  PCNO = 'C11'
   ```

   You learn that C33 is the only child of C11.

2. Determine the next level of indirect descendants of C11 by displaying the children C33.

   ```
   SELECT CNO, CNAME
   FROM   COURSEX
   WHERE  PCNO = 'C33'
   ```

   The result would show information about courses C22 and C44. A result of many rows corresponds to a branch in the tree.

3. We choose to follow the C22 path (the left branch).

   ```
   SELECT CNO, CNAME
   FROM   COURSEX
   WHERE  PCNO = 'C22'
   ```

   The result would show information about course C66.

4.   Find the children of C66.

     SELECT CNO, CNAME
     FROM   COURSEX
     WHERE   PCNO = 'C66'

     A "no records selected" result indicates that you are at
     the bottom of the tree. (C66 is a leaf node.)

5.   Now "go back up the tree" and find the children of C44.

     SELECT CNO, CNAME
     FROM   COURSEX
     WHERE   PCNO = 'C44'

     The result would show information about course C55.

6.   Find the children of C55.

     SELECT CNO, CNAME
     FROM   COURSEX
     WHERE   PCNO = 'C55'

     A "no records selected" result indicates that you are at
     the bottom of the tree. (C55 is a leaf node.)

7.   Finally! We are finished because we have visited every
     node under C11.

Comments:

1.   This process is tedious. Imagine traversing a large tree
     with many branches. This could occur, for example, in
     the explosion of a large part in a parts-explosion
     design. For example, the part might be a submarine or an
     office building.

2.   The process involved executing multiple SELECT
     statements. This inhibits possible optimization of the
     query.

3.   The above sequence of steps visited the nodes in the
     following order:

          C11, C33, C22, C66, C44, C55

     The next sample query will show that this is the same
     sequence that ORACLE will follow in traversing the tree.

START WITH and CONNECT BY:
ORACLE's Tree Traversal Clauses

ORACLE provides specific clauses which allow you to execute a single SELECT statement to tell the system to "traverse down" or "traverse up" the tree. These clauses are illustrated in the following sample queries.

Traversing Down a Tree

Sample Query 22.4:   Same as Sample Query 22.3. Solve using the "START WITH" and the "CONNECT BY" clauses.

```
SELECT CNO, CNAME
FROM    COURSEX
CONNECT BY PRIOR CNO = PCNO
START WITH CNO = 'C11'
```

CNO	CNAME
C11	INTRO TO CS
C33	DISCRETE STRUCTURES
C22	DATA STRUCTURES
C66	RELATIONAL DATABASE
C44	DIGITAL CIRCUITS
C55	COMPUTER ARCH.

Comments:

1.   CONNECT BY Clause

"CONNECT BY condition" is used to indicate that the rows are to be retrieved in a tree-structured sequence. The "condition" identifies the parent-child relationship which is used to structure the rows into a collection of trees. The keyword "PRIOR" is placed before the parent column. Hence, the clause

        CONNECT BY PRIOR CNO = PCNO

indicates that the CNO value in a parent row will equal the PCNO value in the row for each of its children. This clause could also have been written as

        CONNECT BY PCNO = PRIOR CNO

The key point is that PRIOR is placed before the parent column (CNO). This is important because it indicates a "walking down" direction of tree traversal. (Sample Query 22.6 will show that placing PRIOR before the child field is useful for "walking up" a tree.) The CONNECT BY clause must follow the FROM clause if no WHERE clause is present. Otherwise, it must follow the WHERE clause.

2.   START WITH Clause

"START WITH condition" specifies the starting point for the traversal. The condition can identify one or more rows. Each row identified corresponds to the root of the tree (or subtree) to be displayed. In this sample query

        START WITH CNO = 'C11'

identifies one row corresponding to the root of the tree represented by the result table. Subsequent sample queries will show traversing from the middle of a tree.

The START WITH clause is optional, but it is almost always present. If it is omitted, the system will display a collection of trees where there will be as many trees as there are rows in the table. That is, each row in the table will be the root of a tree.

3.   Tree Traversal Sequence

The sequence in which ORACLE traverses a tree was initially described in our "hard way" solution to this problem. This sequence is sometimes called "preorder" tree traversal. The ORACLE Reference manual attempts to describe this process. We believe that illustrating a substantial example will convey the general idea. The traversal occurs by visiting previously unvisited nodes and by applying the following procedure at each node.

a.   Try to go down the tree, visiting the leftmost unvisited child.

b.   If you can't go down, go horizontally to the right.

c.   If you can't go down or horizontally, go up to the next unvisited node.

An example of this process is shown in Figure 22.5, where the nodes are labeled according to the order of retreival. The sequence in which the rows are selected may not be critical for some applications. The ORDER BY clause can be used to display the retrieved rows in a desired sequence. We describe the traversal sequence because we believe it provides conceptual insight into the logic of recursive processing.

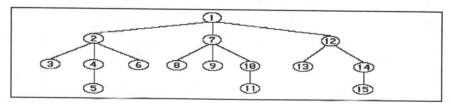

Figure 22.5: Example of ORACLE tree traversal.

LEVEL Pseudo-Column

When you retrieve rows from a "tree" (really a tree-structured table) the selected rows in the result table form a "subtree." However, a result table (a subtree), like that shown in the previous sample query, suffers from the same problem we observed in the COURSEX table shown in Figure 22.1. The hierarchical relationships between the rows of the tree/subtree are not immediately obvious when you examine the table. ORACLE provides a pseudo-column, LEVEL, which can help with this problem. When you select LEVEL in a recursive query, ORACLE assigns a level number to each selected row. This level corresponds to the row's level in the subtree. (Notice we said "subtree" and not "tree." See Sample Query 22.6 below.) A row at the root of a subtree is at level 1. Rows below the root are at level 2, etc.

Sample Query 22.5.1:   Same as Sample Queries 22.3 and 22.4. Display the LEVEL pseudo-column to reflect the hierarchy of the selected subtree.

```
SELECT LEVEL, CNO, CNAME
FROM    COURSEX
CONNECT BY PRIOR CNO = PCNO
START WITH CNO = 'C11'
```

LEVEL	CNO	CNAME
1	C11	INTRO TO CS
2	C33	DISCRETE STRUCTURES
3	C22	DATA STRUCTURES
4	C66	RELATIONAL DATABASE
3	C44	DIGITAL CIRCUITS
4	C55	COMPUTER ARCH.

The following example shows another technique for representing the hierarchy of a selected subtree.

Sample Query 22.5.2:   Same as Sample Queries 22.3 and 22.4. Use LEVEL pseudo-column to provide indentation which reflects hierarchy of the tree.

```
COLUMN LFMT FORMAT A18 HEADING 'PREREQ. CNO.'

SELECT LPAD(' ',3*(LEVEL-1))||CNO LFMT, CNAME
FROM    COURSEX
CONNECT BY PRIOR CNO = PCNO
START WITH CNO = 'C11'
```

```
PREREQ. CNO.          CNAME
C11                   INTRO TO CS
    C33               DISCRETE STRUCTURES
        C22           DATA STRUCTURES
            C66       RELATIONAL DATABASE
        C44           DIGITAL CIRCUITS
            C55       COMPUTER ARCH.
```

Comments:

1. It might be helpful to review the LPAD function and the concatenation operator (||) described in Chapter 9. We use these facilities to build a character string showing the indentation of the course numbers.

2. Again, the level numbers do not necessarily apply to levels of trees in the COURSEX table. In these examples, they do incidentally correspond to levels in COURSEX because the root of the selected subtree (C11) happened to be the root of a tree in the original table. This will not always occur. See the next two sample queries.

Traversing Up a Tree

You can enter a tree at a leaf or middle-level node by identifying it with the START WITH clause. You can then traverse upward in the tree to retrieve and display information stored in a parent and other "ancestor" node. To cause an upward traversal, place the PRIOR keyword before the child column in the CONNECT BY clause.

Sample Query 22.6:   Display the course number and name of course C55 and any course which is a direct or indirect prerequisite for that course (i.e., enter the tree containing C55 and walk up to its root.) Also display the level number of the selected rows.

```
SELECT LEVEL, CNO, CNAME
FROM    COURSEX
CONNECT BY CNO = PRIOR PCNO
START WITH CNO = 'C55'
```

LEVEL	CNO	CNAME
1	C55	COMPUTER ARCH.
2	C44	DIGITAL CIRCUITS
3	C33	DISCRETE STRUCTURES
4	C11	INTRO TO CS

Comments:

1.   Walking up a tree is conceptually simpler than walking down a tree. This occurs because each node in a tree has at most one parent. Hence the upward traversal follows a single path. (This simplification will not apply to networks.)

2.   LEVEL corresponds to a node level in the retrieved subtree. This example showed that C55 is at level 1. However, Figure 22.2 shows C55 as a leaf node.

More Examples

You don't have to begin a traversal at a root or leaf node. The START WITH clause can identify any row. The next example starts the traversal in the middle of a tree and traverses downward.

Sample Query 22.7: Display the number and name of any course which has course C22 as a direct or indirect prerequisite. Display level numbers in the result.

```
SELECT LEVEL, CNO, CNAME
FROM    COURSEX
CONNECT BY PRIOR CNO = PCNO
START WITH CNO = 'C22'
```

LEVEL	CNO	CNAME
1	C22	DATA STRUCTURES
2	C66	RELATIONAL DATABASE

Comment:

Note that LEVEL begins with 1. This reflects the fact that LEVEL corresponds to levels in the selected subtree.

The START WITH clause can identify multiple rows. This means that the result table will correspond to multiple subtrees.

Sample Query 22.8: Display the number and name of any course which has C11 or T11 as a direct or indirect prerequisite. Indent the course numbers to reflect the hierarchy of the subtrees.

```
SELECT LPAD(' ',3*(LEVEL-1))||CNO LFMT, CNAME
FROM    COURSEX
CONNECT BY PRIOR CNO = PCNO
START WITH CNO = 'C11' OR CNO = 'T11'
```

PREREQ. CNO.	CNAME
C11	INTRO TO CS
C33	DISCRETE STRUCTURES
C22	DATA STRUCTURES
C66	RELATIONAL DATABASE
C44	DIGITAL CIRCUITS
C55	COMPUTER ARCH.
T11	SCHOLASTICISM
T12	FUNDAMENTALISM
T44	COMMUNISM
T33	HEDONISM

Sample Query 22.9.1: Display all rows in the COURSEX table. Indent the course numbers to reflect the course prerequisite relationships.

```
SELECT LPAD(' ',3*(LEVEL-1))||CNO LFMT, CNAME
FROM    COURSEX
CONNECT BY PRIOR CNO = PCNO
START WITH CNO IN
              (SELECT CNO
               FROM    COURSEX
               WHERE  PCNO IS NULL)
```

PREREQ. CNO.	CNAME
C11	INTRO TO CS
C33	DISCRETE STRUCTURES
C22	DATA STRUCTURES
C66	RELATIONAL DATABASE
C44	DIGITAL CIRCUITS
C55	COMPUTER ARCH.
P11	EMPIRICISM
P22	RATIONALISM
P33	EXISTENTIALISM
P44	SOLIPSISM
T11	SCHOLASTICISM
T12	FUNDAMENTALISM
T44	COMMUNISM
T33	HEDONISM

Comment:

The subquery selected the root node of every tree in COURSEX. The SELECT statement could be simplified if the database designer had chosen to establish a single tree structure as shown in Figures 22.3 and 22.4.

Sample Query 22.9.2: Same as above, but assume retrieval from COURSEY shown in Figure 22.3.

```
SELECT LPAD(' ',3*(LEVEL-2))||CNO LFMT, CNAME
FROM    COURSEY
WHERE CNO <> 'X00'
CONNECT BY PRIOR CNO = PCNO
START WITH CNO = 'X00'
```

Comment:

Although the traversal started at the dummy row (X00), a WHERE clause removed this row from the result. Because the X00 row was assigned level number 1, we adjusted our indentation by specifying "LEVEL-2".

START WITH Clause vs. WHERE Clause

Sample Queries 22.4 through 22.8 did not have any WHERE clauses. Yet the result for each of these examples contained only a few rows from the COURSEX table. This occurred because the START WITH clause selected (or effectively eliminated) certain rows. If a row was not encountered during the traversal, it did not appear in the result. The WHERE clause, when used with a recursive query, will select some subset of the traversed rows (and only the traversed rows) for display. The next example illustrates this point.

Sample Query 22.10:   Display the number and name of every three-credit course which has course T11 as a direct or indirect prerequisite. Use the indentation technique (even though it may lead to confusion in interpreting the result).

```
SELECT LPAD(' ',3*(LEVEL-1))||CNO LFMT, CNAME
FROM    COURSEX
WHERE   CRED = 3
CONNECT BY PRIOR CNO = PCNO
START WITH CNO = 'T11'
```

PREREQ. CNO.	CNAME
T11	SCHOLASTICISM
T12	FUNDAMENTALISM
T33	HEDONISM

Comments:

1.   T44 was not displayed because it has a CRED value of 6. But its child, T33, was displayed. The WHERE clause will select (or reject) individual rows. The START WITH behaves differently. It selects (or rejects) an entire subtree.

2.   This example shows that you need to be careful when interpreting the result of a recursive query which has a WHERE clause. Many users would, on examining the result, conclude that T12 is the parent of T33. This is wrong. T44 is the parent of T33, but T44 was not displayed.

Reference LEVEL in WHERE Clause

Other clauses can reference the LEVEL pseudo-column. These
include the WHERE, GROUP BY, and ORDER BY clauses.

Sample Query 22.11:   Display the subtree having C11 as the
root. Display only the first three
levels of the subtree.

```
SELECT  LPAD(' ',3*(LEVEL-1))||CNO LFMT, CNAME
FROM    COURSEX
WHERE   LEVEL <= 3
CONNECT BY PRIOR CNO = PCNO
START WITH CNO = 'C11'
```

PREREQ. CNO.	CNAME
C11	INTRO TO CS
C33	DISCRETE STRUCTURES
C22	DATA STRUCTURES
C44	DIGITAL CIRCUITS

Network Structure

Thus far we have limited our discussion to tree structures
where each node has a maximum of one parent. The recursive
relationship being modeled is a one-to-many relationship
where a course can have only one (direct) prerequisite but it
can be the (direct) prerequisite for many courses.

A more flexible design would support a many-to-many
recursive relationship by allowing a node to have many
parents. Such a structure is called a network. Obviously, a
tree is just a special kind of network. The network structure
would be necessary if we allowed a course to have more than
one (direct) prerequisite course. Figure 22.6 shows an
example of a network. Observe that C44 and P22 have two
prerequisite courses, and T33 has three prerequisite courses.

Representing a Network in a Relational Database

The most common way to represent a many-to-many relationship in a relational database is to create a separate table to store the primary keys of the related rows. Figure 22.7 illustrates the PREREQ table, which represents the network shown in Figure 22.6. There is one row in PREREQ for each line in the network. Make the following observations about the PREREQ table.

1.   The CNO column has duplicate values for those courses which have more than one parent (more than one course prerequisite). These values are the C44, T33, and P22. Duplicate values also exist in the PCNO column because a course can be the prerequisite for any courses. But there are no duplicate rows in PREREQ. Its primary key is composite, containing both the columns.

2.   We do not use null values in the PCNO column when a course has no prerequisite. This is because no column in a primary key can be null. Therefore, some other non-null value needs to be specified. We choose some dummy value (e.g., "X00").

Now, because all of the prerequisite course information is embodied in a single table, PREREQ, we no longer need a modified course table (COURSEX or COURSEY). Instead, the design will use the familiar COURSE table.

CNO	PCNO
C11	X00
C33	C11
C22	C33
C44	C33
C44	T44
C66	C22
C55	C44
T11	X00
T44	T11
T33	T44
T33	T12
T33	P33
T12	T11
P44	X00
P11	X00
P22	P11
P22	T11
P33	P11

Figure 22.7:
PREREQ table.

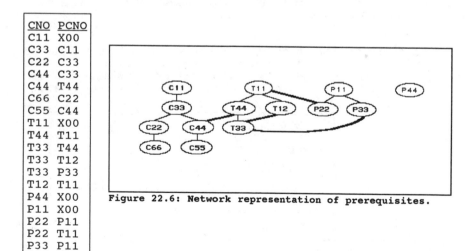

Figure 22.6: Network representation of prerequisites.

Traversing Down a Network

You use the same techniques to traverse a network that were used to traverse a tree.

Sample Query 22.12: Display the course number of any course which has course C11 as a direct or indirect prerequisite course.

```
SELECT CNO
FROM    PREREQ
CONNECT BY PRIOR CNO = PCNO
START WITH CNO = 'C11'
```

```
CNO
---
C11
C33
C22
C66
C44
C55
```

Comment:

In this example we wanted only the CNO values which are stored in PREREQ. What if you also wanted to see the course name? The network design makes enhancement a more complicated programming problem.

Sample Query 22.13: Display the course number and name of any course which has course C11 as a direct or indirect prerequisite course. (Same as Sample Queries 22.3 and 22.4.)

```
SELECT CNO, CNAME
FROM    COURSE
WHERE   CNO IN
        (SELECT CNO
         FROM    PREREQ
         CONNECT BY PRIOR CNO = PCNO
         START WITH CNO = 'C11')
```

CNO	CNAME
C11	INTRO TO CS
C22	DATA STRUCTURES
C33	DISCRETE STRUCTURES
C44	DIGITAL CIRCUITS
C55	COMPUTER ARCH.
C66	RELATIONAL DATABASE

Comments:

ORACLE does not allow a recursive query against a join table. This means that the following statement, which appears to be reasonable, will cause an *error*.

```
SELECT LPAD(' ',3*(LEVEL-1))||COURSE.CNO LFMT, CNAME
FROM    COURSE, PREREQ
WHERE   COURSE.CNO = PREREQ.CNO
CONNECT BY PRIOR COURSE.CNO = PREREQ.PCNO
START WITH COURSE.CNO = 'C11'
```

Traversing Up a Network

When you walk up a network (unlike a tree) you can encounter a node which has multiple parents, all of which need to be visited. An upward traversal is identical to a downward traversal. You realize this objective by placing PRIOR before the child field to indicate the traversal direction is upward.

Sample Query 22.14:   Same as Sample Query 22.6. Display the course number and name of course C55 and any course which is a direct or indirect prerequisite for that course.

```
SELECT CNO, CNAME
FROM    COURSE
WHERE   CNO IN
        (SELECT CNO
         FROM PREREQ
         CONNECT BY CNO = PRIOR PCNO
         START WITH CNO = 'C55')
```

CNO	CNAME
C11	INTRO TO CS
C33	DISCRETE STRUCTURES
C44	DIGITAL CIRCUITS
C55	COMPUTER ARCH.
T11	SCHOLASTICISM
T44	COMMUNISM

Summary

This chapter introduced the ideas associated with recursive data structures and recursive processing. We illustrated how it is possible to store recursive data in tables. The rows in these tables can represent a tree or a network structure. Unfortunately, the tabular representation is not very helpful when you try to visualize the tree or network structure. This leads to a level of complexity which is more in the domain of the professional application programmer. Fortunately, few users will encounter applications with recursive data structures. However, as the "prerequisite of" relationship between courses and the "is a component of" relationship between parts illustrate, there are a number of real-world applications which can capitalize on recursive processing facilities. Fortunately, ORACLE provides such facilities with its CONNECT BY and START WITH clauses.

Summary Exercises

The following exercises assume the tree structure represented by the COURSEX table.

22A. Display the course number and name of any course which has course T11 as a direct or indirect prerequisite course. Use indentation to indicate the hierarchical relationship between the courses.

22B. Display the course number and name of course T33 and any course which is a direct or indirect prerequisite for this course.

22C. Display the course number and name of any course having a nonzero labfee which is a direct or indirect prerequisite for course C66.

22D. Display the course number and name for course C33 and the course number and name of its prerequisite course.

The following exercises assume the network structure represented by the PREREQ table.

22E. Same as 22A.

22F. Same as 22B.

VI

More about ORACLE

The previous parts of this text introduced the data definition, data retrieval, and data manipulation statements of SQL. Part VI introduces another dimension of SQL by presenting statements which facilitate the management of your data. In particular, we focus on those techniques which allow you to share your data with other users of the system. This topic involves the notion of creating views and granting privileges. We also consider the idea of a database transaction as it relates to database integrity and recovery. We conclude with a discussion of the ORACLE Data Dictionary. You will find the SQL statements presented in these chapters to be useful, powerful, and easy to learn.

Organization of Chapters

Chapter 23 presents a comprehensive discussion of the CREATE VIEW statement. This statement permits you to define a view which is essentially a "virtual" table. A view corresponds to the notion of "local view" which is applicable within most multiuser database systems. This is an important chapter because many companies have a policy which states that users can retrieve only data from views.

Chapter 24 introduces some of the key ideas behind database security. This is not a comprehensive discussion of the topic. Instead, we present a programmer-user (vs. database administrator) perspective by introducing those variations of the GRANT and REVOKE statements which are relevant to this audience.

Chapter 25 introduces the transaction concept by presenting the COMMIT and ROLLBACK statements. This is an important chapter for programmers who will write application programs which update tables. Most users can skip this chapter. However, those users who intend to execute interactive update operations (a questionable practice) should read this chapter because of its relevance to database integrity and recovery.

Chapter 26 presents ORACLE's Data Dictionary. This dictionary contains data about data, sometimes referred to as "metadata." Exploring the Data Dictionary will help you determine information about tables you or other users have created, the columns in these tables, the views based on these tables, etc. You will find ORACLE's Data Dictionary to be a very userful database which contains information you will frequently examine.

23

The View Concept

Most database management systems provide some facility which allows for the definition of a "local view" of the database. "Local view" is a generic expression corresponding to some subset of the database which a particular user or group of users can display and/or update. A local view is usually defined by the database administrator and then made available to a user. Because a local view is usually defined for each user, a given database may have many local views defined on it. ORACLE supports the local view concept through the CREATE VIEW statement. Execution of this statement will create an "SQL view" which is similar but not identical to the "local view" concept.

The local view approach serves two purposes.

1.   Security: The user has no access to any data which is
      not part of his or her local view. Also, the user may be
      allowed to perform only certain operations on the local
      view's data. This prevents accidental or intentional
      retrieval or modification of data which are not within
      the defined local view.

2.   Simplicity: The user can disregard all data which are
      not within his or her local view. In fact, the user
      might not even be aware that such data exist. Because a
      local view is usually much smaller than the entire
      database, the user's view is simplified and a possible
      source of confusion is removed.

   Below we describe an "SQL view" and then relate it to the
"local view" concept.

   The CREATE VIEW statement is used to define the content of
an SQL view which is sometimes called a "virtual table." We
say "table" because the user perceives and manipulates an SQL
view in the same manner as the COURSE table has been
processed throughout this text. We say "virtual" because the
rows and columns of a view do not really exist. The view
corresponds to data in a table which were previously
established with a CREATE TABLE statement. To introduce some
SQL terminology, we use the phrase "base table" to designate
any table created by a CREATE TABLE statement. All the
educational database tables in this book (COURSE, STAFF,
DEPARTMENT, etc.) are base tables. The CREATE VIEW statement
is used to establish an SQL view which is defined on some
base table. An SQL view can be thought of as a window into
some subset of a base table. Figure 23.1 illustrates this
perspective of an SQL view. Later we will see that the CREATE
VIEW statement provides more power and flexibility than the
window analogy implies.

   Once an SQL view is established you can execute a SELECT
statement which references the view. The system will
associate the SQL view with a base table and then extract and
display the data from the base table. This approach means
that a view does not contain replicated data from a base
table. It doesn't contain any data at all because it is not
a real table. All processing is done with the data stored in
the base table. Later we will examine how the system does
this.

This chapter will introduce the details of the CREATE VIEW statement. We will see that an SQL view is perceived as exactly one (virtual) table. To relate an SQL view to the generic notion of a local view, note that a user might have a local view which consists of multiple tables. Some of these tables might be base tables, and others might be SQL views. We will also see that the CREATE VIEW statement defines only the content of the virtual table. It does not specify which user can access a view, nor does it specify what operations may be performed against the view. The next chapter will present the GRANT statement, which serves these purposes. There we will see that the local view concept is usually implemented by utilization of both the CREATE VIEW and GRANT statements. For the remainder of this chapter the term "view" implies an SQL view.

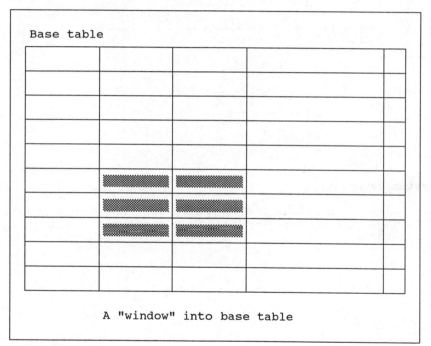

Figure 23.1: View concept.

CREATE VIEW Statement

The first example illustrates the aforementioned window analogy for a view by creating a view which corresponds to a subset of columns and of rows from the COURSE table.

Sample Statement 23.1:   Create a view (a virtual table) called CISC which contains just the rows corresponding to courses offered by the CIS Department. The view should contain all of the columns from the COURSE table with the exception of the CDEPT column. The left-to-right column sequence of the view should be CNAME, CNO, CRED, CLABFEE, CDESCP.

```
CREATE VIEW CISC AS

        SELECT  CNAME, CNO,

                CRED, CLABFEE, CDESCP

        FROM    COURSE

        WHERE   CDEPT = 'CIS'
```

System Response:

Like all previous CREATE statements, the system should display a message confirming the successful creation of the view.

Comments:

1. The name of the view, CISC, immediately follows the CREATE VIEW keywords. View names are formulated according to the same rules that apply to table names. A view name, like a table name, has a prefix which the system defines as the username of the user who entered the CREATE VIEW statement.

2. The keyword AS follows the view name. The definition of the view follows the AS keyword. Observe that this definition is simply a "good old" SELECT statement. In this example it is

    ```
    SELECT CNAME, CNO, CRED, CLABFEE, CDESCP
    FROM   COURSE
    WHERE  CDEPT = 'CIS'
    ```

    If we were to directly execute this SELECT statement, the result would correspond to the content of the desired view definition. Here the SELECT statement is not executed. Instead, ORACLE saves the text of the SELECT statement as a definition of the view in its Data Dictionary. (See Chapter 26.)

3. In this example the view inherited the names of its columns from the COURSE table. Sample Statement 23.4 will demonstrate a version of the CREATE VIEW statement which allows the assignment of different column names.

Processing Views

We can usually manipulate views just as we have done with base tables throughout this text. However, there are some important exceptions which will be described as we progress through the examples. In general, you will find that many views can be treated exactly like base tables, so much so that a view is often referred to simply as a "table" instead of "virtual table."

Sample Query 23.2:   Display the entire CISC table.

```
SELECT *

FROM CISC
```

CNAME	CNO	CRED	CLABFEE	CDESCP
INTRO TO CS	C11	3	100.00	FOR ROOKIES
DATA STRUCTURES	C22	3	50.00	VERY USEFUL
DISCRETE MATHEMATICS	C33	3	.00	ABSOLUTELY NECESSARY
DIGITAL CIRCUITS	C44	3	.00	AH HA!
COMPUTER ARCH.	C55	3	100.00	VON NEUMANN'S MACH.
RELATIONAL DATABASE	C66	3	500.00	THE ONLY WAY TO GO

Comment:

The syntax of the SELECT statement (and all other SQL data manipulation statements) remain unchanged. In this example we see that the view name is referenced in the FROM clause.

Exercise:

23A. Create a view called FPAYROLL on the FACULTY table. The view is to contain the FNAME, FSALARY, FHIRE_DATE, and FNUM_DEP columns. Issue a SELECT statement against this view and examine the results.

Sample Query 23.3:   For any row in the CISC table with a labfee greater than or equal to $100, display its name followed by its labfee. Sort the result by course name in ascending sequence.

```
SELECT  CNAME, CLABFEE

FROM    CISC

WHERE   CLABFEE >= 100

ORDER BY CNAME
```

CNAME	CLABFEE
COMPUTER ARCH.	100.00
INTRO TO CS	100.00
RELATIONAL DATABASE	500.00

Comment:

1. Again observe that the view is referenced like a base table. In the current sample query a WHERE clause and an ORDER BY clause were used to select specific rows from the view and to display them in a specific row sequence.

2. This query could have been satisfied by executing the following statement which refers to the base table.

```
SELECT  CNAME, CLABFEE
FROM    COURSE
WHERE   CDEPT = 'CIS'
AND     CLABFEE >= 100
ORDER BY CNAME
```

This statement presumes that the user is aware of both the existence and content of the COURSE table. In many situations the database administrator only allows the user to access a view.

Specifying Column Names for a View

The column names in the CISC view were inherited from the COURSE table. The next example illustrates a method for explicitly naming the columns of a view and then referencing them in a SELECT statement.

Sample Statement 23.4:   Create a view called VEXPCOURSE which corresponds to rows from the COURSE table where the labfee exceeds $150. The columns of the view correspond to CNO, CNAME, and CLABFEE. Their respective names in the view are CNUMBER, COURSE_NAME, and EXPENSIVE_LABFEE.

```
CREATE VIEW VEXPCOURSE

(CNUMBER, COURSE_NAME, EXPENSIVE_LABFEE)

AS      SELECT CNO, CNAME, CLABFEE

        FROM    COURSE

        WHERE   CLABFEE > 150
```

System Response:

Like all previous CREATE statements, the system should display a message confirming the successful creation of the view.

Comments:

1.   In the CREATE VIEW statement, the column names of the view are specified after the view name. Note that they are enclosed within parentheses and separated by commas.

2.   We chose to begin the view name with the letter "V" to serve as a reminder that this table is really a view. This technique is useful, but it is not necessary.

Sample Query 23.5:   Display the course name and labfee values from the VEXPCOURSE table. Display the result in course name sequence.

```
SELECT COURSE_NAME, EXPENSIVE_LABFEE

FROM    VEXPCOURSE

ORDER BY COURSE_NAME
```

COURSE_NAME	EXPENSIVE_LABFEE
COMMUNISM	200
EXISTENTIALISM	200
RELATIONAL DATABASE	500

Comment:

The SELECT statement must reference the defined column names as defined in the view. These names appear as column headings in the displayed result. An attempt to reference the column names of the corresponding base table would result in an error.

Exercise:

23B. Create a view called FPAYROLL2 on the FACULTY table. The view is to contain the FNAME, FSALARY, and FHIRE_DATE columns from the FACULTY table. The corresponding column names in the FPAYROLL2 view should be called F2N, F2S, and F2H. Issue a SELECT statement against this view and examine the result.

Rules for CREATE VIEW

Figure 23.2 outlines the general format of the CREATE VIEW statement. We address the issues of specification of column names and the formulation of a valid SELECT statement.

As Sample Query 23.1 indicated, the designation of specific column names may be optional. If you do not specify the column names, the view inherits its column names from the base table. Sample 23.4 illustrated a situation where the columns of VEXPCOURSE were assigned names different from the underlying base table. Observe that we could allow the columns of VEXPCOURSE to inherit the column names from the COURSE table. Sometimes the creator of a view is required to specify column names. Sample 23.6 will present a situation where the view contains a column of derived values. In such cases it is necessary to explicitly specify column names because the values in a column do not directly correspond to any predefined (base table) column and, hence, cannot inherit a name.

"Almost any" SELECT statement is permitted as a view definition. There is one limitation. *The ORDER BY clause cannot be included in the SELECT statement.* This is reasonable when you consider that the relational model dictates that a base table or a view should not have any predefined sequence. The ORDER BY clause may be attached to the SELECT statement which retrieves data from the view.

Aside from this restriction, any valid SELECT statement can serve as a view definition. In particular, this includes statements which involve built-in functions, expressions, the join, union, intersection, difference operations, and subqueries. Also, the FROM clause may even specify a view, which means that it is possible to define a view on top of a view. See Sample 23.10.

This approach of using a SELECT statement to define a view is simple, powerful, and conceptually elegant. In all previous examples the direct execution of a SELECT statement was interpreted by the system as the definition of a subset of the database to be retrieved for display. (This perspective is consistent with the theory of a relational database which defines the database structure as a collection of sets and the query language as a notation which defines a subset to be retrieved.) In the context of CREATE VIEW a SELECT statement constitutes the definition of a subset (i.e., a window) which is a view into a base table.

There are no restrictions when you formulate a SELECT statement which references a view. However, there are a number of restrictions which apply to updating views. These will be described at the end of the chapter.

The following pages will show sample statements which define views which represent statistical summaries, the join operation, and the union operation. The techniques illustrated in these views are extremely useful because they allow information to be synthesized from one or more tables and presented to the user as a single (presumably simpler) table.

```
CREATE VIEW viewname (col1, col2, ...)

AS    SELECT    _____
                              ┐
      FROM      _____  ├── "almost any"
                              │   SELECT statement
      WHERE     _____  ┘
```

Figure 23.2: CREATE VIEW statement.

View Defined as a Statistical Summary

The next example shows that we can create a view with columns containing summary data derived from a base table.

Sample Statement 23.6:   Create a view called VCSTAT which has one row for each department which offers courses. The columns are the department id followed by the sum and the average labfee values for each department.

```
CREATE VIEW VCSTAT

      (CDEPT, SUM_CLABFEE, AVG_CLABFEE) AS

      SELECT CDEPT, SUM(CLABFEE), AVG(CLABFEE)

      FROM    COURSE

      GROUP BY CDEPT
```

System Response:

> Like all previous CREATE statements, the system should display a message confirming the successful creation of the view.

Comments:

1.   The SELECT clause contains group functions which perform the required calculations for each department group. The derived results effectively become the values of the second and third columns of the view.

2.   The example shows that the column names of the view are explicitly named. This is necessary because view columns which contain derived data do not directly correspond to, and hence cannot inherit the names of, any base table columns.

3.   Recall that the GROUP BY clause will cause the system to sort by the grouping field. This sorting is incidental to the grouping process. You should explicitly use the ORDER BY clause if you want the result to be sorted. However, we did not include an ORDER BY clause in the definition of VCSTAT because the ORDER BY clause is not permitted in the definition of any view.

4.   This view cannot be updated because it contains derived data. To be precise the system will not permit update operations on any view which is defined with a GROUP BY clause or a built-in function.

Sample Query 23.7.1:   Display the average labfee for courses offered by the Philosophy and Theology Departments. Sort the result by average labfee in descending sequence.

```
SELECT  CDEPT, AVG_CLABFEE

FROM    VCSTAT

WHERE   CDEPT = 'PHIL'

OR      CDEPT = 'THEO'

ORDER BY AVG_CLABFEE DESC
```

CDEPT	AVG_CLABFEE
THEO	110
PHIL	87.5

Sample Query 23.7.2:   Display the department id and average labfee for any course having an average labfee less than $100.

```
SELECT CDEPT, AVG_CLABFEE

FROM    VCSTAT

WHERE  AVG_CLABFEE < 100
```

CDEPT	AVG_CLABFEE
PHIL	87.5

View Defined as Join of Tables

In Chapter 17 we described the subtle issues associated with the join operation. We noted that the SQL syntax was easy but the logic of the join could be misunderstood by the user. The database administrator can help unsophisticated SQL users avoid the potential problems of the join operation by creating a view which is a join of some tables. Then the user would perceive the tables as a single table. Such a user could then utilize just those techniques described in Parts I through III of this text. This approach involves extra effort by the database administrator. However, it simplifies the users' task and removes potential sources of error. The next example illustrates the creation of such a view.

Sample Statement 23.8:   Create a view called VCSD which is the join of the COURSE, STAFF, and DEPARTMENT tables along the columns containing department id values. VCSD should contain all the columns from these base tables with the exception of the department ids, which will be equal to each other and, therefore, should only occur once in the view.

```
CREATE VIEW VCSD AS

SELECT CNO, CNAME, CDESCP, CRED, CLABFEE,

       DEPARTMENT.DEPT, DBLD, DROOM,

       DCHFNO, ENAME, ETITLE, ESALARY

FROM   COURSE, STAFF, DEPARTMENT

WHERE  CDEPT = STAFF.DEPT

AND    CDEPT = DEPARTMENT.DEPT
```

System Response:

Like all previous CREATE statements, the system should display a message confirming the successful creation of the view.

Comments:

1. Recall that certain rows from the STAFF table and the DEPARTMENT table will not appear in the join result. The creator of this view should be aware of this fact and verify that it is acceptable within the context of the application environment. This would be the case for the following sample query where we make the same semantic assumptions specified in Chapter 17. Namely, a staff member can tutor any course offered by his department; the staff member is also located in the same building and room as is specified for his department in the DEPARTMENT table.

2. Because DEPT is a column in both the STAFF and DEPARTMENT tables, the SELECT statement must qualify the column names. The view inherited the column name DEPT from the DEPARTMENT.DEPT column, which contains the department ids. It does not inherit the qualifier (DEPARTMENT). The complete column name in the view becomes VCSD.DEPT. The SELECT statement in the view definition could have referenced STAFF.DEPT instead of DEPARTMENT.DEPT, in which case the view column would still inherit the same name (VCSD.DEPT).

    The content of the view would be the same if the SELECT clause referenced CDEPT, in which case the view would have inherited the name of CDEPT (really VCSD.CDEPT). We could have explicitly named the view columns using the technique shown in Sample 23.4.

3. If we wanted to include all base table columns in the view, especially the three identical columns containing the department id values, then we would have to code the department id column names such that they are unique. Furthermore, we must explicitly name the view columns because inheritance would imply that two columns would be named DEPT, which is invalid. For example, the SELECT clause in the CREATE VIEW statement could be written as

    ```
    CREATE VIEW
    VCSD2 (CNO, CNAME, CDESCP, CRED, CLABFEE, CDEPT, DDEPT,
           DBLD, DROOM, DCHFNO, SDEPT, ENAME, ETITLE, ESALARY)
        AS
    SELECT CNO, CNAME, CDESCP, CRED, CLABFEE, CDEPT,
           DEPARTMENT.DEPT, DBLD, DROOM, DCHFNO, STAFF.DEPT,
           ENAME, ETITLE, ESALARY
    FROM    COURSE, STAFF, DEPARTMENT
    WHERE   CDEPT = STAFF.DEPT
    AND     CDEPT = DEPARTMENT.DEPT
    ```

In this view, the three columns containing the department ids are named CDEPT, DDEPT, and SDEPT. Also note that the SELECT statement had to explicitly reference the name of every column in all three tables. A common error is the writing of a SELECT clause with an asterisk (SELECT * FROM ...). This would cause an error whenever the same column name is used in multiple tables. Such is the case with DEPT in the current example.

Sample Query 23.9: For any staff member who can tutor philosophy courses, display his name, the name of the course he can tutor, and his building and room location. Sort the result by staff member name.

```
SELECT  ENAME, CNAME, DBLD, DROOM

FROM    VCSD

WHERE   DEPT = 'PHIL'

ORDER   BY ENAME
```

ENAME	CNAME	DBLD	DROOM
DICK NIX	EMPIRICISM	HU	100
DICK NIX	RATIONALISM	HU	100
DICK NIX	EXISTENTIALISM	HU	100
DICK NIX	SOLIPSISM	HU	100
HANK KISS	SOLIPSISM	HU	100
HANK KISS	EXISTENTIALISM	HU	100
HANK KISS	RATIONALISM	HU	100
HANK KISS	EMPIRICISM	HU	100

Comment:

This query is comparatively simple. The user extracts all the data from one (virtual) table instead of constructing a complex query using the join operation. The complexity of constructing the VCSD view has been passed onto the database administrator (where it belongs).

View Defined on the Union of Two Tables

ORACLE allows a view to be defined which contains a UNION,
INTERSECT, or MINUS keyword. The following example will
illustrate the view defined as a union of two tables.

Sample Statement 23.10:   Create a view which contains the
name, department, and salary (in
that order) of all staff and
faculty members assigned to the
Theology Department. (This is
similar to Sample Query 21.3.) Give
the view the name of THEO_EMPLOYEES
and name the columns NAME, DEPT_ID,
and SALARY.

```
CREATE VIEW THEO_EMPLOYEES

              (NAME, DEPT, SALARY)

AS      SELECT ENAME, DEPT, ESALARY

        FROM    STAFF

        WHERE   DEPT = 'THEO'

        UNION

        SELECT FNAME, FDEPT, FSALARY

        FROM    FACULTY

        WHERE   FDEPT = 'THEO'
```

System Response:

Like all previous CREATE statements, the system should
display a message confirming the successful creation of
the view.

Comments:

1.   Recall that a UNION requires that the SELECT statements
fulfill the definition of "union-compatible." In the
example, we have satisfied this requirement.

2.   DB2 Compatibility: Current versions of DB2 do not allow
for the creation of a view which contains the UNION
clause.

View Defined on Another View

The SELECT statement which defines a view can itself reference another view. The next example creates a view based on the CISC view which is, in turn, based on the COURSE base table. (See Sample Statement 23.1.)

Sample Statement 23.11: Create a view called VCHEAPCISC, which contains rows for CIS courses with a cheap labfee. These are CIS courses with a labfee less than $100. The view should contain just the CNAME and CLABFEE columns and inherit those column names.

```
CREATE VIEW VCHEAPCISC AS

SELECT CNAME, CLABFEE

FROM    CISC

WHERE   CLABFEE < 100
```

System Response:

Like all previous CREATE statements, the system should display a message confirming the successful creation of the view.

Comments:

1. All the data required for the VCHEAPCISC view are found in the CISC view. It may be the case that the user does not have access to the COURSE table, but does have access to CISC. Hence, the FROM clause in the SELECT statement references CISC.

2. Restrictions: Obviously, the previous restriction on view definition applies. (No ORDER BY clause is allowed.)

3. Can we define another view on the VCHEAPCISC view? (Can we base a view on a view on a view, etc.?) Yes. There is no arbitrary limit on the number of views dependent on other views.

Sample Query 23.12:   Display the entire VCHEAPCISC table.

```
SELECT *

FROM VCHEAPCISC
```

CNAME	CLABFEE
DATA STRUCTURES	50.00
DISCRETE MATHEMATICS	.00
DIGITAL CIRCUITS	.00

Comments:

1. Observe that only CIS department courses appear in the result. This is because the underlying view, CISC, allows access to only CIS courses.

2. The labfee values are all less than $100, as prescribed in the definition of VCHEAPCISC.

Exercise:

23C. Create a view of the FACULTY table, called VFSAL, which presents the highest and lowest salaries of faculty members by department. The columns in the view will have the names of DEPARTMENT, HIGHEST_SALARY, and LOWEST_SALARY. Issue a SELECT statement against this view and examine the results.

23D. Create a view on the view FPAYROLL which presents the average faculty salary and average number of dependents. Call the view FAVERAGES and use the column names FAVG_SAL and FAVG_NUM_DEP. Issue a SELECT statement against this view and examine the results.

View Update Restrictions

Sometimes it is possible to execute INSERT, UPDATE, and DELETE statements which reference a view. When allowed, the updates against the view are automatically applied to the underlying base table. However, there are some restrictions to these operations which are contingent on the view definition. In general, you can operate under the following assumption: "If it makes sense to update a view, and you have been granted permission to update the view, then you can (probably) update it." To validate this guideline, we ask you to consider three examples.

Example 1:

Consider the CISC table (view) defined in Sample Statement 23.1. The content of this view, shown in Sample Query 23.2, is essentially a "mirror image" of the CIS rows in the COURSE table excluding the CDEPT column. Now consider each of the following three update operations as applied to CISC.

DELETE FROM CISC WHERE CNO = 'C66'

This statement would be allowed. The WHERE clause identifies the CISC row(s) to be deleted. The corresponding row(s) would be deleted in the COURSE table. The above statement "makes sense" and ORACLE would apply the delete operation to the underlying base table.

UPDATE CISC SET CLABFEE = 25 WHERE CLABFEE = 0

This statement would be allowed. The WHERE clause identifies the CISC row(s) to be updated. The corresponding row(s) would be updated in the COURSE table. (Another UPDATE statement might be rejected. For example, "SET CLABFEE = 1000" would be rejected because the value exceeds the maximum range value. This restriction applies to the table, not the view.) The above statement "makes sense" and ORACLE would apply the update operation to the underlying base table.

INSERT INTO CISC VALUES
('THE OCCULT', 'X11', 0, 999.99, 'FOR SHIRLEY''S SAPS')

This statement would be *rejected*. In fact, no INSERT operations can be applied to CISC. ORACLE allows an INSERT operation if all the nonnull columns are part of the view. During execution of a valid INSERT statement, base table columns which are not specified in the view are set to null values. CDEPT is defined with the NOT NULL clause and it is not part of the CISC view. Hence, no rows can be inserted into CISC. If you know about the existence of the CDEPT column in the underlying base table, then no insert operation is reasonable. Hence, ORACLE will reject all INSERT statements referencing CISC.

Example 2:

Consider the VCSTAT view defined in Sample Statement 23.6. This view is not a "mirror image" of some rows and columns in the underlying base table. The rows in VCSTAT are compressed by the SUM and AVG functions. Also the GROUP BY operation has effectively resequenced the rows. Most INSERT, UPDATE, and DELETE operations against VCSTAT just don't make sense. How would you apply them to COURSE? Accordingly, ORACLE would reject any attempt at modifying VCSTAT.

Example 3:

Consider the VCSD view defined in Sample Statement 23.8. This definition of this view contains a join operation. During a join operation some rows match with many other rows, producing duplicate data in the view table. This occurred in VCSD (see result in Sample Query 23.9). VCSD is not a "mirror image" of an underlying base table. Most INSERT, UPDATE, and DELETE operations do not make sense. ORACLE would reject all such operations against VCSD.

These examples show that some reasonable update operations can be applied to "mirror image" views. Other views cannot be updated. This is true. But our notion of "mirror image" is just a conceptual analogy which corresponds to the precise rules specified in the ORACLE reference manual, which states that

1.   You can DELETE rows in a base table through a view if the view definition references just one table (e.g., no join or union operations) and does not contain GROUP BY, DISTINCT, any group function, or the ROWNUM pseudo-column.

2.   You can UPDATE rows in a base table through a view if the view definition observes the above restrictions and, furthermore, does not update a column defined with an expression.

3.   You can INSERT rows into a base table through a view if the view definition observes both the above restrictions and, furthermore, the view does not exclude any of the NOT NULL columns from the base table.

We conclude our discussion of view update by mentioning that these rules are imperfect because there are circumstances where it does make sense to update a view but ORACLE prohibits the update operation. We invite you to find an example of such a circumstance. (See Exercise 23N.) We note that all relational DBMS products have some imperfections pertaining to the view update process. This is because the view update problem is still an open area of database research.

DROP VIEW Statement

This chapter illustrated the creation of five views (CISC, VEXPCOURSE, VCSTAT, VCSD, and VCHEAPCISC). The DROP VIEW statement is very simple and can be used to remove the view from the database. The next example demonstrates its use.

Sample Statement 23.13: Drop the VCSTAT table from the database. More precisely, drop the VCSTAT view.

```
DROP VIEW VCSTAT
```

System Response:

The system will display a message confirming that VCSTAT has been dropped.

The next example drops a view on which another view is based. When this occurs, all views dependent on the dropped view become invalid.

Sample Statement 23.14: Drop the CISC table from the database. More precisely, drop the CISC view.

```
DROP VIEW CISC
```

Comment:

This statement drops CISC and invalidates VCHEAPCISC, the only view that is dependent on CISC.

The DROP TABLE statement will cause all views which are dependent on the base table to become invalid. Hence, dropping the COURSE table would invalidate all the views created by the sample statements illustrated in this chapter.

Exercise:

23E. Drop the view VFSAL which was created in Exercise 23C. Issue a SELECT statement against this view and notice the system response.

23F. Drop the view FPAYROLL. Issue a SELECT statement against the view FAVERAGES, which was based on the FPAYROLL view.

Summary

We conclude this chapter by noting that the CREATE VIEW statement is quite simple because it utilizes the SELECT statement as a vehicle for defining a view. The only potential problems pertain to the restrictions for defining and updating views. It is helpful to understand how ORACLE handles views.

How does the system handle views?

Recall that ORACLE stores the view definition (the text of the SELECT statement) in the Data Dictionary. When a query is executed against the view, the system consults the dictionary and extracts (1) the name of the base table and (2) the view predicates specified in the WHERE clause of the view definition. The system merges the predicates of the query with those of the view definition to form a new query. The view name is replaced with the name of the underlying base table, and the predicates are AND-connected. This reformulated query is then executed by the system.

Consider the CISC view defined in Sample Statement 23.1. It specifies a base table (COURSE) and a predicate (CDEPT = 'CIS'). Assume a user enters the query shown in Sample Query 23.3 rewritten below.

```
SELECT  CNAME, CLABFEE
FROM    CISC
WHERE   CLABFEE  = 100
ORDER BY CNAME
```

The system reformulates this query following the process described above. The reformulated query is shown below.

```
SELECT  CNAME, CLABFEE
FROM    COURSE
WHERE   CLABFEE  = 100
AND     CDEPT = 'CIS'
ORDER BY CNAME
```

This reformulated query is submitted for execution. Observe that it does satisfy the objective of Sample Query 23.3. This approach to defining and processing views means that a query against a view is always applied against the underlying base table. This is why the system does not have to store a duplicate copy of the data to represent a view. Sometimes the merging process described above is inappropriate. In this case, ORACLE will execute the SELECT statement which defines the query and store the result as an intermediate result. This intermediate result is accessed by the SELECT statement which accesses the view.

Summary Exercises

23G. Create a view called VTHEO_STAFF based on the STAFF table. It is to reflect the ENAME, ESALARY, and ETITLE information for all staff members assigned to the THEO department.

23H. Create a view which presents the average salary of all staff members assigned to each department. The view will be called VAVG_STAFF and will have the column names of DEPT and AVERAGE_SALARY.

23I. Create a view based on the VTHEO_STAFF view which presents the total of the salaries for all staff members in the THEO department.

23J. Create a view which reflects the join of the FACULTY, COURSE, and CLASS tables. The view is to present the name of the faculty member teaching the class and the name of the course for all courses for which there are class offerings. Use the column names of INSTRUCTOR and COURSE_NAME. The view will be called VINSTR.

23K. Drop the VTHEO_STAFF view.

23L. Can you issue an UPDATE statement against the VCSD view created in Sample Statement 23.8?

23M. Can you insert rows into the THEO_EMPLOYEES view created in Sample Statement 23.10?

23N. Give an example of a view which makes sense to update, but which ORACLE would not allow to be updated.

24

Database Security

Database security is a broad topic which can be examined from the systems administrator, database administrator, professional programmer, or casual user point of view. ORACLE has a comprehensive authorization subsystem which allows for the protection of any database object from illegitimate access or manipulation. The general scheme involves identification of (1) who the user is, (2) what object is referenced, and (3) what processes can be executed against the specified object. This chapter will examine the authorization scheme from the programmer-user point of view. ORACLE supports the GRANT and REVOKE statements which are used to grant and subsequently retract database privileges.

The following sample statements assume that the database administrator has granted you permission to create tables. We assume that you previously executed the CREATE TABLE statement to create the COURSE table. ORACLE then recognizes you as the creator of this table. As creator of the COURSE table, you automatically have all privileges (to be described below) on this table. Also, with the exception of the database administrator, no other user has any privileges on the COURSE table -- until you grant them such privileges. The following examples illustrate how you can use the GRANT statement to pass privileges to other users.

The GRANT Statement

The general syntax of the GRANT statement is described below. Note the execution of a single statement allows for the granting of many of privileges on an object to many users.

```
GRANT  privilege-1, privilege-2, ...
ON     object
TO     username-1, username-2, ...
[WITH GRANT OPTION]
```

We describe each of the above parameters within the context of table privileges.

Object: The object may be a base table or a view.

Privileges: We list only those privileges which pertain to base tables or views.

* SELECT
* INSERT
* UPDATE (columns)
* DELETE
* INDEX
* ALTER

The granting of a particular privilege means that user who is granted the privilege can execute the corresponding statement against the specified object. In particular, note that it is possible to grant permission to another user so that the other user can alter (append a new column) or create an index on your base table. The SELECT, INSERT, UPDATE, and DELETE privileges can be granted on a base table or a view. The INDEX and ALTER privileges can only be granted on a base table. The SELECT, INSERT, and DELETE privileges pertain to entire rows of a base table or view. The UPDATE privilege can be restricted to specific columns. You can also grant all the above privileges by specifying ALL as a privilege in the statement. (GRANT ALL ON ...)

Username: Your username is typically the same sign-on identifier which you used to access SQL*Plus. There is a special username, PUBLIC, which can be specified when you wish to grant a privilege to all users.

WITH GRANT OPTION: When granting privileges the recipient does not automatically obtain the ability to pass privileges to other users. If you want to allow another user to be able to do so, you must include the WITH GRANT OPTION clause at the end of your GRANT statement.

Sample Query 24.1:   You would like to give MOE permission to display your COURSE table. You do not want him to be able to perform any other operations involving this table. More precisely, you would like to grant SELECT privileges on COURSE to MOE.

```
GRANT  SELECT

ON      COURSE

TO      MOE
```

System Response:

The system displays a message which confirms the granting of the privilege.

Comments:

1. The general syntax of the GRANT statement is rather straightforward as described on the previous page.

2. MOE (really the person with the username of MOE) can now issue any valid SELECT statement referencing your COURSE table. He can display all columns of all rows.

3. MOE cannot issue a GRANT statement to pass this privilege to some other user. This is because you did not grant MOE his privilege with the GRANT option. (See the next example.)

WITH GRANT OPTION

Sample Statement 24.2: Allow LARRY and CURLEY to display just those rows from the COURSE table corresponding to courses offered by the CIS Department. Also allow them to modify the course description and labfee amount in these rows. Assume you have already created the CISC view which contains just those CIS rows which LARRY and CURLEY can display and modify. Finally, allow them permission to pass their privileges onto other users.

```
GRANT SELECT, UPDATE(CDESCP,CLABFEE)

ON     CISC

TO     LARRY, CURLEY

WITH GRANT OPTION
```

Comments:

1. This example illustrates the general approach to database security for application data. A responsible individual (project leader, professional programmer, sophisticated user) has responsibility for a base table. This individual may have initially created the base table and inserted the data, or may have been granted all privileges from the database administrator. Then this person grants access to the table to users such that they can do the least damage. This is done by

    a. Creating a view which limits their access to just certain rows and/or columns of the table

    b. Granting some, usually not all, privileges on this view

    This scheme provides a very simple but powerful and flexible approach to database security.

2. LARRY and CURLEY can issue any SELECT statement against CISC. They can issue an UPDATE statement only if it references the CDESCP or CLABFEE columns.

3. LARRY and CURLEY can grant their privileges to other users. They may also choose to grant these privileges using WITH GRANT OPTION. If they do so, recipients can then pass on the same privileges to even more users.

The REVOKE Statement

Any granted privilege can subsequently be revoked by executing the REVOKE statement. The syntax is similar to the GRANT statement, but it has the opposite effect. The general syntax is

```
REVOKE  privilege-1, privilege-2, ...
ON      object
FROM    username-1, username-2, ...
```

The following example demonstrates this statement.

Sample Statement 24.3:   CURLEY has abused his update privilege on CISC. Revoke his UPDATE privileges but allow him to retain his SELECT privilege.

```
REVOKE  UPDATE

ON      CISC

FROM    CURLEY
```

Comments:

1. After you execute this statement, the system will reject any UPDATE statement issued by CURLEY which references CISC. Note that CURLEY had UPDATE privileges on two columns. The REVOKE statement will not allow column-specific revocation of the UPDATE privilege. As the example shows, you must revoke all UPDATE privileges on the object. Under some circumstances, you may wish to reissue the GRANT statement for the other columns after executing the REVOKE statement.

2. Assume CURLEY had previously granted UPDATE privileges to other users, who may in turn have granted them to even more users, etc. In this case, the REVOKE statement will automatically apply to all these users. The effect of the revocation ripples down to all users who obtained an UPDATE privilege on CISC from CURLEY.

3. Note that the UPDATE privileges were not retracted from LARRY. Could LARRY grant the UPDATE privileges to CURLEY after you issued the REVOKE statement? Yes, and it would work. This is because the original privileges were granted using WITH GRANT OPTION.

4. You can revoke all privileges on an object by using the ALL keyword. (REVOKE ALL ON ...)

Referencing Another User's Table

Assume that you have been granted privileges on a table or view created by another user. Under these circumstances you must reference the table or view by its complete name. This means that you must include the username as a prefix to the table name. Otherwise, the system will assume your username as a prefix. This will result in an error because you did not create the table or view.

Sample Statement 24.4:   In Sample Statement 24.1 you granted SELECT privileges on COURSE to MOE. Assume that your authorization identifier is U48989. What statement must MOE execute in order to display your COURSE table?

```
SELECT *

FROM     U48989.COURSE
```

CNO	CNAME	CDESCP	CRED	CLABFEE	CDEPT
T11	SCHOLASTICISM	FOR THE PIOUS	3	150.00	THEO
T12	FUNDAMENTALISM	FOR THE CAREFREE	3	90.00	THEO
T33	HEDONISM	FOR THE SANE	3	.00	THEO
T44	COMMUNISM	FOR THE GREEDY	6	200.00	THEO
P11	EMPIRICISM	SEE IT-BELIEVE IT	3	100.00	PHIL
P22	RATIONALISM	FOR CIS MAJORS	3	50.00	PHIL
P33	EXISTENTIALISM	FOR CIS MAJORS	3	200.00	PHIL
P44	SOLIPSISM	ME MYSELF AND I	6	.00	PHIL
C11	INTRO TO CS	FOR ROOKIES	3	100.00	CIS
C22	DATA STRUCTURES	VERY USEFUL	3	50.00	CIS
C33	DISCRETE MATHEMATICS	ABSOLUTELY NECESSARY	3	.00	CIS
C44	DIGITAL CIRCUITS	AH HA!	3	.00	CIS
C55	COMPUTER ARCH.	VON NEUMANN'S MACH.	3	100.00	CIS
C66	RELATIONAL DATABASE	THE ONLY WAY TO GO	3	500.00	CIS

Comments:

1. The U48989 prefix is required. If it were omitted, the system would attempt to display a table called MOE.COURSE which either does not exist or is the name of some other table created by MOE which he coincidentally named COURSE.

2. Many users will not have permission to create tables. Therefore, every table they reference will have the authorization id prefix of some other user.

3. Typing the prefix for every reference to a table is a minor inconvenience. You can reduce this effort by using synonyms. (See Chapter 5.) For example, MOE could execute the following statement

    CREATE SYNONYM MC FOR U48989.COURSE

    Then the preceding query could be entered as

        SELECT *
        FROM   MC

    This is a common technique which is used very often in practice.

Summary

In this chapter we introduced the notion of database security through the SQL GRANT and REVOKE statements. There are two forms of the GRANT and REVOKE statement. The first form pertains to "system" privileges. The second form pertains to "table" privileges. The scope of our discussion was limited to table privileges.

The GRANT statement is used to allow other users to access a table. With the statement, you specify what privileges (i.e., how the users will be allowed to access the table) are to be given to other users. In general, if a user has not been specifically granted authorization to perform an operation (or the privilege has not been granted to PUBLIC), that user cannot perform that operation. A privilege may be granted to a user along with the ability of that user to pass on the privilege to other users by specifying the WITH GRANT OPTION. The REVOKE statement is used to retract a user's granted privilege. The REVOKE statement has a cascading effect.

Throughout the text we have used the terms "creator" of a table and "owner" of a table interchangeably. This is not entirely accurate. It is possible for the DBA to create an object using the username of any user. In this circumstance, the DBA is the <u>creator</u> of the object while the other user is considered to be the <u>owner</u> of the object.

We conclude this chapter with a brief comment on the first form of the GRANT statement which is used to grant system privileges. Only the database administrator can execute this form of the GRANT statement. This form of the GRANT statement can be used to grant three different privileges to an individual who would like to use the ORACLE system. The CONNECT privilege is necessary to sign-on to ORACLE. You cannot sign-on to ORACLE until you receive this privilege. The second privilege is RESOURCE. You need this privilege in order to issue the CREATE TABLE and other CREATE statements except CREATE VIEW and CREATE SYNONYM. (Anyone who can sign-on to ORACLE can create views and private synonyms.) The third privilege is the DBA privilege. If you have this privilege, people will be nice to you!

Finally, how do you determine which privileges have been granted to you? You could query the Data Dictionary. This will be described in Chapter 26. (See Sample Query 26.3.)

Summary Exercises

24A. Grant SELECT and INSERT privileges on the STAFF table to CURLEY.

24B. Grant all privileges on the DEPARTMENT table to everyone. Then quickly revoke those privileges.

Transaction Processing

Most databases reflect a dynamic environment rather than a
static one. Changes to data within ORACLE systems are
accomplished through the INSERT, UPDATE, and DELETE
statements originally introduced in Chapter 15. For most
production information systems these statements are usually,
but not always, placed within application programs. However,
there are occasions when these statements will be executed
within an interactive environment. When this is necessary,
the user should follow procedures which ensure database
integrity. An important consideration within this context is
the specification of database transactions. This chapter
introduces the concept of a transaction and in so doing
presents two new SQL statements, COMMIT and ROLLBACK.

Preliminary Example

The first example does not introduce any new SQL reserved words, but it does illustrate the objectives of transaction processing. For this example, assume the COURSE table contains a row for a course with a CNO value of "XXX". Also assume there are classes on this course described in the CLASS table and there are student registrations for these classes in the REGISTRATION table.

Sample Statements 25.1: Course "XXX" has been dropped from the curriculum and, therefore, must be removed from the COURSE table. All class offerings for this course must be removed from the CLASS table. Registration information for those classes must be removed from the REGISTRATION table.

```
DELETE

FROM REGISTRATION

WHERE CNO = 'XXX'


DELETE

FROM CLASS

WHERE CNO = 'XXX'


DELETE

FROM COURSE

WHERE CNO = 'XXX'
```

Comment:

The example shows three independent DELETE statements. However, from the user's viewpoint, these changes constitute a single "logical unit of work": Delete all rows which reference the course with the CNO value of "XXX". From the SQL viewpoint, this unit of work requires the execution of multiple DELETE statements because multiple tables need to be changed. A logical unit of work is called a "transaction." The next example will illustrate how to bundle the set of DELETE statements to form a single transaction.

Why is it necessary to define the three DELETE statements as a single transaction just because the user sees this as a single logical unit of work? Assuming that each DELETE statement is correct, why not simply execute each statement? In other words, why bundle? The answer to this question lies in recognition of events which are beyond the control of the SQL user.

Computer systems "go down." This can happen in the middle of a terminal session when you are executing any of the three DELETE statements. What is the status of the database if the computer goes down at some time just before, during, or after you have issued the second DELETE statement? If this happens, you cannot be sure if the updates to the CLASS table actually occurred. (In fact, you cannot even be sure that the changes for the first DELETE statement were written to the disk before the problem occurred.) You could verify the status by displaying the tables. However, this usually is not practical, especially if the tables are large.

What we want is an all-or-nothing situation. Either all the rows in all tables containing a CNO value of "XXX" have been deleted or none of them have. If all rows which reference "XXX" are deleted, we have realized our objective. If none are deleted, we have to start all over again. This requires some extra effort, but it is the necessary cost of database integrity. This all-or-nothing situation is exactly what a transaction provides.

Defining Transactions

In the previous example we observed that the three separate DELETE statements are logically related. It would be unacceptable if only the first one or two statements, but not the third, executed successfully. How is the system able to ensure that if only some of the statements execute successfully that their effect will be canceled? The answer is the system will only consider the initial changes as "tentative" until the completion of the logical unit of work (the transaction) occurs. If a problem is encountered prior to the completion of all operations in the logical unit of work, the tentative changes will be undone. Obviously, the system must be informed of which SQL statements constitute a logical unit of work. In other words, we must define the boundaries of each transaction. This is achieved by specifying "synchronization points."

Synchronization points, often called "sync points," define the scope of a database transaction. A sync point is automatically established at the beginning of each terminal session or application program. Thereafter, the user or programmer can specify other sync points, which establish the end of a previous transaction and the beginning of a new transaction using the SQL keywords COMMIT or ROLLBACK. Under normal circumstances, a transaction is concluded by executing

*   A COMMIT statement which informs the system that all changes made within the transaction are acceptable and that they should be applied to the database.

*   A ROLLBACK statement which informs the system that an unacceptable situation has been encountered and that any changes made since the start of the transaction are to be voided.

If the computer system goes down in the middle of a transaction (before you can issue either a COMMIT or ROLLBACK statement), any changes to the database specified within that transaction are automatically undone. This is because ORACLE has a recovery subsystem which will automatically issue a ROLLBACK statement for all transactions which were pending when the problem occurred. Of course, this means that you have to reissue those update statements which were undone.

The COMMIT and ROLLBACK statements will be illustrated in Sample Statements 25.2 and 25.3. Before presenting examples, we must make a few comments regarding the interactive execution of these statements.

SET AUTOCOMMIT Command

SQL*Plus has a system variable (AUTOCOMMIT) which the user can set to ON or OFF to enable or disable the automatic commit feature. When AUTOCOMMIT is set to ON, the successful completion of an SQL statement will result in the immediate commitment of changes to the database. If AUTOCOMMIT is set to OFF at a certain point in the terminal session, any changes to the database which occurred after that point can be undone by executing a ROLLBACK statement. Alternatively, the user can commit these changes by executing the COMMIT statement. Both the ROLLBACK and COMMIT statements establish sync points as described on the previous page.

COMMIT Statement

The function of the COMMIT statement is to terminate a transaction and cause the tentative changes to be applied to the database and thus made permanent.

Sample Statement 25.2:   Course "XXX" has been dropped from the curriculum. Remove all references to this course from the COURSE, CLASS, and REGISTRATION tables. Bundle the changes into a single transaction to be committed after successful execution of all DELETE statements.

```
SET AUTOCOMMIT OFF

DELETE
FROM REGISTRATION
WHERE CNO = 'XXX'

DELETE
FROM CLASS
WHERE CNO = 'XXX'

DELETE
FROM COURSE
WHERE CNO = 'XXX'

COMMIT
```

Comment:

The COMMIT statement caused the delete operations to become permanent. All three tables were updated to reflect the removal of the rows with a CNO value of "XXX."

ROLLBACK Statement

The following example illustrates the use of the ROLLBACK statement to undo changes made to the COURSE table.

Sample Statement 25.3:   Assume you were told that all classes for course number "C11" were canceled and, therefore, you should delete all rows which reference this course in the CLASS and REGISTRATION tables. After you enter the DELETE statements (but before you commit them), you decide to undo them because you feel that this action should be confirmed by the CIS Department chairperson.

```
SET AUTOCOMMIT OFF

DELETE
FROM REGISTRATION
WHERE CNO = 'C11'

DELETE
FROM CLASS
WHERE CNO = 'C11'

ROLLBACK
```

Comments:

1.   If you displayed the REGISTRATION table after executing the first DELETE statement but before executing the second DELETE statement, you would observe that the C11 rows were deleted. If you examined the CLASS table after executing the second DELETE statement you would observe that the C11 rows were deleted. Finally, after executing the ROLLBACK statement, displaying the rows from other tables would again show the presence of the C11 rows.

2.   The previous example had SET AUTOCOMMIT OFF. Assuming that no intermediate SET AUTOCOMMIT ON command was executed, the above SET AUTOCOMMIT OFF statement was unnecessary.

SAVEPOINT Statement

Version 6 introduced a new SQL statement, SAVEPOINT, which allows the specification of checkpoints within a long transaction. A new variation of the ROLLBACK statement allows you to roll back to a checkpoint instead of the beginning of a transaction. The SAVEPOINT statement will rarely, if ever, be used in an interactive environment. Professional programmers should consult the ORACLE manual for details on this statement.

Database Recovery

The ROLLBACK statement allows you to undo any uncommitted changes to the database. But what if you discover update errors after they have been committed? You could execute further update statements to make corrections. But this is potentially dangerous, especially if the changes are complex. This could lead to a loss of database integrity. It is safer to undo the committed changes. The undoing of committed changes requires the intervention of the DBA who would execute special system utility programs to restore the database to a previous state. An examination of ORACLE's recovery system is beyond the scope of this text. However, because the recovery subsystem is based on the transaction concept, it is important that users define their logical units of work and establish transactions via proper utilization of the COMMIT and ROLLBACK statements.

Summary

This chapter introduced the AUTOCOMMIT system variable and two SQL statements, COMMIT and ROLLBACK, which allow the definition of a logical unit of work called a transaction. The effect of these two statements is to mark the end of one transaction and the beginning of another, thus establishing what is called a sync point. The COMMIT statement causes all pending database changes (those which occurred after the last sync point) to be committed. The ROLLBACK statement causes the pending changes to be undone. The effect is just as if the update statements had never been executed.

We conclude by noting two default actions on the part of the system.

1.   Some SQL statements automatically cause an implicit commit. Some of these are CREATE TABLE, CREATE INDEX, DROP TABLE, DROP INDEX, GRANT, REVOKE, and other statements (not covered in this book) which cause ORACLE to update its Data Dictionary.

2.   Some circumstances cause an automatic rollback to occur. We have already mentioned one. This is when the system crashes.

DB2 Compatibility: DB2 supports the COMMIT and ROLLBACK statements using SPUFI and embedded SQL. It uses a different mechanism in the QMF environment.

Finally, we note that the COMMIT statement can also be formulated as COMMIT WORK. The same applies to the ROLLBACK statement.

Summary Exercise

25A. Execute the SET AUTOCOMMIT OFF command. Then delete all CIS rows from the COURSE table and execute the query. Display the table to verify their (tentative) removal. Now issue the ROLLBACK statement. Again, display the COURSE table and observe that the tentative changes have been undone; the CIS rows are back in the table. Finally, execute the SET AUTOCOMMIT ON command.

Exploring ORACLE's Data Dictionary

Throughout this text we have periodically made brief reference to ORACLE's Data Dictionary. In Chapter 5 we introduced two dictionary tables, USER_SYNONYMS and ALL_SYNONYMS. In Chapter 13 we introduced the DESCRIBE command, which displayed the names and descriptions of columns in a designated table. We will see that the system extracted this information from the Data Dictionary. And in Chapter 14, we indicated that the CREATE TABLE and CREATE INDEX statements indirectly update the Data Dictionary.

The objective of this chapter is to present an organized overview of the Data Dictionary. Our goal is to provide enough information such that you can independently explore the Data Dictionary to discover information about (1) tables, columns, views, etc., which are part of your own application system and (2) aspects of the Data Dictionary which are not covered in this chapter.

The Data Dictionary contains information about the logical and physical structure of the ORACLE database. This structure usually changes with each new version of ORACLE. Hence, the Data Dictionary is also changed or enhanced with each new version. With the introduction of Version 6 (V6) of ORACLE, major changes were made to the Data Dictionary; it is quite different from the Version 5 (V5) Data Dictionary. This chapter describes the V6 dictionary. This is the only chapter where the illustrated sample queries will execute on V6 but not on V5. If you are still using V5, you will find some useful information on V5 in the Summary of this chapter. We recommend that V5 users read this chapter for two reasons. First, it will help you understand the purpose and structure of a data dictionary. Second, most V5 users will eventually upgrade to V6.

Structure of ORACLE's Data Dictionary

We make the following observations about the structure of ORACLE's Data Dictionary. We note that these observations apply to V5, V6, and, most likely, all future versions of ORACLE.

1. The Data Dictionary is a collection of tables. This chapter will describe many of these tables.

2. The Data Dictionary tables contain "metadata"; this is "data about data." It contains information about every table in your ORACLE system, every column in these tables, every index on these columns, etc.

3. You can examine these tables by using SQL. The only thing you need to learn is the names of the tables and their columns. This is not difficult.

4. You do not directly update the Data Dictionary tables using the INSERT, UPDATE, and DELETE statements. Instead, ORACLE will automatically maintain these tables in response to CREATE, DROP, ALTER, and other SQL statements.

In effect, the dictionary is just a collection of tables which you examine using SELECT statements. When you complete this chapter you will be able to query the dictionary to answer such questions as

• What tables and views did I create? What columns are in those tables and views? What is the description (data type, length, etc.) of the columns?

• What synonyms for what tables or views did I create? (Review Sample Query 5.3.)

• What privileges have been granted to me? On what tables or views? Are my UPDATE privileges column specific? Who is the grantor of the privileges?

• What privileges have I granted to other users? On what tables, views, or columns? Who is the grantee of each privilege?

In order to answer these questions you first need to learn the names (and semantics) of certain dictionary tables and columns. This is a primary objective of this chapter.

We begin by illustrating a typical query you would execute to examine the dictionary. This query displays just one of approximately 100 tables found in the V6 dictionary. After this example, we describe the basic organization of the V6 dictionary.

The USER_CATALOG Table

The USER_CATALOG table contains one row for every table, view, synonym, and sequence which you (as the "user") created and have not yet dropped. This table has two columns: TABLE_NAME, the name of the object; and TABLE_TYPE, the type of the object.

Sample Query 26.1: Display the USER_CATALOG table.

```
SELECT * FROM USER_CATALOG
```

TABLE_NAME	TABLE_TYPE
C	SYNONYM
CISC	VIEW
CL	SYNONYM
CLASS	TABLE
COURSE	TABLE
D	SYNONYM
DEPARTMENT	TABLE
F	SYNONYM
FACULTY	TABLE
NULLTAB	TABLE
R	SYNONYM
REGISTRATION	TABLE
S	SYNONYM
ST	SYNONYM
STAFF	TABLE
STUDENT	TABLE
VCHEAPCISC	VIEW
VCSD	VIEW
VCSTAT	VIEW
VEXPCOURSE	VIEW

Comments:

1. We note that the displayed result contains information only about objects that you created. It does not describe any object which some other user granted you access to. The ALL_CATALOG table will contain the above information plus information about tables, views, synonyms, and sequences which some other user has granted you privileges on.

2. CAT can be used as a synonym for the USER_CATALOG table.

Dictionary Tables about Database Objects

Users will access (and sometimes create) a variety of database objects. Information about these objects can be found in a number of dictionary tables. Ten of these tables and their columns are briefly described in Figure 26.1.

1. The name of each table begins with "ALL_" or "USER_". In general, if the name of the table begins with "USER_", it will only reference objects created by the user; if the name of the table begins with "ALL_", it will reference all objects created by the user plus other objects which the user has been granted privileges on.

2. There is a pairing of tables (e.g., USER_CATALOG and ALL_CATALOG) which have the same columns, with one exception. The "ALL_" tables have an additional column (OWNER) which contains the username of the owner of the object.

```
ALL_OBJECTS & USER_OBJECTS tables
  OWNER            (not in USER_OBJECTS)
  OBJECT_NAME      name of object
  OBJECT_ID        internal identifier
  CREATED          timestamp
  MODIFIED         timestamp

ALL_CATALOG & USER_CATALOG tables
  OWNER            (not in USER_CATALOG)
  TABLE_NAME       name of table, view, synonym, or sequence
  TABLE_TYPE       table, synonym, sequence

ALL_TABLES & USER_TABLES tables
  OWNER            (not in USER_TABLES)
  TABLE_NAME       name of table
  • many other columns exist which describe physical
    characteristics of the table like tablespace name,
    cluster name, freespace percentages, etc. These
    other columns are primarily examined by the DBA.

ALL_VIEWS & USER_VIEWS tables
  OWNER            (not in USER_VIEWS)
  VIEW_NAME        name of view
  TEXT_LENGTH      length of data in TEXT column
  TEXT             the SELECT statement which defines view

ALL_SYNONYMS & USER_SYNONYMS tables
  OWNER            (not in USER_SYNONYMS)
  SYNONYM_NAME     name of synonym
  TABLE_OWNER      owner of table or view
  TABLE_NAME       name of table or view
```

Figure 26.1: Dictionary tables about "user objects."

3.   There is a hierarchy among the tables:

"_OBJECT" tables reference every type of object. These include tables, views, synonyms, sequences, indexes, tablespaces, and databases.

"_CATALOG" tables reference only tables, views, synonyms, and sequences.

"_TABLES" tables reference only tables.

"_VIEWS" tables reference only views.

"_SYNONYMS" tables reference only synonyms.

4.   There is a fair amount of redundant data found in these tables. For example, if you created the COURSE table, "COURSE" would be found in the TABLE_NAME column of the ALL_CATALOG, USER_CATALOG, ALL_TABLES, and USER_TABLES tables and in the OBJECT_NAME column of the ALL_OBJECTS and USER_OBJECTS tables. This is true, but much of the redundancy is "apparent." These dictionary tables are really views of base tables which you cannot access.

Sample Query 26.2:   Display the owner and name of every (base) table, other than your own, on which you have privileges. Sort the result by table name within owner name.

```
SELECT  OWNER, TABLE_NAME
FROM    ALL_TABLES
WHERE   OWNER <> USER
ORDER BY OWNER, TABLE-NAME
```

OWNER	TABLE_NAME
CURLEY	CTABLE
LARRY	LTABLE
MOE	MTABLEA
MOE	MTABLEB
SYS	AUDIT_ACTIONS
SYS	DUAL

Comment:

You will see references to tables created by other users and the system (owner is "SYS") which you can access.

Exercises:

26A. What views did you create which do not have a name beginning with the letter "V"?

26B. What is the definition of the CISC view?

Dictionary Tables about Columns

Assume that you forgot the names and descriptions of columns in your COURSE table. You can find this information in the USER_TAB_COLUMNS table or the ALL_TAB_COLUMNS table. The content of these tables is shown in Figure 26.2. Again, the same naming convention applies. The USER_TAB_COLUMNS table contains one row for each column in every table or view that you created. ALL_TAB_COLUMNS contains the same information plus information about columns in tables or views you have been granted privileges on.

```
ALL_TAB_COLUMNS & USER_TAB_COLUMNS Tables

OWNER                (not in USER_TAB_COLUMNS)
TABLE_NAME           name of table or view
COLUMN_NAME          name of column
DATA_TYPE            NUMBER, CHAR, DATE, etc.
DATA_LENGTH          in bytes; pertains to hardware code
DATA_PRECISION       decimal precision for NUMBER, otherwise  null
DATA_SCALE           digits to right of decimal point
NULLABLE             Y/N - column allow nulls
COLUMN_ID            sequence no. of col. (CNO=1, CNAME=2, etc.)
DEFAULT_LENGTH       length of default value
DATA_DEFAULT         default value of col, if defined
```

Figure 26.2: Dictionary tables about columns in tables and views.

Sample Query 26.3:   Display the column number, name, data type, length, scale, and precision of each column in the COURSE table. Sort the result by column number.

```
SELECT  COLUMN_ID, COLUMN_NAME, DATA_TYPE,
        DATA_LENGTH, DATA_PRECISION, DATA_SCALE
FROM    USER_TAB_COLUMNS
WHERE   TABLE_NAME = 'COURSE'
ORDER BY COLUMN_ID
```

COLUMN_ID	COLUMN_NAME	DATA_TYPE	DATA_LENGTH	DATA_PRECISION	DATA_SCALE
1	CNO	CHAR	3		
2	CNAME	CHAR	22		
3	CDESCP	CHAR	25		
4	CRED	NUMBER	22		
5	CLABFEE	NUMBER	22	5	2
6	CDEPT	CHAR	4		

Comments:

1. Most of the displayed information is self-evident. However, we note that the DATA_LENGTH column describing CRED and CLABFEE is 22. This will apply to all numeric values.

2. COLS can be used as a synonym for the USER_TAB_COLUMNS table.

3. The name ALL_TAB_COLUMNS is really a synonym for the ACCESSIBLE_COLUMNS table.

4. The USER_TAB_COLUMNS and ALL_TAB_COLUMNS tables also contain information about columns in clusters. We briefly described clusters in Chapter 14.

Exercises:

26C. Display the name and type of every object which you created.

26D. Display every table which has a name beginning with the letter "C."

26E. Display each of your views which references your STAFF table.

26F. Display the name of each of your tables which has a column with the name "CNO".

26G. Display the name of each of your tables which has a column name containing the character string "DEPT".

26H. Display any column from the COURSE table which can accept null values.

Dictionary Tables about Table and Column Privileges

ORACLE records all table and view privileges, except column-specific UPDATE privileges, in the dictionary tables shown in Figure 26.3. The column-specific UPDATE privileges are recorded in the dictionary tables shown in Figure 26.4.

The USER_TAB_GRANTS_MADE table contains information about grants on objects that you own. Recall that another user can grant privileges on one of your objects if you grant using WITH GRANT OPTION. The GRANTOR column identifies the grantor (you or another user) who granted the privilege.

The ALL_TAB_GRANTS_MADE table contains the same information as USER_TAB_GRANTS_MADE plus information about grants you made on other users' objects. The OWNER column identifies the owner (you or another user) of the object.

The USER_TAB_GRANTS_RECD table contains information about grants on objects that you received (you are grantee).

The ALL_TAB_GRANTS_RECD table contains information about grants on objects that you received plus any privileges granted to the PUBLIC.

The USER_TAB_GRANTS table contains information about grants where the grant is on an object that you own, or you are the grantor, or you are the grantee.

The ALL_TAB_GRANTS table contains the same information as the USER_TAB_GRANTS table plus information about grants where the grantee is "PUBLIC".

Sample Query 26.4:   Who are the grantees of privileges that you have directly granted on your own objects? Identify the grantee and object along with the SELECT and DELETE privileges.

```
SELECT  GRANTEE, TABLE_NAME, SELECT_PRIV, DELETE_PRIV
FROM    USER_TAB_GRANTS_MADE
WHERE   GRANTOR = USER
```

GRANTEE	TABLE_NAME	S	D
MOE	COURSE	Y	N

Comment:

USER is an ORACLE keyword which will contain your username (e.g., U48989). The WHERE clause identifying you as grantor was necessary because you could have granted privileges using WITH GRANT OPTION. Thus, another user could be the (indirect) grantor of a privilege on an object that you own.

```
ALL_TAB_GRANTS_MADE & USER_TAB_GRANTS_MADE tables
ALL_TAB_GRANTS_RECD & USER_TAB_GRANTS_RECD tables
ALL_TAB-GRANTS & USER_TAB_GRANTS tables

Columns in tables:

GRANTEE                 (not in USER_TAB_GRANTS_RECD)
OWNER                   (not in USER_TAB_GRANTS_MADE)
TABLE_NAME              name of table or view
GRANTOR                 username of grantor of privilege
SELECT_PRIV
INSERT_PRIV
DELETE_PRIV
UPDATE_PRIV
REFERENCES_PRIV
ALTER_PRIV
INDEX_PRIV
CREATED                 timestamp of grant

The "_PRIV" columns contain the following values:

N = No    - user doesn't have privilege
Y = Yes  - user has privilege, but no GRANT OPTION
G = Grant - user has privilege, WITH GRANT OPTION
S = Select- user has privilege on selected columns only
A = All  - user has this privilege on all columns
```

Figure 26.3: Dictionary tables about table privileges.

The six dictionary tables for column-specific queries (Figure 26.4) contain data corresponding to the six tables described above. However, these dictionary tables identify the column (COLUMN_NAME) to which the privilege applies.

```
ALL_COL_GRANTS_MADE & USER_COL_GRANTS_MADE tables
ALL_COL_GRANTS_RECD & USER_COL_GRANTS_RECD tables
ALL_COL-GRANTS & USER_COL_GRANTS tables

Columns in tables:

GRANTEE                 (not in USER_COL_GRANTS_RECD)
OWNER                   (not in USER_COL_GRANTS_MADE)
TABLE_NAME              name of table or view
COLUMN-NAME             name of column
GRANTOR                 username of grantor of privilege
UPDATE_PRIV
REFERENCES_PRIV
CREATED                 timestamp of grant
```

Figure 26.4: Dictionary tables about column privileges.

The DICTIONARY Table

We have described a number of ORACLE's dictionary tables, and there are many others we did not describe. Therefore, a new problem arises. How do you remember the names of the dictionary tables? The answer is simple. Display a special dictionary table called DICTIONARY. This table contains the name of and a brief comment on every table in ORACLE's V6 Data Dictionary.

Sample Query 26.5:   Display the DICTIONARY table.

```
COLUMN TABLE_NAME FORMAT A25
COLUMN COMMENTS   FORMAT A50 NEWLINE JUSTIFY LEFT

SELECT * FROM DICTIONARY
```

TABLE_NAME
COMMENTS
ACCESSIBLE_COLUMNS
Columns of all table, views, and clusters
ACCESSIBLE_TABLES
Tables and views accessible to the user
ALL_CATALOG
All tables, views, synonyms, sequences accessible to the user
   .   .
   .   .
   .   .
DBA_CATALOG
All database tables, views, synonyms, sequences
   .   .
   .   .
   .   .
USER_CATALOG
Tables, views, synonyms, sequences owned by the user
   .   .
   .   .
   .   .

Comments:

1.   When you display the DICTIONARY table, you will see references to over 100 dictionary tables. Some of these tables begin with "DBA_". These tables, unlike those that begin with "USER_" and "ALL_", contain information about other user's objects, tables, privileges, etc. Only the DBA can examine these tables.

2.   You can use DESCRIBE to determine the columns in a dictionary table. This information is also contained in the DICT_COLUMNS dictionary table. Its columns are TABLE_NAME, COLUMN_NAME, and COMMENTS.

3.   "DICTIONARY" can be abbreviated as "DICT".

Summary

This chapter has introduced the ORACLE Data Dictionary. The only real problem is remembering the names of the tables and their columns. However, this is not a real problem because the dictionary describes itself. All you have to do is remember the DICTIONARY table. Displaying this table (Sample Query 26.5) lists the names of the dictionary tables. This should be all you need to get started to explore the ORACLE's Data Dictionary. We conclude with some final comments about the dictionary.

1. ORACLE's Data Dictionary contains many other tables in addition to the ones we described in this chapter. In particular, it has information about the physical structure of the database. These tables describe indexes, clusters, tablespaces, and other objects which are of interest to the DBA concerned with machine performance. A discussion of these objects is beyond the scope of this text. However, if you choose to learn ORACLE's physical database structures, you will not find it difficult to examine the Data Dictionary to explore the physical organization of your system.

2. All the dictionary tables referenced in this chapter are really views on a collection of tables which only the DBA can access. These views are created and made available to you when ORACLE is installed on your system.

3. Each new version of ORACLE provides facilities which were not present in the preceding version. New objects related to the new facilities will be described in the new dictionary. This means that you can expect the structure of the dictionary to evolve over time.

Comment to V5 users still running under V5:

As we mentioned in the introduction to this chapter, the dictionary tables introduced in this chapter are not present in V5 and thus the sample queries will not execute in V5. However, if you understand the basic concepts of a data dictionary as described in this chapter, then you should be able to independently explore the V5 dictionary. The V5 dictionary contains a table called DTAB which serves the same purpose as the DICTIONARY in V6. It contains one row for every table in the V5 dictionary. Displaying DTAB will get you started.

Comment on Upward Compatibilty from V5 to V6:

Usually a vendor attempts to provide "upward compatibility" when introducing a new version of a software product. This means that new features are provided in the new version, but the old features still apply. In other words, there are enhancements to the product which usually imply new commands in the language, but the old commands still work. Because ORACLE has made a major modification (not just an enhancement) to its Data Dictionary, the *V5 dictionary tables are not necessarily present*. During the process of installing V6, the DBA can *optionally* execute a command file (CATALOG5.SQL) which will establish the old V5 Data Dictionary for purposes of upward compatibility.

Comment on V7:

Version 7, as mentioned in Chapter 14, will contain many new features pertaining to database integrity. In anticipation of this event, ORACLE allows the syntax of some of the features to be placed in V6 CREATE TABLE statements. (See Appendix D.) ORACLE has also provided dictionary tables pertaining to database integrity. You will see these tables referenced when you display DICTIONARY.

Comment on DB2 Compatibility:

All the sample queries in this chapter were enclosed by a double box. The DB2 dictionary (called the DB2 Catalog) is similar in spirit. It, too, is a collection of tables about tables, views, etc., which can be examined using SQL. However, the names of the DB2 tables are different from the ORACLE tables. Hence, this is one more dimension of incompatibility between ORACLE and DB2.

Summary Exercises

26I. Display the dictionary tables having a name which begins with "USER_".

26J. Display the name of the columns found in the USER_TABLES dictionary table.

26K. Display information about every privilege you have received.

26L. Same as 26K. Exclude privileges granted to PUBLIC.

26M. Display all privileges which you have directly or indirectly granted on the STAFF table.

26N. What columns are in the ALL_OBJECTS table?

Entering and Exiting SQL*Plus

This appendix describes the sign-on and sign-off procedures used to execute SQL statements using SQL*Plus.

Preliminary Comments

1. If this is your first experience with ORACLE, we recommend that you read Chapter 1 and the first section (Entering SQL Statements) of Chapter 2 before you actually sign-on to SQL*Plus.

2. If your host operating system is a multiuser system, make sure that you have obtained the proper operating system and ORACLE sign-on ids and passwords.

3. If you plan to execute the sample queries and exercises in this text, then you (or your DBA) need to create the sample educational database and related LOGIN.SQL file. This process is described in Appendix C.

The Sign_On Process

1. Access your host operating system.

    Follow the regular sign-on procedure to access your host operating system (DOS, UNIX, CMS, etc.). For a multiuser system this typically involves entering an system id and password. This process may also require that you enter a specific subdirectory or do a remote logon to another machine which is part of your communications network.

    This step is specific to your system. This means that rookie users may have to ask their DBA to describe this process.

2.   Sign-on to SQL*Plus

    a.   Enter "SQLPLUS" and press the Enter key (Return key). If your operating system is case-sensitive (e.g., UNIX), you should enter "sqlplus".

    b.   The system should respond with some self-identifying information and then prompt you for your ORACLE username (which may or may not be the same as your system id).

        Enter user-name:

    c.   Next, the system prompts you for your ORACLE password (which may or may not be the same as your host system password).

        Enter password:

    d.   Assuming ORACLE recognizes your username and password, the system will respond with the SQL prompt and await entry of your first SQL statement or SQL*Plus command. You are ready to go!

        SQL>

Comment: Sometimes your DBA will make the sign-on process easier by establishing a procedure which automatically puts you into the SQL*Plus environment. This effectively allows you to skip step 2.

The Sign-Off Process

1.   Enter "exit" at the SQL prompt.

    SQL> exit

This command will terminate SQL*Plus and return control to your host operating system.

2.   Follow the standard procedure to exit your host system. (Again, you may have to ask your DBA to describe this process.)

B

Educational Database

The design shown in Figure B.1 represents the basic content and structure of the sample tables used throughout this text. This figure used the IBM notation for referential integrity where the arrow points from the parent table to the dependent table. (This differs from the tutorial notation used in Chapter 14.) Only the primary key and foreign key columns are shown in Figure B.1. The primary key columns are underlined. Sample data are shown in Figure B.2a and B.2b.

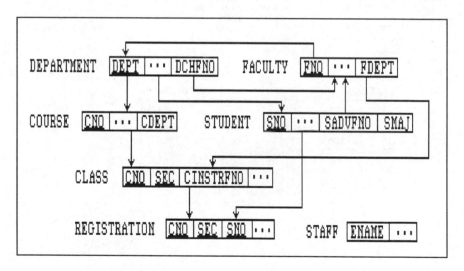

Figure B.1: Educational database design.

DEPARTMENT

DEPT	DBLD	DROOM	DCHFNO
THEO	HU	200	10
CIS	SC	300	80
MGT	SC	100	–
PHIL	HU	100	60

STAFF

ENAME	ETITLE	ESALARY	DEPT
LUKE	EVANGLIST3	53	THEO
MARK	EVANGLIST2	52	THEO
MATTHEW	EVANGLIST1	51	THEO
DICK NIX	CROOK	25001	PHIL
HANK KISS	JESTER	25000	PHIL
JOHN	EVANGLIST4	54	THEO
EUCLID	LAB ASSIST	1000	MATH
ARCHIMEDES	LAB ASSIST	200	ENG
DA VINCI	LAB ASSIST	500	–

COURSE

CNO	CNAME	CDESCP	CRED	CLABFEE	CDEPT
C11	INTRO TO CS	FOR ROOKIES	3	100.00	CIS
C22	DATA STRUCTURES	VERY USEFUL	3	50.00	CIS
C33	DISCRETE MATHEMATICS	ABSOLUTELY NECESSARY	3	.00	CIS
C44	DIGITAL CIRCUITS	AH HA!	3	.00	CIS
C55	COMPUTER ARCH.	VON NEUMANN'S MACH.	3	100.00	CIS
C66	RELATIONAL DATABASE	THE ONLY WAY TO GO	3	500.00	CIS
P11	EMPIRICISM	SEE IT-BELIEVE IT	3	100.00	PHIL
P22	RATIONALISM	FOR CIS MAJORS	3	50.00	PHIL
P33	EXISTENTIALISM	FOR CIS MAJORS	3	200.00	PHIL
P44	SOLIPSISM	ME MYSELF AND I	6	.00	PHIL
T11	SCHOLASTICISM	FOR THE PIOUS	3	150.00	THEO
T12	FUNDAMENTALISM	FOR THE CAREFREE	3	90.00	THEO
T33	HEDONISM	FOR THE SANE	3	.00	THEO
T44	COMMUNISM	FOR THE GREEDY	6	200.00	THEO

CLASS

CNO	SEC	CINSTRFNO	CDAY	CTIME	CBLD	CROOM
C11	01	08	MO	08:00-09:00A.M.	SC	305
C11	02	08	TU	08:00-09:00A.M.	SC	306
C33	01	80	WE	09:00-10:30A.M.	SC	305
C55	01	85	TH	11:00-12:00A.M.	HU	306
P11	01	06	TH	09:00-10:00A.M.	HU	102
P33	01	06	FR	11:00-12:00A.M.	HU	201
T11	01	10	MO	10:00-11:00A.M.	HU	101
T11	02	65	MO	10:00-11:00A.M.	HU	102
T33	01	65	WE	11:00-12:00A.M.	HU	101

Figure B.2a: Educational database.

REGISTRATION

CNO	SEC	SNO	REG_DATE
C11	01	325	04-JAN-1988
C11	01	800	15-DEC-1987
C11	02	100	17-DEC-1987
C11	02	150	17-DEC-1987
P33	01	100	23-DEC-1987
P33	01	800	23-DEC-1987
T11	01	100	23-DEC-1987
T11	01	150	15-DEC-1987
T11	01	800	15-DEC-1987

FACULTY

FNO	FNAME	FADDR	FHIRE_DATE	FNUM_DEP	FSALARY	FDEPT
06	KATHY PEPE	7 STONERIDGE RD	15-JAN-1979	2	35000.00	PHIL
10	JESSIE MARTYN	2135 EAST DR	01-SEP-1969	1	45000.00	THEO
08	JOE COHN	BOX 1138	09-JUL-1979	2	35000.00	CIS
85	AL HARTLEY	SILVER STREET	05-SEP-1979	7	45000.00	CIS
60	JULIE MARTYN	2135 EAST DR	01-SEP-1969	1	45000.00	PHIL
65	LISA BOBAK	77 LAUGHING LN	06-SEP-1981	-	36000.00	THEO
80	BARB HLAVATY	489 SOUTH ROAD	16-JAN-1982	3	35000.00	CIS

STUDENT

SNO	SNAME	SADDR	SPHNO	SBDATE	SIQ	SADVFNO	SMAJ
325	CURLEY DUBAY	CONNECTICUT	203-123-4567	780517	122	10	THEO
150	LARRY DUBAY	CONNECTICUT	203-123-4567	780517	121	80	CIS
100	MOE DUBAY	CONNECTICUT	203-123-4567	780517	120	10	THEO
800	ROCKY BALBOA	PENNSYLVANIA	112-112-1122	461004	99	60	PHIL

Figure B.2b: Educational database.

C

Using the Educational Database

This appendix describes how to set up the educational database so that you can execute the sample queries and exercises in this text. You don't need to know anything about ORACLE, SQL, or SQL*Plus in order to perform this task. However, you do need to know how to load or create a file on your host operating system. Rookie users may have to ask their DBA to perform this task for them.

Two files need to be loaded (or created) in your user directory. These are the CEDUC.SQL and the LOGIN.SQL files. (Note that the file names should be lowercase, "ceduc.sql" and "login.sql", for UNIX and other case-sensitive host systems.) Copies of these files are placed on the companion disk for this text. These files are not very large and may be created using any means available to you. (Copies of these files are shown in Figures C.1 and C.2.)

We present a conceptual overview of these files. Then we present the mechanics of loading the files. From a practical point of view, the mechanics is the important thing. To understand the content of the CEDUC.SQL and LOGIN.SQL files requires reading this text. However, we believe it is helpful to present a little information about the purpose and content of these files. Again, we note that you really don't need to understand the content of these files to follow the mechanical steps necessary to load them.

The CEDUC.SQL File

Chapter 1 of this text begins by describing the SELECT statement which is used to retrieve data from tables. This chapter presumes that the tables have already been created and loaded with sample data. To establish this situation, the appropriate CREATE TABLE and INSERT statements (described in Chapters 14 and 15) need to be executed. These statements are present in the CEDUC.SQL file shown in Figure C.1. You must load this file into your user directory. Then, after signing onto SQL*PLus, you will execute it using the START command. This will create the sample educational database shown in Appendix B. This file, and the LOGIN.SQL file, are really "command" files (described in Chapter 12) which allow a collection of SQL statements and SQL*Plus commands to be put into a batch (like DOS ".BAT" files) and executed. We describe the mechanics of executing this file below.

The LOGIN.SQL File

Usually, but not always, every SQL*Plus user will have his or her own version of the LOGIN.SQL file in their user directory. This file is not necessary, but it is very useful. When present, it usually contains SQL*Plus commands which control terminal display characteristics (linesize, page length, etc.). Also, it contains commands which define the column headers of displayed reports. When it is not present, or if it does not have the correct commands, you get the default behavior for terminal display. Your SQL statements will work, but query results will probably not be formatted as a "pretty" report. Some column headings may be truncated and some report lines may wrap. If the LOGIN.SQL is not present, you will receive a warning message indicating this fact when you sign-on to SQL*Plus.

SQL*Plus will automatically execute the LOGIN.SQL file (if present) when you sign-on. Its content is shown in Figure C.2. (Again, you are not expected to understand the content of this file. The meaning of these commands is described in Part III of this text.) If you (or your DBA) place this file in your user directory, then the results of the sample queries should appear on your terminal in the same format as they appear in this text.

Mechanics of Loading Files

Loading the LOGIN.SQL File:

Create a copy of this file in your user directory. You can use any editor available on your host system, or you can copy this file from the companion disk. Make sure the content is the same and the name of the file is "LOGIN.SQL" (or "login.sql"). *This should be done before you sign-on to SQL*Plus.*

Loading the CEDUC.SQL File:

1. Create a copy of this file in your user directory. You can use any editor available on your host system; or, you can copy this file from the companion disk. Make sure the content is the same. (You can rename this file if you wish. But the file type must be ".SQL" (or ".sql"). This step should be done before you sign-on to SQL*Plus.

2. Sign onto SQL*Plus by entering "SQLPLUS" (or "sqlplus) and entering your username and password. Appendix A describes this step in more detail.

3. When you get the SQL prompt enter "START CEDUC" as shown below. (If you decided to rename this file to XXX.SQL, then you would enter "START XXX".)

        SQL> START CEDUC

    The system will respond by executing each of the CREATE TABLE and INSERT statements present in the CEDUC.SQL file. You will see these statements and the SQL*Plus responses to them displayed on the screen.

4. Assuming the previous step was successful, all of the tables described in Appendix B are now available for processing. You are ready to start executing the sample queries and exercises.

Start of Figure C.1: CEDUC.SQL file.

```
CREATE TABLE COURSE
(CNO      CHAR(3)      NOT NULL,
 CNAME    CHAR(22)     NOT NULL,
 CDESCP   CHAR(25)     NOT NULL,
 CRED     NUMBER,
 CLABFEE  NUMBER(5,2),
 CDEPT    CHAR(4)      NOT NULL);

INSERT INTO COURSE VALUES
    ('C11','INTRO TO CS','FOR ROOKIES',3, 100,'CIS');
INSERT INTO COURSE VALUES
    ('C22','DATA STRUCTURES','VERY USEFUL',3, 50,'CIS');
INSERT INTO COURSE VALUES
    ('C33','DISCRETE MATHEMATICS','ABSOLUTELY NECESSARY',3, 0,'CIS');
INSERT INTO COURSE VALUES
    ('C44','DIGITAL CIRCUITS','AH HA!',3, 0,'CIS');
INSERT INTO COURSE VALUES
    ('C55','COMPUTER ARCH.','VON NEUMANN''S MACH.',3, 100,'CIS');
INSERT INTO COURSE VALUES
    ('C66','RELATIONAL DATABASE','THE ONLY WAY TO GO',3, 500,'CIS');
INSERT INTO COURSE VALUES
    ('P11','EMPIRICISM','SEE IT-BELIEVE IT',3, 100,'PHIL');
INSERT INTO COURSE VALUES
    ('P22','RATIONALISM','FOR CIS MAJORS',3, 50,'PHIL');
INSERT INTO COURSE VALUES
    ('P33','EXISTENTIALISM','FOR CIS MAJORS',3, 200,'PHIL');
INSERT INTO COURSE VALUES
    ('P44','SOLIPSISM','ME MYSELF AND I',6, 0,'PHIL');
INSERT INTO COURSE VALUES
    ('T11','SCHOLASTICISM','FOR THE PIOUS',3,150,'THEO');
INSERT INTO COURSE VALUES
    ('T12','FUNDAMENTALISM','FOR THE CAREFREE',3,90,'THEO');
INSERT INTO COURSE VALUES
    ('T33','HEDONISM','FOR THE SANE',3,0,'THEO');
INSERT INTO COURSE VALUES
    ('T44','COMMUNISM','FOR THE GREEDY',6,200,'THEO');
COMMIT;

CREATE TABLE DEPARTMENT
(DEPT     CHAR(4)      NOT NULL,
 DBLD     CHAR(2),
 DROOM    CHAR(3),
 DCHFNO   CHAR(2));

INSERT INTO DEPARTMENT VALUES ('THEO','HU','200','10');
INSERT INTO DEPARTMENT VALUES ('CIS', 'SC','300','80');
INSERT INTO DEPARTMENT VALUES ('MGT', 'SC','100', NULL);
INSERT INTO DEPARTMENT VALUES ('PHIL','HU','100','60');
COMMIT;

CREATE TABLE STAFF
(ENAME    CHAR(10)     NOT NULL,
 ETITLE   CHAR(10),
 ESALARY  NUMBER,
 DEPT     CHAR(4));

INSERT INTO STAFF VALUES ('LUKE', 'EVANGLIST3', 53, 'THEO');
INSERT INTO STAFF VALUES ('MARK', 'EVANGLIST2', 52, 'THEO');
INSERT INTO STAFF VALUES ('MATTHEW', 'EVANGLIST1', 51, 'THEO');
INSERT INTO STAFF VALUES ('DICK NIX', 'CROOK', 25001, 'PHIL');
INSERT INTO STAFF VALUES ('HANK KISS', 'JESTER', 25000, 'PHIL');
INSERT INTO STAFF VALUES ('JOHN', 'EVANGLIST4', 54, 'THEO');
INSERT INTO STAFF VALUES ('EUCLID', 'LAB ASSIST', 1000, 'MATH');
INSERT INTO STAFF VALUES ('ARCHIMEDES', 'LAB ASSIST', 200, 'ENG');
INSERT INTO STAFF VALUES ('DA VINCI', 'LAB ASSIST', 500, NULL);
COMMIT;
```

```
CREATE TABLE STUDENT
(SNO      CHAR(3)       NOT NULL,
 SNAME    CHAR(25)      NOT NULL,
 SADDR    CHAR(25),
 SPHNO    CHAR(12),
 SBDATE   CHAR(6),
 SIQ      NUMBER,
 SADVFNO  CHAR(2),
 SMAJ     CHAR(4)       NOT NULL);

INSERT INTO STUDENT VALUES ('325','CURLEY DUBAY', 'CONNECTICUT',
'203-123-4567','780517',122,'10', 'THEO');
INSERT INTO STUDENT VALUES ('150','LARRY DUBAY', 'CONNECTICUT',
'203-123-4567','780517',121,'80','CIS' );
INSERT INTO STUDENT VALUES ('100','MOE DUBAY', 'CONNECTICUT',
'203-123-4567','780517',120,'10','THEO');
INSERT INTO STUDENT VALUES ('800','ROCKY BALBOA', 'PENNSYLVANIA',
'112-112-1122','461004',99, '60','PHIL');
COMMIT;

CREATE TABLE CLASS
(CNO       CHAR(3)      NOT NULL,
 SEC       CHAR(2)      NOT NULL,
 CINSTRFNO CHAR(2),
 CDAY      CHAR(2),
 CTIME     CHAR(15),
 CBLD      CHAR(2),
 CROOM     CHAR(3));

INSERT INTO CLASS VALUES
    ('C33','01','80','WE','09:00-10:30A.M.','SC','305');
INSERT INTO CLASS VALUES
    ('C55','01','85','TH','11:00-12:00A.M.','SC','306');
INSERT INTO CLASS VALUES
    ('C11','01','08','MO','08:00-09:00A.M.','SC','305');
INSERT INTO CLASS VALUES
    ('C11','02','08','TU','08:00-09:00A.M.','SC','306');
INSERT INTO CLASS VALUES
    ('P11','01','06','TH','09:00-10:00A.M.','HU','102');
INSERT INTO CLASS VALUES
    ('P33', 01','06','FR','11:00-12:00A.M.','HU','201');
INSERT INTO CLASS VALUES
    ('T11','01','10','MO','10:00-11:00A.M.','HU','101');
INSERT INTO CLASS VALUES
    ('T11','02','65','MO','10:00-11:00A.M.','HU','102');
INSERT INTO CLASS VALUES
    ('T33','01','65','WE','11:00-12:00A.M.','HU','101');
COMMIT;

CREATE TABLE FACULTY
(FNO        CHAR(2)      NOT NULL,
 FNAME      CHAR(20)     NOT NULL,
 FADDR      CHAR(25),
 FHIRE_DATE CHAR(10),
 FNUM_DEP   NUMBER,
 FSALARY    NUMBER(7,2),
 FDEPT      CHAR(4));
```

```
INSERT INTO FACULTY VALUES
('06', 'KATHY PEPE', '7 STONERIDGE RD', '1979-01-15', 2, 35000, 'PHIL');
INSERT INTO FACULTY VALUES
('10', 'JESSIE MARTYN', '2135 EAST DR', '1982-03-07', 1, 45000, 'THEO');
INSERT INTO FACULTY VALUES
('08', 'JOE COHN', 'BOX 1138', '1979-07-09', 2, 35000, 'CIS');
INSERT INTO FACULTY VALUES
('85', 'AL HARTLEY', 'SILVER STREET', '1979-09-05', 7, 45000, 'CIS');
INSERT INTO FACULTY VALUES
('60', 'JULIE MARTYN', '2135 EAST DR', '1978-05-17', 1, 45000, 'PHIL');
INSERT INTO FACULTY VALUES
('65', 'LISA BOBAK', '77 LAUGHING LN', '1981-09-06', 1, 36000, 'THEO');
INSERT INTO FACULTY VALUES
('80', 'BARB HLAVATY', '489 SOUTH ROAD', '1982-01-16', 3, 35000, 'CIS'
);
COMMIT;

CREATE TABLE REGISTRATION
(CNO       CHAR(3)    NOT NULL,
 SEC       CHAR(2)    NOT NULL,
 SNO       CHAR(3)    NOT NULL,
 REG_DATE  DATE);

INSERT INTO REGISTRATION VALUES
    ('C11', '01', '325', '04-JAN-88');
INSERT INTO REGISTRATION VALUES
    ('C11', '01', '800', '15-DEC-87');
INSERT INTO REGISTRATION VALUES
    ('C11', '02', '100', '17-DEC-87');
INSERT INTO REGISTRATION VALUES
    ('C11', '02', '150', '17-DEC-87');
INSERT INTO REGISTRATION VALUES
    ('P33', '01', '100', '23-DEC-87');
INSERT INTO REGISTRATION VALUES
    ('P33', '01', '800', '23-DEC-87');
INSERT INTO REGISTRATION VALUES
    ('T11', '01', '100', '23-DEC-87');
INSERT INTO REGISTRATION VALUES
    ('T11', '01', '150', '15-DEC-87');
INSERT INTO REGISTRATION VALUES
    ('T11', '01', '800', '15-DEC-87');
INSERT INTO REGISTRATION VALUES
    ('C11', '01', '111', '26-DEC-92');
COMMIT;

CREATE TABLE NULLTAB
(PKEY      NUMBER,
 COLA      NUMBER,
 COLB      NUMBER,
 COLC      NUMBER);

INSERT INTO NULLTAB VALUES (1,    10,    20,    5);
INSERT INTO NULLTAB VALUES (2,    30,    30,    5);
INSERT INTO NULLTAB VALUES (3,    160,   NULL,  10);
INSERT INTO NULLTAB VALUES (4,    NULL,  170,   5);
INSERT INTO NULLTAB VALUES (5,    NULL,  NULL,  10);
INSERT INTO NULLTAB VALUES (6,    10,    40,    5);
INSERT INTO NULLTAB VALUES (7,    30,    60,    5);
INSERT INTO NULLTAB VALUES (8,    NULL,  NULL,  NULL);
INSERT INTO NULLTAB VALUES (NULL, NULL,  NULL,  NULL);
INSERT INTO NULLTAB VALUES (NULL, NULL,  NULL,  NULL);
INSERT INTO NULLTAB VALUES (NULL, NULL,  NULL,  NULL);
COMMIT;
```

Figure C.1: CEDUC.SQL file.

```
REM   This is the login.sql file which is automatically
REM   executed when you sign onto SQL*Plus.

REM   The following COLUMN commands are used to specify the column
REM   format of columns for tables in the sample education database.
REM   One objective of the FORMAT specifications was to define a
REM   column width for screen display such that the full column name
REM   appears (no truncation of the column name). Another objective
REM   was to allow selection of all columns in a table such that no
REM   line wrapping occurs. To accomplish this objective we have made
REM   some columns wider and other columns shorter. Columns in the
REM   education database which are not specified below will have the
REM   default format characteristics.

REM formatting COURSE table
COL CNAME    FORMAT A20
COL CDESCP   FORMAT A20
COL CRED     FORMAT 99
COL CLABFEE FORMAT 999.99
COL CDEPT    FORMAT A5

REM formatting DEPARTMENT table
COL DEPT    FORMAT A4
COL DBLD    FORMAT A4
COL DROOM   FORMAT A5
COL DCHFNO FORMAT A6

REM formatting STAFF table
COL ENAME   FORMAT A10
COL ETITLE FORMAT A10

REM formatting STUDENT table
COL SNAME    FORMAT A20
COL SADDR    FORMAT A20
COL SIQ      FORMAT 999
COL SADVFNO FORMAT A7

REM formatting  CLASS table
COL SEC         FORMAT A3
COL CINSTRFNO FORMAT A9
COL CDAY        FORMAT A4
COL CBLD        FORMAT A4
COL CROOM       FORMAT A5

REM formatting FACULTY table
COL FNO         FORMAT A3
COL FNAME       FORMAT A14
COL FADDR       FORMAT A15
COL FSALARY     FORMAT 99999.99
COL FDEPT       FORMAT A5

REM formatting for REGISTRATION and NULLTAB tables unnecessary

COLUMN COUNT(*) FORMAT 99999

REM set terminal characteristics
SET NEWPAGE 1
SET PAGESIZE 24
SET SCAN ON TAB ON SQLTERM ';'
SET ECHO ON
```

Figure C.2: LOGIN.SQL file.

Answers to Exercises

Chapter 1

```
A.   SELECT * FROM COURSE WHERE CLABFEE < 150;
B.   SELECT * FROM COURSE WHERE CRED > 3;
C.   SELECT * FROM COURSE WHERE CDEPT = 'THEO';
D.   SELECT * FROM COURSE WHERE CNAME = 'RELATIONAL DATABASE';
E.   SELECT * FROM COURSE WHERE CNO = 'P44';
F.   SELECT * FROM COURSE WHERE CNO < 'P01';
G.   SELECT * FROM COURSE WHERE CNAME > 'RATIONALISM';
H.   SELECT CNAME, CDESCP FROM COURSE;
I.   SELECT CDEPT, CNO, CLABFEE, CRED FROM COURSE;
J.   SELECT CNO, CLABFEE FROM COURSE WHERE CLABFEE > 100;
K.   SELECT CNAME FROM COURSE WHERE CDEPT = 'CIS';
L.   SELECT CLABFEE FROM COURSE;
M.   SELECT DISTINCT CLABFEE FROM COURSE;
M.   SELECT CRED, CLABFEE FROM COURSE WHERE CDEPT = 'CIS';
O.   SELECT DISTINCT CRED, CLABFEE FROM COURSE WHERE CDEPT =
     'CIS';
P.   SELECT * FROM STAFF;
Q.   SELECT * FROM STAFF WHERE ESALARY < 1000;
R.   SELECT * FROM STAFF WHERE DEPT = 'THEO';
S.   SELECT ENAME, ETITLE FROM STAFF;
T.   SELECT ENAME, ESALARY FROM STAFF WHERE ESALARY > 1000;
U.   SELECT ENAME, ETITLE FROM STAFF WHERE ENAME < 'MARK';
V.   SELECT DISTINCT ETITLE FROM STAFF;
```

Chapter 3

```
A.   SELECT * FROM COURSE ORDER BY CDEPT;
B.   SELECT CNAME, CLABFEE FROM COURSE WHERE CDEPT = 'PHIL'
     ORDER BY CNAME DESC;
C.   SELECT CNAME, CNO, CRED FROM COURSE ORDER BY CLABFEE,
     CNO;
D.   SELECT * FROM COURSE ORDER BY 3;
```

E. SELECT CDEPT, CLABFEE, CNAME FROM COURSE WHERE CRED = 3 ORDER BY CDEPT, CLABFEE DESC, CNAME;
F. SELECT * FROM STAFF ORDER BY ENAME;
G. SELECT ENAME, ESALARY FROM STAFF WHERE ESALARY < 1000 ORDER BY ESALARY DESC;
H. SELECT * FROM STAFF WHERE DEPT = 'THEO' ORDER BY ETITLE;
I. SELECT DEPT, ENAME, ESALARY FROM STAFF ORDER BY DEPT, ESALARY;
J. SELECT DEPT, ETITLE, ESALARY FROM STAFF ORDER BY DEPT, ESALARY DESC;

Chapter 4

A. SELECT * FROM COURSE WHERE CRED = 3 AND CDEPT = 'PHIL';
B. SELECT * FROM COURSE WHERE CLABFEE >= 100 AND CLABFEE <= 500;
C. SELECT * FROM COURSE WHERE CRED = 3 AND CDEPT = 'THEO' AND CLABFEE >= 100 AND CLABFEE <= 400;
D. SELECT * FROM COURSE WHERE CDEPT = 'PHIL' OR CDEPT = 'THEO';
E. SELECT * FROM COURSE WHERE CDEPT = 'THEO' OR CRED = 6;
F. SELECT * FROM COURSE WHERE CLABFEE = 0.00 OR CLABFEE = 90.00 OR CLABFEE = 150.00;
G. SELECT CNO, CNAME, CLABFEE FROM COURSE WHERE NOT CLABFEE = 100;
    or
    SELECT CNO, CNAME, CLABFEE FROM COURSE WHERE CLABFEE <> 100;
H. SELECT CNO, CLABFEE FROM COURSE WHERE NOT CLABFEE = 100 AND NOT CLABFEE = 200;
I. SELECT * FROM COURSE WHERE (CRED = 6 AND CDEPT = 'PHIL') OR CLABFEE > 200;
J. SELECT * FROM COURSE WHERE CRED = 3 AND (CLABFEE < 100 OR CLABFEE > 300);
K. SELECT * FROM COURSE WHERE NOT CLABFEE > 100 OR (CDEPT = 'THEO' AND CRED = 6);
L. SELECT * FROM COURSE WHERE NOT (CRED = 3 AND CDEPT = 'PHIL');
M. SELECT * FROM COURSE WHERE CLABFEE IN (12.12, 50.00, 75.00, 90.00, 100.00, 500.00);
N. SELECT * FROM COURSE WHERE CLABFEE NOT IN (12.12, 50.00, 75.00, 90.00, 100.00, 500.00);
O. SELECT CNO, CLABFEE FROM COURSE WHERE CLABFEE BETWEEN 50.00 AND 400.00;
P. SELECT CNO, CLABFEE FROM COURSE WHERE CLABFEE NOT BETWEEN 50.00 AND 400.00;
Q. SELECT CNAME, CDESCP FROM COURSE WHERE CDESCP BETWEEN 'FOR' AND 'FORZ';
R. SELECT CDEPT, CNO, CDESCP FROM COURSE WHERE CDEPT IN ('CIS', 'THEO') AND CLABFEE NOT BETWEEN 100 AND 400 ORDER BY CDEPT, CNO;

S. SELECT * FROM STAFF WHERE DEPT = 'PHIL' OR DEPT = 'THEO';
T. SELECT * FROM STAFF WHERE DEPT = 'THEO' AND ESALARY > 52;
U. SELECT ENAME FROM STAFF WHERE ESALARY >= 52 AND ESALARY
   <= 1000;
   or
   SELECT ENAME FROM STAFF WHERE ESALARY BETWEEN 52 AND
   1000;
V. SELECT ENAME, ETITLE FROM STAFF WHERE DEPT = 'THEO' AND
   (ESALARY = 51 OR ESALARY = 54);
W. SELECT ENAME, ESALARY FROM STAFF WHERE ESALARY IN (51,
   53, 100, 200, 25000);
X. SELECT ENAME, ESALARY FROM STAFF WHERE ESALARY NOT
   BETWEEN 100 AND 1000 ORDER BY ENAME;
   or
   SELECT ENAME, ESALARY FROM STAFF WHERE ESALARY < 100 OR
   ESALARY > 1000 ORDER BY ENAME;
Y. SELECT DISTINCT DEPT FROM STAFF WHERE ESALARY > 5000;

Chapter 5

A. SELECT * FROM USER_SYNONYMS;
B. CREATE SYNONYM ARBITRARY FOR COURSE;
C. SELECT * FROM USER_SYNONYMS;
D. DROP SYNONYM ARBITRARY;
E. SELECT * FROM USER_SYNONYMS;
F. SELECT * FROM ALL_SYNONYMS;

Chapter 6

A. SELECT * FROM COURSE WHERE CDESCP LIKE 'FOR THE%';
B. SELECT CNAME, CDESCP FROM COURSE WHERE CDESCP LIKE '%E';
C. SELECT CNAME, CDESCP FROM COURSE WHERE CDESCP LIKE '%.%'
   OR CDESCP LIKE '%-%' OR CDESCP LIKE '%!%';
D. SELECT CNAME, CDEPT FROM COURSE WHERE CDEPT LIKE '___';
E. SELECT CNAME, CDESCP FROM COURSE WHERE CDESCP LIKE
   '____THE__A%';
F. SELECT CNAME, CDESCP FROM COURSE WHERE CNAME NOT LIKE
   '%E' AND CNAME NOT LIKE '%S';
G. SELECT * FROM STAFF WHERE ENAME LIKE 'MA%';
H. SELECT * FROM STAFF WHERE ETITLE LIKE '%1' OR ETITLE LIKE
   '%2' OR ETITLE LIKE '%3';
I. SELECT ENAME, ETITLE FROM STAFF WHERE ENAME LIKE '%S%'
   AND ETITLE LIKE '%S%';
J. SELECT DISTINCT DEPT FROM STAFF WHERE DEPT LIKE '__E%';
K. SELECT ENAME FROM STAFF WHERE ENAME LIKE '_____I%' ORDER
   BY ENAME;

Chapter 7

A. SELECT CNO, CRED, CRED * 2 FROM COURSE WHERE CDEPT =
   'PHIL';
B. SELECT CNO, CRED * 10.50 FROM COURSE WHERE CDEPT =
   'THEO';

C. SELECT CNO, CLABFEE, CLABFEE / 2.0 FROM COURSE WHERE
    CLABFEE > 0.00;
D. SELECT CNO, (CLABFEE * 1.50) + 35 FROM COURSE WHERE
    CLABFEE < 200;
E. SELECT ENAME, ESALARY + 100 FROM STAFF;
F. SELECT ENAME, ESALARY, ESALARY * 1.15 FROM STAFF;
G. SELECT ENAME, ESALARY - 100 FROM STAFF WHERE ESALARY -
    100 < 25000;
H. SELECT ENAME, ESALARY + 1000 FROM STAFF WHERE ESALARY <
    25000 ORDER BY 2 DESC;

Chapter 8

A. SELECT MIN(CNAME) FROM COURSE;
B. SELECT SUM(CLABFEE) FROM COURSE WHERE CDEPT = 'PHIL';
C. SELECT AVG(CLABFEE), MAX(CLABFEE), MIN(CLABFEE) FROM
    COURSE WHERE CDEPT = 'CIS' AND CLABFEE <> 0;
D. SELECT COUNT(*) FROM COURSE;
E. SELECT COUNT(DISTINCT CLABFEE) FROM COURSE WHERE CLABFEE
    <> 0;
F. SELECT AVG(CRED * 50.0) FROM COURSE WHERE CDEPT = 'THEO';
G. SELECT CDEPT, SUM(CRED) FROM COURSE GROUP BY CDEPT;
H. SELECT CDEPT, COUNT(*) FROM COURSE GROUP BY CDEPT ORDER
    BY CDEPT;
I. SELECT CDEPT, SUM(CLABFEE) FROM COURSE WHERE CRED <> 6
    GROUP BY CDEPT ORDER BY 2 DESC;
J. SELECT CDEPT, MAX(CLABFEE) FROM COURSE GROUP BY CDEPT
    HAVING MAX(CLABFEE) > 300;
    or
    SELECT CDEPT, MAX(CLABFEE) FROM COURSE WHERE CLABFEE >
    300 GROUP BY CDEPT;
K. SELECT CDEPT, SUM(CRED) FROM COURSE GROUP BY CDEPT HAVING
    SUM(CRED) > 15;
L. SELECT CDEPT, SUM(CLABFEE) FROM COURSE WHERE CRED = 3
    GROUP BY CDEPT HAVING SUM(CLABFEE) < 150;
M. SELECT CDEPT, MAX(CLABFEE) FROM COURSE WHERE CLABFEE <=
    400 GROUP BY CDEPT HAVING MAX(CLABFEE) > 175;
N. SELECT MAX(SUM(CLABFEE)) FROM COURSE GROUP BY CDEPT;
O. SELECT   SUM(ESALARY),   AVG(ESALARY),   MAX(ESALARY),
    MIN(ESALARY) FROM STAFF;
P. SELECT COUNT(*) FROM STAFF WHERE DEPT = 'THEO';
Q. SELECT COUNT(DISTINCT ETITLE) FROM STAFF;
R. SELECT SUM(ESALARY) + 5000 FROM STAFF;
S. SELECT DEPT, AVG(ESALARY) FROM STAFF GROUP BY DEPT;
T. SELECT DEPT, SUM(ESALARY) FROM STAFF WHERE ESALARY > 600
    GROUP BY DEPT ORDER BY 2;

Chapter 9

A. SELECT TRUNC(CLABFEE) FROM COURSE;
B. SELECT CNO, ROUND(CLABFEE/CRED,2) FROM COURSE;
C. SELECT SUBSTR(CNO,2), SUBSTR(CNAME,1,5), SUBSTR(CDESCP,4,2) FROM COURSE WHERE CDEPT = 'PHIL';
D. SELECT INSTR(CDESCP,'FOR') FROM COURSE WHERE CDESCP LIKE '%FOR%';
E. SELECT LENGTH(CNAME) FROM COURSE;
F. SELECT INITCAP(LOWER(CNAME)) FROM COURSE;
G. SELECT DISTINCT CDEPT, LENGTH(CDEPT) FROM COURSE;
H. SELECT FLOOR(CLABFEE/CRED), CEIL(CLABFEE/CRED) FROM COURSE;
I. SELECT SUBSTR(CNO,LENGTH(CNO)) FROM COURSE;
J. SELECT CNO, TO_CHAR(CLABFEE*10,'$9,999.99') FROM COURSE;
K. SELECT CNO, CDESCP FROM COURSE WHERE LENGTH(CDESCP) < 15;
L. SELECT TRANSLATE(CNO,'123456789','000000000'), TRANSLATE(CNAME,' ','-') FROM COURSE;
M. SELECT DECODE(CRED,3,'THREE',6,'SIX') FROM COURSE;
N. SELECT CLABFEE, LENGTH(TO_CHAR(CLABFEE)) FROM COURSE WHERE CLABFEE <> 0;
O. SELECT CDESCP||CNO FROM COURSE;

Chapter 10

A. SELECT TO_CHAR(REG_DATE,'DAY Month DD, YYYY') "FORMATTED_DATE" FROM REGISTRATION;
B. COLUMN FA FORMAT A22 HEADING 'TODAY''S DATE and TIME';
SELECT TO_CHAR(SYSDATE, 'MM/DD/YY HH12:MI:SS A.M.') FA FROM REGISTRATION;
C. COL FB FORMAT A14 HEADING 'CURRENT HOUR';
COL FC FORMAT A14 HEADING 'CURRENT MINUTE';
COL FD FORMAT A14 HEADING 'CURRENT SECOND';
SELECT TO_CHAR(SYSDATE,'HH12') FB, TO_CHAR(SYSDATE,'MI') FC, TO_CHAR(SYSDATE,'SS') FD FROM COURSE WHERE CNO = 'C11';
D. SELECTTO_CHAR(TO_DATE('04-JUL-1776','DD-MON-YYYY'),'DAY WW') FROM COURSE WHERE CNO = 'C11';
E. SELECT NEXT_DAY(SYSDATE,'SATURDAY') FROM COURSE WHERE CNO = 'C11';
F. SELECT ADD_MONTHS(REG_DATE,3) FROM REGISTRATION WHERE SNO = '325';
G. SELECT REG_DATE, CNO, SEC, SNO FROM REGISTRATION WHERE REG_DATE > TO_DATE('31-DEC-87');
H. SELECT SNO FROM REGISTRATION WHERE TO_CHAR(REG_DATE,'MON') = 'DEC';

Chapter 11

A.   CLEAR BREAKS
     CLEAR COMPUTES
     TTITLE LEFT 'LABFEE STATISTICS'
     COLUMN CLABFEE FORMAT $9,999.99
     BREAK ON CDEPT SKIP 1 ON CRED SKIP 1 ON REPORT
     COMPUTE SUM AVG MAX MIN OF CLABFEE ON CDEPT
     COMPUTE SUM AVG MAX MIN OF CLABFEE ON CRED
     COMPUTE SUM OF CLABFEE ON REPORT
     SELECT CDEPT, CNAME, CRED, CLABFEE FROM COURSE ORDER BY
     CDEPT, CRED;

B.   CLEAR BREAKS
     CLEAR COMPUTES
     COLUMN ESALARY FORMAT $99,999.99
     TTITLE CENTER 'SALARY REPORT'
     BREAK ON DEPT SKIP 3 ON REPORT
     COMPUTE MAX MIN OF ESALARY ON DEPT
     COMPUTE SUM OF ESALARY ON REPORT
     SELECT DEPT, ENAME, ESALARY FROM STAFF ORDER BY DEPT;

Chapter 12

C.   (SPOT command file)
     CLEAR BREAKS
     CLEAR COMPUTES
     TTITLE LEFT "SPOT REPORT"
     SELECT * FROM STAFF WHERE ESALARY >= &1;

Chapter 13

A.   SPOOL SPIKE
     SELECT .....;
     SPOOL OFF
B.   HOST TYPE SPIKE.LST > PRN   (for DOS)
     HOST lpr SPIKE.lst   (for UNIX)
C.   DECSRIBE STAFF
D.   SET TIMING ON
     SELECT * FROM COURSE WHERE CLABFEE IN (0,50,100);
     SELECT * FROM COURSE WHERE CLABFEE =0 OR CLABFEE = 50 OR
     CLABFEE = 100;
     SET TIMING OFF
E.   HELP ORDER BY
F.   DEFINE ZERO = 0
     (place following in a command file)
     SELECT * FROM COURSE WHERE CLABFEE = &ZERO;

Chapter 14

```
B.    CREATE TABLE JUNK
      (C1        CHAR(10)     NOT NULL,
       C2        NUMBER       NULL,
       C3        NUMBER(7,2)  NOT NULL
      PRIMARY KEY (C1));
      {V5 users should not include the PRIMARY KEY clause}
C.    CREATE UNIQUE INDEX XSNO ON STUDENT(SNO);
      CREATE INDEX XSMAJ ON STUDENT(SMAJ);
D.    CREATE TABLE CISCOURSE
      (CISCNO        CHAR(3)   NOT NULL,
       CISCNAME      CHAR(25)  NOT NULL,
       CISCRED       NUMBER,
       CISCLABFEE    NUMBER(5,2),
      PRIMARY KEY (CISCNO));
      {V5 users should not include the PRIMARY KEY clause}
      CREATE UNIQUE INDEX XCISCNO ON CISCOURSE(CISCNO);
```

Chapter 15

```
A.    INSERT INTO STAFF (ENAME, ETITLE, ESALARY, DEPT)
      VALUES ('ALAN', 'LAB ASSIST', 3000, 'CIS');
B.    INSERT INTO STAFF (DEPT, ENAME)
      VALUES ('CIS', 'GEORGE');
C.    UPDATE STAFF SET ESALARY = 4000 WHERE DEPT = 'CIS';
D.    DELETE FROM STAFF WHERE DEPT = 'CIS';
E.    CREATE TABLE EXPENSIVE
      (EXPCNO        CHAR(3),
       EXPCNAME      CHAR(22),
       EXPCLABFEE    NUMBER(5,2),
       EXPDEPT       CHAR(4));
      INSERT INTO EXPENSIVE
      SELECT CNO, CNAME, CLABFEE, CDEPT FROM COURSE WHERE
      CLABFEE > 100;
F.    UPDATE EXPENSIVE
      SET EXPCLABFEE = EXPCLABFEE - 50
      WHERE EXPCLABFEE > 400;
G.    DELETE FROM EXPENSIVE WHERE EXPDEPT = 'THEO';
H.    INSERT INTO EXPENSIVE (XCNO, XDEPT) VALUES ('X99',
      'XXX');
I.    UPDATE EXPENSIVE SET XNAME = 'JUNK';
J.    DELETE FROM EXPENSIVE;
K.    DROP TABLE EXPENSIVE;
```

Chapter 16

```
A.    SELECT  AVG(FNUM_DEP),  SUM(FNUM_DEP),  COUNT(*)  FROM
      FACULTY;
B.    SELECT SUM(FSALARY + (250 * FNUM_DEP)) FROM FACULTY;
C.    SELECT * FROM NULLTAB WHERE COLA <> COLB;
D.    SELECT  FNAME,  FNO,  FNUM_DEP  FROM  FACULTY  ORDER  BY
      FNUM_DEP DESC;
E.    SELECT AVG(FSALARY) FROM FACULTY GROUP BY FNUM_DEP;
```

F.   SELECT FNAME, FNUM_DEP, FDEPT FROM FACULTY WHERE FNUM_DEP
     IS NULL;
G.   SELECT ENAME, DEPT FROM STAFF WHERE DEPT IS NULL;
H.   SELECT DEPT, COUNT(*) FROM STAFF GROUP BY DEPT;

Chapter 17

A.   SELECT * FROM COURSE, DEPARTMENT WHERE CDEPT = DEPT;
B.   SELECT CNO, CNAME, CDESCP, CRED, CLABFEE, CDEPT, DBLD,
     DROOM, DCHFNO FROM COURSE, DEPARTMENT WHERE CDEPT = DEPT;
C.   SELECT CNAME, CLABFEE, DCHFNO FROM COURSE, DEPARTMENT
     WHERE CDEPT = DEPT AND CLABFEE > 100.00;
D.   SELECT CNO, CNAME FROM COURSE, DEPARTMENT
     WHERE CDEPT = DEPT AND DCHFNO = '60' ORDER BY CNO DESC;
E.   SELECT ENAME, ESALARY FROM STAFF, DEPARTMENT
     WHERE STAFF.DEPT = DEPARTMENT.DEPT AND DBLD = 'SC';
F.   SELECT DISTINCT DBLD, DROOM FROM DEPARTMENT, STAFF
     WHERE DEPARTMENT.DEPT = STAFF.DEPT AND ESALARY > 200;
G.   SELECT MIN(CLABFEE), MAX(CLABFEE) FROM COURSE, DEPARTMENT
     WHERE CDEPT = DEPT AND DBLD = 'SC';
H.   SELECT COUNT(*) FROM STAFF, DEPARTMENT
     WHERE STAFF.DEPT = DEPARTMENT.DEPT;
I.   SELECT ENAME, ESALARY, CLABFEE, CLABFEE - ESALARY FROM
     STAFF, COURSE WHERE DEPT = CDEPT AND (CLABFEE - ESALARY)
     >= 52;
J.   SELECT DEPARTMENT.DEPT, SUM(ESALARY), AVG(ESALARY) FROM
     STAFF, DEPARTMENT WHERE DEPARTMENT.DEPT = STAFF.DEPT
     GROUP BY DEPARTMENT.DEPT;
K.   SELECT CNAME, COUNT(*) FROM STAFF, COURSE
     WHERE DEPT = CDEPT GROUP BY CNAME;
L.   SELECT DEPARTMENT.DEPT FROM DEPARTMENT, STAFF
     WHERE DEPARTMENT.DEPT = STAFF.DEPT
     GROUP BY DEPARTMENT.DEPT HAVING COUNT(*) >= 3;
M.   SELECT DEPARTMENT.DEPT, COUNT(*) FROM DEPARTMENT, STAFF
     WHERE   DEPARTMENT.DEPT   =   STAFF.DEPT   GROUP   BY
     DEPARTMENT.DEPT;
N.   SELECT DCHFNO FROM DEPARTMENT, COURSE
     WHERE DEPT = CDEPT AND CRED = 6;
O.   SELECT COURSE.CNO, CNAME, SEC FROM COURSE, CLASS WHERE
     COURSE.CNO = CLASS.CNO AND CDAY = 'MO';
P.   SELECT COURSE.CNO, CNAME FROM REGISTRATION, COURSE
     WHERE REGISTRATION.CNO = COURSE.CNO AND SNO = '800';
     {there is no need to reference the CLASS table with this
     example if we assume referential integrity is in effect}
Q.   SELECT COURSE.CNO, SEC, CINSTRFNO, CDAY, CTIME, CBLD,
     CROOM FROM CLASS, COURSE WHERE CLASS.CNO = COURSE.CNO AND
     CLABFEE < 100.00 AND CDAY <> 'FR';
R.   SELECT SNO, REG_DATE FROM REGISTRATION, COURSE
     WHERE REGISTRATION.CNO = COURSE.CNO AND CDEPT = 'THEO';
S.   SELECT COUNT(*) FROM COURSE, REGISTRATION
     WHERE REGISTRATION.CNO = COURSE.CNO
     AND CNAME = 'EXISTENTIALISM';
T.   SELECT COUNT(*) FROM REGISTRATION, COURSE
     WHERE REGISTRATION.CNO = COURSE.CNO AND CDEPT = 'PHIL';
U.   SELECT DISTINCT FNO, FNAME FROM FACULTY, CLASS WHERE FNO
     = CINSTRFNO AND CDAY IN ('MO', 'FR');

```
V.   SELECT FNAME FROM FACULTY, DEPARTMENT, COURSE
     WHERE FNO = DCHFNO AND DEPT = CDEPT AND CRED = 6;
Wa.  SELECT COURSE.CNO, CLASS.SEC, CNAME, CINSTRFNO, SNO
     FROM REGISTRATION, COURSE, CLASS
     WHERE COURSE.CNO = CLASS.CNO
     AND CLASS.CNO = REGISTRATION.CNO
     AND REGISTRATION.SEC = CLASS.SEC
     AND REGISTRATION.SEC = '01' AND CNAME = 'EXISTENTIALISM';
Wb.  SELECT    COURSE.CNO,    CLASS.SEC,    CNAME,    CINSTRFNO,
                STUDENT.SNO, SNAME FROM REGISTRATION, COURSE,
     CLASS, STUDENT WHERE COURSE.CNO = CLASS.CNO
     AND CLASS.CNO = REGISTRATION.CNO AND REGISTRATION.SEC =
     CLASS.SEC AND REGISTRATION.SEC = '01'
     AND REGISTRATION.SNO = STUDENT.SNO
     AND CNAME = 'EXISTENTIALISM';
Wc.  SELECT COURSE.CNO, CLASS.SEC, CNAME, FNAME, STUDENT.SNO,
     SNAME FROM REGISTRATION, COURSE, CLASS, STUDENT, FACULTY
     WHERE COURSE.CNO = CLASS.CNO
     AND CLASS.CNO = REGISTRATION.CNO
     AND REGISTRATION.SEC = CLASS.SEC
     AND REGISTRATION.SEC = '01'
     AND REGISTRATION.SNO = STUDENT.SNO AND CINSTRFNO = FNO
     AND CNAME = 'EXISTENTIALISM';
X.   "paper and pencil exercise" ---
Y.   SELECT * FROM COURSE, FACULTY;
Za.  SELECT D1.DEPT, D2.DEPT FROM DEPARTMENT D1, DEPARTMENT D2
     WHERE D1.DBLD = D2.DBLD AND D1.DEPT < D2.DEPT;
Zb.  SELECT S1.ENAME, S1.ESALARY, S2.ENAME, S2.ESALARY,
     S1.ESALARY - S2.ESALARY FROM STAFF S1, STAFF S2
     WHERE (S1.ESALARY - S2.ESALARY) > 1000;
Zc.  SELECT S1.ENAME, S1.ESALARY, S2.ENAME, S2.ESALARY,
     S1.ESALARY - S2.ESALARY FROM STAFF S1, STAFF S2
     WHERE (S1.ESALARY - S2.ESALARY) > 1000
     AND S1.DEPT = S2.DEPT;
Zd.  SELECT S1.ENAME, S1.ESALARY, S2.ENAME, S2.ESALARY,
     S1.ESALARY - S2.ESALARY
     FROM STAFF S1, STAFF S2, DEPARTMENT
     WHERE S1.DEPT = S2.DEPT AND DEPARTMENT.DEPT = S1.DEPT
     AND (S1.ESALARY - S2.ESALARY) > 1000 AND DBLD = 'HU'
```

Chapter 18

```
A.   SELECT * FROM COURSE, STAFF WHERE CDEPT = DEPT (+);
B.   SELECT * FROM DEPARTMENT, COURSE WHERE DEPT = CDEPT (+);
C.   SELECT * FROM DEPARTMENT, FACULTY WHERE DEPT = FDEPT (+);
D.   SELECT * FROM FACULTY, DEPARTMENT WHERE FDEPT = DEPT (+);
E.   SELECT DEPT, DBLD, FNO, FNAME, CNO, SEC
     FROM DEPARTMENT, FACULTY, CLASS
     WHERE DEPT = FDEPT (+)
     AND   FNO = CINSTRFNO (+);
```

Chapter 19

A. SELECT ESALARY FROM STAFF
    UNION
    SELECT FSALARY FROM FACULTY;
B. SELECT CDEPT, CRED, CDESCP FROM COURSE
    WHERE CDEPT = 'PHIL'
    UNION
    SELECT FDEPT, FNUM_DEP, FADDR FROM FACULTY
    WHERE FDEPT = 'PHIL';
C. SELECT CLABFEE FROM COURSE INTERSECT SELECT ESALARY
    FROM STAFF;
E. SELECT FNO FROM FACULTY MINUS
    SELECT DCHFNO FROM DEPARTMENT;
F. SELECT CRED FROM COURSE INTERSECT
    SELECT FNUM_DEP FROM FACULTY;
    or
    SELECT DISTINCT CRED FROM COURSE, FACULTY
    WHERE CRED = FNUM_DEP;
G. SELECT CLABFEE, CRED, 'COURSE' FROM COURSE
    WHERE CDEPT = 'CIS'
    UNION
    SELECT FSALARY, FNUM_DEP, 'FACULTY' FROM FACULTY
    WHERE FDEPT = 'CIS';
H. SELECT CNAME, CDEPT, CLABFEE, 'EXPENSIVE' FROM COURSE
    WHERE CLABFEE >= 200.00
    UNION
    SELECT CNAME, CDEPT, CLABFEE, 'CHEAP' FROM COURSE
    WHERE CLABFEE <= 50.00;
I. SELECT * FROM STAFF, DEPARTMENT
    WHERE STAFF.DEPT = DEPARTMENT.DEPT (+)
    UNION
    SELECT * FROM STAFF, DEPARTMENT
    WHERE STAFF.DEPT (+) = DEPARTMENT.DEPT;

Chapter 20

A. SELECT CNO, CNAME, CDEPT FROM COURSE
    WHERE CLABFEE = (SELECT MIN(CLABFEE) FROM COURSE);
B. SELECT CNO, CNAME, CDEPT, CLABFEE FROM COURSE
    WHERE CLABFEE = (SELECT MAX(CLABFEE) FROM COURSE
                     WHERE CLABFEE < 500.00);
C. SELECT CNO, CNAME, CDEPT, CLABFEE FROM COURSE WHERE
    CLABFEE = (SELECT MIN(CLABFEE) FROM COURSE
                     WHERE CLABFEE > 0);
D. SELECT CNO, CNAME, CDEPT, CLABFEE FROM COURSE
    WHERE CRED = 6
    AND CLABFEE = (SELECT MAX(CLABFEE) FROM COURSE
                     WHERE CRED = 6);
E. SELECT CNO, CNAME, CLABFEE FROM COURSE WHERE CLABFEE <
    (SELECT AVG(CLABFEE) FROM COURSE WHERE CDEPT = 'THEO');
F. SELECT * FROM COURSE WHERE CLABFEE >
    (SELECT MAX(CLABFEE) FROM COURSE
    WHERE CDEPT IN ('THEO', 'PHIL'));

G. SELECT ENAME, ESALARY FROM STAFF
    WHERE ESALARY <= (SELECT MAX(CLABFEE) FROM COURSE);
H. SELECT * FROM COURSE WHERE CDEPT = 'CIS' AND CLABFEE <
    (SELECT AVG(ESALARY) FROM STAFF WHERE DEPT = 'THEO');
I. SELECT DEPT, DCHFNO FROM DEPARTMENT WHERE DEPT IN
    (SELECT CDEPT FROM COURSE WHERE CRED = 6);
J. SELECT CNO, SEC, CBLD FROM CLASS
    WHERE CBLD = (SELECT DBLD FROM DEPARTMENT, STAFF
                        WHERE DEPARTMENT.DEPT = STAFF.DEPT
                        AND ENAME = 'DICK NIX');
    or
    SELECT CNO, SEC, CBLD FROM CLASS WHERE CBLD =
    (SELECT DBLD FROM DEPARTMENT WHERE DEPT =
    (SELECT DEPT FROM STAFF WHERE ENAME = 'DICK NIX'));
K. SELECT FNAME, FDEPT FROM FACULTY
    WHERE FNO NOT IN (SELECT CINSTRFNO FROM CLASS);
L. SELECT CNO, CNAME, CLABFEE FROM COURSE WHERE CLABFEE >
    (SELECT MIN(ESALARY) FROM STAFF);
M. SELECT FNAME, FNUM_DEP FROM FACULTY WHERE FNUM_DEP = ANY
    (SELECT CRED FROM COURSE);
    or
    SELECT FNAME, FNUM_DEP FROM FACULTY WHERE FNUM_DEP IN
    (SELECT CRED FROM COURSE);
N. SELECT CNO, CNAME FROM COURSE WHERE CNO IN
    (SELECT CNO FROM REGISTRATION WHERE SNO = '800');
O. SELECT * FROM CLASS WHERE CNO IN
    (SELECT CNO FROM COURSE WHERE CLABFEE < 100.00)
    AND CDAY <> 'FR';
P. SELECT SNO, REG_DATE FROM REGISTRATION WHERE CNO IN
    (SELECT CNO FROM COURSE WHERE CDEPT IN
    (SELECT DEPT FROM DEPARTMENT WHERE DBLD = 'SC'));
Q. SELECT CNO, CNAME, CDEPT, CLABFEE FROM COURSE
    WHERE CLABFEE = (SELECT MAX(CLABFEE) FROM COURSE
                        WHERE CLABFEE <>
                        (SELECT MAX(CLABFEE) FROM COURSE));
R. SELECT FNAME, FNUM_DEP FROM FACULTY WHERE FNUM_DEP <
    (SELECT MIN(CRED) FROM COURSE);
S. SELECT C1.CNO, C1.CNAME FROM COURSE C1, COURSE C2
    GROUP BY C1.CNO, C1.CNAME, C1.CLABFEE
    HAVING C1.CLABFEE = MAX(C2.CLABFEE);

Chapter 21

A. SELECT FNAME, FDEPT, FSALARY FROM FACULTY FX WHERE
    FSALARY > (SELECT AVG(FSALARY) FROM FACULTY
                WHERE FDEPT = FX.FDEPT);
B. SELECT FNAME, FDEPT FROM FACULTY FX
    WHERE FNUM_DEP >
    (SELECT AVG(CRED) FROM COURSE WHERE CDEPT = FX.FDEPT);
C. SELECT FNAME, FDEPT FROM FACULTY WHERE EXISTS
    (SELECT * FROM COURSE
    WHERE CDEPT = FACULTY.FDEPT AND CRED = 6);
    or
    SELECT FNAME, FDEPT FROM FACULTY WHERE FDEPT IN
    (SELECT CDEPT FROM COURSE WHERE CRED =6);
    or

```
        SELECT FNAME, FDEPT FROM FACULTY, COURSE
        WHERE FDEPT = CDEPT SNF CRED = 6;
D.      SELECT CNO, CNAME, CLABFEE FROM COURSE WHERE CLABFEE >
        (SELECT MIN(ESALARY) FROM STAFF);
        or
        SELECT DISTINCT CNO, CNAME, CLABFEE FROM COURSE, STAFF
        WHERE CLABFEE > ESALARY;
E.      SELECT FNAME, FDEPT FROM FACULTY WHERE NOT EXISTS
        (SELECT * FROM COURSE WHERE FACULTY.FDEPT = CDEPT
         AND CRED = 6);
F.      SELECT CNAME, CDEPT, CLABFEE FROM COURSE CX
        WHERE CLABFEE =
        (SELECT MAX(CLABFEE) FROM COURSE WHERE CDEPT = CX.CDEPT);
G.      SELECT DEPT, DBLD, DROOM, COURSE.CNO, CNAME, SEC, CDAY
        FROM DEPARTMENT, COURSE, CLASS
        WHERE DEPT = CDEPT AND COURSE.CNO = CLASS.CNO
        UNION
        SELECT DEPT, DBLD, DROOM, COURSE.CNO, CNAME, ' ', ' '
        FROM DEPARTMENT, COURSE WHERE DEPT = CDEPT AND NOT EXISTS
        (SELECT * FROM CLASS WHERE CNO = COURSE.CNO)
        UNION
        SELECT DEPT, DBLD, DROOM, ' ', ' ', ' ', ' '
        FROM DEPARTMENT WHERE NOT EXISTS
        (SELECT * FROM COURSE WHERE CDEPT = DEPARTMENT.DEPT);
        or
        SELECT DEPT, DBLD, DROOM, COURSE.CNO, CNAME, SEC, CDAY
        FROM DEPARTMENT, COURSE, CLASS WHERE DEPT = CDEPT (+)
        AND COURSE.CNO =CLASS.CNO (+);
H.      SELECT DISTINCT DEPT FROM STAFF WHERE EXISTS
        (SELECT * FROM DEPARTMENT WHERE DEPT = STAFF.DEPT);
I.      SELECT DISTINCT DEPT FROM STAFF WHERE NOT EXISTS
        (SELECT * FROM COURSE WHERE CDEPT = STAFF.DEPT);
```

Chapter 22

```
A.      COLUMN LFMT FORMAT A18 HEADING 'PREREQ. CNO.'
        SELECT LPAD(' ',3*(LEVEL-1))||CNO LFMT, CNAME
        FROM COURSEX WHERE CNO <> 'T11'
        CONNECT BY PRIOR CNO = PCNO  START WITH CNO = 'T11';
B.      SELECT CNO, CNAME FROM COURSEX
        CONNECT BY CNO = PRIOR PCNO  START WITH CNO = 'T33';
C.      SELECT CNO, CNAME FROM COURSEX
        WHERE CLABFEE <> 0 AND CNO <> 'C66'
        CONNECT BY CNO = PRIOR PCNO  START WITH CNO = 'C66';
        SELECT LPAD(' ',3*(LEVEL-1))||CNO LFMT, CNAME;
D.      SELECT C1.CNO, C1.CNAME, C2.CNO, C2.CNAME
        FROM COURSEX C1, COURSEX C2
        WHERE C1.PCNO = C2.CNO AND C1.CNO = 'C33';
E.      SELECT LPAD(' ',3*(LEVEL-1))||CNO LFMT, CNAME
        FROM COURSE WHERE CNO <> 'T11'
        AND CNO IN (SELECT CNO FROM PREREQ
        CONNECT BY PRIOR CNO = PCNO
        START WITH CNO = 'T11');
F.      SELECT LPAD(' ',3*(LEVEL-1))||CNO LFMT, CNAME
        FROM COURSE WHERE CNO IN (SELECT CNO FROM PREREQ
        CONNECT BY CNO = PRIOR PCNO  START WITH CNO = 'T33');
```

Chapter 23

A.   CREATE VIEW FPAYROLL
     AS SELECT FNAME, FSALARY, FHIRE_DATE, FNUM_DEP FROM
     FACULTY;
B.   CREATE VIEW FPAYROLL2 (F2N, F2S, F2H)
     AS SELECT FNAME, FSALARY, FHIRE_DATE, FNUM_DEP FROM
     FACULTY;
C.   CREATE VIEW VFSAL
     (DEPARTMENT, HIGHEST_SALARY, LOWEST_SALARY)
     AS SELECT FDEPT, MAX(FSALARY), MIN(FSALARY) FROM FACULTY
     GROUP BY FDEPT;
D.   CREATE VIEW FAVERAGES (FAVG_SAL, FAVG_NUM_DEP) AS
     SELECT AVG(FSALARY), AVG(FNUM_DEP) FROM FPAYROLL;
E.   DROP VIEW VFSAL;
     {"SELECT * FROM VFSAL" will now cause an error}
F.   DROP VIEW FPAYROLL;
     {"SELECT * FROM FAVERAGES" will now cause an error}
G.   CREATE VIEW VTHEO_STAFF
     AS SELECT ENAME, ESALARY, ETITLE
     FROM STAFF WHERE DEPT = 'THEO';
H.   CREATE VIEW VAVG_STAFF (DEPT, AVERAGE_SALARY)
     AS SELECT DEPT, AVG(ESALARY) FROM STAFF GROUP BY DEPT;
I.   CREATE VIEW MYVIEW (TOTAL)
     AS SELECT SUM(ESALARY) FROM VTHEO_STAFF;
J.   CREATE VIEW VINSTR (INSTRUCTOR, COURSE_NAME)
     AS SELECT DISTINCT FNAME, CNAME
     FROM FACULTY, COURSE, CLASS
     WHERE COURSE.CNO = CLASS.CNO AND FNO = CINSTRFNO;
K.   DROP VIEW VTHEO_STAFF;
L.   No. View is defined on multiple tables.
M.   No. View is defined on multiple tables.
N.   Two examples are presented.
     (i)   Consider view DC created as
     CREATE VIEW DC
     AS SELECT DEPT, DBLD, DROOM, CNO, CNAME, CRED, CLABFEE
         FROM DEPARTMENT, COURSE WHERE DEPT = CDEPT;
     The following statement makes sense.
     UPDATE DC SET CNAME = 'XXX', CRED = 6, CLABFEE = 99.99
     WHERE CNO = 'C11';
     Updating COURSE columns makes sense, but updating any of
     the DEPARTMENT columns is questionable.
     (ii)   Assume we split the course table into two tables:
            COURSE1 contains columns CNO, CNAME, and DESCP.
            COURSE2 contains columns CNO, CRED, CLABFEE, and
            CDEPT. Also assume a one-to-one correspondence
            based on matching CNO values is maintained. Then
            we create a view as follows.
            CREATE VIEW COURSE
            AS   SELECT COURSE1.CNO, CNAME, CDESCP, CRED,
            CLABFEE, CDEPT FROM COURSE1, COURSE2
            WHERE COURSE1.CNO = COURSE2.CNO;
     The following UPDATE statement makes sense.
            UPDATE COURSE SET CNAME = 'XXX', CRED = 6,
                            CLABFEE = 99.99
            WHERE CNO = 'C11';

Chapter 24

A. GRANT SELECT, INSERT ON STAFF TO CURLEY WITH GRANT OPTION;
B. GRANT ALL ON DEPARTMENT TO PUBLIC;
    REVOKE ALL ON DEPARTMENT TO PUBLIC;

Chapter 25

A. SET AUTOCOMMIT OFF
    DELETE FROM COURSE WHERE CDEPT = 'CIS';
    SELECT * FROM COURSE;
    {result shows all rows except CIS rows}
    ROLLBACK;
    SELECT * FROM COURSE;
    {result shows all COURSE rows, including CIS rows;
    SET AUTOCOMMIT ON

Chapter 26

A. SELECT VIEW_NAME FROM USER_VIEWS
    WHERE VIEW_NAME NOT LIKE 'V%';
B. SELECT TEXT FROM USER_VIEWS
    WHERE VIEW_NAME = 'CISC';
C. SELECT OBJECT_NAME, OBJECT_TYPE FROM USER_OBJECTS;
D. SELECT TABLE_NAME, OWNER FROM ALL_TABLES
    WHERE TABLE_NAME LIKE 'C%';
E. SELECT VIEW_NAME FROM USER_VIEWS
    WHERE TEXT LIKE '%STAFF%';
F. SELECT TABLE_NAME FROM USER_TAB_COLUMNS
    WHERE COLUMN_NAME = 'CNO';
G. SELECT TABLE_NAME FROM USER_TAB_COLUMNS
    WHERE COLUMN_NAME LIKE '%DEPT%';
H. SELECT COLUMN_NAME FROM USER_TAB_COLUMNS
    WHERE TABLE_NAME = 'COURSE' AND NULLABLE = 'Y';
I. SELECT TABLE_NAME FROM DICTIONARY
    WHERE TABLE_NAME LIKE 'USER%';
J. SELECT COLUMN_NAME FROM DICT_COLUMNS
    WHERE TABLE_NAME = 'USER_TABLES';
    or
    DESCRIBE DICT_COLUMNS
K. SELECT * FROM ALL_TAB_GRANTS_RECD;
L. SELECT * FROM ALL_TAB_GRANTS_RECD
    WHERE GRANTEE <> 'PUBLIC';
M. SELECT DELETE_PRIV FROM USER_TAB_GRANTS_MADE
    WHERE TABLE_NAME = 'STAFF' AND DELETE_PRIV <> 'N';
N. SELECT COLUMN_NAME FROM DICT_COLUMNS
    WHERE TABLE_NAME = 'ALL_OBJECTS';
    or
    DESCRIBE ALL_OBJECTS;

Index